CONTENTS

First published 1974 by
Octopus Books Limited
59 Grosvenor Street, London W1

© 1973/74 Phoebus Publishing Company
© This compilation 1974 Phoebus Publishing Company
This book is adapted from 'The Story of Pop'. It has been produced by Phoebus Publishing Company in cooperation with Octopus Books Ltd.

ISBN 0 7064 0409 2

Distributed in Australia by Rigby Limited 30 North Terrace, Kent Town, Adelaide, South Australia 5067

Printed in England by Jarrold & Sons Ltd, Norwich

The introductions to the chapters have been specially written by Jeremy Pascal.

Note The numbers in the *Back Tracks* indicate chart positions in Great Britain unless otherwise stated.

Alan Aldridge Associates

Introduction

Rock has struck a chord in the lives of millions of the world's young people, and this book chronicles its stars and superstars, whose story spans continents, life styles and a kaleidoscope of changing attitudes. But the history of their music is surprisingly short — a mere twenty years since its first eruption as Rock & Roll. Determined to be larger than life, they have been outrageous, unconventional, sometimes comical, sometimes defiant, often outcasts in a world they found too grey for them. The names are legendary now, from Bill Haley, the first star of all, through Elvis Presley, arguably the greatest, to Jimmy Osmond, the youngest. From Little Richard who brought theatre to Rock, through Bob Dylan who made it literate, to David Bowie who pushed the barriers even farther. Those people, and dozens of others — the Beatles who revolutionised the music and sent it round the world, the Rolling Stones who frightened and outraged parents and authority, Jimi Hendrix who became its victim — stamped their individual imprints not only on a style of music but also on the consciousness of a new generation.

From Bill Haley to David Cassidy they are all here; their songs, their styles, their trends, their triumphs and their tragedies are all minutely chronicled — from the kiss-curled rocker who smashed to fame with an entirely new music in the mid-'50s to the glitter-flashing idols of the '70s who have taken the music into its third decade and to an even younger audience. Here are the stars and the superstars.

Robert Ellis

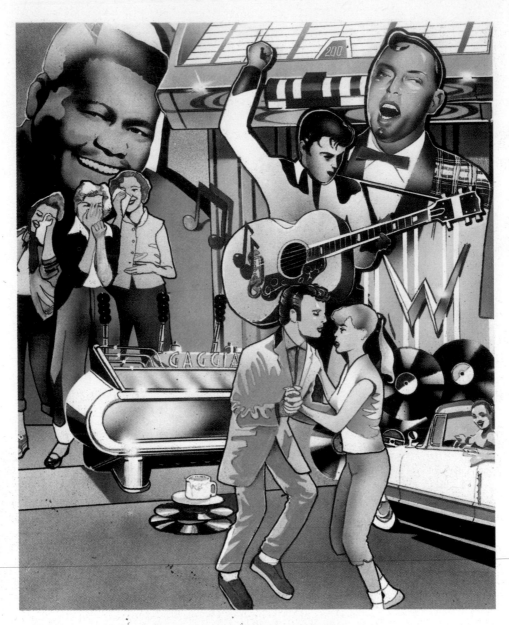

CHAPTER I
Rock & Roll

The children of the '50s changed the world. Before them there were no 'teenagers', before them youth had no separate identity, before them kids were just young replicas of adults. And then came Bill Haley with 'Rock Around The Clock' — the song and the singer inspired a bloodless revolution and created rock & roll.

After rock & roll nothing was to be quite the same again. A handful of men, all Americans, gave the music its shape, form and content. Haley was the first, but Presley was a new style of star — sexual, aggressive, surly; he was to equal in his wealth, success and popularity the fabulous high style of the great days of Hollywood. Fats Domino, Little Richard and Chuck Berry were to show the black man a new way, give

him a previously unconsidered equality. The Everly Brothers, Buddy Holly, Eddie Cochran, among others, were to take rock & roll and adapt it into a pop style that would spread outwards and become the best-known music across the globe, levelling barriers of nationality, language and custom, uniting a generation divided by politics, religions and oceans.

Rock & roll turned on the struggle of the young to get free from the past. Only six years separated the successes of Bill Haley and Roy Orbison but so rapid was the change, so widespread the enthusiasm that the music had already exploded out of cellars and dance halls to become a million-dollar industry and a permanent influence on successive generations of the young.

Bill Haley: the man least likely...

The world's first rock & roll star, the man whose music turned on millions of teens the world over, was nearly 30 when he burst to fame, married and with five children. As if that wasn't ironic enough – seeing that he sparked the revolt of one generation against their elders – the song that started a new era had originally been written as a novelty foxtrot by two members of the Tin Pan Alley establishment who stood for everything that R&R wasn't, one of whom was 63 years old! From these unpromising beginnings a music was born, and it's a sure-fire certainty that those three principal characters could never have dreamed what a monster they were creating.

Mike Cook

The man, of course, was Bill Haley: the song, 'Rock Around The Clock'. How was it, then, that this man – twice the age of his audience – and this song should awaken the latent power of teens?

Bill Haley was born in a Detroit suburb in 1927. From his earliest years he was destined for a career in music but, as the years rolled on, it became apparent that while he'd make a steady and unspectacular living, he'd never, but NEVER, be a star. Just to look at him you could see that stocky, chubby, moon-faced Haley was not the stuff that stars are made of.

At 13 he was picking guitar for a buck a gig, firmly into country & western, doing the rounds of the Mid West – steady, dependable and dull. He'd played at auctions, at touring medicine shows, and on local radio billed as 'The Rambling Yodeller'. In the backwoods towns of America artists like him are as much part of the landscape as Coke ads and road houses. Radio offered him a secure niche and he became institutionalised as Programme Director of an independent station in Pennsylvania, at the same time fronting and organising hillbilly bands with lacklustre names like 'The Four Aces Of Western Swing' and 'The Saddlemen'. The more you saw him, the less you could imagine him playing anywhere larger than a local college.

But Haley – like Alan Freed – had one great advantage – a good ear. He didn't just shut his senses off from what was happening around him. Certainly he played hillbilly and C&W but that didn't deafen

him to the music that was causing young whites to tune their radios to the illicit black stations or sneak off at night to the black quarters — the wrong sides of the mid-western tracks — and learn how to click their fingers, move their bodies, and talk in a language unknown in their homes. What's more they learned to jitterbug. Haley heard this music and analysed its appeal — the beat. He played regularly at high school hops and saw the kids doing these lunatic dances and shouting 'crazy, man, crazy', 'go man go' and other outlandish expressions.

Haley started to experiment, pulling in other streams to his predominantly C&W repertoire. "What we played", he said, "was a combination of country and western, Dixieland, and old-style R&R."

Haley was no fool. He saw that the strict tempo formality of the hugely popular Big Bands was offering the kids no excitement. By the late '40s he saw that things were ripe for change and he had the musical know-how, picked up from years of playing and touring, to put together a synthesis of the most exciting musical styles around. "We decided to try for a new style", he said, "mostly using stringed instruments but somehow managing to get the same effect as brass and reeds." And excitement — the excitement that, a few years later, was going to make kids rip up seats, stomp around cinemas and generally run riot.

First the excitement had to be in the music. Haley, by his own admission, was not the first to appreciate this but he was the first to define it AND, more importantly, to create it. "Around the early '50s the musical world was striving for something new, the days of the solo vocalist and big bands had gone. About the only thing that was making any noise was progressive jazz but this just went above the heads of the average listener. I felt that if I could take a beat the listeners could clap to as well as dance this would be what they were after. From that the rest was easy . . . ."

Hybrid Sounds

What in fact he did was to take two recognisable forms of music — C&W and R&B — and create a synthesis that appeared as a new form. This was the classic formula and the reaction was very potent chemistry indeed. But the rest was certainly not as easy as Haley would have us believe. At first he put out very run-of-the-mill C&W and R&B numbers on the topsides of discs issued through a small, local, independent label. But the flipsides had strange hybrid sounds with weirder names like 'Rock The Joint'. Even in the titles the Haley ear was accurate; He just took everyday sayings picked up from high school gigs, like 'crazy, man, crazy', 'see you later, alligator' and 'shake, rattle and roll' and, wedding them to his new beat, turned them into songs. But Bill Haley and the Saddlemen were hardly the image demanded by 'hep-cats' so a name change was indicated. The Saddlemen were buried and re-emerged as the Comets. The name had a feel of speed

about it and is a rather obscure pun on Halley's Comet, a celestial body that appears in the sky with infrequent regularity. No doubt there was also a hope that the group's career would be similarly meteoric.

Initially, there were problems; not everyone was ready for or convinced by Haley's new brainchild. Any doubt, however, should have been swept away when 'Crazy Man Crazy' was the first rock & roll song ever to enter the national charts in

Bill Haley and the Comets. His arrival at Waterloo from Southampton for his first British tour produced scenes of pure hysteria. However the outward success of the tour belied the fact that, in the flesh, Haley was exposed as being quite old. One of 'them' pretending to be one of 'us'.

extraordinary 'kiss curls', dressed like a cowboy's dream of city chic — in fact the epitome of bad taste — garish tartan jacket and sporting braces, he just couldn't have been further from the standard image of a star. But his music was right and the Comets added to the excitement by presenting rather stagey — not to say stiff-jointed — athletics like rolling on their backs, jumping onto the piano and doing something unusual with a double bass.

His rise from 'Clock' in '55 was truly meteoric. He created rock & roll, Alan Freed named it. Haley took it out into America at large by way of records, TV and films and then, swiftly, to the world. Soon after American youth had found THEIR music, it was adopted by Europe. In Britain, Haley's movie — *Rock Around The Clock* — was a smash, and he was a hero of cosmic proportions. He made a few more hits and was swept on the crest of a wave, quite bewildered by his own success. As kids rioted, cinemas broke up and destruction, violence and mayhem (at least according to the press) ran rampant, Haley could only grin, nonplussed, and say: 'I'm just a country boy'. In fact, he was an unwitting Frankenstein who had bred a monster of terrifying proportions.

It couldn't last, of course, and it didn't. Following the movie Haley came to Britain. Fuelled by a blaze of publicity stoked by the press, his arrival at Southampton and his progress via special train to the capital were pure hysteria. Outwardly, the tour was a success but, as one commentator has said, "Haley killed his own image by crossing the Atlantic. Whereas it had been possible to ignore the fact on film, in the flesh it became painfully obvious that this perspiring fat person was quite old. One of 'them' pretending to be one of 'us'".

Father of Rock

Almost as soon as it had begun, it finished. Standing at Haley's shoulder was the man who in every way fitted the music — Presley. Haley had made his pile, his name was in the books, his records — thin, reedy, impoverished things that they now seem — were in the archive collections. He faded as fast as the comet that christened his band and, like that same celestial body, duly reappeared every so often as an object of nostalgia — older, portlier, increasingly less hirsute.

Haley's place in the story is important and, indeed, honourable. He gave the music its first impetus, a recognisable form. All who followed him should be grateful for his ear and musical acumen but he, like all true trailblazers, burnt out to be replaced by the true heroes. Perhaps he is the 'Father Of Rock & Roll', but his trouble was that he fitted the paternal role too well. Now, perhaps, he deserves a certain reverence as the grandfather of it all — the man who set the world on fire to become the first superstar of rock, and show from the very beginning that rock music is about much more than sheer musical ability or smart looks.

1953. It was a small beacon that showed the way ahead but Haley didn't follow up his first success for another year when 'Shake, Rattle And Roll' really hit the jackpot with twelve weeks in the Top Ten. In the same year — 1954 — Haley also recorded and released the 'novelty foxtrot' — 'Rock Around The Clock', but it didn't mean a thing. Rock was conceived and entering labour pains, it was yet to be born, kicking and screaming, into the world.

Moment of Birth

The moment of birth was probably the release of *Blackboard Jungle* which carried 'Rock Around The Clock' as its theme music. After that Bill Haley was 'made'. With a rapidity that startled the portly singer, Haley found that he was a star, making films, notching hits, and the cult figure for millions of kids. Even in the exultant throes of stardom he cut a bizarre figure. Round, puppy-fat face topped with

Above: Bill Haley and the Comets during their 1974 tour of Europe, still getting all the rock & rollers on their feet. Below: Receiving an award from Olivia Newton-John to commemorate the sixth successful release of 'Rock Around The Clock' in 1974.

Chris Walter

Fats Domino...
of Blueberry Hill

Of the five *undisputed* 'giants' of rock & roll — Elvis Presley, Little Richard, Fats Domino, Chuck Berry and Jerry Lee Lewis — Fats Domino is the most neglected and the most underrated.

He's neglected perhaps, because in the style of rock & roll he played — New Orleans dance blues — he was overshadowed by the more flamboyant, more outrageous, Little Richard. (It would be hard for *anyone* to try and upstage Little Richard, particularly with such a relaxed style as Fats had.)

Fats Domino is underrated not only for the quality of his music and what he achieved in terms of recording successes, but also for his central role in the development of New Orleans music — his absorption and transformation of the cultural styles in New Orleans into rock & roll, and his subsequent influence on countless other performers. It is this latter point, his importance in terms of *New Orleans*, which is the most rewarding to explore.

Universal Appeal

As to the quality of Fats' music, it was perhaps best defined by Charlie Gillett, in his book *The Sound of the City*, when he said his apparently eternal and universal appeal defies musical analysis. His records were simple, convincing, memorable, and danceable. Other people may have occasionally come up with something better, but Domino could be relied on.

In fact, he was relied on so much that he sold over 65,000,000 records, collecting 22 Gold Discs — an achievement only surpassed in rock & roll by Elvis Presley. In all, he had more than 80 singles and 25 albums released. When he first came to the attention of the white record buyers, it was because Pat Boone had covered

15

Fats' own 'Ain't That A Shame', earning his first-ever Gold Disc for his pains. But Fats didn't mind too much, he also got a Gold Disc for it, his ninth altogether.

Antoine 'Fats' Domino was born in New Orleans on May 10th, 1929 (say his record company, others date him earlier, on February 26th, 1928) . . . one of nine children. Although his father was a violinist and his uncle, Harry Verette, had played trumpet in Kid Ory's and Oscar Celestin's New Orleans jazzbands, Antoine was the only child to show any musical inclination. He started playing the piano when he was six, after a relative had left an old upright in the house.

Soon he began playing for small charge in the evenings, and working in a bedspring factory during the day to help support the family. An accident at the factory seriously damaged his hands, and doctors recommended amputation. Fats refused, and after two years of exercises he was back playing again, in bassist Billy Diamond's band — it was Diamond who first dubbed him 'Fats'.

Eventually, Fats met up with Dave Bartholomew. The start of their relationship is one of the most confused periods of Fats' career. The most likely account is that Bartholomew invited him to join his New Orleans band, but others say they didn't meet until Fats was signed to the Imperial record label. Whatever the truth, Bartholomew had an excellent reputation as a trumpeter — Charlie Gillett writes that he even played with Duke Ellington's band, but in fact their association is limited to the fact that Bartholomew and Ellington's bass player, Aaron Bell, played together with Herb Leary and His Society Syncopaters.

Imperial Sign Domino

Lew Chudd founded Imperial in Los Angeles in 1947, and after hearing excellent reports of a young New Orleans pianist, he travelled out to see Fats playing in a 'jump' band (probably Bartholomew's). He was so impressed with the 20-year-old, that he signed him there and then. Fats was to provide Imperial with the bulk of its income for the next eight years, until Ricky Nelson was signed from Verve (after selling 1,000,000 copies of a cover of Fats' 'I'm Walkin''.

At the time of Lew Chudd's visit, New Orleans was an incredible hive of exciting music, particularly from the 'jump' bands that had established a direct link with rock & roll. They used various instruments, usually including a couple of saxophones to *emphasise* the difference between each beat of the boogie-woogie played by the pianist's left hand, creating a 'jump' rhythm; or to *blurr* it, creating a 'shuffle' rhythm.

Apart from Fats, who was leading the field in New Orleans at the time, the city also boasted such performers as Amos Milburn, Roy Brown, Smiley Lewis (who was originally from Texas and originally named Overton Lemon), Lloyd Price and Guitar Slim. But Fats' main rival, both

personally and musically, was Roy Byrd, who performed and recorded under the name 'Professor Longhair and His Shuffling Hungarians'. While Fats played 'jump' rhythm, Professor Longhair played 'shuffle'. Although big locally, he didn't have any sustained national success beyond two records, 'Bald Head' and what must be the definitive shuffle record of all time, 'Like Longhair'.

Cosmopolitan Music

New Orleans was and is a major confluence for races and cultures. The city had once been a major port in the slave trade, and from earliest times was exposed to the music brought over from Africa and the West Indies. And as the capital of the French colony in America, the local blues was heavily influenced by the more commonly-spoken French language. As well as New Orleans jazz, these strains mingled to create both Cajun and Zydeco music.

Fats' music, particularly his ballad style,

was drawn from this music. Zydeco is a blues style played by the Arcadian people in southern Louisiana. They sang in French and played that most 'French' of instruments, the accordion. The most significant effect of their music was the creation of a swirling instrumental sound behind the singers. Cajun music substituted saxophones for the accordions, but retained the swirling effect. (The most successful example probably being 'Sea Of Love' by Phil Phillips and the Twilights, which was produced by George Khoury in Lake Charles, Louisiana. The swirling effect, emphasised by the Twilights' mournful vocal backing, created a convincing audio-picture of the sea behind Phillips' singing. It was covered in Britain, arrangement and all, by Marty Wilde.)

Louisiana Accent

Another obvious New Orleans influence on Fats was in his singing. He had a strong Louisiana 'creole' accent, which became even more pronounced in his singing. Fats

An early picture of 220 pounds Antoine 'Fats' Domino, one of the giants of rock & roll.

was, in fact, brought up to speak French, picking up his English later. But like most of the 'jump' band singers, he sang in English, with strong French intonations, most apparent in the vowels.

Most of Fats' songs were composed and arranged with David Bartholomew at Imperial (which although based in Los Angeles, recorded Fats almost entirely in New Orleans). Bartholomew played trumpet on Fats' records until about 1956, as well as being composer/arranger/producer, but gave up playing when they broke into the white market. He had, up to that point, also been recording without Fats, and had several successes in the R&B field including, 'That's How You Got Killed Before', 'Ain't Gonna Do It', 'Who Drank My Beer?' and 'Frantic Chick'.

Thin High Voice

'The Fat Man', recorded in October 1949, was their first record, their first hit, and their first Gold Disc. Fats' voice then was much higher, 'thinner', and more

Fats Domino at the piano.

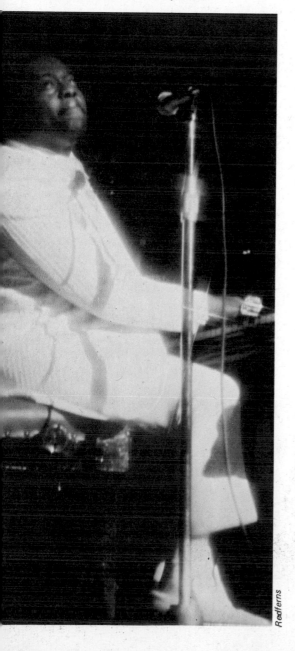

nasal than it was to become later, but 'The Fat Man' is as compelling today as it must have been then. The solid two-handed chording and rolling boogie beat contain so much exuberance and inherent warm humour, even before he weighs in with 'they call, they call me the fat man, cause I weigh two hundred pounds . . .'

It is classic boogie-woogie and nascent rock & roll. The instrumental line-up he used here was more-or-less maintained throughout his career: his own piano, trumpet, two or three saxes, guitar, bass and drums. Herb Hardesty played the sax solos up to 1955, when he started sharing them with Lee Allen, Cornelius Coleman was the regular drummer, Frank Fields the bassist and either Walter Nelson or Ernie Maclean on guitar.

With these musicians and Bartholomew's expertise, Fats became a giant in the R&B field — and the only one who would carry on successfully in rock & roll (which involved hardly any appreciable change in his style). The very early music is almost all 12-bar, each song distinguishable from the next only by its lyrics. But later he 'personalised' it with his own seemingly effortless complex phrasing and timing.

In fact, Fats' breakthrough into the white market came with the perfecting of this 'personal' fractured singing style in his and Dave Bartholomew's song, 'Ain't That A Shame'. But it was the fact that Pat Boone had a hit covering it that drew the white public's attention to him and his music. From then on in, it was hit after hit. But Fats had been involved even earlier in the creation of rock & roll as the music of a new generation.

Sell-Out

The story of Alan Freed, the Cleveland DJ, and his role in the birth of rock & roll is well known: he started *Moondog's Rock & Roll Party* on a Cleveland radio station after being introduced to the music at Leo Mintz's downtown record store. The music was, simply, black rhythm and blues. The response to his radio show was so good that he arranged a stage show in Cleveland Arena in March 1953. There was room for 10,000 people, but the demand was so fantastic that three times that number turned up and the ensuing chaos caused the show to be called off and re-arranged later that year. The performers Freed had on the show included Joe 'Shake Rattle And Roll' Turner, and Fats Domino.

After suffering Pat Boone's successful cover version of 'Ain't That A Shame' (in the white market only, Fats earned a Gold Disc in the R&B charts), Fats came up with his first white hit, 'I'm In Love Again' — another Gold — in 1956. 'Blueberry Hill', which followed it, is his best known record, and its phenomenal success cemented Fats' position as a popular entertainer in the rock & roll field. This record, though, was out of character for two reasons: first, it was the only record (up to 1962 at least) that wasn't recorded in New Orleans, but in Los Angeles; and secondly, it wasn't an original song, but a

standard revised well-known song.

Standards rarely come off when done by rock & roll performers (witness Little Richard's 'Baby Face' and 'By The Light Of The Silvery Moon') but Fats managed to overcome this handicap and make them his own (his other notable successes were with 'My Blue Heaven' and 'Margie').

Imperial wasn't, of course, the only label to promote its R&B music as rock & roll, but it was the most successful — simply by virtue of having Fats Domino in its catalogue. Dave Bartholomew too had been recording without Fats for the label and had several successes in the R&B field: 'That's How You Got Killed Before', 'Ain't Gonna Do It', 'Who Drank My Beer?' and 'Frantic Chick'; but he stopped to concentrate on Fats when they broke into the white market.

R & B Label

Sydney Nathan's King label, in Cincinnati, Ohio, had one of the strongest R&B catalogues — Bill Doggett, Bullmoose Jackson, Roy Brown, Hank Ballard and the Midnighters (who incidentally originally did 'The Twist' that Chubby Checker copied), Otis Williams and the Charms, not to mention guitarists Albert King, Freddie King and Johnny 'Guitar' Watson (who first recorded with Amos Milburn's Jump Band and later with rock singer Larry Williams). Other labels were Aladdin, in Los Angeles, who had Dave Bartholomew as producer for a time and performers such as Amos Milburn and Shirley and Lee on their books; and Speciality, in Hollywood, who had Lloyd Price, Guitar Slim and the inimitable Little Richard (as well as the white singer Larry Williams).

Fats Domino's success was enormous in both the white and black markets and he appeared in most of the notable rock & roll films of the day: *Jamboree, Shake Rattle and Rock, The Big Beat* and *The Girl Can't Help It*. He was topped only by Presley in the white sales, but kept ahead of him in the black market (both of them well ahead of their nearest rivals, Little Richard and Chuck Berry). Needless to say Fats was also a great influence and inspiration for other black singers as well as focusing attention on the music of New Orleans and the Deep South.

One of the more direct results of his popularity was the emergence of Little Richard, whose more frenetic boogie-woogie piano was also derived from the same influences as Fats' but included Fats' own piano-playing as well. In fact most of the musicians on Fats' records also backed Little Richard. Their relationship, musical and cultural, was the black mirror image of that applied to Bill Haley and Elvis Presley; one was harmless, the other dangerous.

It was in New Orleans itself that Fats had his biggest influence, directly and indirectly. Apart from his effect on such singers as Lloyd Price and Smiley Lewis Fats' success threw a lot of light on to Johnny Vincent's Ace label.

In 1956, Vincent, whose label was

Redferns

Born May 10th, 1929 in New Orleans.
1949: Cut his first record, 'The Fat Man'/ 'Detroit City Blues'.
1955: Broke into the white market with 'Aint That A Shame', 'I'm In Love Again' and 'Blueberry Hill'. Following this came his first album, 'Rock And Rollin' with Fats Domino' (Imperial).
1956: Fats hit the road on a series of tours with people like Jerry Lee Lewis, B. B. King, Duane Eddy, James Brown and Johnny Preston. He also appeared in a number of rock & roll films, most notably, *Jamboree* and *The Girl Can't Help It*.
1957: 'I'm Walking'/'I'm In The Mood For Love' and the unforgettable ballad, 'The Valley Of Tears'. In the next 10 years, Fats released countless albums and more than 50 singles. Below are a few of his hit singles from this time.
1958: 'Sick And Tired', 'Little Mary' and 'Whole Lotta Loving'.
1959: 'When The Saints Go Marching In', 'I'm Gonna Be A Wheel Some Day' and 'Margie'.
1960: 'Walking To New Orleans', 'Before I Grow Too Old' and 'Natural Born Lover'.
1961: 'Aint That Just Like A Woman', 'Shu Rah' and 'I Hear You Knocking'.
1962: 'Dance With Mr. Domino' and 'Did You Ever See A Dream Walking?'
1963: 'There Goes (My Heart Again)' and 'Red Sails In The Sunset'.
1964: 'Lazy Lady'.
1968: 'Lady Madonna'.
Many of Fats' best tracks can be found on the recent, outstanding United Artists double-album, simply called 'Fats Domino'.

based in Jackson, Mississippi, started recording a New Orleans band whose music was a lot closer to Roy 'Longhair' Byrd's than Fats' Huey 'Piano' Smith and the Clowns. The band had three vocalists apart from Huey himself – Bobby Marchan, Junior Gordon and Frankie Ford. With Bobby Marchan singing they had the tremendous 'Rockin' Pneumonia And Boogie Woogie Flu' and 'Don't You Just Know It' as big hits, and of course with Frankie Ford there was the inimitable 'Sea Cruise'. Ford's vocal was, in fact, dubbed on to a previously unissued version of the song by the band with Huey Smith singing, in the wake of the success of another white singer on Vincent's Ace label, Jimmy Clanton.

Soft Rock

Jimmy Clanton – cast in the mould of Frankie Avalon – had several hits with ballads such as 'Just A Dream', 'Letter To An Angel' and 'Ship On A Stormy Sea' (all Gold Discs) as well as 'Venus In Blue Jeans'. Although born in Baton Rouge, Louisiana, Clanton was as 'Philadelphian' as Bobby Rydell, Frankie Avalon and Fabian, and was instrumental in the sad process of softening Southern rock & roll, just as the Philadelphia singers had softened rock & roll in the North. Other singers who came under Fats' influence were Lee Dorsey, Irma Thomas, Ernie K. Doe, Clarence 'Frogman' Henry, Joe Jones and in name at least, Chubby Checker.

As the years rolled on, Fats' music became less and less adventurous on the whole and, with one or two major exceptions, his singing became much more mellow, losing a lot (but not all) of its local colour. The hits petered out around 1962, ironically with the emergence of the Beatles and all the other British groups who had been raised on his music. That year, Fats left Imperial, and after unsuc-cessful liaisons with ABC-Paramount, Mercury and Broadmoor, he was con-tracted to Warner-Reprise and made a couple of startling, though excellent records, both Lennon/McCartney songs, 'Lady Madonna' and 'Lovely Rita'.

Simple Music

There's no really simple way of showing how big Fats Domino's music was, both in its own right and in terms of the influence it had. His music is simple, exuberant, loving and happy, and even the melancholy songs have a comforting feel to them. Fats Domino weighed in at around 220 pounds, and he played rock & roll long before the term was invented. "Some people call it rhythm & blues," he once said, "and some calls it rock & roll, but I just calls it music with a beat." However people describe his music, one thing is certain: he is one of the great musicians of rock.

'Elvis Presley is a 21-year-old sex maniac with greasy hair, dirty songs and no future...'

Yes, that's what they're saying — all the preachers and teachers and youth club leaders, the bankers and brokers and Respectable Folkers: they're all saying Elvis is mean and evil; a walking disgrace to the human race. They're screaming about all these Shocking Things — the way he sings, his flashy rings, his sneering lips, his writhing hips. My God! guess what — He's a Communist Plot! — I'm tellin' ya, Mac — he's gotta *pink* Cadillac! To the older generation in the '50s that's the way Elvis came over. Right from the start he was larger than life — he wasn't so much just another singer, as a threat to the youth of America.

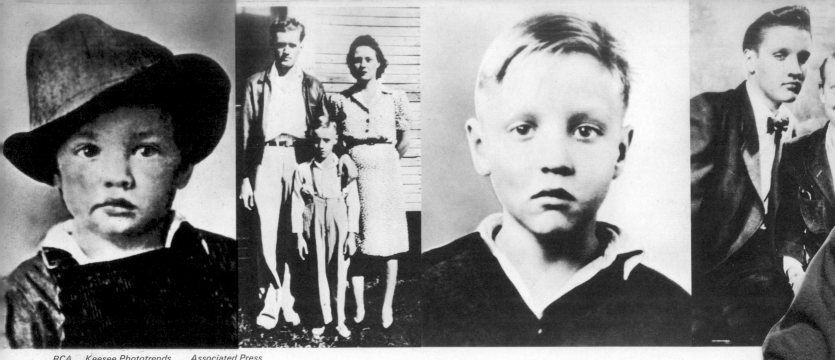

RCA   Keesee Phototrends   Associated Press

From childhood to rock & roll star. Left to right: Elvis Presley about two years old; Elvis, aged eight, with his parents; Elvis, aged six, with blond hair. His natural colour is reddish-brown which he dyed black early on in his career; Elvis the adolescent with his cousin, Gene Smith; teenage Presley, complete with acne; Elvis at 18, leaning against his father's car. Far right: 50,000,000 Fans Can't Be Wrong; Elvis the well-groomed star. Centre left: Elvis aged 13 posing in a cowboy suit. Centre: Elvis in the pose that launched a thousand female fantasies. Centre right: golden-suited Elvis being escorted into the International Amphitheatre, Chicago, in 1957.

So, here you are stuck in a small American town and it's 1956, and you don't care what they're saying about Elvis Presley, because he's something else. *He's* like a hurricane blowing the roof off everything, and all those people who are moaning and groaning about it are so dull they practically smother you to death. School, and home is just sit-up-for-teas full of silence and scolding and holding you down. Dull growing up in a dull, dull town.

And then – *AWOP-BOP-A-LOO-BOP-A-LOP-BAM-BOOM*!!! – along comes Elvis Presley, with the wildest music in the world, more energy than the atomic bomb and more sexuality than your most secret dreams.

He's got greasy hair, flicked up and back so it all falls across his face when he's singing and moving, long sideburns that your parents really hate; and he never stands still, and he never looks humble, and he never tries to be witty like all those crooners in their bow-ties and dinner-jackets. Presley, in fact, looks like he's going to make all those crooners with their cute lyrics and clear, precise voices obsolete. He doesn't treat songs that way. He growls and mumbles and sneers and sulks with a will that's hard to mistake:

> *'If you're lookin' for trouble*
> *You came to the right place.*
> *If you're lookin' for trouble*
> *Just look right in my face . . .'*
>
> *('Trouble')*

And his voice! He's got all that sexy sug-

gestiveness you only ever heard before on those old black guys' records that play late at night on weird little radio stations your momma doesn't know about. Under-the-pillow listening; furtive, primitive, strange. And now here's Elvis, sounding that same way but gutsier and young. He even did it on the Ed Sullivan TV Show – which is like pulling down your pants in front of President Eisenhower or something.

From now on they could burn rock & roll records till they choked on the smoke; they could pulp it out in the pulpits till they frothed at the mouth; all to no avail. What's more, they couldn't anymore just blame it on the blacks:

'NOTICE! STOP: Help Save The Youth Of America', those posters from the lunatic fringe had screamed, 'DON'T BUY NEGRO RECORDS. The screaming, idiotic words, and savage music of these records are undermining the morals of our white youth in America!'

But it was too late. It wasn't under-the-pillow listening to small black radio stations any more – it was everywhere, out in the open, and Elvis Presley was showing that, yes, that 'white youth of America' could be a living part of that music. So Dullsville could think what it wanted. *Rock & Roll is here to stay!*

The Magic Formula

Elvis had the formula for rock & roll within him: he had been brought up with the Blues and country music all around him; in its living environment. He was born in the Deep South – in Tupelo, Mississippi, and his family moved to Memphis, Tennessee when he was at the moody, restless and rebellious age of 13.

Elvis Aaron Presley was his real name, and all he had to change for his public career was the colour of his hair. He really has a kind of auburn, reddish-brown hair-colour, but he dyed it black early on in his

20

fortune-hunt, and it has now been black for more than 15 years.

He was born on January 8th, 1935, son of Vernon and Gladys Presley, who were sharecroppers plagued by poverty, half-helped by welfare programmes, and much-comforted by The First Assembly Church of God. They had a still-born son, Elvis' twin, who would have been called Jesse Garon Presley. Presley's mother died in 1958 with her son at the height of his rock & roll career; more famous and successful than any other American of his generation; the most potent sex symbol since Rudolph Valentino; and selling records faster than anyone in history.

The Way Up

How did Elvis get to that position? It started with him playing guitar all day long, hanging round the local clubs where the black gospel groups came to perform, listening to bluesmen like Junior Parker and Arthur 'Big Boy' Crudup on battered old radio-sets. Elvis had always wanted something more than to drive a truck for 35 dollars a week, and kept his hair immaculately combed for a fantasy-world of admirers. Then enter two other men who helped and launched Presley. The first was Sam Phillips, and the second was 'Colonel' Tom Parker.

Sam Phillips was also very much a Southerner, born in Alabama, and like Elvis himself, he was a white guy with a good ear for black music. An ex-DJ, he formed his own record company, Sun Records, which started issuing 78s from Memphis in 1950.

Elvis has rarely been interviewed about his music, but when he talked to *Hit Parade* magazine in January 1957, he explained how Sam Phillips helped him:
"You wanna make some blues? he suggested over the phone, knowing I'd always been a sucker for that kind of jive. He mentioned Big Boy Crudup's name and maybe others too. I don't remember . . . I hung up and ran fifteen blocks to Mr. Phillips' office . . . We talked about the Crudup records I knew, . . . settled for 'That's Alright Mama', one of my top favourites . . ."

So Elvis cut five singles for the Sun label, each having a bluesy song on one side and a countryish song on the other.

But by this time, Elvis had been performing all around the Memphis area, and had come to the attention of a man with much less a love of music – but with far bigger dreams and ambitions – than Sam Phillips. That man was Colonel Tom Parker, one-time fairground barker and small-time promoter with an unerring eye for a smart deal, outrageous publicity, and Elvis' almost limitless future. The Colonel became Presley's manager and RCA Victor bought Elvis' Sun recordings. The price paid, which also included a Cadillac, was in 1955 considered extraordinarily high, being $35,000; but as things turned out, RCA Victor was getting gold for glass beads and Sam Phillips had signed away millions and millions of dollars.

Nevertheless, everyone seemed to be quite happy with Elvis Presley's new deal. He got top TV exposure, he broke concert attendance records all over the United States, and he built up a fanatical following in Britain and many other countries which he never bothered to tour. (Elvis always said it was because he was terrified of flying – Colonel Parker, more bluntly, said there just wasn't enough money in it.) Either way, it didn't harm the phenomenal Presley success; if anything it helped, by making Elvis the most untouchable, golden superstar in world history.

Poor Boy Elvis

In any event, turning down huge financial offers became a Colonel Parker pastime, and merely ensured that future offers for the services of 'The King' were ever bigger, ever more sensational. Reportedly, one of the attempts to get Presley to Britain, by a Birmingham promoter, involved offering him £100,000 for one performance in Wembley Stadium. It had been planned that he should appear inside a magnifying bubble so that, in perfect harmony with his image, he would appear to be both completely untouchable and much larger than life. The Colonel, needless to say, rejected the offer, with the characteristic remark: "Well, that's fine money for me and my staff, but what about my poor boy Elvis?"

In the first two years after they acquired him, Elvis gave RCA Victor the no. 1 slot on the singles charts in America (which accounts for 70% of the world record market) for 55 weeks. That's more than one week out of every two when Elvis beat all other comers, and almost single-handedly vanquished the old give-me-the-moonlight regime.

In fact Elvis had *twelve* no. 1 records in the US, all Gold Discs, before he was inducted into the US Army after making his fourth film, *King Creole*, in 1958. These twelve included 'Heartbreak Hotel', 'Hound Dog', 'Love Me Tender', 'All Shook Up', 'Jailhouse Rock', and 'Hard Headed Woman'. While Colonel Parker was later to prove acutely aware of the dangers of over-exposure and cut down the number of concerts, records, and especially interviews, at this early point in Elvis' career, RCA Victor was fairly saturating the market. After 'Hound Dog', they released seven singles at the same time! Every one became a major hit.

Presleymania

It was just like Beatlemania in fact. Presley generated exactly the same hysteria. No-one else could possibly have hits with seven different records all issued the same week. No-one else seemed to need half so many ambulance-men, or doctors, or nurses, or cops, or security-guards, as Elvis made necessary when he did a concert.

His films too were smashes — including the very first one, a Western called *Love Me Tender*, which — as the credits at the beginning admitted — was simply 'introducing Elvis Presley'; and the title song from that film earned Elvis another first in recording history, by notching up over 1,000,000 advance orders before it was even recorded!

And of course, his albums were smashes, some selling over the million mark in their own right. By the time RCA Victor were trying to fill the gap caused by Presley being in the Army and unable to cut new material, they could legitimately issue an album called '50,000,000 Elvis Fans Can't Be Wrong: Elvis' Golden Records Volume 2'. No other singer had ever achieved more than one such volume before.

And British chart history gives an equally favourable record of Presley's early years: six of his LPs and EPs sold well enough to crash the singles charts; and in 1958, with 'Jailhouse Rock' (another film title-song) he broke yet another boundary when that single jumped into the charts from nowhere straight to no. 1 in its first week of release.

Two things made for this shattering success. The first was the acumen of The Colonel. He never put a foot wrong; he guided Presley's affairs with total dedication and uncanny flair that verged on the Midas touch. Example: seeing, in the earliest days, that Presley was going to be huge, he also saw that there would be a sizeable anti-Elvis movement, not just among the oldies, but also among those young people who

just didn't happen to dig his voice, or were perhaps jealous of the effect he had on their favourite girl, or whatever. And he also saw that he and Presley could cash in on that. Suddenly, there was a flood of 'I Love Elvis' buttons, and T-shirts, and balloons, and more besides: along with it, there was a smaller but still considerable flood of 'I Hate Elvis' products . . . and they were all making equally good money — for Elvis Presley Inc.

Parker also knew, and expertly, the way to dangle 'his boy' in front of the financial giants of Hollywood and Madison Avenue in the most challenging, tempting terms possible. He was once approached by the company that was making a film of the hit Broadway musical *Bye Bye Birdie*, who wanted Elvis to appear in the film and perform two songs. "Sure," said the Colonel, "the price is 100,000 dollars." The film man gulped, turned white, swallowed, recovered himself a bit, and said that that kind of figure was unthinkable. "Tell you what I'll do to oblige," said Parker good-naturedly, "I'll toss a coin and you can call. If you lose, you pay 200,000 for two songs. If you win, you get four songs for nothing." The film man ran away in a cold sweat and Elvis never did appear in that film — but the repercussions were tremendous. Everyone began doubling their offers, and Parker certainly didn't have to worry about letting 'Bye Bye Birdie' fly away.

But the second thing that made Elvis so huge, such a unique giant among stars, was simply his own talent. He was the classic poor-boy-who-makes-good — but he was never the boy-next-door. He was never that touchable or reachable. Nik Cohn once said that the difference between British and American rock & roll was that Tommy Steele made it to the London Palladium, and Elvis Presley became God. And it's true, Elvis Presley *did* become God. He came to represent something much bigger than himself — the whole vast potential of adolescence finding its own rebellious identity as something quite separate from the role of imitation-adult.

Yet only someone with as much innate talent as Presley could have come to represent all that. He could do it, and did it, because he lived and breathed the tight connexion between music and sex which White America had long been at great pains to deny. Elvis was indeed, in this sense, 'the nigger in the woodpile': he was the greatest sexual threat to White Virginity in the USA. His style of presentation showed it (his hip-movements were blanked-out on US TV), his way of dressing and posing for photographs showed it, and, most of all, his music showed it. The *New York Times* in fact once went so far as to complain that he 'injected movements of the tongue and indulged in wordless singing that were singularly distasteful.'

Apple Pie and Pork Chops

He had a fantastic mixture of bluntness and suggestiveness — as Mick Jagger was to come along and use for another generation — and he combined both those qualities with a third: that magic magnetism which nowadays is known as charisma. Presley had masses of charisma — masses of whatever magic it takes to keep your ears and eyes riveted on a performer of extra-special power.

Part of that power stemmed from Presley's natural-looking arrogance, which in fact concealed the polite southern boy underneath. Elvis really wasn't very rebellious at all — he said yes sir, no ma'am, to reporters; he liked home-cooking, especially apple pie and pork chops; and he was as patriotic as many of the senior citizens who hated him. Part of it stemmed from his sense of humour — for indeed he had a lightly mocking self-awareness and self-amusement that few people have ever credited him with. And part of it came from having a stronger voice than any of his rivals. It was a voice that could be light-and-delicate (as on early Sun recordings like 'I Don't Care If

The Sun Don't Shine'), or light-and-breathless (as on 'Don't Be Cruel'), or unusually soulful ('Is It So Strange?'), or just beautifully raucous and tough, as on all his pre-Army rockers. In short, he had a range and a control, an ability to punch and to hint delicately with equal sureness and ease, that gave him legitimate claim to the tag 'white blues singer'; and made him the best country-rocker and tough urban rocker there was.

King Kong

But in the beginning, it was his lack of inhibition and his sexuality that had the devastating impact. There was none of the coyness and cleanness of 'going dating' in an adult-approved way as far as Elvis was concerned. Other teenage-aimed singers might make records with titles like 'Put Your Head On My Shoulder', 'At The Hop' and 'Teenage Crush'. Not Elvis. *His* titles were earthy and blunt and mean.

'Trouble'; 'One Night'; 'Baby Let's Play House'; 'Paralyzed'; 'Got A Lot O' Livin' To Do': those were the typical Elvis titles. And they all fitted in with the ingredients that made Presley a unique, thrusting, ominous force. His music always managed to suggest an underlying violence — 'He don't stop playin' till his guit-ar breaks', is a line from the self-describing song 'King Creole'. And as for 'Jailhouse Rock', well not only is violence in the air, but Elvis' voice seems to be raging from the depths of some confinement — raging like King Kong in chains.

In his love-songs Elvis never pretended that he'd 'saved himself' for the girl he was addressing the song to; the lyrics always suggested that he had plenty of experience behind him, and could sweep aside all hesitations and shyness:

> 'If you wanna be loved, baby you gotta love me too:
> Cos I aint for no one-sided love affair:
> Well a fair exchange aint no robbery
> An' the whole world knows that it's true . . .'

('One-Sided Love Affair')

That really lays it on the line; there's not going to be any time-wasting games, and anyone who doesn't agree is just being hypocritical. That's the message, and it typifies the message that Presley was burning into the consciousness of the kids. It added up, over those late '50s years, to nothing less than a sharp concerted attack on all the two-faced conventions and straitjackets which were imposed by adults on the youth of White America.

Presley's delivery gave a stylishness and authority to all these open, blunt songs, which was utterly lacking in other rock artists. He did it not just with sneers and swagger (which plenty of others mimicked), but by a pent-up tremble in his bass notes, sudden full-throated rasps, and equally sudden mellow country moans.

So Presley was saying love minus zero — no limit! — not only years before 'the permissive society' replaced the upright pre-Kennedy America, but also a full six years before the Beatles were wanting to hold your hand. Millions of eager 17-year-olds,

weary of the pudge-next-door who *did* only want to hold their hands, could get off a good deal more honestly when Elvis belted out 'Stuck On You' and 'Doncha Think It's Time'.

It certainly was time, too, that the music related to the real feelings and dreams and emotions and aspirations of teenagers. And it was Elvis Presley's achievement that he made it happen — and made it happen so big that there was no stopping it. Not even Elvis, when he got older and flabbier, could put the clock back. When he came out of the Army in 1960, and grew up, and changed forever, that was *his* concern, not everybody's. The music and the greater freedom and assertiveness it had achieved, kept on rolling. Rocking and rolling. And what happened to Elvis is another story.

Keesee Phototrends

Elvis Presley in **GI Blues**.

When Elvis Presley came out of the US Army in March 1960, it should have been like Christ coming back to earth. Somehow, it wasn't quite like that. The fanfares sounded, the fans (if not the angels) sang, but the King of Pop Kings didn't quite set the world on fire again like he should have done.

It would have been impossible perhaps to match the myth which his absence had only strengthened — the Presley legend was *too* big to live up to. 'Elvis Presley' — the very words on the page produced, in those last days of the '50s, a kind of emotional charge in the mass of the music-buying public. They stood for power and anarchy and sex and the ultimate music, with a vividness that no superstar's name today can match.

The fact that through most of 1958 and all of 1959, Presley was away from the scene — even away from America, stationed mostly in some obscure part of West Germany — only served to make him more thrillingly untouchable, more charismatic, a star of greater magnetism.

Old Shep

In the meantime his record company, RCA Victor, had material they could release. Quite a lot of material in fact — especially for those days, when it was unusual if an artist cut many more tracks than were needed for immediate release. The self-indulgence of today's superstars, given to whiling away large parts of their lives in studios, was an unheard-of thing. But where Elvis was concerned, RCA Victor were fortunate. They not only had spare masters on hand, but indeed spare masterpieces — excellent, highly com-mercial stuff. The smash hit singles 'I Got Stung'/'One Night', 'A Fool Such As I'/ 'I Need Your Love Tonight', and 'Big Hunk O'Love' were all issued and turned gold in 1959, while Elvis was away in the US Army.

And then by pretending — quite shrewdly — to have run out of unissued material, RCA Victor managed at a stroke to pep up people's eagerness even more, and to sell a scraped-together EP so heavily that it climbed high up the British singles chart. The tracks were assembled from much earlier sessions and included the all-time greatest tear-jerker, Presley's incredible version of 'Old Shep'. New gold.

Back in the USA

This was the situation when Elvis got back to the USA, but things went slightly wrong, from the fans' point of view, straight away. A newly-recorded single — first proof of the continued existence of Elvis' phenomenal voice — was released, was great, and sold 1,000,000 copies in six days. But it was chart positions that mattered above all else, and in the charts this new Presley single, 'Stuck On You'/ 'Fame And Fortune', didn't quite pull it off. It failed to hold the top slot in the States for as long as the return of the Messiah would have warranted, and was toppled unceremoniously by the Everly Brothers. In Britain, where fever-pitch fanaticism was supposed to run higher, the let-down was worse still. Far from crashing straight in at no. 1 as expected, 'Stuck On You' came in at no. 6, went to no. 2, stayed there only a fortnight and then plunged to no. 8. It never made the top position at all.

Now obviously, a record that goes gold in under a week, tops the US charts — US record sales then represented 70% of the world market — and jumps straight from

nowhere to the middle of the British Top Ten is doing pretty well. No other artist, except the Beatles at the height of Beatlemania, would have felt any pangs of regret or twinges of disappointment over that. But it was less than the total blitz that Elvis Presley's return to the scene was meant to achieve.

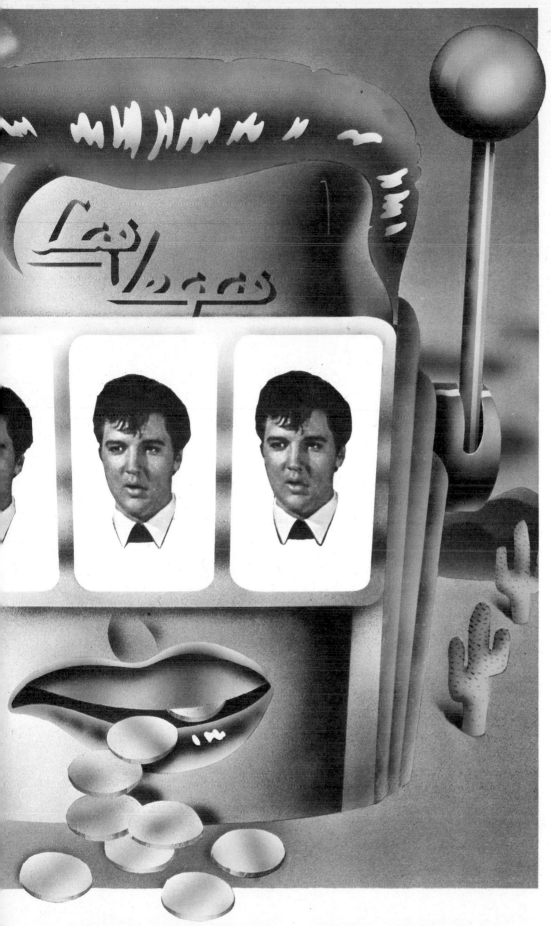

Anyhow, there it was. And it wasn't the only thing wrong. Presley promptly appeared on a US TV-Special, being welcomed back by the very man whose music and life style was supposed to have been vanquished by Presley's early rock & roll pioneering — Frank Sinatra. Sinatra was widely regarded by many rock fans as 'the enemy': the nastiest pseudo-jazz smoothie of them all.

A bad move. Well-nigh betrayal, in fact. And if Elvis Presley's fans had let themselves stop to read it, there was the proverbial writing on the wall. There had been a lot of worrying publicity stories during Elvis' military service about what a good boy he was, about how his officers were proud of him, about how he was just an ordinary, humble, regular guy. And now, back he was with a shameful lack of sideburns and a good deal less grease on his hair, slapping Frank Sinatra on the back and swapping his army uniform for another — an evening-suit. Elvis Presley in an evening-suit!

Hollywood

There was no escaping it. The tiger was turning tame; the mean, moody rock & roll supremo was going soft.

And of course he was. Presley was being steered, as ever, by Colonel Tom Parker, his manager; and Parker was steering him, also as ever, towards wherever most money was waiting. It was waiting, naturally enough, in a broader record-buying market — which is why the songs after 'Stuck On You' did indeed 'go soft' — and it was also waiting in Hollywood.

So Presley churned out waterfalls of ballad singles, and a matching torrent of light-entertainment Hollywood films. The singles were bigger smashes all over the world than any of his pre-Army rock records, and the films were far better box-office draws than any of his pre-Army celluloid adventures.

A couple of these new movies happened to be interesting, or even good, like the consecutive *Flaming Star* and *Wild In The Country*; and a couple of the records were pretty fine as well. But such results were beside the point. The point as far as Colonel Parker was concerned was that Presley was getting $3,000,000 plus out of Hollywood every year for a total of nine weeks' work; and record-royalties were bringing the annual income of Elvis Presley Inc. up beyond the four million mark. And the point as far as the rock music audience was concerned was that they had lost a unique, unmeasurable talent — and gained instead a plastic replica whose only uniqueness was as a money-making show-biz machine.

Certainly the thing that showed most clearly the yawning gap between the real Elvis and the new plastic one was the quality of the albums from 1961 onwards.

There were two early exceptions — 'Elvis Is Back', the first fruit of his return to the studios which drew, like his early records, on old blues songs; and a religious

There was no escaping that unpalatable fact; and crazy as it may now seem, many fans, especially in Britain, found it *very* unpalatable indeed. Many Presley fans at the time regarded it as a personal affront that 'Stuck On You' was kept off the no. 1 slot — kept off not only by other (lesser) artists, not only by other British (and therefore *much* lesser) artists, but by what seemed like a terrible cockney conspiracy. Lonnie Donegan's 'My Old Man's A Dustman' and then 'Do You Mind' by Anthony Newley were the guilty parties. It was as if the tiger had been refused entry to the Ark, in order to make more room for the sheep.

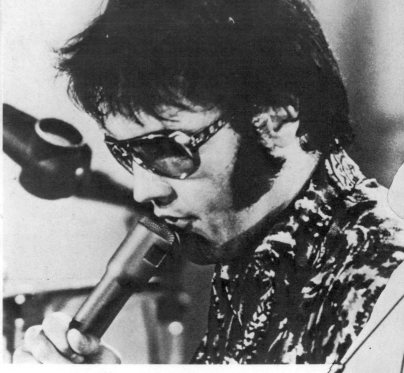

Above: Elvis may not have changed much but after the Army (far left), he lost his sideburns which (far right) have grown again — although his hair is noticeably less greasy than in his 1957 portrait (bottom right). Live (centre pics), Elvis still comes on like a regular superstar, though without the moody petulance that characterised him in *Love Me Tender* (bottom left).

album cut very soon afterwards, 'His Hand In Mine', on which Elvis' voice retained most of its power and sexiness, but achieved a new high of delicacy and precision. (It was from this session that, five years later, RCA Victor took and released 'Crying In The Chapel' — the first Presley single to top the British charts after the advent of Beatlemania.)

Apart from those two albums, Elvis' output was dismal. Most of the albums were the soundtracks for his films though not, in fact, the actual soundtracks: the films always had strings dubbed over the vacuous bubblegum songs, whereas the records didn't for a surprisingly long time. It's strange, and to Elvis' credit, that on his records he held out against the Mantovani syndrome until 1965. 'All That I Am', a particularly lame single of that year, was in fact the first-ever Presley track with strings on.

Elvis is Dead

And the Beatles, of course, made Elvis Presley's mid-'60s output look as obsolete as it was. They had set out, in John Lennon's words, ''to be bigger than Presley,'' and by the end of 1964 they had done it. When they arrived at Kennedy Airport at the start of their first US tour, they were met by scenes of hysteria the like of which had not been seen since Presley's 1957 concerts. And placards bobbed above the heads of the crowds with pointed messages like 'ELVIS IS DEAD: LONG LIVE RINGO'.

As a source of any kind of musical freshness Elvis was indeed dead. Even as a money-making machine, he was getting in need of an overhaul. Colonel Parker and RCA Victor began to have a hard time of it.

They had set Elvis firmly in the direction of the lucrative All-Round-Entertainment field — comedy films, like *Follow That Dream*, and mickey-mouse novelty songs like 'Big Boots', and 'There's No Room To Rhumba In A Sports Car'. Yet they found that they weren't making quite the killing they'd expected.

King of Schmalz

They found it was no longer enough to make empty, plot-less, star-vehicle movies rigidly rooted in the tradition of '30s and '40s Hollywood. With every film — and Elvis made over 30 of them between 1960 and 1968 — not only did 'Golden Boy' seem weaker and more hopelessly out of touch, but the box-office returns diminished. And Hollywood itself was in decline.

Besides all that, the switch of image from rock star to Everyman was not overwhelmingly successful. Elvis Presley's name was too heavily associated with rock & roll and teenage hooliganism for the mums and dads to take him to their hearts.

Sensing this, Colonel Parker tried to have Elvis straddle all the different markets: tried vainly to keep his star as the 'King of Rock', as well as have him turn into the 'King of Schmalz'. He was over-ambitious.

It was the 'jack-of-all-trades-master-of-none' problem. The records Elvis issued swayed waywardly between rock and pop and popcorn, and they didn't succeed in pleasing anyone very much. At times he released new but spineless semi-rockers that few old fans and no mums and dads were going to buy — records like 'Blue River' and 'Do The Clam'. At other times he issued dire middle-of-the-road material like 'All That I Am' and 'You'll Never Walk

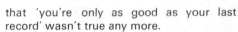

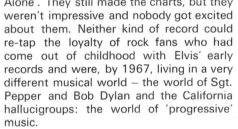

Alone'. They still made the charts, but they weren't impressive and nobody got excited about them. Neither kind of record could re-tap the loyalty of rock fans who had come out of childhood with Elvis' early records and were, by 1967, living in a very different musical world — the world of Sgt. Pepper and Bob Dylan and the California hallucigroups: the world of 'progressive' music.

Holy Writ

Elvis Presley was resolutely anything but progressive. He was positively retrogressive: so much so that sometimes, in desperation, RCA Victor had released singles that Elvis had recorded way back in the mid-'50s because at least they were better (and no less old-fashioned) than the stuff in his current bag. 'Aint That Lovin' You Baby' and 'Tell Me Why', both recorded in 1957 and rejected as substandard at that time, were issued as bidding-for-the-charts singles in the mid-'60s.

It was a sorry situation, except in one respect. There was still a considerable vestige of magic in Elvis Presley's name — enough to give him an aura of professional immortality, and enough to make a lot of people keep hoping that one day he would kick the mud off his boots and make some more music again. Great music, that is.

And then, by the end of 1967, time — which had seemed to be running out for him — suddenly started to be on his side. The rock audience had matured enough to start breaking free of its old (pop) prejudices. Suddenly the charts weren't Holy Writ any more. Suddenly 'modern versus old-fashioned' seemed a silly dispute, and the word 'new' stopped meaning 'therefore better and hipper than anything made three months ago'. Suddenly people found virtues in older music, and got genuinely interested in the history, the roots, of rock music.

Suddenly, the long-standing pop maxim

that 'you're only as good as your last record' wasn't true any more.

For Elvis, this meant that he was in with a chance. It meant that if he cared to stop Hollywooding about, he could try to make some quality albums and expect recognition for them — as well, of course, as a new recognition for his pre-Army recordings. He could free himself of the impossible obligation to be up-to-date (which had even led to a film set in 'Swinging London', though filmed entirely in Hollywood!) and could take advantage of the widening of taste that people were undergoing.

He tried. He gradually disentangled himself from all those awful filming plans, and began to take a hold on his recording career. He was largely foiled by the cautious Colonel Parker, who seemed, by 1968, to have lost forever his once-infallible instinct. And the story of Elvis Presley's recording career from 1968 until now is the sad but still not quite hopeless tale of that caution and that loss.

Elvis in Memphis

There were plenty of people around, by 1968, who wanted to take Elvis into a studio and make him come up with a good no-shit new album. Chris Moman was one of them, and he was given the chance.

He brought Elvis back to Memphis to record — for the first time in 14 years; he selected a bunch of songs because they were good rather than because Elvis Presley Inc. would get more money by relying on certain washed-out composers; he got an exceptional team of musicians together and got them jamming and loosening up nicely with Elvis; and he threw all the Colonel Parker henchmen and hangers-on out of the studio!

There were two results: one was a good album, 'From Elvis In Memphis'; the other was a guarantee that the mortified Colonel Parker would never allow such a thing to happen again.

On a smaller scale, the occasional sortie into good records continued – 'Suspicious Minds', 'If I Can Dream' and 'Burning Love' were good singles, and 'Elvis Country', a 1971 album, was impressive. And in addition, the TV-Special Elvis did in late 1968 (his first television appearance since the one with Sinatra nearly nine years earlier) had many great and powerful moments.

But basically, Presley was perversely kept pointing firmly down the road to plasticity. The films stopped, but super-rich Las Vegas supper-clubs took their place and Elvis got into a new rut, imitating his old hip-swivels and 'All Shook Up' grunts every night for an audience of rich, middle-aged women.

And that is the Elvis Presley that today's posters and documentary films of him show – a man who exudes money-glamour, whose wardrobe is enough to shame Barbarella, and who is surrounded by an entourage and a stage-management that is truly fit for a King. Solid-gold Tutankhamen come back to a fair imitation of real life.

That's the superficial picture. Underneath lies something far healthier. Take away all the theatre and there is a dynamic stage presence. Take away all the horrific brass and orchestra-noises from recent 'live' albums like 'Elvis: Aloha From Hawaii Via Satellite', and there is a fine basic rock group working for Presley. Plough through all the rubbish he has put out in the last

few years, and you'll find about an album's-worth of actively good and promising tracks.

That's the frustrating thing about him. He still shows signs of an enormous talent. It peeps through the plastic now and again.

But he has to choose. Against him is the whole deathly weight of the American money-machine. He can either go down in history as the last of the great manipulated stars who, for lack of integrity and lack of self-respect, clutched at every last show-biz straw and droned on for decades after he should have been put out of his hollow misery; or he can go down in history as one of the true 20th-century musical greats.

Elvis was born on January 8th, 1935 in Tulepo, Mississippi. His parents were poor Southern whites, living in a two-roomed log cabin. When he was 13 years old the family moved to Memphis.

1954: Elvis met Sam Phillips who signed him to Sun Records. They had an 'instant' local hit with 'That's All Right Mama'.

1955: At the end of this year Elvis signed with 'Colonel' Tom Parker and moved to the RCA label.

1956: 'Heartbreak Hotel' was released in January, and became Elvis' first Gold Record; followed by three more that same year.

1958: After two years of solidly dominating the rock scene, Elvis was drafted into the US Army.

1960: An out-of-touch Elvis came out of the Army to an anti-climactic return to the charts. 'Stuck On You' only made no. 2 in Britain.

There then followed 'The Hollywood Years', with Elvis making $3,000,000 per year from films alone. His records from then on went into a steady decline, with titles like 'Kiss Me Quick' (1963), 'Kissing Cousins' (1964), and 'If Every Day Was Like Christmas'

BACK TRACK

(1966). Elvis keeps threatening to return to his former glory with the odd record such as 'In The Ghetto' (1969), and the 'From Elvis In Memphis' album.

There are over 40 Elvis albums currently available. The following list represents the key material:

1 'Elvis World Wide 50 Gold Award Hits': a four-album package with one or two weak tracks.

2 'Elvis 'Golden Records' Vol 1': a must for every rock fan; contains 'Hound Dog', 'All Shook Up', and 'Heartbreak Hotel'.

3 'Elvis Rock 'n' Roll': 'That's All Right Mama', 'Mystery Train', 'Blue Suede Shoes', and 'Trying To Get To You'.

4 'A Date With Elvis' (deleted, but much missed): 'Baby Let's Play House', 'Blue Moon', and 'Good Rockin' To-night'.

5 'Elvis 'Golden Records' Vol 2': 'Jailhouse Rock', 'Teddy Bear', and 'One Night'.

6 'Elvis Is Back' (uneven): 'Girl Of My Best Friend', 'Reconsider Baby', and 'Such A Night'.

7 'Rock 'n' Roll Vol 2': 'Paralyzed', 'Rip It Up', and 'So Glad You're Mine'.

8 'Elvis' Golden Records Vol 3' (patchy): 'His Latest Flame', 'It's Now Or Never', and 'Stuck On You'.

9 'Elvis TV Special': an NBC TV programme soundtrack.

10 'From Elvis in Memphis': 'In The Ghetto'.

11 'Memphis To Vegas'.

12 'Vegas To Memphis'.

Cyrus Andrews

LFI

Little Richard

The man who put the Bop in

A-Wop-Bop -A-Loo-Bop -Lop-Bam-Boom

Some people like rock. Some people like to roll. But Little Richard was something else. He had a bounce and flash that made even Elvis look slow, and a voice with more speed than a runaway express train; sweeping all the pale imitations before him into oblivion.

These days Richard has become a pale imitation of himself, dressing his band in grey, himself in gay, and losing touch with the audience almost every time. Typically he once threw Jimi Hendrix out of his band for wearing brightly coloured shirts, but there was a time when he was the biggest ball of energy around.

Richard was two years late crossing the Atlantic because his label, Specialty, didn't initially have an international distribution

deal. So Britain got 'Rip It Up' from Bill Haley and 'Long Tall Sally' from Pat Boone, of all people, in 1956, which in no way prepared for the arrival of the real thing.

Little Richard's first American hit had been 'Tutti Frutti' in 1955, followed in 1956 by 'Long Tall Sally' and then 'Rip It Up'. He finally crashed into the British charts in February 1957 with a mammoth double-sider, 'Long Tall Sally'/'Tutti Frutti'. Either could have been the 'A' side for there was little to choose between them – what was going for them they both had – and from the moment Little Richard opened his mouth or fingered a piano key, it was clear that unlike Haley or Boone he was not wholesale.

Behind him the tempo was hard and furious, but he upped it, thrashing his keyboard double-time as if his body clock was synched in twice as fast as everyone else's. All the while he bellowed, roared, screamed,

and sometimes even sang. Tarzan had nothing on Richard. This vocal overkill meant you could hardly catch the words, and truthfully at first it seemed these were only gibberish. But 'awopbopaloobopalop-bamboom' had meaning for all who wanted to understand. Here was a private language that conveyed nothing to squares and straights. Here was the language of rock & roll.

For all those who sent that record high into the charts a subsequent view of Little Richard was no kind of let-down, since his appearance was as outrageous as his music. He showed up first on album sleeves and in the music press, most often in a stance midway between an Al Jolson impersonation and a back-flip demonstration, only crazier than both – feet apart, knees bent and together, torso leant back, arms in a hands-up position; preparing perhaps to

29

spring upon the piano keys. Whatever the purpose of the stance it was impossible to describe the set of Richard's limbs with greater accuracy owing to the nature of his clothes, which were unusual.

His jacket fell clear of his body way down towards his knees, whilst the trousers hung like giant gaberdine flags. His tailor must've been on a percentage from the mill. A shiny pompadour hairstyle made his head appear larger than it actually was, and his facial expressions would emphasise its roundness; these expressions switched between terror and serenity as his eyes revolved at all times like dark marbles on white saucers. As a final stroke he grew above his top lip a moustache so thin it might have been traced with a sharp pencil. It was hard to believe he was real. Then *Don't Knock The Rock* was at last put out, and it was all true. In the scene where he appeared onstage, a dance-floor fist fight broke out which turned into a mass brawl. That figured.

Richard actually toured Britain with those package shows that played one-nighters up and down the country; fifteen minutes to race through your hits — half an hour if you had top billing — and wherever you went on the backing was Sounds Incorporated. He didn't cause any fights, but he was pretty wild all the same. He would come on in that same baggy suit and start right into one real hairy rocker — 'Rip It Up', 'Lucille', 'Good Golly Miss Molly' — it didn't matter which — and straightaway the audience would be up and jumping and shouting and screaming — then he'd do another, then another, then some more. He didn't bother with a piano stool; instead he would stand twisted away from the keys, face on to the auditorium, jerking his hands up and down to one side. Then, without missing a chord, he'd cock one leg up onto the instrument and raise another cheer playing that way.

The Hammy Stripper

He'd be breaking sweat by now, so he'd shake off his jacket and tug out his shirt tails, making like a hammy stripper. The crowd would shout and whistle and stamp and cat-call, and thus encouraged he would tread coyly to the stage edge — the back-up boys not for one moment letting up on the rooty riffs — and step carefully out of his pumps. Then he'd pull off his socks, unbutton his shirt and take that off too — so you could see he was in fine shape physically, looking brown and sexy with the glistening sweat and all. Next he would make ready to toss these garments (the shirt, the pumps, the socks) to the front stalls, with the calculated result that everyone who wanted to be in line for a memento of the wild man had worked down into the aisles dividing the expensive seats — thus causing plenty of concern amongst the stewards who weren't at all used to this kind of havoc and seemed mostly to be O.A.P's fattening their pension. And who was this mad coon anyhow?

The shoes he wouldn't throw too far: they'd most likely hurt someone, and even if he wasn't going to wear them again he probably didn't like to think of them getting scuffed. The socks he just dangled and dropped, since not even *he* could make too much production about sweaty hose. (His keenest fans liked to imagine they were silk and monogrammed, but losing two pairs a night — early and late houses — he doubtless sent out to the nearest store for nylon.)

Finally, he swung the shirt lassoo-style so no one was quite sure at which point of the arc he would let go, and thus where it would land. At best it would float out above the stretching crowd — caught brilliant white in the spotlight before dropping to be snatched and torn and taken home and pinned up: 'A Piece Of Little Richard's Shirt, Slough Adelphi, October 23rd'. He'd hitch up his trousers after, just to show that was the finish of that part of the act.

Too Much

The band was still at it, by this time working up some kind of a sweat themselves, and Richard would dive straight back in with 'Ready Teddy' or 'Jenny Jenny' or 'She's Got It' — 'Ruby lips, shapely hips, when she walks down the street all the cats flip, she's got it . . .' Whichever, he'd be tearing his throat and lungs apart and beating away on that rock-crazed grand.

What next Richard? Climb up on the piano, trailing mike wires, sing and shout and go a little crazier up there! Then jump off. . . . But he's fallen, collapsed, he can't get up! The music's suffocated and stopped, helpers are rushing onto the stage from the wings with robes and towels and damp cloths and all kinds of stuff. Wow, he really drove himself to that, he just crazied himself right into the ground. Why don't they put the poor guy on a stretcher or something instead of just crowding him? That's no way to treat a guy who's nearly dead or in a coma or unconscious at the very least. Then ''Oooo mah soooooooul'' the invalid squeals in a soaring falsetto, and the sonofabitch is on his feet shoving the other comedians away, throwing off the robes and the towels and the damp cloths, and the audience — never once caring that he's made monkeys of them all — lift the roof off with a colossal roar of delight.

Simply . . . the Best

Even Richard couldn't follow that, so he'd finish the number as soon as he could and they'd bring the curtain down. Of course he would have to come out again otherwise no-one would have gone home. So he did, wrapped in a big white robe like a contender who'd gone 15 rounds with the champ and got his arm raised when it was over. Richard was simply the best.

The fact is he hadn't made it to the top overnight. He was only 20 when 'Tutti Frutti' sold a million, but he'd already been around for a while. He'd sung in church during his early teens and been a blues singer at 15, recording for RCA in what they called a 'cry' style. He sang gospel blues for Specialty before he started into rock & roll (keeping the catch in his voice), then laid down everything he was going to

Redferns

The different moods of Little Richard.

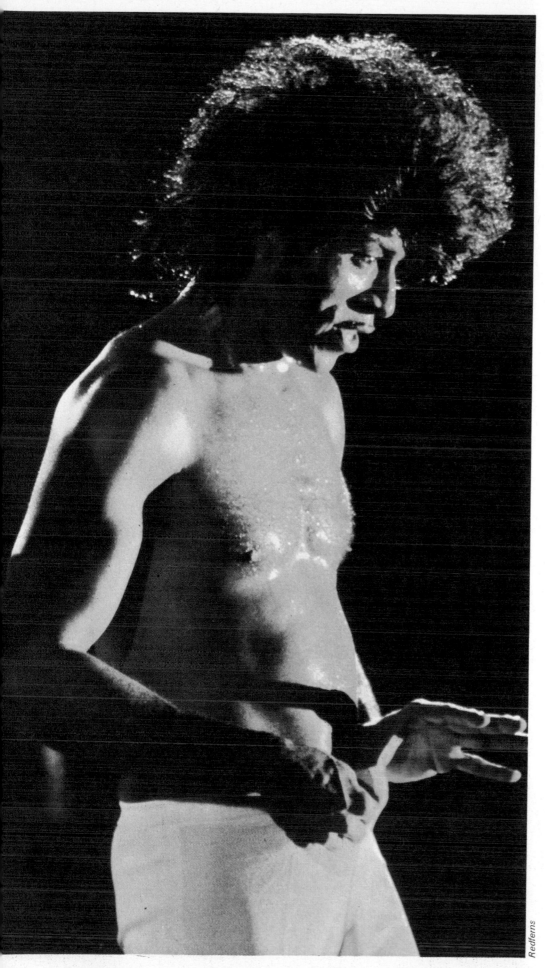

do in a spell that lasted only nine months. They spread it thin though, so it lasted through into his retirement.

Richard, the story goes, did a deal with God when he was in trouble, and when He came up with His end, Richard kept his word too, threw a bunch of jewellery into the sea, and quit rock & roll. He played gospel instead. It was hard to believe. He served the Lord in this manner for several years, but then he made a come-back. The new songs weren't as good as the old ones, but no one cared. It was the old ones the people wanted to hear — 'Tutti Frutti' and 'Long Tall Sally', 'Keep A Knockin'' and 'Miss Ann'. He came on just as strong as ever and for all that religion he was still vain and worldly and profane. Still Little Richard.

Laughs and Jeers

He was yet to clean up totally however and make the big killing. He had to wait until someone decided it was time for a real rock & roll revival. That happened at the tail end of the '60s. The idea was that the kids were so full of everything *new* that had come along since the Beatles first kicked things around in 1963, that at least they must have forgotten what came before and at most never known. After all, a 17-year-old who was digging Cream in 1968 could scarcely have been out of nappies in rock & roll's heyday. Right boys? Right boss! So they wheeled out Bill Haley and Jerry Lee Lewis and Bo Diddley and Chuck Berry and Fats Domino and natch Little Richard, and stuck them up in front of the long-hairs and said do the old songs. And they did.

Chuck Berry was just about the only one who hadn't lost it. In fact he was almost better than ever. Bill Haley, well he'd been no kind of teenager back in 1955; Jerry Lee didn't bother to hide his preference for country; Bo Diddley was a one-song man; and Fats Domino had never been a genuine rock & roller anyway, but was a New Orleans rhythm and blues artist from way back. They were getting fat fees though, so it goes.

"I Am the King"

None of that counted for anything set beside what had happened to Little Richard. Instead of the monstro wild man of rock & roll was someone who only resembled a star when the sequins on his go-go tunic twinkled. He did his strip just like before — only this time it was a cheap drag act. Those that didn't laugh jeered. It seemed he didn't care too much about his songs any more — anything would do. So he even did Presley stuff. Although he could still thrash his piano, he preferred shimmying at the front of the stage or on the grand's top, from where he'd once fallen in epic mock exhaustion. For this reason he employed a stand-in pianist. American audiences seem to have tolerated this somewhat better than the British fans, who prefer Chuck Berry these days.

Richard said: "I am still the greatest. I am the King of Rock & Roll." But his most loyal subjects have turned away to watch their memories instead.

In front of an incredulous audience Little Richard strips; turning himself on as he tears his shirt into shreds and flings the pieces to the audience.

31

Chuck Berry

Still rockin' 20 years later

Chuck Berry stands alongside Elvis Presley, the Beatles and Bob Dylan as one of the key figures in the history of rock music. His career provides a thread linking '50s rock & Roll with contemporary white rock; blues with pop; black music with white audiences. As well as being an enormously effective and influential stylistic innovator, his lyrics in many ways articulate the underlying spirit of rock & roll more vividly and lastingly than any other artist.

Chicago calling/1930–1955

Berry has never been very forthcoming about his date of birth except to say that it was October 18th. The year is believed to have been between 1929 and 1932; the place was St. Louis, Missouri.

His background is in many ways typical of the black performers who shaped the musical direction of rock. He began singing in a church choir at the age of six – which, as he's said himself, 'seems to be the ritual.' While still at high school, he began learning to play guitar, and by the early '50s he had formed a group. He recalls how his earliest 'professional' appearance came in a high school glee club revue, playing 'Confessing The Blues' – already it seems that his style was showing, and his outrageous lyrics and raw, crude guitar-work received a rousing welcome.

His next step was similarly typical. The late '40s and '50s saw a large number of major southern blues artists become part of the mass migration of blacks to the northern industrial cities, particularly Chicago. There, Muddy Waters, Elmore James, Howlin' Wolf, Little Walter and others transformed the rural styles of the South into the heavily amplified, raucous Chicago bar blues sound, with its loud, emphatic beat. Chuck Berry played with the Muddy Waters band at one of its club gigs in the city early in 1955. The blues star liked his style and suggested that he get in touch with Leonard Chess, the head of Chess Records, for whom all the major Chicago blues artists recorded. Leonard Chess told him to come back with some of his material, and when he returned with six tracks – including 'Maybellene' and 'Wee Wee Hours' – taped on his $79 mono. recorder, he was signed up immediately.

Phillip Parr

Two weeks later he had his first recording session with Chess, and his first record, 'Maybellene', was released in May. It reached no. 5 in the singles charts and sold a million!

Close your books, get out of your seat/1955–1959

In spite of the blues background from which it arose, 'Maybellene' was not a blues record. It provides a striking example, in fact, of the way in which black and white musical traditions intermingled to produce rock & roll. It was conceived as a country and western song; hence the incongruous hillbilly name of the heroine, a subject on which Berry once remarked: ''. . . the only Maybellene I ever knew was the name of a cow.'' The way Berry performed it was in a coarser version of the 'rockabilly' style, successfully pioneered in Memphis by strongly country-influenced white artists on the Sun label.

The Dollar Dictates

The records he issued immediately after the initial hit – 'Thirty Days' and 'No Money Down' – came closer to the spirit of the bluesy music he liked most, but both failed to make the pop charts. In retrospect, it's clear that Chuck Berry's classic recordings would probably never have occurred if there had not been an overriding desire to break through into the lucrative white market; a speculation backed by Berry's oft-quoted belief that 'the dollar dictates what music is written.' The fact that Alan Freed, the DJ most responsible for bringing black music to white radio audiences, was present at the 'Maybellene' session (he is even credited as part-composer) confirms the impression that one of Chuck Berry's chief aims was to make money. He was once asked if he would have written his hit songs even if it had not paid him to do so. He replied simply: ''No, I wouldn't have had time. Commercialism is a great instigator.''

Between 1956 and 1958, Berry found a way of regularly harnessing his creativity to the demands of the market. 'Roll Over Beethoven' was a medium-sized pop hit in 1956, and set the pattern. He evolved a readily identifiable style characterised by chugging rhythms based on switching rapidly back and forth between two or three chords; wailing and clanging lead guitar sounds, with biting high-speed solos serving as explosive intros; staccato rhythms in the lyrics reinforcing the overall impression of speed; and slick, clearly enunciated vocals.

The sly, sinuous clarity of his singing was important to his success. It meant that the words were almost always audible and became a far more central part of his songs than they were with most rock & roll. Also, of course, it helped him to reach the white audiences who had always complained that they couldn't understand what black artists were saying. Above all he was cool – rather than committing himself entirely to the wild abandon which rock & roll seemed to imply, Chuck Berry often adopted the stance of a person commenting on the action from a slightly removed position, leaving space for wit and humour.

Prolific

He entered fully into his stride with 'School Day', which reached the Top Ten early in 1957; to be followed later that year by 'Rock And Roll Music'. 1958 was a great year for him: his biggest hit, 'Sweet Little Sixteen', reached no. 2 and was followed into the charts by 'Johnny B. Goode' and than 'Carol'. But Berry was to have no more major hits in the '50s, though other recordings between then and early 1961 were well remembered, and exerted almost as much influence on later rock: songs like 'Beautiful Delilah', 'Sweet Little Rock And Roller', 'Jo Jo Gunne', 'Almost Grown', 'Little Queenie', 'Back In The USA', 'Too Pooped To Pop', 'Let It Rock', 'Bye Bye Johnny', 'Jaguar And The Thunderbird', 'Talkin' 'Bout You' and 'Come On'. He was, in fact, an extremely prolific composer, and some of the songs for which he is best known were not even issued as 'A' sides at the time. Songs like 'Brown-Eyed Handsome Man', 'Reelin' And Rockin'', and 'Memphis Tennessee'.

Life-Style

In writing his lyrics, Chuck Berry consciously aimed at appealing to the new white teenage rock & roll audience. In doing so, he defined a life-style which revolved around the music, and created a series of anthems that celebrated speed, sex and dancing – life as fun, and fun as physical excitement. Songs about driving frequently recurred: the car was personal territory; simultaneously providing opportunities for sex, listening to rock & roll and moving around how and where you wanted. His vision was essentially anti-Puritan, anti-Romantic, and rooted in city life. And it was *rebellious*, because Berry's songs precisely located the enemy – work, school, the law, parents and old age. 'School Day' summed up the attitudes he affirmed:

'Soon as three o'clock rolls around
You finally lay your burden down
Close your books, get out of your seat
Down the hall and into the street
Up to the corner and round the bend
Right to the juke joint you go in
Drop the coin right into the slot
You gotta hear something that's really hot
With the one you love you're making romance
All day long you've been wanting to dance
Feeling the music from head to toe
Round and round and round you go . . .
. . . . Hail, hail rock'n'roll!
Deliver me from the days of old!'

As in most of his songs the vitality stems partly from the rich details of his observations. His openly patriotic hymn to America, 'Back In The USA', is bursting with this kind of energy:

'Did I miss the skyscrapers, did I miss the
long freeway?

From the coasts of California to the shores
of the Delaware Bay?
You can betcha your life I did till I got back
in the USA . . .
. . . Looking hard for a drive-in, searching for
Arconica Bay
Where hamburgers sizzle on an open grill
night and day
And the juke box jumping with records back
in the USA . . .
. . . I'm so glad I'm living in the USA
Anything you want, got it right here in the
USA.'

Berry wrote and sang about teenagers; about sex and cars, the boredom of school, the way that parents didn't understand them. His music and words perfectly expressed what the kids felt but possibly could not say. His talent was for imagining himself in the place of a teenager (even though he was almost certainly 10 years older than his audience), and an ability to understand and express their problems. In 'Sweet Little Sixteen' he summed up their dilemma personally:

'Sweet Little Sixteen,
She's got the grown up blues,
Tight dresses and lipstick,
She's sporting high heel shoes,
Oh but tomorrow morning,
She'll have to change her trend,
And be sweet sixteen
And back in class again.'

When Pete Townshend gave one of his astute commentaries on the meaning of rock, Berry's name came automatically to mind: ''Mother has just fallen down the stairs, Dad's lost all his money at the dog track, the baby's got TB. In comes the kid, man, with his transistor radio, grooving to Chuck Berry. He doesn't give a shit about Mum falling down the stairs. He's with rock & roll.''

Have Mercy, judge/1960–1964

By 1960, however, rock & roll was on its knees. Elvis was being cleaned-up in the Army, Little Richard had gone back to church, Holly and Cochran were dead, Jerry Lee was returning to country ballads after falling into disrepute over his 'child bride'. And Chuck Berry suffered a similar fate at the hands of vindictive Puritanism when, in late 1959, he was charged with transporting a minor over a state line for immoral purposes.

The most common version of the abduction story is that the girl, an Indian from Texas, went with Berry to work as a cloakroom assistant and salesgirl at his night-club in St. Louis. When he fired her, she went to the police and revealed that she was only 14. A series of trials followed, with Berry making fewer records and getting much less airplay. According to local court records, the wrangle culminated in his conviction and a two-year jail sentence, begun in February 1962. Berry denies all this: he says he was acquitted, and adds that he certainly didn't know the girl was so young.

Born 18th October, somewhere between 1928 and 1932.

Professional debut in the early '50s at high school 'Glee Club' review.

1955: Moved to Chicago, gigged with Muddy Waters and signed with Chess Records. 'Maybellene' reaches no. 5 in USA.

1956: 'Roll Over Beethoven' makes no. 29. 'Thirty Days', 'No Money Down', 'Brown-Eyed Handsome Man', and 'You Can't Catch Me' all miss the US charts.

1957: 'School Day' (no. 5); 'Rock And Roll Music' (no. 8); 'Oh Baby Doll' (no. 57).

1958: 'Sweet Little Sixteen' (no. 2 USA, no. 16 UK); 'Johnny B. Goode' (Top Ten USA); 'Beautiful Delilah' (no. 81); 'Carol' (no. 18); 'Sweet Little Rock And Roller' (no. 47); 'Jo Jo Gunne' (no. 83); 'Merry Christmas Baby' (no. 71); 'Run Rudolph Run' (no. 73).

1959: 'Antony Boy' (no. 60); 'Almost Grown' (no. 60); 'Little Queenie' (no. 80); 'Back In The USA' (no. 37); 'Broken Arrow' (miss).

BACK TRACK

1960: 'Too Pooped To Pop' (no. 42); 'Let It Rock' (no. 64); misses were 'Bye Bye Johnny'; 'Mad Lad'; 'Jaguar And The Thunderbird' and 'Talkin' 'Bout You'.

1961: 'Come On' (miss).

1963: 'Let It Rock'/'Memphis Tennessee' (no. 6 UK).

1964: 'No Particular Place To Go' (no. 10 USA, no. 3 UK); 'Nadine' (no. 23); 'You Never Can Tell' (no. 14); 'Little Marie' (no. 54); 'Promised Land' (no. 1).

1965: 'Dear Dad' (no. 95); misses were 'It Wasn't Me' and 'Lonely Schooldays'.

1966: 'Club Nitty Gritty' (miss).

1967: 'Back To Memphis' (miss).

1968: 'Feelin' It' and 'Louie To Frisco' (misses).

1970: 'Tulane' (miss).

1972: 'My Ding-A-Ling' (no. 1 USA and UK).

1973: 'Reelin' And Rockin'' (no. 27 USA, no. 18 UK).

*(Information courtesy of **Let It Rock**). Chart positions refer to USA unless otherwise stated.*

Whatever the facts of the case, the upshot was that while schmalz dominated the pop scene in the early '60s, Chuck Berry was notable by his absence.

They're really rockin' in Bolton/1964–1966

When Berry did re-appear he landed firmly on his feet. The British rock renaissance was in full spate, and he was its chief hero.

On one level, his influence here lay in the simple fact that almost all the major British beat groups and R&B bands emerging in 1963 included his material in the hard core of their repertoire. The Beatles used 'Too Much Monkey Business' in their stage act, recorded 'Roll Over Beethoven' on their second LP, and did 'Rock And Roll Music' for their third.

The Rolling Stones owed even more to him. They started their recording career with 'Come On', included 'Carol' and Berry's arrangement of 'Route 66' on their debut album, and later recorded 'Bye Bye Johnny' and 'Round And Round'. Other Berry numbers, such as 'Johnny B. Goode' and 'Little Queenie' were central to their stage act.

The other new hitmakers joined in. The Kinks featured 'Beautiful Delilah', Gerry and the Pacemakers did 'Maybellene', and in Sheffield Dave Grundy changed his surname to Berry, and had a minor hit with 'Memphis Tennessee' — until the re-issue of the Berry original.

But any attempt to explain Berry's

impact must go beyond his musical and lyrical substance. His great strength lay in the way that he appealed to different audiences. The beat groups like the Beatles and the Stones saw him as one of the great rockers, and delighted crowds by playing his songs. At the same time, trad and folk fans saw him as a genuine blues man in the great black tradition. Because his appeal was so wide, he helped to bring together the strands of popular music. He limited the 'pop' and the purist factions, and helped to mould the future course that pop was to take.

Berry was also respected because, unlike most of the '50s stars, he wrote his own material. He was a poet and musician as well as a showman; and one of the most important features of the '60s breakthrough was a universal belief in the need to extend the artist's control over all aspects of the product, and prevent performers becoming mere vehicles for hit songs manufactured by the industry.

Berry himself capitalised on the resurgence of interest in his work with a string of new singles releases, beginning early in 1964 with 'Nadine'. Most of these were re-worked from earlier successes. The lyric of 'Nadine' was a colourful extension of the car chase theme of 'Maybellene', though the song was slower and funkier. 'No Particular Place To Go' — a Top Ten hit on both sides of the Atlantic — was 'School Day' with new, comic words. 'Little Marie' continued where 'Memphis' left off. But the songs were mellower, and placed a fresh emphasis on his warmth and wry humour.

'You Never Can Tell' was the outstanding example. Two rock & roll fans get married and settle down. Berry delights in the story, not letting on whether he sees the situation as the triumph of true love, the end of freedom, or the only possible way to retain at least part of the way of life based on excitement which he had celebrated in the '50s:

'They had a hi-fi phono, boy did they let it blast
Seven hundred little records, all rockin' rhythm and jazz
But when the sun went down, the rapid tempo of the music fell
"C'est la vie", say the old folks,
"It goes to show you never can tell."'

Like the best of his other songs of the era, 'You Never Can Tell' has an even denser visual quality than his '50s material and is full of little specifics like: 'The coolerator was crammed with TV dinners and ginger ale' and 'They bought a souped-up Jidney, it was a cherry-red '53'. In 1964, Chuck Berry was not only at the height of his influence, but also at an imaginative peak as a lyricist.

Berry was also an enormous influence on the new post-Beatle groups and their music, and American bands of the '60s often paid homage to him. But he also had a more direct effect on major figures in the States. The Beach Boys founded their career on Berry's material, minimally adapting the words of 'Sweet Little Sixteen' to create 'Surfin' USA', copying his guitar licks, and

35

transposing his whole car/girl mythology into an affluent Californian context.

More lastingly significant, perhaps, was Bob Dylan's debt to Chuck Berry. He had included Berry numbers in his rock & roll repertoire during his schooldays, and when he first tried his hand at recording rock the result was 'Subterranean Homesick Blues'. This song appears both lyrically and musically as an extension of 'Too Much Monkey Business', and provides an interesting comparison: Berry's lament about 'working at the filling station' becomes Dylan's 'Twenty years of schooling and they put you on the day shift'; and even the metrical pattern is almost identical, with Chuck singing 'Blond-haired, good-looking, trying to get me hooked', and the '60s song echoing it with 'Get sick, get well, hang around the ink well'. More generally, the sheer linguistic fireworks of Dylan's mid-'60s lyrics find a clear rock precedent in Chuck Berry's restless rhythms, imagery and phrasing.

Got myself a little job/ 1966–1969

In 1966, Chuck Berry left Chess to sign a contract worth $150,000 with Mercury. During the next three years his recording career reached its lowest ebb. Perhaps it was the mood of the times: rock was becoming increasingly preoccupied with 'inner space' and studio effects in the wake of the 1967 drugs, love and 'Sgt. Pepper' phenomenon; and it's hard to imagine Berry writing songs which could be as meaningful in that context as his classic hits were in their time.

It was during the mid-'60s, however, that his reputation as a live artist reached its peak; and his shows became legendary occasions. When he toured Britain in 1964 – heading a bill that included Carl Perkins, the Animals and the Nashville Teens – the audiences were split between those who had loved him in the '50s, including a sizeable proportion of hardcore Teds; and those, like the Stones' and Beatles' fans, who had just discovered him and tended to be the educated, middle-class youth. No other performer could attract such a cross-section. Sometimes the mixture was explosive, as in the 1969 concert at the Albert Hall, when he shared the bill with the Who. Berry was forced to go on first, and the rockers showed their displeasure by, among other things, invading the stage and bringing his act to an untimely end.

The act itself has been developed and refined over the years, but still features the famous 'duck walk', which involved half-gliding, half-shuffling across the stage in a crouched position while playing guitar. Berry once explained the origin of this trademark which earned him the nickname 'Crazy Legs'. He was appearing in an Alan Freed show in New York in 1956: "We had one suit, we didn't know we were supposed to *change*. So I actually did that duck walk to hide the wrinkles in my suit. I got an ovation . . . so I did it again, and again . . ." Like his cherry-red Gibson guitar, it has become part of the myth.

Back home/1969–1974

Berry returned to Chess in 1969. In the following months he put out two new albums, 'Back Home' and 'San Francisco Dues', which showed that the reunion had been a happy one. The LPs were more firmly in a blues vein than anything he'd done before. Although it was good music, it seemed then that Chuck Berry was a man of the past as far as pop success and the development of rock were concerned; that his career as a major musical figure was over.

Then, early in 1972, he visited Britain. At the time, a stronger consciousness of the traditions of the music appeared to be developing. Perhaps it was simply nostalgia. But when he played in Coventry the audience response was unprecedented, and the music press was ecstatic.

From the opening bars of 'Sweet Little Sixteen' the audience joined in, almost completely drowning out his voice. Berry, amazed and delighted, contented himself with simply playing along to most of the songs – witness his comment "I got a chance to sing one" at the beginning of the 'Reelin' And Rockin' recorded at the concert. The response was so overwhelming that most of the tapes of the concert were unusable; in the end, Berry, noted for his habit of demanding cash in advance and playing strictly the 45 minutes agreed, overran his spot by an hour and was finally dragged, still playing, from the stage. A legend had come to life, to play one of the most memorable concerts in rock history.

This performance gave him the live half of his next album, 'The London Chuck Berry Sessions'. More important, it gave him 'My Ding-a-Ling'. He had recorded a slightly different version of the song for Mercury under the title 'My Tambourine', and the number had appeared in a variety of forms by black artists since about 1950. The new Berry version, however, was issued as a single, cleverly promoted, and hit the jackpot. It gave him his biggest-ever hit, and his first no. 1 in both Britain and America. He had at last reached two markets from which he'd previously been extremely remote: the 'novelty' market and the early-teen and pre-teen buyers, both attracted to the obvious (but very mild) dirtiness of the song. Berry followed up its success with his live, sexier version of 'Reelin' And Rockin''; and it too sold well. The new interest prompted yet another spate of Chuck Berry revivals, and the Electric Light Orchestra's version of 'Roll Over Beethoven' soared into the British Top Ten, 17 years after the song was written.

These developments, along with the systematic programme of re-issues embarked on by Chess, and his bill-topping appearance at the Rock and Roll Festival in London, made 1972 the most successful year of his career. Such a comeback makes it difficult to argue with him when he sings, 'I may go down sometimes but I always come back rocking'. But in terms of influence and musical achievement. Chuck Berry will always remain, first and foremost, the paragon of '50s rock.

Jerry Lee Lewis The Killer

Mike Cook

On a hot, sultry day in August, 1956, four musicians gathered round a piano in the Sun recording studio, Memphis, Tennessee, and in two takes cut a version of 'Peace In The Valley' – the four musicians were Carl Perkins and Johnny Cash on guitars, Jerry Lee Lewis just singing, and Elvis Presley on piano. In those days, four guys trying for the big time; but at today's prices a multi-million pound combination of talent. To this day, that recording has never been released.

Jerry Lee Lewis was to become one of the small band of rock & roll entertainers who, even today, still invites criticism. Criticism, not so much for his music, but rather for his eccentric personal life-style.

Up-tempo Hymns

It took Lewis just nine years from his birth in Ferriday, Louisiana, on September 29th, 1935, to start tinkering with a piano. That part of America is still known as the Bible Belt, with religion playing a central part in community life. Some of the first songs Lewis learned were gospel numbers and hymns, but he wasn't content with a straight reproduction of the tunes, and always had to take them a stage further. While attending bible college he was discovered playing up-tempo versions of hymns and asked to leave. Then, as a door-to-door salesman (the only job he could find at the time), he spent most evenings arranging country and hillbilly music to suit his taste for wilder rhythms.

He didn't really regret his dismissal from the college in Waxahatchie, Texas, and still belongs to the church. "I don't claim to be a very good Christian, but you are either hot or you are cold, there's no inbetween," he once said.

His eager driving piano music, accompanied by a voice that often reached a scream, and an uninhibited streak of showmanship, led to several gigs in Louisiana night-clubs. Then, in February 1956, he walked into Sam Phillips' Sun studio and asked for an audition. At his first session he cut a version of Gene Autry's 'You're The Only Star In My Blue Heaven'. In those days he worked mainly with just a guitarist and drummer, and among his first 'back-up' men were Jimmy Van Eaton (drums) and Roland James (guitar) – from Billy Riley's band. Recording sessions at Sun tended to turn into parties. Things became so loose and the booze so plentiful that by the time it came round to Lewis cutting 'The Crawdaddy Song' he could only remember three of the ten verses and he took two piano breaks.

During his early days with Sun, Lewis became more and more influenced by boogie and blues piano styles, and as he developed in this field a lot of his country recordings were suppressed. Lewis still argues with the decision to hold back this material, and considers his more famous rock & roll numbers to be just as much country numbers as classics like 'You Win Again'.

"I've always been singing country & western," he pointed out in an interview some years later. "Even if they're sung as rock, 'Whole Lotta Shakin' Goin' On' and 'Great Balls Of Fire' are still country. Country music would have caught on a lot quicker as a commercial proposition if Jim Reeves hadn't been killed. It hurt country music a lot. It hurt a lot when Hank Williams died. He was spreading out real big when he died, he was set to go all the way."

Even before he had a hit record, Lewis was touring. He did a string of dates with Johnny Cash as far back as 1956, and at the end of 30 days had less then $50 in his pocket. Another tour he undertook almost wrecked his career. It happened in Britain when he arrived with his third wife, Myra, who was also his cousin. A minor storm broke when it was discovered that he had married Myra in December, 1957, five months before his divorce from his second wife became final. When the news broke that Myra was all of 13-years-old, verbal thunder and lightning landed on the couple and a tour which was only into its fifth day had to be cancelled in the face of mounting public protest.

Abrupt End

During the first concert following the national newspapers' revelation of Myra's age, Lewis was greeted with the odd cat-call and an audience that had very little enthusiasm for the music. "I sure hope you ain't as dead as you sound," he announced with the trace of a sneer.

He is not beyond treating his audiences as mere witnesses to his act, and not as paying customers at all. In his own mind he can do no wrong, and if he wants to play mainly country music when the fans have come to hear good old rock & roll, well that's just too bad for them.

As his first British tour came to its abrupt end, and Lewis left on a midnight flight back to the States, his one feeling of regret was that he hadn't made the front pages of the British evening newspapers. "Who is this guy de Gaulle?" he asked, "He seems to have gone over bigger than us. What's so great about him?" When he arrived in New York, Lewis was said to be picking up $100,000 for the cancelled tour — President Eisenhower's salary for a year in office! Perhaps it's not surprising that he told waiting reporters his short-lived tour had been "great, just great."

Jerry Lee Lewis appearing on the ATV *Tom Jones Show* in 1969.

Four years later, Lewis' three-year-old son drowned in a swimming pool accident five days before the start of another British tour. After the funeral, he went ahead with the tour. Then, in 1971, Myra hired a private detective to shadow her husband, a noted womaniser. When she had enough evidence, she divorced him on the grounds of cruelty and infidelity. Myra proceeded to marry the detective, and a month later Lewis wed the former wife of a police lieutenant.

Throughout all his personal troubles Lewis' fans remained faithful to him, and he has visited Britain successfully several times since his ejection by the press.

In the early days it was his habit of climbing on top of his piano, holding the microphone in one hand and stamping on the instrument's lid, that brought him to the attention of the masses. He became known as something of a wild man, with a penchant for wine, women and song, and totally lacking in modesty. A brief appearance in the film *High School Confidential* set the seal on a budding career and put Lewis among the top money earners in the pop field. Though rock & roll was no longer the big business it had been towards the end of the '50s and during the early '60s, he managed to remain a huge attraction.

What'd I Say

His albums continued to attract healthy sales, though by this period the material showed a shifting of interest. Instead of concentrating so much on traditional and contemporary country songs, he veered towards rhythm & blues. On his 'More Of The Greatest Live Show On Earth' album recorded 'live' at the Panther Hall, Fort Worth, Texas, in 1966, he includes Chuck Berry's 'Little Queenie', 'Johnny B. Goode' and 'Roll Over Beethoven', plus Ray Charles' 'What'd I Say'.

Stray Bottle

While talking to Larry Wilkinson of Radio WLOC at a disc jockey convention in Munfordville, Kentucky, in October, 1965, Lewis said: "I'd rather sing and play than eat when I'm hungry." The truth of that statement can be doubted, but Lewis often makes remarks about his love of music, alternating between rock & roll and country to suit the occasion.

Despite being initially banned on most 'white' radio stations in America because it was 'too sexy', 'Whole Lotta Shakin'' remained one of the most popular Jerry Lee Lewis records. An appearance on Steve Allen's networked TV show led to re-bookings for the following two weeks after Lewis obligingly lived up to his reputation by wrecking the piano. When he wasn't actually climbing on the piano, he would aim kicks at the stool or hit the keys with his feet. His habit of curling his right leg round the microphone stand, only to kick it sideways now and then and bring his foot down on the stage with a stamp, is alleged to have started when he wanted to trap a stray whisky bottle that was rolling away from him, though he has never commented on that one.

His attachment to the bottle is well known. Two examples of this occurred during his last British tour in early 1972. The tour opened in Middlesbrough and Lewis was, as is his custom, leaving things to the last moment before arriving at the theatre. When he finally made it, he was clutching a bottle of whisky which he took with him

to his dressing room and carried on drinking. By the time he was meant to go on stage the bottle appeared to be welded to his hand, and just as he was about to step from behind the curtain on to the stage in his familiar red trousers and matching shirt, the tour manager wrested the bottle from his grasp.

Some days later, a press reception was hosted for Lewis in a smart London hotel. He held court in a hired room, his right hand constantly clutching a filled glass of booze. It transpired that Lewis had achieved the seemingly impossible feat of checking into the hotel with a drink, heading for the bar, travelling to a TV studio to tape a show, still with a drink, and being driven drink in hand back to the hotel where he headed again for the bar before attending the reception.

In America in the mid-'60s Lewis occasionally played a guitar or drums on stage as well as the piano. It is a little known fact that he is skilled at all these instruments, picking up the rudiments of all three while still living on his father's farm in Ferriday.

Jerry Lee Lewis with his 13-year-old wife, Myra, in 1958

Jerry Lee Lewis in *Keep On Rocking*.

Oddly enough, in view of his popularity, Lewis hasn't been the inspiration for many other artists, though Tom Jones admits to recording 'Green Green Grass Of Home' after hearing the American's recording of the song. In 1969, Jones brought Jerry Lee to London to appear on ATV's *Tom Jones Show* series. While Lewis got to work, the Welshman leaned on the piano with an eager look of admiration in his eyes.

Jesus Christ

During his stay in London on that occasion, Lewis told one reporter: "Booze and women are my two big weaknesses, and I've gotta have both when I need them." On a later visit he claimed that he didn't think his fourth marriage would last a long time because of his habits. He capped that by revealing in London in early 1972 that he had signed to play the part of Jesus Christ in a stage musical *The Carpenter*. He grew a beard for the part, but the project received no more publicity. Publicity is one commodity Lewis loves. He is rarely lost for a word and if an exaggeration sounds better than the plain truth, well then, he ain't about to hold his tongue. He even has a habit of perso-

nalising his songs, mentioning his own name. "Well, I never do the same thing twice, so sometimes I sing something like 'don't let good old Jerry Lee down'," he explained. "I think if I'm singing a country song it makes it just that bit more intimate if I sing it with my name, like on 'Take Another Chance On Me', it's a little more real."

During another concert tour in 1973 he introduced his sister, Linda Gail Lewis, on stage. She has done some recordings with her famous brother, the most popular being their 'Together' album. He has a lot of faith in her talent, but while she is fairly well recognised in the country field in America, she has yet to make her mark elsewhere.

That tour showed how much Jerry Lee Lewis has veered back towards his country roots. A good 40% of the material was anything but rock & roll, with even 'That Old Rugged Cross' included in the programme. "I would say what I do now is country rock," he explained. "You can't beat country music, no matter what anybody says, country songs tell the truth." Lewis' feel for country music is well-known, and he has won many awards for his C&W recordings. His records frequently appear in the country charts in America,

and sometimes simultaneously crop up in the pop section. Yet when he came to London again in early 1973 for a recording session (accompanied by a young woman called Charlotte Bumps!), he featured a list of famous rock & roll songs. The resulting album, 'London Session', had Lewis backed up by a number of the country's top instrumentalists — people like Klaus Voorman, Rory Gallagher, Alvin Lee and Peter Frampton.

'The Killer'

While loved — almost idolised — by the old-time rockers, Lewis does not command the same importance in the history of pop music as, for example, Chuck Berry. The reason is simple: he has never written his own material. Had he been able to write for himself he would, undoubtedly, be one of the giants of rock.

His performances have always been marked by that cool, professional, detached control of the audience that marks out an exceptional artist from the hordes of enthusiastic exhibitionists. And yet it was always other people's material that he was performing *and* recording — never his own.

As it is, Jerry Lee remains 'The Killer' — one of rock & roll's greatest characters.

The Everly Brothers

SKR

Nobody sounded like the Everly Brothers, before or since. They put their adolescent heads together, leaned coaxingly into the microphone, crooned cheek-by-cheek in a wailing, sensuous harmony; the sound of heartbreak made vocal. Phil and Don Everly made a noise that was an orchestra in itself, or could sound like one remarkable voice.

The combination of the two voices, Phil's light and seductive, Don's a shade deeper, both of them husky and persuasive, was something more than just a simple duet. Their roots were in American country music, good neighbourliness and fiddles round the fire. They grew up into the new excitement and independence of rock & roll, and away from their folksy family act at a time when the rest of American youth was growing away from *their* parents. The plaintive sweetness of country music and the driving power of rock & roll merged into a unique Everly Brothers sound — a sound so distinctive and unforgettable that for many people the opening bars of 'All I Have To Do Is Dream', the nostalgic twang of 'Crying In The Rain', the low-down growl of 'Bird Dog', bring on the pangs of forgotten adolescence more than any of the other giants of rock & roll.

Family Act

The Everly Brothers were once the Everly Family. They were born in Brownie, Kentucky, the Bluegrass State on the borders of America's South, and through the years of travelling, of jetting the world, the strain of stardom and one night stands, they've kept the feeling of their country roots. Ike and Margaret Everly, their parents, were established country artists. Ike, a guitar-picker of considerable Southern charm is still capable of stealing the show from his sons once he is behind a guitar, but back in the '40s the birth of Don, and then Phil, gave Ike the promise of a family act. When Don was eight and

Phil was six they were singing on the radio in Shenandoah, Iowa. Phil was telling jokes and Don was reading the commercials for Deacon's Rat Poison. The Everly family had a regular breakfast show, and anyone who wants to know the melodies and folksiness which accompanied their exceptional childhood should listen to the LP 'Roots', where the recorded voice of Ike Everly introduces little Don and baby boy Phil to the world. It was sweet music.

Big Brothers Break

The Everlys grew up to the sound of country and folk, to grassroots country guitar and harmonica. But as Don and Phil changed from children to adolescents their parents could see the break up of the act. They knew they would never make it big on their own, but they thought Don and Phil might, so they stepped back and the brothers found themselves on their own, already experienced performers looking for a break in a bigger world than the small-town radio stations and country shows they knew.

For a while they were lost. They found themselves in Nashville, the home of country music, but something more was happening — rock & roll was on the move.

Although the Everlys weren't yet part of it, neither were they content with the songs of their childhood. Other artists recorded their songs, but nothing happened for them until they met a man called Wesley Rose, a country music producer looking to expand his operation into newer, more profitable markets. Together they found a song which united their innate gift for melody and harmony with a driving, hand-clapping rhythm. It was called 'Bye Bye Love', and it sold a million, just like that.

Incredible Harmony

The Everly Brothers were no one-hit wonders, no rock & roll flukes. They were as professional as any musicians could be who had been performing in public from the age of six. Their sound was already unique — united, polished, harmonious. One only has to look at what harmony meant in the cruder music of the late '50s, in the turgid early efforts of rock & roll. It was heavy, it was unsubtle. It usually involved a high voice which sang a few solo bars, a deep bass voice which sang a few solo bars, and some voices which chugged out a pedestrian rhythm in between. The Everly Brothers soared. After they arrived, voices never combined

41

in quite the same way again. Their sound was liquid, the perfect vehicle for emotion, but never sugared. The words they sang touched hearts tussling with the agonies of adolescence and unrequited love, rejection, crying in the rain. And their music was white.

Unlike Elvis Presley, another Southerner who drew his musical power from a heritage of black blues, the Everlys built their strength on a white sound. Their music wasn't down to earth and dirty, though it was sensuous and sexy. Nor were they themselves blue-jeaned and raunchy. They started as country boys in all the wrong clothes, then they turned into college boys. They wore greased-back quiffs and Ivy League jackets, they were presentable, charming boys-next-door, but something else as well. They were, are, good looking in a slightly feminine way, but more than this, they had something disquietingly delinquent about them. They photographed as hood-eyed and sinister for all their charm, and part of their attraction was this air of fragile corruption, a hinted decadence.

Success Built On Power

But it takes more than physical appeal to make a rock & roll superstar. Up until the early '60s the Everly Brothers never put a foot wrong in their career. They simply kept coming up with great songs, they never repeated themselves or fell back on any gimmick, they relied on their unique double voice, on a simple, relaxed stage act, and on songs which they themselves liked. Their success was built on the power of their music. The greater part of their most lasting hits were written for them by Boudleaux Bryant, who came up with the handclapping mournfulness of 'Bye Bye Love' and kicked them off to an unbeatable start. The Everly Brothers were at their most plaintive and wistful with Bryant's song 'All I Have To Do Is Dream', one of the indispensable standards of rock & roll.

'When I feel blue in the night,
When I want you to hold me tight,
Whenever I want you all I have
* to do is dream . . .*
I can make you mine,
Taste your lips of wine,
Any time night or day,
Only trouble is, gee whizz,
I'm dreaming my life away.'

The Everly Brothers spun that 'dream' out to five notes, and no other singers could have stripped 'gee whizz' of its mawkishness the way they did.

Bryant's songs for Don and Phil weren't *all* sad. There were quirky, irresistibly catchy, tongue-in-cheek numbers which Don and Phil put across dead-pan. There was 'Wake Up Little Susie', where Don and Phil and Susie fall asleep in the movies and sing, with terrific verve and rhythm, about the moral thunderbolt that is going to hit them for staying out all night. That was in the days when kids drank Coke,

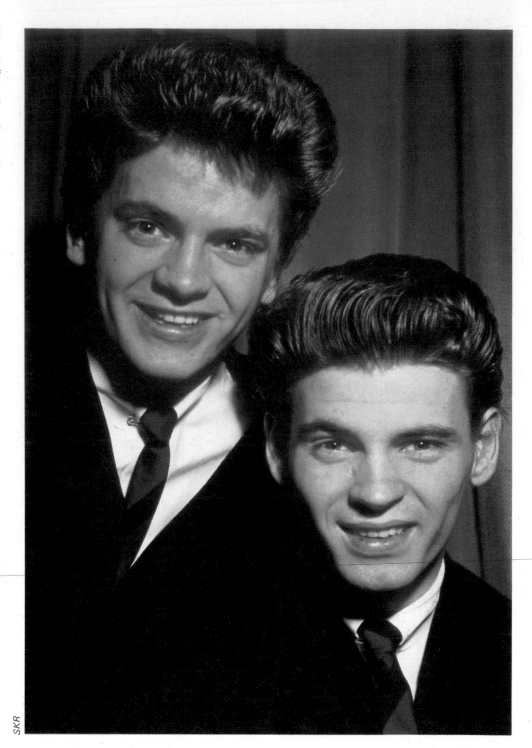

A nostalgic look at the young Everly Brothers. From L to R: Don and Phil Everly.

went to the high school hop, and accounted to their parents for every movement made after midnight.

'Wake up, little Susie, wake up.
Wake up, little Susie, wake up.
We've both been sound asleep,
Wake up, little Susie, and weep,
The movie's over, it's four o'clock
And we're in trouble deep . . .
What're we gonna tell your momma,
What're we gonna tell your pa?
What're we gonna tell our friends when
they say ooh la la?''

And Bryant wrote 'Bird Dog', that flat song of resentment about Johnny, the teacher's pet who manoeuvred himself next to Don and Phil's baby. Buddy Holly wrote 'Not

Fade Away' for the Everly Brothers, and Don and Phil also wrote some of their own. 'Till I Kissed You' was the Everlys in a chirpy mood. 'So Sad To Watch Good Love Go Bad', and the classic 'Cathy's Clown' showed them more unashamedly distressed. Perhaps it was something to do with their grounding in the open, homely sentimentality of country music, but the Everly Brothers, more than any other rock & roll singers, had the ability, with their talent for rhythm and melody, to turn corn into gold. And their sound was more and more distinctive. It sometimes seemed as if Phil Spector later filled studios with orchestras and choirs just to catch that particular spaciousness that the Everlys achieved with two voices, guitars, and a little echo.

Their records sold all over the world in millions, but the stresses of popularity were becoming intolerable. Don and Phil had the normal quarrels that brothers have, then in 1962 on a tour to Britain, Don was taken into hospital with an overdose of drugs. The strain of being a flying star, the years of one-night-stands, crummy dressing rooms, worse hotels, and the harsh lights of airport lounges had told on him. Reportedly high on amphetamines, he tried to commit suicide. He was saved that time, but the superstar, rock & roll jungle phase of the Everlys' career was drawing to a natural close. They never had a big smash hit single again in the way that they had up to 1962, but then the rock scene was changing. The English groups were taking over, and the peculiar sounds and harmonies of the Everlys were a big influence on new groups like the Beatles. Don and Phil themselves carried on thinking, playing, working out new music. They had been the idols of a teenage audience, but the audience itself was growing up and Don and Phil, professionals from kindergarten, were growing up with them.

Back To The Roots

Now they look different. Their hair is long, their clothes are individual and relaxed, they are proud of being different, and they don't have to pretend to be musical twins any more. They have stopped chasing the Hit Parade, and now they can concentrate on the more satisfying business of just turning out good music, on following their own instinct, on going back to roots.

Their recent albums have pulled in the help of other musicians whose music runs along similar lines: Delaney and Bonnie, John Sebastian, David Crosby, Graham Nash. The sound is terrific, always musical, professional, imaginative and full of melody, drive and ease. The songs are about themselves, and about America.

The Everlys were country singers before they were rock & roll stars, and what they do best and most distinctively pulls together the best of both worlds. Whenever they play now, in the world's biggest concert halls or in small clubs, they are greeted with affection and respect. They are faultlessly professional, simple still; just two people, two guitars and a small band. They will sing all the songs everyone wants to hear — 'Dream', 'Crying In The Rain', 'Temptation', 'Bird Dog' — and they sing new songs that go farther back and deeper in, songs like 'Green River', the river that winds through Kentucky.

'Green River you're still my home,
Green River, why did I roam,
Green River, some day I'll come
home to stay.'

The Everly Brothers gave rock & roll some of its most beautiful and most fondly remembered songs: but still, together or on their own, they are basically country boys singing country songs

BACK TRACK

The Everly Brothers' first professional appearances were on their parents' radio show when Don was eight and Phil was six.

Singles on Cadence (USA) and London (UK).

1957: July, 'Bye Bye Love' (no. 6). November, 'Wake Up Little Susie' (no. 2).
1958: May, 'All I Have To Do Is Dream' (no. 1). September, 'Bird Dog' (no. 2).
1959: January, 'Problems' (no. 5). May, 'Poor Jenny' (no. 11). September, 'Till I Kissed You' (no. 2).

With Warner Brothers Label.

1960: April, 'Cathy's Clown' (no. 1). July, 'When Will I Be Loved' (no. 4). September, 'So Sad'/'Lucille' (no. 4). December, 'Like Strangers' (no. 12).

1961: January, 'Walk Right Back' (no. 1). June, 'Temptation' (no. 1). September, 'Muskrat' (no. 16).
1962: January, 'Crying In The Rain' (no. 8). June, 'How Can I Meet Her?' (no. 12). November, 'No One Can Make My Sunshine Smile' (no. 11).
1965: 'Price Of Love' (no. 2). November, 'Love Is Strange' (no. 11).

There were no further single hits and in February 1971 Don Everly released a solo album on A & M (Don Everly). 1972 the Everlys moved to RCA label.

1972: April, 'Stories We Could Tell' (LP). November, 'Pass The Chicken And Listen' (LP).
1973: August, solo single, 'The Air That I Breathe', and solo album, 'Star Spangled Springer', by Phil Everly.

The persistent rumours that the Everly Brothers were splitting up were confirmed in September 1973.

Buddy Holly:
'50s Star...
'70s Legend

Everything that rock & roll offered, Buddy Holly grabbed. Rock & roll said you could play guitar and sing about yourself, write your own songs, experiment and make mistakes, be a star and get the girls. Just what the kid from Lubbock, Texas, needed.

Buddy got off to a fast start. He and a friend called Bob Montgomery sang country and western songs on their own 30-minute radio show — every Sunday afternoon, while they were still at school. This was 1953–55, the years when rock & roll was beginning to confuse the boundaries between country and R&B, and between 'specialist' music and pop. Tapes made by Buddy and Bob (issued later as an LP to cash in on Buddy's success) show Buddy's early awareness of what was happening. Basically the duo sang pure country harmonies, the style that the Everly Brothers made popular throughout the world a few years later. But on a couple of songs, 'You And I Are Through' and 'Baby It's Love', they used drums to kick the beat along and Buddy let his voice play tricks with the vowels . . . it was coming.

Calling All Drums

Without rock & roll, such idiosyncrasies would have been frowned upon by the men in charge of record companies. Country music was recorded for an adult audience who thought of drums only in the context of rhythm & blues. Drums weren't used on the early Elvis records for Sun. Elvis might have been singing blues songs, but instrumentally the records were conservative, obliging bass player Bill Black to hit his instrument as hard as he could to make up for the absence of a drummer. But those records proved a point — there *were* white people in the South who

would buy records which had a 'black' beat. Swallowing its pride and reaching for the money, Nashville eventually conceded. Drummers came in off the streets and took their places in the studios.

Early in 1956, around the time Elvis signed to RCA Victor, Buddy Holly made his first commercial recordings. Buddy and Bob had opened the bill as the local act on a rock & roll package tour which played in their hometown of Lubbock, Texas, and had impressed someone connected with Decca's Nashville office. Buddy was then invited to Nashville.

By this time Buddy had his own back-up group, the Three Tunes, including Sonny Curtis on guitar and Jerry Allison on drums. But Decca substituted a session drummer for the first Nashville recordings, where the main intention seemed to be to recreate the sound of Elvis' Sun records. Sonny Curtis executed an almost perfect 'Scotty Moore' guitar break on 'Love Me', but the most remarkable feature of the songs was Buddy's singing: his breathless, urgent, and mysterious tone on 'Midnight Shift' must have had a profound influence on Bob Dylan at the time he recorded 'John Wesley Harding'.

At the second Nashville session in July, 1956, Jerry Allison was allowed to play drums, and many rock & roll fans consider that 'Rock Around With Ollie Vee' from this session was Buddy's purest and best 'rocker'. There's a frantic rush here which was cooled down and controlled later: in contrast, the first version of 'That'll Be The Day' from this session was wooden, weighed down by a heavy bass and

44

L.H. pic., from top to bottom: Jerry Allison, Buddy Holly and Joe B. Mauldin. Bottom pic: Buddy on guitar, Jerry on drums and Joe on double bass.

to Norman Petty who owned the studio and told him that if Buddy Knox could cut a hit there, so could we. So we recorded four songs, as demonstration records, 'That'll Be The Day', 'I'm Looking For Someone To Love', and two others.''

The demos were sent to New York, where they were passed around several publishing and record companies until Bob Thiele of Coral Records heard them. Although they had only been intended as demos, Thiele issued them as they were, 'That'll Be The Day', backed with 'I'm Looking For Someone To Love'.

And so, in the typically accidental way that pop music makes its history, a new music was born, a new star was fledged. The record came out under the name of the Crickets, as if it were a vocal group record. But although there were some background vocal noises, the focus was on the instruments and the words that Buddy sang. Jagged electric guitar opened it up, and then those cynical lines, mocking the girl who had tried the bluff of threatening to leave her boy. Underneath, Jerry Allison's bump-and-shuffle drums shook the floor of every café that owned a juke-box.

If there was one record which could claim to have inspired the 'beat' music of the '60s, this was it. There was a do-it-yourself feel about 'That'll Be The Day', a home-made non-professionalism that gave every fumbling guitarist the hope that he might get lucky too.

But the immediate reaction of his advisers was almost the opposite. Norman Petty, the engineer of 'That'll Be The Day', took on the job of directing Buddy's talents.

And as manager, producer, session leader, and sometime keyboards man, Petty's influence on most of Buddy's subsequent recordings was considerable.

Norman Petty's own musical preference seems to have been for cocktail music, and his chief preoccupation was to file the rough edges off Buddy Holly's sound. This didn't conflict with everything that Buddy himself wanted, but it did lead to more stereotyped arrangements, an increasingly clean sound, and some silly background vocal harmonies. Consequently, none of Buddy Holly's later records had quite the raw attack of 'That'll Be The Day', while the ones that hold up best over time tend to be his slower songs, where his own intentions were more amenable to Petty's notions of good taste. According to other musicians who were present at most of the recording sessions, Petty rarely made contributions to the actual compositions of the songs to justify the presence of his name on the composer credits. ''That was just a business thing,'' said a spokesman.

But Petty made one piece of astute business that did benefit Buddy. When he

unconvincing mannerisms from Buddy.

A third and last Nashville session produced nothing of note, and Decca lost interest in Buddy. He and the Three Tunes continued to play gigs around north Texas, and Buddy made practice tapes of songs he had heard on the radio, or bought records of, or had written himself. Then two singers from a nearby college had simultaneous national hits, Buddy Knox

with 'Party Doll' and Jimmy Bowen with 'I'm Stickin' With You'. Using the same back-up group, the Rhythm Orchids, Knox and Bowen had recorded their hits at a studio just across the Texas border in Clovis, New Mexico, which Buddy Holly and the Three Tunes had already used to make demos of their songs. ''When we heard that 'Party Doll' had been recorded in Clovis,'' Jerry Allison recalls, ''we went

Above: The grave of Buddy Holly in Lubbock, Texas. Right: Buddy Holly in a sad and pensive mood, gazing out to sea.

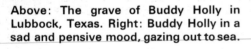

was negotiating with Bob Thiele to release the recording of 'That'll Be The Day', Petty also made a separate contract to record Buddy Holly as a solo artist. Holly would be on the Coral label, and the Crickets on Brunswick, although the same people would be involved in making both series of records. While the Crickets' records were rock & roll, Holly's solo records were softer, what the trade used to call 'ballads with a beat'.

The first solo Holly record, 'Words Of Love', sank without trace, although it inspired a respectful and faithful version from the Beatles years later; but the second, 'Peggy Sue', was as remarkable as 'That'll Be The Day' had been. Without any irony or defence, Buddy droned a childishly simple verse over a hypnotic guitar rhythm; it worked because he sang it so adventurously, playing around with the melody and vowels until the whole thing became just sound. Anybody else who tried to sing it was obliged to follow Buddy's vocal lines, or risk losing the song's effectiveness — an important quality of Buddy's style which explains the continuing demand for his records.

The success of 'That'll Be The Day' and 'Peggy Sue' immediately created a demand for personal appearances by Buddy Holly (and the Crickets) around the world, and they made tours of the States,

Australia and Britain. On stage, Buddy confirmed and extended the impressions created on record, as one report stated:

'At the Globe, Stockton, the stage seemed huge and empty with just a drummer (Jerry Allison) behind his kit, and the bass player (Joe Mauldin) standing next to his stand-up bass. And when Buddy walked on, his face cracked by a huge grin under his glasses, it was impossible not to identify with him and feel nervous on his behalf: could this kid, who looked like he had just changed out of his school uniform, meet the audience's expectations? One blast on his guitar and those of us in the front row were ready to move to the back. How could one guitar be so loud? "I think the secret of Buddy's style," Jerry Allison ruminated later, "was

that we didn't have a rhythm guitar, so Buddy had to play a style which was lead and rhythm at the same time, he had to play a melody on chords."'

Relaxed And Impressive

There were two LPs out by this time, one just called 'Buddy Holly' with an almost recognisable picture of him without his glasses, and 'The Chirping Crickets'. On stage, Buddy would run through most of the songs, which mostly sounded just like the records, but sometimes were even better because Norman Petty wasn't around to make them smooth. The audiences marvelled at how Jerry Allison could play so strongly while looking so relaxed, and remembered forever the engaging character of Buddy himself; he never said very much between songs, but was impressive because those words he sang were his, he'd written them, and that was a novelty for any touring act in 1958.

It wasn't just the fact that he wrote his own material, it was also the content that was important. 'Only love grows cold, and old', he sang in 'Think It Over'. That was strong stuff for a love song, and so was his casual dismissal of tragedy in 'I'm Looking For Someone To Love', where his girl was run over by a street car. Buddy shrugged his shoulders and went off looking for someone else to take her place.

On the other hand, he could be sentimental without being sloppy, especially on his solo record, 'Heartbeat' and 'Well . . . All Right'. In these days of easy listening charts and golden oldies compilations, that sort of stuff would do well today, but it barely got played when it was issued at the turn of 1958–59. Neither did the Crickets' 'It's So Easy', and it must have seemed that Buddy was about to sink into obscurity when he was killed in a plane crash during a tour early in 1959.

Buddy's death brought attention to his

most recent record, 'It Doesn't Matter Anymore' – its title suddenly took on prophetic meaning, and the arrangement signalled a new direction that Buddy had just taken – a direction attributed by many to a recent marriage and its 'softening' effect on his approach. In place of the Crickets and Norman Petty's production was a full-blown string arrangement by Dick Jacobs, and instead of writing his own song, Buddy was here doing one by Paul Anka. Evidently sensing that the music business no longer had much sympathy for the do-it-yourself approach, Buddy had moved into the mainstream of pre-planned pop music. And whereas his previous records had defied immediate imitators, this one pop production inspired innumerable derivatives, notably from Bobby Vee in the States and from Marty Wilde and Adam Faith in Britain. Suddenly everybody was singing 'bay-beh', backed by pizzicato strings.

Buddy Holly's premature death allowed endless speculation about what he might have done if he had lived, and also generated a necrophilic interest in every sound he had already committed to tape. He even made a bizarre return to the British charts when the cycle turned to bring spontaneous-sounding records back to favour at the expense of arranged pop music. Back in late '56 and early '57, Buddy used to do versions of current hits that he liked, some of which were issued at the time, but others of which didn't have proper rhythm tracks on them, just Buddy's voice and guitar. After he died, Norman Petty collected these tapes, and demos of songs that Buddy had written, and dubbed rhythm tracks onto them, supplying the finished product to Coral and Brunswick (branches of American Decca) as LP material. Two of these tracks, 'Bo Diddley' and 'Brown-Eyed Handsome Man', became hit singles in Britain in 1963.

Genius Of Pop

Years later, Buddy Holly's records still hold their magic, both for the people who heard them in their time, and for young listeners who have come to him for the first time and immediately recognise a man whose fascination with sound is more fashionable now than ever before. His guitar technique was rudimentary, and his vocal range wasn't particularly big, but he created an instantly recognisable sound through a strange tone, accent and pronunciation, so that whatever words he sang, they belonged to that sound and the character behind it. But if this description makes his singing sound artificial and contrived, that wasn't the effect: he seemed to do it instinctively.

Buddy Holly exploited the freedom that rock & roll brought to pop music. In making room for himself, he created spaces which other people are still exploring. If he was never quite a superstar in his own lifetime, he was a genius of pop music, which other so-called superstars can never hope to be.

BACK TRACK

Born Buddy Holley in Lubbock, Texas, on September 7th, 1936. He had a musical background and started to play acoustic guitar at the age of nine.
1950–52: Performed at local clubs and high schools with Bob Montgomery.
1955: Played a show on the same bill as Bill Haley and the Comets.
1956: First recording sessions in Nashville on January 26th.
1957: 'That'll Be The Day' released under the name of the Crickets, makes UK no. 1. 'Peggy Sue' and 'Oh Boy' singles released.
1958: Toured successfully in Australia and Britain. 'Maybe Baby', 'Rave On', 'Think It Over' and 'Early In The Morning' singles released. Married Maria Elena Santiago.
1959: Buddy dies in an air crash on February 3rd, at Clear Lake, Iowa, along with J. P. (The Big Bopper) Richardson and Ritchie Valens. His single 'It Doesn't Matter Anymore' makes UK no. 1. 'Peggy Sue Got Married' single released.
1961–63: Other posthumous singles were 'Baby I Don't Care', 'Reminiscing', 'Brown-Eyed Handsome Man', 'Bo Diddley' and 'Wishing'.

The three albums available which contain most of Buddy's most popular material are 'Buddy Holly's Greatest Hits' (Coral), 'Buddy Holly's Greatest Hits, Volume Two' (Coral) and 'Remember Buddy Holly' (Coral). For the sake of completeness, the following list gives an impression of what other albums are available to the enthusiast: 'Wishing' (MCA): Buddy and Bob material recorded around 1955.
'That'll Be The Day' (Coral): Nashville sessions. 'Listen To Me' (MCA): Buddy's first album. 'The Chirping Crickets' (Coral). 'Rave On' (MCA). 'True Love Ways' (MCA). 'He's The One' (MCA). 'Brown-Eyed Handsome Man' (MCA). 'Giant' (MCA).

GENE VINCENT The Classic Rocker

Rex Features

The late Gene Vincent belonged to an elite of '50s rock & roll singers who collectively shaped rock's early history with records and visual images unlike anything ever heard or seen before. Like his contemporaries Little Richard and Jerry Lee Lewis (by whom he was always overshadowed), Vincent only had a handful of hits. He faded from popularity in the States as early as 1958; by which time rock & roll had attained middle-class respectability through cleaned-up rock artists like Connie Francis and Ricky Nelson.

However, European fans gave him a new lease of life, and he subsequently spent nearly 10 years on the road as the epitome of the greasy rock & roller — never really to escape the confines of this image. Like most of the early rock legends, he is remembered more for what he stood for than what he actually did.

Eugene Vincent Craddock was born in the seaport of Norfolk, Virginia, in 1935, and came from a poor background. Prospects were not high, so at the age of 15 he joined the US Navy as a despatch rider at the local naval base. In 1955, while riding despatch, he was knocked down by a naval car on the base and sustained multiple fractures of his left leg. Vincent was hospitalised and his leg re-set, but it didn't heal completely and complications set in. Eventually the leg became so wasted that it had to be permanently encased in plaster, and later on Vincent wore a leg brace.

As with most young white Southerners, hillbilly music was part of Vincent's heritage, and during his lengthy hospitalisation he began jangling around on a guitar. He was discharged from the Navy late in 1955 on a permanent disability pension and, early in the new year, began to hang around Norfolk's local radio station (WCMS), which broadcast hillbilly music and booked local bands through an affiliated agency. Under the guidance of WCMS DJ 'Sherriff Tex' Davis, Eugene Craddock, as he was still known, began broadcasting, backed by local musicians.

Day Off Work

These were primeval days in rock history and just at this time (February/March 1956) Elvis Presley hit the big-time with 'Heartbreak Hotel' on RCA. Over at Capitol, RCA's rival, an elderly but astute country producer named Ken Nelson had been warning his colleagues of the impending importance of rock & roll, but had been largely ignored. Nelson, who had previously been vying for Presley's Sun contract, nonetheless made up his mind to sign the first halfway-passable rock singer to come his way.

Meanwhile, back in Norfolk, Vincent had written 'Be-Bop-A-Lula' — a novel rocker based on 'Money Honey' — and Tex Davis saw distinctly commercial possibilities in

it. He had Vincent record a demo one evening late in April 1956, using four hillbilly musicians from the station houseband, and immediately mailed it to Ken Nelson at Capitol. Nelson was so excited that he had Vincent and his group flown to Nashville for a proper session. The lead guitarist, a plumber, and the bassist, a factory-worker, took the day off from work and the 15-year-old drummer cut class to play the session. Another song, 'Woman Love' (which Nelson supplied) became the 'A' side, but it was the flip, 'Be Bop-A-Lula', which climbed into the US Top 10 in the summer of 1956. It was a landmark record — the first hard electric rock sound. Taken at a relaxed walking pace, it was hardly a rocker in the accepted sense, but because of the extreme tension in Vincent's voice — which was swathed in eerie tape-echo — the song moved in its own way. The lead guitarist, an elderly fellow named Cliff Gallup, played some of the finest rock guitar of the '50s, and on some records his lengthy improvised solos played as great a part in the overall sounds as Vincent's high-pitched vocals.

Fresh out of the Navy, with his injured leg only half-healed, a bewildered Vincent suddenly found himself catapulted from obscurity to national prominence. At this early stage in rock history no precedent

existed by which to gauge the correct approach to rock & roll management, and the following months were a shambles as Tex Davis used Vincent as a guinea-pig for his trial-and-error management methods.

Two more fine records, 'Race With The Devil' and 'Bluejean Bop', were released, but they flopped and the impetus was lost. On the strength of their first hit, however, Vincent and his Bluecaps (as they were called) toured extensively, and late that year sang 'Be-Bop-A-Lula' in the classic rock movie *The Girl Can't Help It*. Vincent's deathly-pale tortured face, overhung by a cascading cluster of untidy curls, was not an easy image to forget. Even by current standards he looked like a freak; by mid-'50s standards he was downright bizarre.

Without hit records, though, the gig money decreased rapidly, and at the end of the year, the original group — simple country boys — disbanded and returned to Norfolk to resume normal life. Vincent went into hospital for further treatment on his leg, came out, found new management, and formed another group. By this time, mid-1957, he had been half-forgotten; but another hit, 'Lotta Lovin''/ 'Wear My Ring', brought him back into the limelight. The new Bluecaps, with their snappy stage-show and another superb guitarist in Johnny Meeks, caused riots in

Below: Gene Vincent on TV in the '60s.

staring at some vision only he could see. Suddenly, he'd swing his left leg right over the mike, spin round 360 degrees and tear into the first number. Transformed into a crouching wildcat, he'd carry the mike-stand a few feet off the ground, spin, throw and catch it in a single short burst of movement. Then he'd be stock still for minutes on end. In his heyday, he was the most extraordinary and terrifying spectacle on stage.

His management worked him to the bone on big money for three years and he became an integral part of the British pop scene, eventually settling in England, in 1961. Major hits eluded him, but his popularity was unaffected. This, in itself, was unique in an era when artists depended on hits for survival.

Suitcase Existence

By 1964, however, the years of constant touring and the pain from his ailing leg had taken their toll and his drinking had reached the critical stage — he made the national press on several occasions through ill-behaviour in his private life. He became something less than a demi-god, and more a provincial rock & roller who could be seen performing daily at minor venues around the country. He finally returned to the States in 1965 for operations on his leg, and nothing more was heard from him for several years.

When he re-emerged suddenly in 1969 for a British tour, he was barely recognisable. The years of inactivity had made him obese, and it was hard to equate his appearance with that of the erstwhile wild rocker. Later that year he appeared at the Toronto rock festival (backed by Alice Cooper), but found work hard to come by in America and returned to Britain in 1971 — only to be involved in alimony proceedings with his English former wife. He fled to the States, and died a fortnight later after a seizure attributed to a bleeding ulcer.

End of the Road

Throughout his career, Gene Vincent lived a day-to-day existence out of a suitcase, and never once settled down to contemplate either his future or his health. He could be vindictive when drunk, and caused endless management feuds, but in his public performances he remained polite and professional. Shortly before his death, he appeared on British radio to sing 'Be-Bop-A-Lula' — his one indisputable claim to fame — one more time. "You know," he told his host, "I just don't know how many times I must have sung this song." Nevertheless he sang it again, his voice shaky in places, the old feeling almost gone, but the same old song in spite of it all.

He was dogged by injuries, his drinking and marital troubles were seized on by the gutter press, but as long as he was on the road he was happy. "I'll play anywhere any-one wants me," he once said towards the end. It was the thought of that road finally running out that eventually killed him.

Australia and in some American cities. Vincent had at this time reached his peak in the States; but success was not to last long.

Capitol, it seems, were one of the few companies not to indulge in payola during the '50s, and few DJs were disposed towards playing Vincent's records — especially as he showed a certain anti-pathy towards the media anyway. More-over, he looked distinctly working-class, had a severe drinking problem, and as such was unacceptable to a media geared — as it always had been in the States — to middle-class respectability. Vincent also alienated Dick Clark of *American Band-stand* — at that time the single most influential TV pop show in America — and, by the summer of 1958, was a virtual out-cast in an American pop scene now domi-nated by a new breed of pretty boys like Frankie Avalon and Ricky Nelson.

To cap it all the US tax authorities began hounding him for non-payment, the musicians union revoked his membership, and he was forced to work abroad. He arrived in Britain to a star welcome in November, 1959.

Black Leather Hamlet

Whereas in America Vincent had merely been one of a great array of rock stars; in faraway Britain each of the early

American rockers was individually worshipped by fans who had yet to taste real rock & roll first hand. Images were formed from available records and album covers, and fans and the media alike thought Vincent to be a lean, mean, no-nonsense character. In person, how-ever, he turned out to be the total opposite — soft-spoken, gentle and shy. Jack Good, scholarly ombudsman of English pop and director of rave TV shows like *Oh Boy* and *Boy Meets Girl*, was at the airport to meet Vincent, whom he'd booked for a show. Expecting a leather-jacketed, stilletto-wielding hood, he was, instead, greeted with great courtesy by a polite Southern youth.

Fast-thinking Good, a brilliant creator of images, took one look at Vincent and decided that he needed a grittier demeanour if the British public were not to be disappointed. Before long, Vincent was seen on British TV clad from head to toe in black leather, with a huge silver medallion hanging around his neck (Good recently said he'd based this image on Hamlet!).

Gene now entered a new phase in his career — as a European idol he became renowned for his black leathers and unique stage act: the curtain would go up and Vincent would be there like some demon possessed by the beat, face contorted in an agonised smile, and his huge eyes

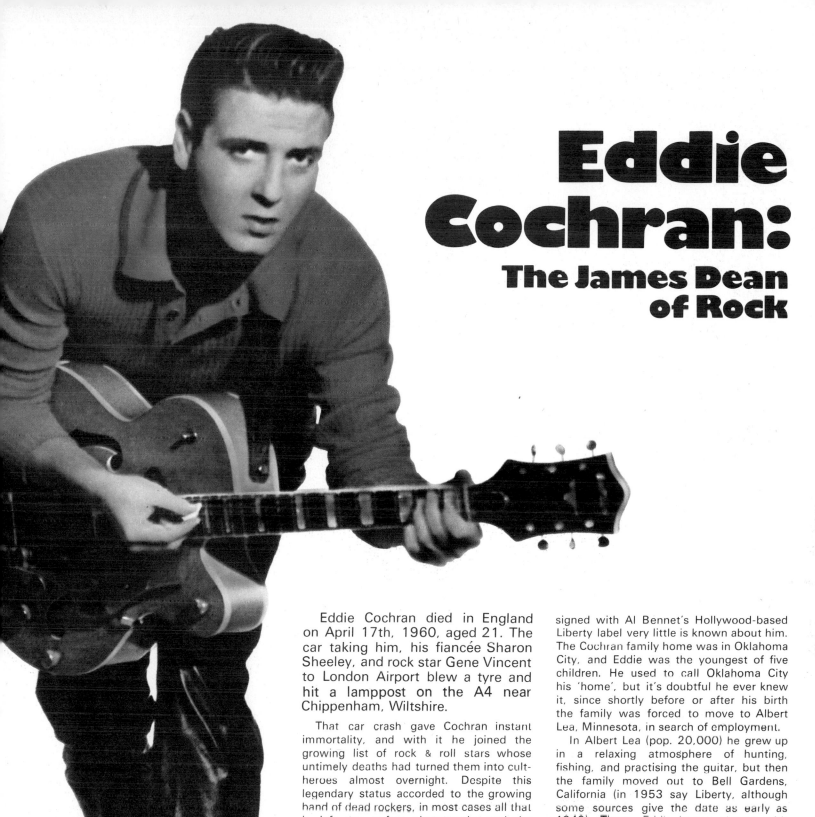

Eddie Cochran:
The James Dean of Rock

Eddie Cochran died in England on April 17th, 1960, aged 21. The car taking him, his fiancée Sharon Sheeley, and rock star Gene Vincent to London Airport blew a tyre and hit a lamppost on the A4 near Chippenham, Wiltshire.

That car crash gave Cochran instant immortality, and with it he joined the growing list of rock & roll stars whose untimely deaths had turned them into cult-heroes almost overnight. Despite this legendary status accorded to the growing band of dead rockers, in most cases all that is left are a few photographs and the music. Eddie Cochran was no exception to this.

Rock & roll is essentially *American* music, *white* American music. The exception proving the rule, of course, is the fact that two of the greatest rock & roll performers, Chuck Berry and Little Richard, were — and still are — black. But although *they* were black, their *music* was white, and in it they had managed to capture the spirit of being a white American teenager. Eddie Cochran *was* that white American teenager, the all-American boy, and in his brief career he managed to home in on the heart of white American rock & roll.

Eddie Cochran was born on October 3rd, 1938, but up to the time that he

signed with Al Bennet's Hollywood-based Liberty label very little is known about him. The Cochran family home was in Oklahoma City, and Eddie was the youngest of five children. He used to call Oklahoma City his 'home', but it's doubtful he ever knew it, since shortly before or after his birth the family was forced to move to Albert Lea, Minnesota, in search of employment.

In Albert Lea (pop. 20,000) he grew up in a relaxing atmosphere of hunting, fishing, and practising the guitar, but then the family moved out to Bell Gardens, California (in 1953 say Liberty, although some sources give the date as early as 1949). There, Eddie began playing with Hank Cochran (no relation say Liberty — his cousin say others), playing rockabilly music at local reviews. And then in a local music store in Bell Gardens, Eddie met Jerry Capehart, an aspiring songwriter who was to become integral to his success — and yet remain totally ignored by most rock historians. Undoubtedly Capehart was instrumental in finding the right style for Cochran, and he also wrote the words for most of his major hits.

Soon after their first meeting Capehart got some recording studio time, and he took Hank and Eddie along to cut some songs they had co-written (and which were ultimately released on the Los Angeles Ekko label). After this session three titles were released as singles under

Camera Press

the name of 'The Cochran Brothers': 'Tired And Sleepy', 'Mr. Fiddle', and 'Guilty Conscience'. Hank Cochran, however, felt that their musical interests weren't really very close, and so set off for Nashville to play pure country music (he had some small success later with 'Little Bitty Tear').

Soon after Hank's departure in 1956, Jerry Capehart and Eddie made some dubs for American Music, a publishing company, and among the songs they laid down were 'Long Tall Sally' and 'Blue Suede Shoes' — an indication of how fast they had moved on to pure rock & roll once away from Hank's country influence. On the dubs, since released by Liberty, Eddie sang and played guitar, and Jerry Capehart played a cardboard box amplified to sound like a snare drum. Connie 'Guybo' Smith played fine bass on these sessions, as he did on most of Eddie's hits (some accounts place him on the Cochran Brothers' recordings as well).

From these dubs, Eddie had his first solo record released — 'Skinny Jim'/'Half-Loved' — on the Crest label (a promotional subsidiary of American Music). Armed with the dubs and the solo record, Jerry Capehart did the rounds of the record companies in the area and found Liberty interested enough to sign Eddie. Then, instead of using any Capehart/Cochran material (they later released a more polished version of 'Skinny Jim', which Capehart had written), Liberty gave them a John D. Loudermilk song. 'Sittin' In The Balcony', to record. Released in late 1956 it sold over 1,000,000 copies, with Eddie singing in his gulping, ersatz-Elvis voice, and Capehart on the cardboard box drums. As a direct result of the hit came a cameo part for Eddie in the film *The Girl Can't Help It,* starring Tom Ewell and Jayne Mansfield.

The film, directed by Frank Tashlin, was one of the better ones to come out of the period labelled as 'rock & roll films'. It featured most of the usual names — Little Richard, Gene Vincent, Fats Domino — but had them as incidentals . . . the story-line (about Jayne Mansfield's rise to stardom as a rock & roll star who couldn't sing) coming first. Eddie was in fact being watched on television during the film, singing a number he had co-written with someone called Fairfield, 'Twenty Flight Rock'.

In fact, neither 'Twenty Flight Rock' nor 'Sittin' In The Balcony' were really very good records. 'Twenty Flight Rock' was simply a variation on the numbers theme used by Bill Haley for 'Rock Around The Clock'; and 'Sittin' In The Balcony' was really little more than the one line about sitting in the back row of the balcony at the cinema holding hands with a girl. Liberty did, however, use a Capehart/Cochran song as the follow-up to Loudermilk's. Capehart now describes the release of 'Mean When I'm Mad' as 'a mistake', and if sales are any reflection he was quite right. The record was a disaster, and it marked the beginning of a lean period for them both. They spent the

time trying out various different styles, trying to find the right one for them. Also during this time Eddie made another film, *Untamed Youth,* which was about kids picking cotton in California.

It wasn't until March of 1958, though, that the whole thing came together. According to Jerry Capehart both of them were by then unashamedly searching for commerciality in their songs, looking for a sound that would sell and make them both successful. That sound eventually came along the evening before they were due in Los Angeles' Gold Star studios (where they did most of their recording). Eddie had travelled from his home to Capehart's Park Sunset apartment in Hollywood, and at the end of a fruitless night, Eddie came out with a riff that Capehart was keen to use somehow and find some lyrics for.

''I knew,'' he says, ''that there had been a lot of songs about summer, but none about the *hardships* of summer. Of all the seasons, there'd never been a blues song about summer.'' And so, in less than an hour they had written the first summertime blues, in fact *the* 'Summertime Blues'.

That number proved to be what they had spent two years looking for. In its few verses the song captured the hang-ups and absurdity of having to work in the summer holidays, so wrecking your 'social' life. Beyond that, the song also seemed to harbour a more general discontent with authority — from parents and the boss,

right up to the most self-important politicians:

> 'Ev'ry time I call my Baby,
> Try to get a date, My boss says
> 'No dice, Son you gotta work late'.'

After its release in May, 1958, 'Summertime Blues' quickly became an enormous hit and Eddie's second Gold Disc. As an all-time, much-covered classic of rock & roll it stands as fresh and relevant today as it was then.

It wasn't merely Jerry Capehart's words that made the record such a classic: those few chords strummed on Cochran's semi-acoustic Gibson, the sudden pauses for the gruff voice of authority (which was dubbed on later by Eddie himself), the naturally exciting way he sang it, blended everything into a perfect cohesive whole.

The sparse instrumentation of Eddie's voice(s) and guitar, Connie Smith's bass and Jerry Capehart's cardboard box, were again used in the follow up-record, 'C'mon Everybody'. All the same ingredients were there, carefully re-mixed so that the formula would work again with the record sounding somehow 'similar yet different' (the key to the success of more than just Eddie Cochran).

'C'mon Everybody' was another Capehart/Cochran song, and retained that same teenage 'feel' that had hallmarked 'Summertime Blues': the same use of a simple-yet-effective strummed chord

Eddie Cochran giving one of his many unforgettable performances.

Eddie Cochran ironically died when his single 'Three Steps To Heaven' was a hit.

sequence, the same 'voice', and the same teenage sentiments in the lyrics. This time though, Jerry Capehart focused on the complexities, problems and joys of kids holding a party while their parents are away.

Although 'C'mon Everybody' didn't do as well as 'Summertime Blues' — except in Britain for some strange reason — it still sold well over 1,000,000 copies and joined 'Summertime Blues' — which had been there most of the summer — in the autumn charts of 1958, carrying on over well into 1959.

During 1959, though, Eddie dissipated his energies somewhat. His next record after 'C'mon Everybody' was 'Somethin' Else' (written by Eddie and Sharon Sheeley, his girlfriend), which simply adapted the expression to a variety of things and girls. Although all the same ingredients were used, this time it just didn't come off.

Nevertheless, to aid his touring commitments, Eddie had formed a band which featured Connie 'Guybo' Smith on bass, Gene Ridgio on drums, and a variety of musicians on piano and sax. The group even cut some records together, notably the instrumental 'Guybo'/'Strollin' Guitar'. This record clearly bore the marks of Eddie's growing interest in the production techniques involved in recording (he'd been a pioneer of the multi-dubbing process), and at the time he was seriously thinking of retiring from the rock business of touring and constantly performing. He wanted more time to use the studios, both for himself and for some other unknown performers he admired. One of these was a friend called Bob Denton, who played on some of Gene Vincent's records and whom Eddie had met on the set of *The Girl Can't Help It*. Another was a duo called Jewel and Eddie (Jewel Atkins, who was to later have the hit, 'The Birds And The Bees', and Eddie Daniels); and he and Jerry Capehart were also both very keen to record with a young studio musician they'd come across called Glenn Campbell.

Another factor behind Eddie's wish to move out of the limelight was the death of a close friend of his, Buddy Holly. They'd arranged to tour together, but at the last minute problems had prevented Eddie from making the trip. It was to be Holly's last tour, as the plane carrying him and two other performers, Ritchie Valens and the Big Bopper (J. P. Richardson), crashed in a snowstorm.

Holly's death on February 3rd, 1959, affected Eddie very deeply, and it's said that he never played any of Buddy's records again (except, so one story goes, on the eve of his own death). As a tribute, Eddie cut 'Three Stars' (which was, incidentally, written by John D. Loudermilk), with the intention that the royalties should go to the bereaved families. Because of some lack of agreement with Liberty, the record was never released at the time.

Anyway, Eddie decided to make one last tour — of England — with Gene Vincent. Like Holly, who had played in England before them, they were received like gods. American performers were never exactly regular visitors to Britain at that time, and their TV appearances and live performances blazed a triumphant trail around the country. The tour was jointly promoted by Jack Good and Larry Parnes, and it was so successful that Gene and Eddie were asked — and agreed to — a 10-week extension after a short break.

After the final date of the first half at the Bristol Hippodrome on April 16th, 1960, Eddie set off in a hired taxi to London Airport with Gene Vincent and Sharon Sheeley. Gene was going to Paris for a few dates and Eddie was returning to the States with his fiancée Sharon, to get married. They'd been together since the touring days of the Kelly Four, and she was a songwriter, known primarily for Ricky Nelson's 'Poor Little Fool' and Eddie's own 'Somethin' Else'.

In the early hours of the following morning, a burst tyre sent the car crashing into a lamppost. The three of them were sleeping in the back when it happened, and Eddie was thrown up into the car roof. Several hours later, he died of severe head injuries without ever regaining consciousness. Both Sharon and Gene were badly injured, and Gene was in pain from the injuries until his death in 1971.

Eddie Cochran's next scheduled release was the ironically-titled 'Three Steps To Heaven' (although it referred to the 'heaven on earth' of being in love, and not 'the great juke-box in the sky'), and in the month following his death it became his biggest hit ever. Both it, and the oft-preferred 'B' side, 'Cut Across Shorty', had been recorded at his last session in 1959, but this didn't stop more posthumous releases all varyingly successful.

The legendary reputations Holly and Cochran still have in England are no doubt due in part to the simple fact that they took the trouble to tour the country; but there is no doubt either that Cochran's reputation was made long before he crossed the Atlantic. Those two anthems for teenage America, 'Summertime Blues' and 'C'mon Everybody' — although only making a total of three minutes and forty-eight seconds together — were both the stuff of which legends are made.

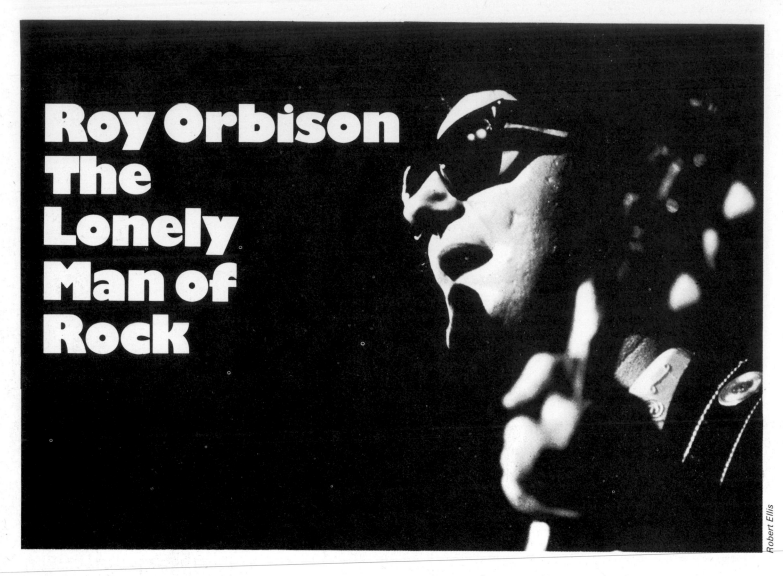

Roy Orbison The Lonely Man of Rock

Robert Ellis

When the Beatles and Mersey-mania swept all before them in 1963, creating an entirely new music scene overnight, only one solo performer survived: Roy Orbison. The reason he emerged unscathed was simply that the anglicised 'rhythm & blues' being peddled by the groups didn't impinge on his realm. Orbison was the only one singing seriously and convincingly about loneliness, grief and despair.

'Only the Lonely
Know the way I feel tonight
Only the Lonely
Know this feeling ain't right
Only the Lonely
Know the heartaches I've been through
Only the Lonely
Know I've cried, cried for you'

'Only The Lonely' was the first time most people had ever heard of Roy Orbison. In the late summer of 1960 the record made the top position in the music charts on both sides of the Atlantic, earning him a Gold Disc. It looked like another 'overnight success' story, but in fact Orbison had been around for quite some time. The delay was due to his failure to find the right type of music for his highly individual voice.

Roy Kelton Orbison was born on April 23rd 1936, in Vernon, Texas. Not long after, his family moved to nearby Wink, and when he was about six his father started teaching him how to play the guitar. In his teens, he was the leader of a group known as the Wink Westerners, who played country & western music at local functions and even had their own programme on Radio KVWC back in Vernon.

The Wink Westerners gradually evolved into the Teen Kings, and Roy struck up a friendship with another young Texan singer, Buddy Holly from nearby Lubbock. When Holly started working under the supervision of Norman Petty at his studio in Clovis, just over the border from Texas, in New Mexico, Holly arranged for Roy Orbison and the Teen Kings to audition for Norman Petty. By this time, the Teen Kings had developed their country music into country-rock, or rockabilly as it was then known, and two of the songs they recorded with Petty, 'Tryin' To Get To You' and 'Ooby Dooby', were released on the Jewel record label.

Two states to the east, in Memphis, Tennessee, Sam Phillips' Sun Record Company had become the mecca for all rockabilly singers seeking to emulate the success of Phillips' protégé, a local truck driver named Elvis Presley. Jerry Lee Lewis, Carl Perkins, Conway Twitty, Johnny Cash and Roy Orbison made the trip.

Phillips had heard Orbison's only release, and had him re-cut that and record several new songs in his studios at 706 Union Avenue. The new version of 'Ooby Dooby', a fast-paced rocker very much in the style of 'Long Tall Sally' about a dance called the Ooby Dooby, was almost an instrumental — just a few verses and two long solos in the classic style of early rock & roll.

'Ooby Dooby' was released as Sun 242 backed by 'Go, Go, Go', and it sold something in the order of 350,000 copies—quite a fair-sized hit. Orbison went on to record a lot of material for Sam Phillips, and had three more singles released on the Sun label — 'You're My Baby', 'Sweet And Easy' and 'Chicken-Hearted' — but none came anywhere near selling as many as 'Ooby Dooby' (which resulted in his nickname, the Big O).

A song Roy Orbison had written about his wife, 'Claudette', another driving rocker, was recorded by the Everly Brothers as the 'B' side to 'All I Have To Do Is Dream', which turned out to be a double-sided million-seller. The Everly Brothers had been signed to the Acuff-Rose music publishers by Wesley Rose, and he was impressed enough by 'Claudette' to offer Orbison a contract.

Syndication International

Above: Roy Orbison, unmoved as ever, and, right, engaged in his favourite pastime.

Rose also negotiated a recording contract for Orbison with RCA Victor, who were based 200 miles cross-state from Memphis, in Nashville. At the old Victor studios there on 17th Street and Hawkins, Orbison cut several tracks under the supervision of Chet Atkins – who'd also been in charge of recording Rose's other clients, the Everlys. RCA released 'Almost Eighteen'/'Jolie' as a single, but with little response, and turned down his next offering 'Paper Boy'. So Wesley Rose thought a change of labels might do Orbison some good and took him across town to Fred Foster's newly-formed Monument label. Orbison's first session with Monument produced 'Paper Boy' – the 18,000 sales, however, seemed to reflect RCA's good judgement in rejecting it.

His second session with Monument resulted in 'Uptown' – another fast rocker very reminiscent of Eddie Cochran's 'Teenage Heaven' in structure, instrumentation and lyric-content. That sold 75,000 copies, a big improvement on 'Paper Boy' but still well below his lone Sun label hit, 'Ooby Dooby'.

At their next recording session, Orbison gave Foster two songs he wanted to record. Foster suggested that the two be combined and brought in a string section and a male vocal backing group. The result was 'Only The Lonely', a Number One hit record, and a million sales. 'Only The Lonely' was a complete departure for Orbison and for Foster. The use of the almost self-parodying male backing singers ('Dum, Dum, Dum, Dummy-Doo-Wah') and the string section made the record pure pop.

It was a beautiful ballad of teenage emotions, but unlike most teen-ballads of the time, it was sung in the most hauntingly dramatic way:

'Maybe tomorrow
A new romance
No more sorrow
But that's the chance
You gotta take
If your lonely heart breaks
Only the lonely . . . .'

Although the strings were a bit heavy-handed, Orbison had managed, in that one record, to perfect the art pioneered by such other former Sun artists as Conway Twitty (then known as Harold Jenkins) and of course Presley; namely of channeling rock & roll into the traditional ballad form.

Orbison's immediate follow-up to 'Only The Lonely' was another song from the same session, 'Blue Angel'. Although it was essentially an inferior imitation of his first hit, employing the same male chorus and surging strings, it did give Orbison a chance to show off his semi-operatic voice – singing some incredible wordless passages in between his sympathising with the blue angel over her broken romance.

At the time of Orbison's two hits grief was quite a popular theme, although no one else was treating it as seriously as Orbison. The usual treatment was more in the vein of 'Tell Laura I Love Her' (Ray Peterson's hit about a guy dying in a stock-car race trying to earn enough money to buy his girl a ring), or 'Teen Angel' (Mark Denning's record of how a girl dies going

back to her boyfriend's car, which is stuck on the railway tracks, to get the ring he gave her).

The introspective tragedy that Orbison sang about was not his exclusive province: the Everly Brothers notably had been covering that ground for quite some time with hits such as 'When Will I Be Loved' and 'So Bad'. Of course the Everlys used a much faster tempo and a much more 'teenage' style, and with them it only seemed a flesh wound from which they would undoubtedly soon recover (even if it did seem like a mortal wound at the time); but Orbison sounded like a terminal case.

Slow-Burning Fuse

In his third hit, 'Running Scared', which brought him his second Gold Disc, Orbison added another devastating ingredient: the slow-burning fuse, or the crescendo. Most of his hits from 'Running Scared' on employed this technique, in various ways, starting off very slowly, building up until it almost bursts over with emotion: the pop 'Bolero'.

'Running Scared' began in a spoken whisper, coming in over the simple but staccato strumming of his guitar, and

Above: Roy Orbison with his wife.
Right: Roy singing his sad songs.

built up in four definite stages. First the backing of a bass and drum comes in; then that is filled out; followed by a heavenly chorus and finally the whole orchestra. The narrative builds up in the same way with Orbison's growing sense of disaster as his girlfriend's ex-lover comes back:

'Just running scared/Each place we go
So afraid/That he might show
Yeah running scared/What would I do
If he came back/And wanted you
Just running scared/Feeling low
Running scared/You loved him so
Just running scared/Afraid to lose
If he came back/Which one would you
   choose.'

Orbison's own 'live' performance of 'Running Scared' was also perfect. His natural complexion is a pasty, death-like white, and he heightened this dramatically by dyeing his hair jet-black (slicked back 'pompadour' style), and wearing dark glasses and all-black outfits rather reminiscent of those worn by flamenco guitarists.

There he stood on the stage; all black and white and completely alone. When he sang, he hardly moved a muscle — not even his lips. Movement of any kind would have detracted from the dramatic image of 'self-control in the midst of despair'. It was a very powerful image complementing perfectly the very powerful emotions laid bare in his songs.

Orbison wrote most of his own songs (in collaboration with someone called Melson), and they fell into three distinct categories: songs about love which has been 'lost' ('Only The Lonely', 'It's Over', 'Blue Angel'); songs about the absence of love, and about loneliness ('In Dreams', 'Oh Pretty Woman'); and songs in which there was the potential threat of the love

being lost ('Running Scared', 'Falling').

All were sung by Orbison in his soaring voice which just seemed to strike the right chord inside the listener, to exactly capture the feeling expressed in the words. Some of those songs — six of which sold over a million copies each — were pure poetry set to music, and turned into pop arias by Orbison's rich and soaring voice.

'Running Scared' was a pure distillation of Orbison's technique, almost a skeletal framework; and the other songs — particularly 'In Dreams' and 'It's Over' — were the fleshing out of those bones. In both songs Orbison's voice again exceeds itself at the climax, with notes of such timbre and quality that the words just melt into pure emotion.

'In Dreams' is the simple plea that Bobby Darin had sung about in 'Dream Lover' and the Everlys had in 'All I Have To Do Is Dream'. In dreams everything is as we want it to be:

'I close my eyes/then I drift away
Into the magic night/I softly say

A silent prayer/like dreamers do
Then I fall asleep to dream
My dream of you'

the only thing we don't control, is how long it goes on:

'Just before the dawn
I awake and find you gone
I can't help it
I can't help it
If I cry . . .
I remember
That you said
Goodbye
Too bad that all these things
Can only happen in my dreams
Only in dreams
In beautiful dreams'

The last four lines encapsulate it perfectly, and Orbison's voice singing them can only be described as magnificent. 'It's Over' contrasts with all Orbison's other songs in that it, for once, goes beyond the poetry of ordinary day-to-day language, and uses very romantic couplets to emphasise the gulf between what there was and what is left. When the love was there, everything was warm and colourful; now it's gone, there's just blackness and emptiness. It begins:

'Golden days before they end
Whisper secrets to the wind
Your baby won't be near you anymore
Tender nights before they fly
Send falling stars that seem to cry
Your baby doesn't want you any more'

and ends:

'Setting suns before they fall
Echo to you, that's all, that's all
But you'll see lonely sunsets after all
It's over, it's over, it's over, it's over.'

Again, the build up to the singing of the last two 'it's overs', in which Orbison manages to evince pain rather than sing mere words.

All of Orbison's songs dealt in tragedy ("pack as much poetry and philosophy into a two-minute pop record as you can" was how he once described his formula for success) and in the end life dealt out some tragedy of its own to him. On June 7th, 1966, he and his 25-year-old wife Claudette were motorcycling home from a race meeting when her bike was involved in a head-on collision and she was killed instantly. Needless to say, he was almost wiped out emotionally, but poured all of his love into his three sons, Roy junior, Tony and Wesley. He even wrote a song about the tragedy — 'It's Too Soon To Know' — which made the Top Three in Britain.

Then two years later, while he was in Bournemouth on a tour of Britain, his Tennessee home burnt down with two of his kids inside — Roy junior, who was 13, and eight-year-old Tony. Since then, he hasn't had a hit record at all, and now, like so many old rockers whose former success has vanished, he has reverted to the music of the Wink Westerners, pure country & western

Tom Hanley

CHAPTER 2
Black Music

The roots of rock & roll lie deep in the music of black people. From the early days of blues and of jazz, white musicians hadn't done the blacks any favours, and mostly they found themselves excluded from the mainstream of commercial success by lame versions of their own innovations. Their only self respect came from playing jazz. Their only hope of making the bright lights came from playing Uncle Tom. Consequently they had their own records, their own radio stations, their own charts, and they could rarely find popularity outside the ghettoes. Rock changed that and within a few years of its first eruption, black artists were making regular and important contributions both to the changing face of the music and to the international charts.

Ray Charles with his soul/jazz style; James Brown with his shouting urban soul; Otis Redding, Aretha Franklin and others gave their people a new pride and identity. Berry Gordy started an all-black recording company in Detroit, created a sound and a style, called it Tamla-Motown, and then stormed the world, with his artists. From Motown came the first black superstars – Diana Ross and the Supremes, the Four Tops, Stevie Wonder. Not only could they compete with the huge established stars and companies, they could beat them at their own game. By the '60s, Jimi Hendrix – an American working out of London – became the first black rock superstar and helped to create a new language for the guitar.

'I'm black and I'm proud' was the cry from these stars who had conquered the bastions of a white industry and drawn together, in a way that was previously impossible – through the medium of music – people who were united not by colour but by age. Their contribution to the music and to the culture was crucial. Without black music there could not have been rock & roll and without the further innovations there could not have been rock music as we know it.

RAY CHARLES High Priest of Soul

''If I don't feel what I'm doing on a record, then I'd rather forget it. If the artist feels the song he's doing, then he can do a great job . . . I'd say the problem with any artist is very simple. If all artists would do what is really right for them and would feel within themselves what they are doing, they would stay up there much longer. A new star is born everyday, but it's a question how long he will shine. But a true artist will be around a long time.''

(Ray Charles, quoted on the sleeve notes of the 'What'd I Say' album, September 1959.)

Consider those remarks in their correct perspective: in September 1959, Craig Douglas was in the middle of a lengthy run at the top of the British charts with 'Only Sixteen'. Across the Atlantic, the best-seller was the Browns' version of the early '50s song, 'The Three Bells'. It was a period of malaise in the history of rock. The original figures who had created the genre had moved on in one way or another: Elvis was in the Army having his image changed; Jerry Lee was an outcast after his marriage to 13-year-old Myra; and Little Richard was doing strange things — rumour had it he'd thrown his wordly goods into Sydney Harbour and entered a monastery. Their places had been taken by the wooden figures, that curious breed of rock & roll mutants who only ever appeared in Britain as a parade of smiling mimers on the Perry Como TV show.

It was in this context that Ray Charles appeared. In fact he had been around singing and performing for a decade, but his music hadn't become known to a large audience until the last years of the '50s. Part of the reason for this obscurity had been that Ray didn't really find himself musically until then. But perhaps of greater importance was that Ray's music from the mid-'50s onwards spotlighted

with an almost cruel precision all that had been lacking in rock since the industry took control — simple, but critical things, like passion, like sincerity, like any semblance of real feeling. It was this *perception* of his music by an increasingly large audience from 1959 through to the beginning of 1962, that elevated Ray to the ranks of rock's all-time Gurus. It's even probably true to say that Ray Charles was the first Underground Hero, but more of that later: first, the man himself.

Ray The Orphan

Ray's early life was veritably tragic. In 1939, at the age of six, he was left incurably blind by an attack of glaucoma, and was placed in the St. Augustine School for the Blind a few miles from his home in Greenville, Florida. It was here that he learned the rudiments of his music, taking up the piano and the clarinet. When

Ray was 15 both his parents died, and Ray the orphan took to the road to earn his living from his music. After a couple of years with local bands he moved West, like all good Yankee dreamers do, and played with a trio in Seattle on the West Coast.

Between 1949 and 1952 he took his first tentative steps in the recording studios, making records for a small Los Angeles label, Swingtime. Many of these recordings became commercially available in this country in the early '60s, and show Ray as a pretty competent plagiarist. Nat 'King' Cole and Charles Brown were his two idols, and at times it's hard to tell the

David Redfern

difference between the young pretender and his heroes. Occasionally, however, even on these very early sessions Ray gives a tantalising glimpse of the great days to come. On one number in particular 'St. Pete Florida Blues', he over-reaches himself dramatically, and, once rid of the Charles Brown voice, his own personality makes its presence felt very strongly. Several of his other 12-bar recordings during this time were done with a similar intensity, but even the best of them – such as 'Hey Now' – fell short on some indefinable quality. In these numbers, historically of far more interest than the more polished copies of Cole and Brown, Ray seemed to be aware that the idiom he was searching for was possible, but at that moment in time unknown.

Up-Tempo

Ray was not to come to terms with himself until he joined Atlantic. Ahmet Ertegun first inquired about him at the end of 1952, and he was signed by Atlantic (run by Ertegun and Jerry Wexler) a little later. Swingtime, a small company in big trouble, sold the genius for about £1,000 – a financial give-away on a par with Sam Phillips' sale of Elvis Presley to RCA.

Atlantic was one of those seminal companies run by dedicated enthusiasts full of ideas. As soon as he got hold of him Ertegun wanted to try Ray on some up-tempo numbers and, for his first Atlantic sessions, provided him with a couple of suitable quickies – one he wrote himself called 'Mess Around', and the other Memphis Curtis' 'It Should Have Been Me'. The session showed great progress since the Swingtime days – if only for the marvellous piano on 'Mess Around' – but it wasn't until December 1953 that Ray started getting into his stride. At this time he did a session for Atlantic using material he had written ('Don't You Know'), his own arrangements and his own band. It was an important innovation.

Pure Gospel

A year later, and the Ray Charles sound was born. In November 1954 he recorded 'I Got A Woman', his first 16-bar since one or two earlier abortive attempts on Swingtime. For this recording, Ray used the line-up that was to become his standard band for several years to come – two trumpets (usually Marcus Belgrave and John Hunt), baritone sax (Bennie Crawford), alto and tenor (the great David 'Fathead' Newman), drums (Teagle Fleming) and bass (Edgar Willis). He dropped the guitar sound that had distinguished many of his earlier 12-bar blues attempts (listen to the rapport that Ray struck up with Mickey Baker on the 1953 'Losing Hand'), and relied increasingly on the piano as his 'lead' instrument. The band doubled-up on his piano figures, and this touch – a piece of pure gospel, especially since Ray's piano phrases became more and more church-based – was, according to Jerry Wexler, 'the kicker'.

It was the gospel bias in his work that Ray explored over the next couple of years at Atlantic, and it was the fusion of this tradition with the Blues that gave Ray Charles the formula he had been looking for. Alan Lewis points out (in the liner notes to the recent Ray Charles compilation album): 'Charles used the gospel chord changes and call and response patterns (first with horns and later with the voices of the Raelets) to create an unprecedented level of tension and excitement'. The best examples of this can be seen in the studio versions of numbers like 'It's All Right' (probably the first recording on which he used a vocal back-up group to emphasise the horns sound), 'Talking About You' (another 16-bar, like 'I Got A Woman' – but made significantly different by the addition of the Raelets), 'A Fool For You' and 'Drown In My Own Tears'.

Ray was bringing all the pieces together – it's a tribute to Atlantic that they let him

A handsome, mature Ray Charles gives a cool smile as he rolls his fingers over the keyboards.

wander off into every conceivable area of the black musical experience. At one moment he was recording with the MJQ vibist Milt Jackson, at another he was doing straight blues, at another he was working on jazz-based instrumentals with his sidemen, at another he'd be trying out gospel sounds with the Raelets. And all the time, his development was nothing short of astonishing. His voice, in particular, was becoming more exciting with each recording he made — just as a couple of years earlier he'd assimilated and transcended the Nat King Cole influence, so now — seemingly in the space of a few months — he absorbed and transcended the gospel vocals of singers like Alex Bradford. He'd become a prolific songwriter, though more often than not his 'compositions' were secularised re-writes of old gospel numbers. 'This Little Light Of Mine' for example became 'This Little Girl Of Mine', and 'Talkin' 'Bout Jesus' became 'Talkin' 'Bout You'. But, in retrospect, the most important thing he did was to go on the road with his new found voice, his new found confidence, his band, and his Raelets. The Ray Charles synthesis was presented to the people.

State of Rapture

Two recordings — 'Ray Charles At Newport' (the 1958 Festival) and 'Ray Charles In Person' (recorded at Herndom Stadium, Atlanta, Georgia, on May 28th, 1959) — remain as testimonies to those magnificent touring days. In these, the gospel flavour is unmistakable. Ray's empathy with his audience is as close as the priest's with his congregation — the music confirms this closeness with the audiences, whose state of rapture forced Ray to constantly look beyond the narrow confines of the studio versions of the songs he was performing. It's a fascinating two-way process — with Ray's influence on the audience being matched by their influence on him. The results are marvellous — 'Drown In My Own Tears' at Herndom and 'A Fool For You' at Newport remain, to this day, the pinnacles of his recording career. There is, it is true, an element of showmanship about the proceedings, but that is never allowed to interfere with the spirit of the music — Ray at this time never fell into the tempting traps that crushed much of the greatness of some of his successors like James Brown and Solomon Burke. Ray was much more a man of the people than a star for the people to idolise — he reflected their feelings just as much as he guided them.

Through this dialectical process, through this church-like empathy with his audience, Ray had invented Soul music. He knew, too, that what he had done was pretty important — only a man confident enough to know he had done great things could say things like: "If an artist feels the song he's doing, then he can do a great performance." It's something that Ray could say with the ease of a man who *had* given great performances. Ray knew that what he was doing was right for him — he'd found the elusive formula. Ray could have made it as a jazz man (and in turn his influence in that field — at that time wallowing in the technically brilliant, but increasingly feelingless New Bop — was considerable); he could have made it as a church singer; he could have made it as a rock & roller; he could have made it as a blues singer — he could have done any of these things, but he didn't. He knew himself that there was no need to adapt to one particular role, when a fusion of all the strands of black musical experience was within the realms of possibility.

An Empty Parody

The old-timers couldn't take it. Big Bill Broonzy shook his head and remarked: "He's got the blues, he's cryin' sanctified and I know that's wrong . . . he should be singing in a church." But his younger followers reacted, instinctively and immediately, along with Ray. Ray had smashed down the barriers of prejudice — and the implications were enormous. They in turn began calling the man 'The Genius'.

Ray's days at Atlantic reached their climax with his recording of 'What'd I Say', which had more or less everything Ray had been striving for parcelled into five minutes. The song, of course, became perhaps the greatest rock standard of all time, with every other group in the universe including it in their repertoire. It's strange to reflect how, at the time of its first release in 1959, the song was dismissed by the BBC DJ's.

Ray left Atlantic in 1960, and moved across to ABC-Paramount. His career with ABC has been — in a nutshell — tragic, and is, perhaps, best forgotten. Anyone who was an avid fan of Ray's in the '50s can only squirm when they listen to Ray's work over the past decade. The first sense of unease came across the Atlantic with his first tours in 1963 — he was starting to

move in some very awkward directions. True, he did perform some of his old classics, beginning the show with 'I Got A Woman' — but his treatment of this song was similar to the way Dylan garbled his way through 'The Times They Are A Changin'' on his 1965 tour — it was as if to say, 'Well, I suppose I have to do this number, so here goes'. It came over like an empty parody.

There was something even worse about the shows — the element of showmanship that had been marginal at Herndom and Newport was beginning to take over. The way in which Ray hammed up his own blindness in his version of 'Careless Love' ('Once I was blind but now I see . . .') was too awful to contemplate — the genius might have finally hit the European road, but he was fast going off the rails.

Unfortunately, Ray's later work — with an ever greater desperation to please all the people all the time, witness his calamitous versions of Beatles' songs — have coloured critical reactions to Ray's earlier work, which are now hardly discussed at all. The case for Ray Charles' influence on the history of rock does need stating.

First, his fusion of Blues and Gospel — his discovery of Soul Music — paved the way forward for Black Rock. Every great black record since 'What'd I Say' owes just about everything to Ray Charles — without his '50s performances, the careers of Otis Redding, James Brown, Bobby Parker, Percy Sledge and Sly and the Family Stone would have been very different. All of these artists accepted Ray's definition of Soul and worked on from there. Similarly, the most commercial black music of the past decade — Tamla Motown — would have been unthinkable without Ray's work with the Raelets.

Second, his impact for the white

musicians — though not so direct — was equally momentous. During the late '50s, countless white artists stated their allegiance to The Genius — Bobby Darin, Lonnie Donegan, Cliff Richard ("What I'd like to achieve," he said in 1960, "is the Ray Charles sound"), Billy Fury, Gene Vincent, Eddie Cochran, Adam Faith . . . the list could go on forever. But perhaps of greater importance was his effect on those who would lead the British Boom in the '60s. Ray Charles stood out in the late '50s because he used real and genuine emotion in pop music — at the time of Bobby Vinton, John Leyton and Frankie Avalon, this was something indeed. Ray became a cult figure amongst young white record buyers because his feelings were intact — the man *was* his music. He showed, in the dark days of rock & roll, that it was possible for the medium to be used as an art form. True, it had happened before, but what was crucial about Ray was that he was proving it at a time when no one else was really bothering.

The Genius Lives On

However tragic his later career has become, nothing can detract from the man's influence in those Atlantic days. It seems fair to say in conclusion: if Chuck Berry and Elvis Presley were the vital figures of Rock from 1955–1958, and Bob Dylan and the Beatles held a similar position from 1963–68, then the years between must belong, in the same fashion, to Ray Charles.

It wasn't his music that bridged the gap between the two eras — it was more his spirit. Ray was true to himself during those years and he proved that by being true to your own feelings, it was possible to produce great music. His message — and his Atlantic recordings — will survive.

SKR

Keystone

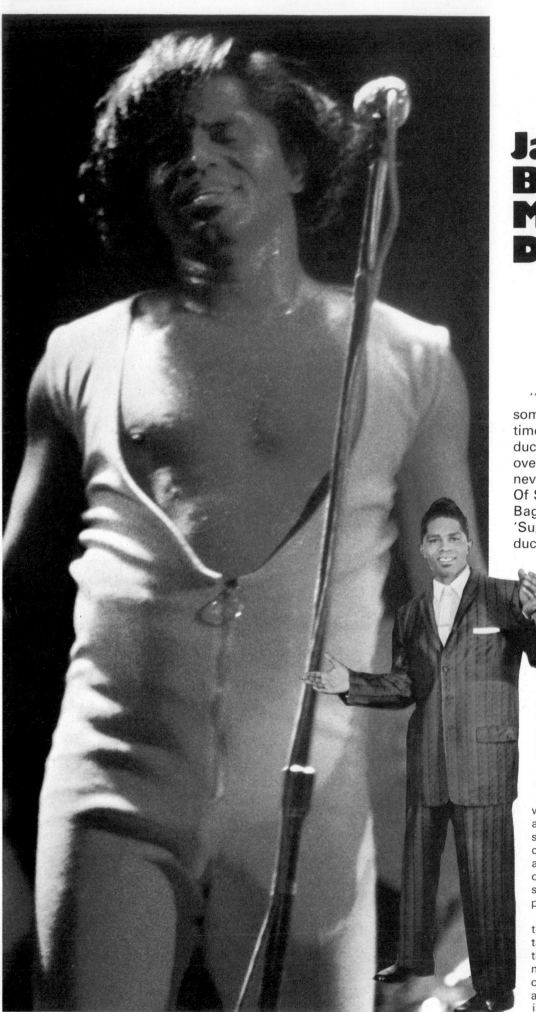

James Brown: Mr Dynamite

''I'd like to know are you ready for some super dynamite soul? It's star-time, ladies and gentlemen. Introducing the young man that's had over 35 soul classics. Tunes that will never die. Tunes like 'Try Me', 'Out Of Sight', 'Papa's Got A Brand New Bag', 'I Feel Good', 'Sex Machine', 'Superbad', and 'Soul Power'. Introducing the world's greatest entertainer – Mr Dynamite – the amazing Mr 'Please Please' himself – the hardest working man in show business. Ladies and gentlemen, the star of the show – **JAMES BROWN!**''

For over 12 years, variations on this bombastic theme have introduced into the spotlight the most dynamic ball of energy so far unleashed by the post-war pop explosion. A man who has 83 consecutive hit records and over 50 albums to his credit; who still maintains an average of over 300 personal appearances every year, and who, between gigs, finds time to jet around his chain of restaurants, radio stations, production and promotion complexes. James Brown is an expert at getting that little bit extra out of all on his payroll – at keeping the whole shebang rolling on a charge from his personal powerpack.

James Brown is at one and the same time the last great vaudeville entertainer, and one of the most powerful of the new wave of black executives. A man who learned how to fight and overcome seemingly impossible odds at an age when most of us are safely in society's warm cocoon. He took

America's cultural heritage by the scruff of the neck, remoulded it after his own image and spat it back to surmount racial oppression, with a gesture that took him straight through the stratas of showbiz into the uneasy zones of political power.

His music has the vitality of rock & roll and the honesty of the blues wrapped up with the personality of a man constantly in tune with the times. Each performance, presented with every available aid to excitement, is inextricably bound to the hopes, fears and demands of this self-made, black giant. Each song is a single expression of defiance tempered in the heat of achievement. He is, in the original terms of reference, truly a soul singer.

Born in South Carolina in 1932 of parents who were soon to part, young James was raised by an aunt in a wooden shack on the wrong side of Augusta, Georgia. As if the burden of this black, barefoot cast-off wasn't heavy enough, he was an unattractive child, shorter than the other kids of his age. The pains of prejudice and poverty can be endured as part of a community, but in his personal torment of size and appearance, James was alone. It is not surprising that from an early age he developed a compulsive need to prove himself. A friend who had to pull him out of many a fight with boys twice his age and size remembers: "James was always the best at everything. He had more determination and guts than the rest of us" — and later a more prophetic memory — after James had scraped together enough from shining shoes to buy baseball equipment — "Along with being a hard player, James was a poor loser and if he got really angry he'd simply take his bat and ball and quit. One of the reasons the kids put up with him — we needed his equipment to play the games."

The Famous Flames

By the early '50's James had formed a gospel group, The 3 Swanees, with Bobby Byrd and Johnny Terry. Mounting success by two relatively local acts, the Five Royals from Winston-Salem and Little Richard from Macon, prompted the group to move into Macon to try for themselves. When Little Richard rocketed to national prominence with 'Tutti Frutti' and got too big for his manager (and his boots), Clint Brantley was able to devote his attention to James and the boys — now calling themselves the Famous Flames, after Charles Brown's Three Blazers, and performing rhythm & blues hits of the period.

Their chance came in February, 1956, when Ralph Bass, producer and talent scout for King Records of Cincinnati heard their dub of 'Please, Please, Please', a Brown original. He drove down to Macon, signed the group on the spot and rushed them back to the studio to re-record the song for immediate release.

Formed as a race label by Syd Nathan in 1945, by '56 King had seen considerable success with R&B acts including Billy Ward and the Dominoes and Hank Ballard

and the Midnighters, as well as a strong country catalogue. As one of the true independents they manufactured, designed and packaged their own products for distribution and promotion in the southern states and along the eastern seaboard. 'Please Please, Please' first hit in Georgia, then slowly snowballed in the confines of King's territory, selling steadily throughout 1956. When the market had been saturated, it died. Only years later after Brown became a star was the record re-activated to become a million seller.

From Bad To Worse

As sales dropped so did the group's enthusiasm and Nathan's smile. Two follow-ups had been pushed out while the record was still selling and several more followed over the next 18 months — each less successful than its predecessor. Although Brown was already writing most of the group's material, he had not yet improved on an uncomfortable blend of styles drawn from the church and those popular acts around him.

Crisis point was reached in the summer of 1958 when, responding to a last chance ultimatum from Nathan, Brown came up with 'Try Me'. This was the big one — the song that Brown affectionately remembers as the turning point of his life. Recorded at his first New York session in September of that year, 'Try Me' was based on the same gospel pattern as previous releases, but with a subtly smoother performance than had been offered before. The feeling is of tender longing, rather than anguished suffering. It hit the Hot 100 and struck gold.

After two years of touring, Brown was beginning to learn more about showmanship. With the kudos of his first national chart entry behind him, he was able to employ a regular 6-piece road band, which made it possible to begin the creation and development of what was to become the hottest act in the business. Being able to rely on a well-rehearsed band, had a telling effect on Brown's writing. Whereas 'Please, Please, Please' had been followed by an erratic selection of derivative attempts to find a winning formula, the half dozen sessions from January '59 to February '61 produced 12 hits in succession — songs that finally broke away from and surpassed earlier influences. The James Brown sound was born, helped along by the close relationship between James and the Flames, punctuating and emphasising rhythms and vocal interplays.

While he was bonding the music around his own personality, Brown was also strengthening and clarifying his image. The precision timing now being demonstrated on stage, gave the band a short solid riff to link the last notes of each to the opening sequence of the next; exhaustive rehearsals ensuring that nothing interrupted the flow. He grew his hair and had it elaborately styled, discarded his baggy suit in favour of Italian mohairs, silk shirts and all the trimmings, and threw in as many lightening dance routines as possible — complete with

a dramatic collapsing scene and robe-shrouded recovery. Sharp as a razor and fast as a flyweight, the final effect was electrifying.

By the beginning of the '60s, the James Brown revue, complete with supporting acts including singers, dancers and comedians, had reached a polished near-perfection and was breaking box office records in ghetto theatres across America. Brown himself was receiving from black audiences the same sort of hysterical reaction that Presley had provoked from young whites, a few years earlier.

An album recorded in Harlem's Apollo Theatre on October 24th, 1962, captured the full power of this amazing road show. Implicit throughout is the authority of the man on stage and his complete mastery over the emotions of the audience. 'Live At The Apollo' became a million dollar seller and the following season Brown was voted no. 1 R&B singer of America.

It would have been a reasonable assumption that, considering his colour and the uncompromising style of his music, Brown was then at the peak of his career. Many other black singers have reached these hallowed gates only to fall back into obscurity (Solomon Burke) or be drawn through with the stupefying hands of white manipulation (Ray Charles, Sam Cooke). But Brown wasn't about to be bought or rejected. By modifying his music to the pulse of the times rather than the tastes of an existing establishment, he went on to reach an international multi-racial audience, and by adopting business policies learned from a white-dominated capitalist society, he achieved a personal stature way above the limitations of being a black rhythm & blues singer.

From this point on, James Brown was making the decisions. He rejected other people's business ideas and built himself into the living legend that he is today. The appearance of full page ads in trade magazines announced each new release, giving an indication of the money being ploughed back into the enterprise. Banner headlines drove home the message — the hardest working man in show business, soul brother no. 1.

Brown's Fair Deal

Back in 1962, there had been a tentative approach to new markets when, at the insistence of King Records, Brown had unwillingly cut four standards with a lush string orchestra and choir. Although 'Prisoner Of Love' was able to be transformed so dramatically that it became an integral part of James' repertoire, it was a policy that could have ended in disaster if followed through to its logical conclusion. A more decisive move was made in 1964. Realising that King was just not geared to keep pace with his expanding horizons, Brown formed his own production company, Fair Deal, and promptly delivered his next batch of tapes to Smash Records of Chicago — a division of the nationwide Mercury Corporation.

With such a prize at stake, all parties

James Brown, the man who has produced 83 consecutive hit records.

Cuban and Puerto Rican, anticipated and influenced a generation of soul music.

Taking advantage of mass communication, Brown began to cut down on his personal appearances to the extent that it was intimated that he was about to retire. Away from the stage he was producing a flood of releases from his many protégés and taking time out to use his own success as an example for soul brothers still trapped in the confines of the street. As early as 1966 he had cut 'Don't Be A Drop-Out' for the Office of Economic Opportunity, but by 1968 he was becoming involved in less controllable ideals.

Following the assassination of Dr Martin Luther King, two marathon TV appearances by James in Boston and Washington, were said to be directly responsible for preventing inflamed rioting on the streets. It was undoubtedly a personal triumph for Brown, the effects of which were perhaps more volatile than he would have wanted.

Although his social conscience gained him a place at LBJ's dinner table, black militants weren't so impressed by his involvement with white establishment and rank capitalism. Brown was none too happy to be caught in such a vice and was soon to play down his role as a black leader. He stepped out of the threshing machine when, on the eve of endorsing Hubert Humphrey for President, he stated, "After tomorrow I'm going back to singing, dancing, and telling kids to stay in school."

After a year away, Brown had returned to King in 1966 with all the reins at his command. They couldn't afford to lose him, so they gave him the works. As his music became progressively more rhythmic, he dropped all pretence at pandering to any particular audience and more than ever his records were expressions of his own thoughts and emotions. Remembering the advantages of his earlier flirtation with Smash, he eventually left King once and for all, leaving behind him a company with nothing to do but go bankrupt. In his new deal with the International Polydor Corporation he is assured of world-wide distribution without compromising himself or his music.

Human Bulldozer

Today at 40-plus, James Brown may have to approach his athletic stage routines with a hint more caution than he would have ten years ago, but, as long as the box office receipts reward it, the show will roll on. Recent involvement with film soundtracks and his first attempt at acting testify to his restless need to conquer every frontier. Records are still issued as fast as his adrenalin can pump them out and, despite criticism (from whites) of their production-line similarity, each shows a keen awareness of the changing times. Because Brown is constantly on the move so is his music, as unique as the man who makes it, influenced by many and influencing many more. He has forged armour plating about him to bulldoze his way to the top.

involved, immediately set their lawyers at one another. Before an injunction could restrict Smash to only issuing instrumentals under James Brown's name, plus any records made by the various artists in the revue, they did manage to get on to the market one vocal album and two singles.

The first of his records to sell in large quantities to whites, 'Out Of Sight' was also the first of a string of successes based on compulsive dance riffs laid down behind Brown's singing of an easily remembered tag line. There had been a shift of emphasis from vocal harmony to strong rhythm accompaniment. The band were now punching out the responses previously tackled by the Famous Flames, who were soon to be phased out altogether.

In bringing up the band on rhythms that appealed to a more lucrative market and a new generation of black record buyers, Brown was hot on the heels of the Motown and Stax Record Companies. Later, by gradually extending these rhythms in a series of repeating riffs and phrases and reducing the songs to broken cryptic verses and staccato outbursts, he alienated all but a minority of his white audience. He just got too black for comfort. The results, a hypnotic brew of blues and gospel, Afro-

ARETHA
The First Lady of Soul

If a truly 'underground' music exists in America today, it's the sound of black gospel: fiercely exciting, unashamedly emotional, unknown to the white pop-buying community, and ignored by the media, even music trade papers, sometimes inspiring soul music, sometimes drawing inspiration from it. Gospel throws up its own stars, who, like their secular counterparts, run their professional life as a business, with highly commercial results.

Since they tend to last longer than soul artists, they often show little desire to 'cross over' and sing 'baby' or 'my darling' instead of 'Him' and 'my Lord', either for moral reasons, or simply because they like the life they live which may or may not exhibit the snow-white purity of the songs they sing.

Few established gospel names may choose to cross over, but it's a rare soul singer that didn't cut his or her musical teeth in childhood at the neighbourhood house of worship. 'Aretha's never LEFT the church!' shouts her father on a recent live album; well, maybe not, musically — but when the 18-year-old Aretha Franklin signed to Columbia Records in 1960, as a secular act, she was embarking on a rocky road that would overshadow any heights aspired to by gospel people, reaching the top of the mountain in June '68, when a whitened, unrecognisable likeness of her made the cover of 'Time' magazine. Now, aged 30, she's still a world star — even if, as will be seen, she has her share of troubles.

Recorded Sermons

Aretha's father has made more records than his daughter; around 80 albums, in fact, of sermons he has preached as pastor of Detroit's New Bethel Baptist Church, which boasts 4,500 members, and, according to the 'Time' piece, 'two uniformed nurses . . . to aid overwrought parishioners'. Outside home ground, the Rev. C. L. Franklin can ask up to 4,000 dollars per public appearance — his reputation enhanced by the LPs; In 1987 he was even convicted for federal tax offences, copping a 25,000 dollar fine — to him about a year's earnings. He's now

56. At 14, Aretha, who'd grown up on Detroit's East Side with her unusually patriarchal family — father, brother Cecil, and sisters Erma and Carolyn, both professional singers today (mother had gone off when Aretha was six, and died shortly after) — in the 'nice' part of the ghetto, she went on the road with her father's gospel show, singing solo and having to cope with the eternal rigours of touring — constant bus travel (the Rev., he went by plane!), precious little sleep, and boredom - submitting for relief, like the others, to alcohol — and other temptations.

She had been introduced to John Hammond of Columbia through one 'Mule' Holly, bassist for jazz piano man Teddy Wilson. Her long sojourn at Columbia, from 1960 to 1965, saw Aretha as a stylist on the fringes of jazz and R&B; correspondingly, she played the 'upper chitlin' circuit' of black supper clubs. On record, her gospel phrasing frequently clashed with the nature of the material (she even had a minor hit with 'Rock-a-bye your baby with a Dixie me-lo-dy'!), and was served with generally lack-lustre accompaniment — though some sides gave promise of what was to come — 'Runnin' out of fools', 'Take a look', and 'Lee Cross' for instance.

By 1966, her talents had come to the notice of Jerry Wexler, enlightened Vice-Pres. of Atlantic Records, who astutely realised that *it* was in her, and it *had* to come out! So, on expiration of contract, he signed her to Atlantic, and set out to let the lady do what she'd always wanted to do — sit at the piano and wail. The first single — 'I never loved a man (the way I love you)', a ponderous ballad of great beauty, economically arranged and recorded in Muscle Shoals, Alabama, with a cataclysmic climax that stands as a classic moment in soul history, proved, to Wexler's delight and amazement, to be an R&B *and* pop smash, and the dam was open. Aretha had been let loose.

Blockbusting Revival

For the next few years, everything in the garden — publicly, at least — was lovely. Hit followed hit, every one a timeless winner: 'Baby I Love You', 'Since You've Been Gone', 'Chain Of Fools', 'Natural Woman', 'Do Right Woman — Do Right Man', 'I Say A Little Prayer' — and a number of fine albums — 'Never Loved A Man . . . ' (arguably her best), 'Lady Soul', 'Aretha Arrives', and so on. Even Britain, for whom a pure soul single in the pop chart was a rarity, lapped up Aretha's blockbusting revival of Otis Redding's 'Respect'.

All was underpinned by Aretha's own sanctified, hard-driving piano, her whooping vocals supported by the traditional girlie group (often including sister Carolyn), and inspired by superlative backings by New York and the South's finest session men. Without surrendering her fiercely black identity, Aretha had somehow come to be internationally adored, right across the board.

Then came 1969, and an indeterminate rot began to set in. The high standard of originals on record dropped in favour of an apparently deliberate policy of 'covering' other artists' recent hits (the LP: 'This Girl's In Love With You' only contained 3 new songs). The big band that toured with Aretha was lumbering and pedestrian and Aretha acquired something of a reputation within the business for non-cooperation and unpredictability. Her record sales, while maintaining her at the top of the tree, dropped noticeably. The 'Soul '69' album, more jazzy than her singles, was indifferently received, and the fans who'd loved the no-holds-barred funk of 'Respect', felt alienated by her habit of starting shows with 'There's no business like show business'. Slowly, she had slipped from her position as leader.

Next year, however, there began a slow process of regeneration — erratic to this day. When Aretha appeared at a benefit for black revolutionary Angela Davis, the old conflicts seemed to be resolved — the Queen was gettin' back *down*. To underline the change, out came the 'Spirit In The Dark' LP (titled 'Don't Play That Song' in Britain) way back up to par, reverting to

Redferns

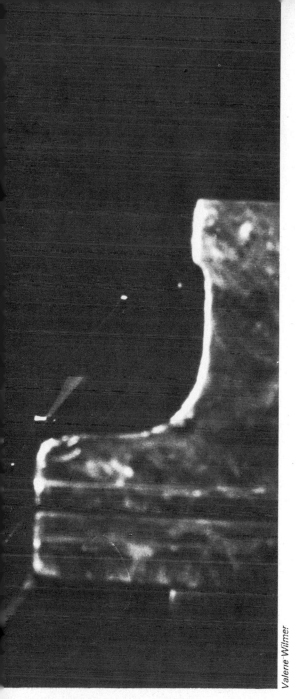

Valerie Wilmer

Above: Aretha Franklin in soulful mood, performing her songs at the piano, and, left, decked out in the finery she has tended towards in recent years. A symptom of her general loss of musical and personal direction, which seemed to endanger her 'First Lady of Soul' title, the flashy clothes have now been discarded, and Aretha is turning again to her blues and gospel roots.

the old style, with plenty of piano, and a hip, rocking choice of material. It was recorded in Miami, and included no less than five originals by Aretha herself, together with some blues from the likes of B. B. King and Jimmy Reed, Goffin-King's 'Oh No Not My Baby', and other goodies. Aretha's 'Spirit In The Dark' being remarkable for its stone gospel sound. Ditching the old 18-piece band, Aretha started to use a small group of peerless session players for her infrequent gigs, often the same ones as had actually been on the record — directed by the

redoubtable King Curtis, whose tenor sax had graced so many of her hits, and others', right from the '50s. And Aretha herself looked better for the change — a good five years younger, nearer her actual age.

In the months that followed, Aretha put out a few excellent sides — a brilliant revival of Ben E. King's 'Spanish Harlem', made great through Dr. John's organ work and Atlantic staffer Arif Mardin's delicate, precise arrangement; 'Rock Steady', a chunk of funk penned by Aretha; and a surprisingly effective version of Motown's 'You're All I Need To Get By'. An album called 'Young, Gifted, and Black', issued in 1972, was merely drawn from the stockpile of unused session tracks from 1970–71, Aretha had in fact stayed away from the studio for some time. But the next one was a milestone.

Worried by Aretha's failure to appeal to the hard-rock market, Wexler had managed to arrange a gig for her at San Francisco's famed rock haven — the Fillmore. A solid success, it garnered more sympathetic press than she'd had in years. The LP recorded live at the show plainly reveals Aretha's joy in performing at her best in front of a new, ecstatic audience, with a faultless band, and the benefit of an unscheduled appearance by none other than Ray Charles. The evening proved such a gas, Atlantic even put out an album of the band's warm-up set!

Choral Backing

Those rooting for Aretha hoped this was the turning point, the harbinger of a new, glorious period in her career. Their hopes were at first fulfilled beyond all expectations, then as quickly dashed to the ground. The master-stroke was to have her go back to her roots. In January 1972, she sang in an L.A. church, with her father in attendance, and accompanied by gospel star James Cleveland, her regular back-up band, a massive choir, and much hullabaloo — out of which came the double-album 'Amazing Grace', described by John Hammond as her 'most shining hour that certainly vies with that first Atlantic set as her best record to date'. Perhaps a trifle long for her pop public, it captured her voice in full bloom, with audience and choir clearly sharing her joy at 'coming home'. It's a record of catharsis; a moving testament to Aretha, cleansing her soul of years of trauma, just letting it all — as they say — hang out.

Unfortunately, the album was such authentic gospel in feel, long tracks and all, that Atlantic were unable to pull a successful single from it. 'Amazing Grace' climbed rapidly in the chart, and plunged rapidly down again.

With the tragic death of King Curtis, Aretha's direction once more became blurred. She worked in the studio with veteran jazz/film arranger/composer Quincy Jones. The resultant album 'Hey Now Hey (the other side of the sky)' was as confused as its title — uncomfortable and over-arranged, with a repellent sleeve

design that alone must have put off a few thousand potential buyers. The strongest track, 'Angel', achieved some success as a single however. At the time of writing (late 1973), she is readying a new LP under the baton of Eumir Deodato, of 'Zarathustra' fame. Furthermore, her Atlantic contract is supposedly up for renewal — so changes may well be in the air.

Aretha has always been a mysteriously private figure, the only clues to her discomfort to be found in her music. Not, I think, out of deliberate management policy — management itself has caused not a little of the problems — but because the facts, if one is to even half believe rumours, are unsavoury. Stories abound of her differences with first husband/manager Ted White, by all accounts a street hustler of sorts before he met the much younger Aretha — on one occasion in 1967, he reportedly openly fought with her in an Atlanta hotel lobby — and of her tendency to turn to drink to relieve her pressures. There, for all to see, were the changes in her appearance — Aretha consistently looked older than her years, suffered from a persistent weight problem, and hid her unease by donning over-brash, bizarre stage garb. So great was public concern that the new, slim Aretha recently held a press conference, chiefly to read out a note from her doctor proclaiming her to be in the best of health.

In '68 Cecil Franklin, now her manager — she has remarried — remarked 'for the last few years Aretha is simply not herself . . . you see flashes of her, but then she's back in her shell'.

Aretha's style is spine-tingling at best, irritating at worst; sometimes samey, but never affected. Her influence on contemporary female singers is undeniable. But in truth, any one of a number of gospel soloists could be in her place; if you love her voice, try listening to others such as Dorothy Norwood, Shirley Caesar, or Dorothy Love Coates — each of them, artistically, is fully Aretha's equal.

Legendary Figure

Perhaps the major strain involved in being at the top of the tree in any field, is that almost certain knowledge that there are others equally, if not more, talented than yourself, who have merely not had the breaks. Even if that isn't true, what artist can be absolutely sure of his talent? Aretha has leaned heavily on others for support and guidance; King Curtis provided the necessary direction and help — Quincy Jones, for all his obvious talent, did not.

Aretha Franklin has sold more records than any other female artist in history; she still sells out halls; she can still make millions happy; and she's still young. Let's hope we haven't yet seen her at her peak. How mortifying it is to realise that for virtually every legendary figure in every field of the arts, success hides a troubled soul. For Aretha, her sadness is joyful, but the joy she evokes has a bitter tang. In Smokey's immortal phrase, her smile is just a frown — turned upside down.

THE FOUR TOPS

Chris Walter

L.F.I.

Of all the innumerable vocal groups that have emerged from the States over the last decade or so, the Four Tops are one of the very few that can be justifiably termed superstars.

Although during the time they were contracted to Tamla Motown, they were just slightly over-shadowed by the phenomenal success of their stable-mates the Supremes, they presented an inspired and individual interpretation of what was generally known as the Motown Sound. Apart from collectively having an abundance of talent and musical expertise, their eventual success owed much to their own determination and persistence as well, and, where others might have become disheartened and disillusioned along the way, they had enough faith in themselves to keep on keeping on. One is happy for them they did eventually make it.

This long musical apprenticeship began way back in 1953, and even had roots stretching beyond then, because each of them had been singing in various other groups before coming together to form the Four Tops. Levi Stubbles (later amended to Stubbs), Abdul Fakir, Renaldo Benson and Lawrence Payton, would all no doubt have paused a little had they realised that it was going to take 11 long years before they would come up with a smash hit record, but in some ways it could be reasoned that this time was not wasted.

A Time For Learning

They perfected their style, their unity, (groups can suffer from much internal disharmony and disagreement), and above all, strengthened their own confidence in themselves. They loathed their previous amateur status and were burning to be true professionals by the time they had a hit record. So often they had seen an inexperienced artist or group hit lucky with just one record and had then shared the audience's embarrassment when watching them live, in realising that there was too small a reservoir of real talent in the performer to follow through with either continued hits, or successful in-person appearances. It was a period during which they paid their dues, but they paid them and learnt from the experience, and reckoned that it was better to pay them before you hit the big time, rather than just as you hit the top.

At the time of their formation, although Detroit had a large black population which ensured plenty of night club and concert work, there was as yet no record company based there, and it took three years of arduous work on this circuit before they were spotted and signed to Chess Records. Along with such companies as Atlantic and Vee Jay, Chess were leaders in producing and marketing records for Black America, but despite this, none of their records for the company were successful and their contract was allowed to lapse. It was perhaps due more to the prevailing trends that were popular at that particular time,

rather than to any lack of merit in their recordings. Black America was not yet ready for them, so the rest of the US certainly wasn't! But rather than modify their style, they put on a brave face and went back to the night spots which at least had the advantage of giving them valuable experience.

The setbacks and disappointments continued however. Having signed and cut some tracks for Red Top Records, the company decided not to release them, and after this, their excitement at being signed to giant and influential Columbia Records was quickly dashed, when a couple of singles released by them did very little to further their careers. It was not until they met their old friend Berry Gordy Jnr. that they began their long climb to the top in earnest.

New Label and Producers

In March 1963, they signed to his then infant Motown Record Corporation, which at that time had a label called Workshop, devoted to jazz and experimental recordings which were not easy to place in any one category or musical style. In order to give them their head and to work out their own level in the musical spectrum, they were launched with an album called 'Breaking Through'. Although highly praised by fellow musicians, the album made little impact on the public, but, whereas their previous recording companies' interest in black music was financial before aesthetic, Gordy felt they had the potential to succeed and it was decided that they should move to the Motown label with new producers and A&R men steering them. To gain more exposure and experience, they toured for a whole year with Billy Eckstine's Revue, and back in Detroit, Eddie Holland was relinquishing his career as a solo vocalist in favour of concentrating on composing and producing with his brother Brian and Lamont Dozier.

Between them, Brian, Eddie and Lamont had written a song called 'Baby I Need Your Loving' which was not in the usual vein of most of the other songs they were creating at that time, but as soon as Berry Gordy heard it on the demo tape, he realised that this would be a superb vehicle for the Four Tops. Unlike many singers, the musical diversity of interest in all types of records that the Tops shared, had been quite influential on their own developing style, and, although undoubtedly a soul act, these absorbed idioms from artists like Billy Eckstine, Sarah Vaughan and mainstream jazz musicians, had overlaid their style with an indefinable quality and mellowness that had made them unique among musical groups. It is a quality that they have maintained to this day, and it was a characteristic that made them readily and easily acceptable to the mass record-buying public in America, rather than just the black market. It is perhaps well evidenced that in one of their very first press interviews they were quoted as saying; 'We are inspired by anyone with talent'.

The record became a smash in the States, but success in Britain eluded them since the song was covered by a local group who took chart honours from them. In the States, however, all they touched seemed to turn to solid gold and their releases became hits with the same regularity that the Supremes were enjoying, and by the time they were ready to break through in Britain, they were already one of Motown's hottest properties.

Their delayed popularity in Britain was boosted by a personal tour in the summer of 1965 to promote their release of 'I Can't Help Myself' which, (despite the fact that it has since become something of a soul classic), failed to click, as did their follow-up 'It's The Same Old Song'. But this type of disappointment was nothing new to them, and by the time the record-buying public was ready for them when they released 'Reach Out I'll Be There', the group that had previously cheated them of chart honours had slipped into total obscurity and oblivion.

Now established as hit recording artists in Britain as well, the chances to perform concerts and live shows (together with TV spots) increased greatly, and it was through the unique and really extra special magic of their live performances that they began to build up a legion of devoted followers, and soon their albums were making the charts, and their earlier 'misses' were being so enthusiastically received that their record company was forced to re-release them (a tricky manoeuvre since their revived hits were in danger of competing with their newest recordings), and it can be safely said that for a time, the Four Tops were the most popular Motown act in Britain.

British audiences for live concerts can be notoriously difficult to handle, and many American artists fail to appreciate the very vast differences that exist between them and those they have known back home, but whereas for many this sometimes proved a fatal stumbling block, the Four Tops had an act that was almost better suited in Britain than their local venues in the States. It is difficult to locate the secret of their appeal, because all greats have that indefinable 'something' that is known simply as 'star quality'. But not only were they armed with a first rate repertoire of songs to sing, they also had a certain class and maturity about themselves and their music that made them appeal to a very wide age group. They pleased the die-hard soul fanatic as much as the well-heeled set who were into Ray Charles and Nancy Wilson; their fans were as varied and as assorted as their own musical influences.

Polish and Perfection

Serving such a long apprenticeship as they had, before making the big time, had also given them a perfection and polish that was not only detectable in their vocalising, but also in their choreography, stage techniques and routines. They were slick, soulful and very together, and this magic combination proved to be irresistible and stunning. Although their lead vocals have always been taken by Levi Stubbs, it is interesting that they have always maintained a corporate image rather than being identified as Levi Stubbs and the Tops, and it is probably indicative of the true and lasting affection they have for one another that this should be so.

It has been said that the Four Tops' records have outsold those of any other Motown group in the UK, and so identified were they with Motown and the Detroit Sound that it came as a shock when they announced that they were joining Dunhill Records in the States, when their contract with Motown expired. They had successfully weathered the departure of Holland, Dozier & Holland, and had gone under the production wing of Frank Wilson, but even so, many loyal fans were uneasy when they learned they were joining a label that until then had been almost totally inactive in the soul field. Not that the Four Tops could any longer be claimed by soul fans as their own exclusive property, but in any event, such fears and apprehension proved to be groundless.

They themselves admitted that the decision to quit Motown was the biggest one they had ever had to face. They had had a winning streak that had lasted 12 years, but above all they feared stagnation and felt a departure would enable them to spread their wings more and explore other musical avenues that they had tentatively flirted with, way back when they were anonymous enough to do so.

Their Special Magic

Before long, the success of 'Keeper Of The Castle' proved that, despite their change of label, their popularity has remained undiminished. Analysing artists who are in, or who are very close to, the superstar category, is a difficult and hard job to do. What makes them so special above all other male vocal groups who are scattered in profusion across the US as well as in Britain? How can one define that special magic that sets them apart from their contenders and describe in words what is essentially a musical and emotional experience?

In the case of the Four Tops, one is forced to conclude that it is simple sincerity and dedication of purpose. Charm-ing, unassuming and clearly no heads turned by fickle success, they learnt much in their struggle to the top, and, in profiting from their sometimes bitter experiences, they achieved a maturity and poise that some never find. They are brim full of characteristics that everybody can easily identify with, and their sophistication is that of class performers. They neither have, nor need, any special gimmicks and they don't pass themselves as 'heavy' heads, or make pretentious statements about matters which they are not involved in. This may rile some who see significance in the most mundane gesture and who seek good copy rather than accurate perspectives, but Levi, Duke (Abdul), Lawrence and Obie (Renaldo) must enjoy some of the greatest personal satisfactions that are possible — they set out to become great singers, and they achieved just that.

Looking back now, they can see the bad times in perspective, and as they look to the future together they can also take personal satisfaction from the fact that over the years they have brought a lot of happiness to a lot of people . . . and the world is a richer and better place for the Four Tops having been here.

BACK TRACK

Stateside
1964: September. 'Baby I Need Your Loving'.

1965: January. 'Without The One You Love'.
Tamla Motown
1965: March. 'Ask The Lonely'. May. 'I Can't Help Myself'. August. 'It's The Same Old Song'. November. 'Something About You'.
1966: March. 'Shake Me Wake Me (When It's Over)'. July. 'Loving You Is Sweeter Than Ever'. October. 'Reach Out I'll Be There' (No. 1).
1967: January. 'Standing In The Shadows Of Love'. March. 'Bernadette'. June. 'Seven Rooms Of Gloom'. October. 'You Keep Running Away'. December. 'Walk Away Renee'.
1968: March. 'If I Were A Carpenter'. August. 'Yesterday's Dream'. November. 'I'm In A Different World'.
1969: May. 'What Is A Man'. September. 'Do What You Gotta Do'.
1970 March. 'I Can't Help Myself'. May. 'It's All In The Game'. September. 'Still Water'.
1971: April. 'Just Seven Numbers (Can Straighten Out Your Life)'. June. (With the Supremes) 'River Deep, Mountain High'. September. 'Simple Game'. November. (With the Supremes) 'You Gotta Have Love In Your Heart'.
1972: February. 'Bernadette' (Re-release). (With the Supremes) 'Without The One You Love'. July. 'Walk With Me, Talk With Me Darling'. September. 'I'll Turn To Stone'. November. (With the Supremes) 'Reach Out & Touch (Somebody's Hand)'.
1973: March. 'So Deep Within You'. June. 'I Can't Quit Your Love'. July. 'Are You Man Enough'. October. 'Sweet Understanding Love'.
1974: January. 'I Just Can't Get You Out Of My Mind'. June. 'Meeting Of The Minds'.

Rex Features   S.I.   S.K.R.

Stevie Wonder

Despite the enormous influence of their music on the development of (white) pop, black American artists have for many years come up against an endless series of racial barriers blocking their general acceptance and classing most of their work as mere 'jungle music'.

So, when black singers did start breaking through to white audiences, all they lost was their original ethnic following. Chuck Berry had to write a country styled song, 'Maybellene', in order to hit the pop charts; and with the passing years fewer black faces were to be seen at concerts of people like Berry, Little Richard, Fats Domino and Ray Charles.

But the '70s have seen very rapid change. Now, ironically, despite the current trend in black music for songs of black consciousness and heavy political meaning to largely replace the old 'love-lost-and-won' stereotype; rhythm and blues, or 'soul' as it is now generally known, has won universal acceptance. In fact soul music now commands something like 30% of the US pop singles chart, and not much less than that in Britain.

Indeed, the very term 'soul' seems to have lost meaning amid all the changes, with artists like Stevie Wonder, Ike and

Tina Turner, Marvin Gaye and Billy Preston now accepted as rock superstars playing to a largely white audience. It was of course the fantastically successful Tamla Motown sound of the '60s that paved the way for this new acceptance, and Motown weren't far from the truth when they used the phrase 'the sound of young America' in their advertising.

Stevie Wonder was very much a product of the Motown machine, which churned out patiently groomed artists and commercially astute records with almost the same regularity as the neighbouring Detroit automobile plants churned out cars. It was Motown who proved that black artists could not only be highly respected performers, but actually have a star entertainer appeal to white audiences. And in this vein it was Wonder, launched in 1962 as a black sub-teen idol, who broke the ice.

Black American Consumers

Previously, black artists had been judged only on the quality of their latest record (as they still are by black American consumers), and it didn't matter how pretty the artist was so long as he (or she) couldn't sing — then no amount of hype could get them anywhere. This factor led to a remarkable consistency in soul music.

While there have been many run-of-the-mill soul records, there have been few that could be criticised for lacking professionalism or musicianship. All this worked both in favour of and against aspiring black stars. Primarily, though, if they had talent then they could get hit records — no matter how ugly or old they were.

Thus, in Britain in the '60s, black middle-aged bluesmen like John Lee Hooker, Howlin' Wolf and Sonny Boy Williamson II became the darlings of the Mod movement; while in the States and Britain too it sure didn't matter that Otis Redding and James Brown weren't exactly the best-looking men born. The point was that so long as they were turning out such great records the kids didn't want to fall in love with their singers, they were happy just to dig what was in the grooves.

All of this put the black artist of the '60s at an advantage over his white rivals, for whom teen sex-appeal was everything, with a lead singer over 22 almost spelling doom for the group. This situation was, thankfully, changed in the '70s, when the music became the most important factor and oldies-but-goodies like 40-plus Alexis Korner found no trouble in making hits.

So while blacks found it hard to become sex symbol idols to white teens — who constituted by far the largest section of the record-buying public — they could at least be assured of a longer, if not quite so fanfared, career. But though their parents might scoff, black American kids *did* hunger for idols of their own, and their demands reached a zenith with the emergence of the Jackson Five in the '70s. Those same demands though had started out way back in 1962 with Stevie Wonder.

Blind since birth, Stevie Wonder — real name Stephen Judkins — was born in Saginaw, Michigan, on May 13th, 1950. When he was three, Stevie's family moved to Detroit and the youngster soon became an adept musician, playing harmonica, organ, bongos and drums. Stevie played with the White family's children, and Ronnie White also happened to be a member of the Miracles, at that time the top Motown act. Impressed by the youngster's musicianship, Ronnie took him to Motown founder Berry Gordy Jr., who was astute enough to recognize Stevie's latent talent and marketing potential. Commercially speaking in fact, Wonder had a lot going for him. He was only 12, which made him cute; he was blind, which, while a tragic fact, could only help his appeal to the mums and dads as well as the kids; and most important of all he really could lay down an exciting and different sound. Wonder was no Little Laurie London, no Osmond Brother of the early '60s: he didn't just *look* right, he *was* right.

Initially, Gordy groomed him as a sort of junior version of Ray Charles, calling him Little Stevie Wonder and cutting a 'Tribute To Uncle Ray' album. With his third record, the pounding, exciting 'Fingertips' — a record that stands entirely on its own, neither Wonder nor anyone else ever having done anything like it since — the 12-year-old 'Boy genius', as Gordy rather presumptuously dubbed him, hit the no. 1 slot in the American charts. The record had been recorded live during a show at the Apollo Theatre in Harlem, which accounted for much of its infectious, immediate excitement. Even at this early stage of his career though, Wonder was a master showman. Unable due to his handicap, to dance around the stage like his contemporaries, Wonder would bob and sway over his keyboards, one ear cocked as if listening for musical notes out of the sky, then shuffle over to the drums or bongos for a stunning display of virtuosity.

In 1965 the Motown Sound was just beginning to make an impression in Britain, and a package-tour was organised including all the label's top acts. It was somewhat premature, playing to half-empty houses, but as a promotional venture it was invaluable, and Stevie Wonder proved to be one of its most impressive acts. With his 1967 recordings of 'A Place In The Sun' and 'I Was Made To Love Her', Wonder's style took a new turn. Gone was the brash, strident R&B. His voice was starting to mature from its earlier high pitch, and he was now into somewhat lush ballads which, while broadening his appeal towards the pop mainstream, tended to be less soulful.

Link With The Label

In 1971, Wonder, who had now dropped the 'Little' tag, though still only just out of his teens, began to exert stronger control over his own career. His contract with Motown ended, Wonder was now able to do exactly what he wanted in musical terms, instead of being manipulated by the Motown production team as before. The finished tapes were then leased back to Motown, thus maintaining his link with the label. The first result was the prophetic 'Where I'm Coming From' album, which showed a whole new turn in Wonder's creative direction. Already, with 'We Can Work It Out', he had come up with one of the few versions of Beatle songs to better the original, and now he showed that while he still sure had some soul, it was the potential of rock which really interested him.

Touring with the Rolling Stones helped him break through barriers of classification that had dismissed him as a 'soul man' of restricted appeal and musical dimension. He played on recording sessions with Jeff Beck, Eric Clapton and Steve Stills among others (Beck recording his 'Superstition'), and became engrossed in experimentation with the Moog synthesizer, the clavinet and other electronic keyboard instruments. Such was his dexterity that he could almost make the synthesizer sing, and his stage acts became even more brilliant as he almost seemed to make his machine sing. Producing other artists, notably his now estranged wife Syreeta Wright, also took up more and more of his attention. Here too he showed that R&B, once in grave danger of drowning in a sea of sock-it-to-me clichés, had far from exhausted its potential. But it was with the release of the critically and publicly acclaimed 'Music Of My Mind' album in 1972 that Wonder really clinched things. It had soul in plenty, but wasn't soul — it had rock too but wasn't rock — the brew was, quite simply, Stevie Wonder.

Following through with 'Talking Book' and 'Innervisions', Wonder became one of the first black artists to move himself away from being a singles' performer, to working chiefly in on albums. For a decade, black music had appeared consistently in the best-selling pop singles listings. Now Wonder and his contemporaries, most notably Curtis Mayfield, Marvin Gaye, Isaac Hayes, Bobby Womack and Billy Preston, fought clear of the limitations of the single to establish themselves consistently in the album charts.

Where Motown recordings had been specifically engineered to make them ideal for playing on cheap portables and juke-boxes, R&B had at last come of age and assumed its rightful place not as a separate, purely ethnic art form, but as an integral and vital part of the rock scene.

Stevie Wonder with Soul stars Martha and the Vandellas.

Atlantic Records

OTIS REDDING
The Big Boss Soul Man

When Otis Redding died, you could see skinny kids walk the streets with black arm bands over their mohair suits. Back in his home town of Macon, Georgia, the City Auditorium had to be hired to accommodate all the people that came to his funeral. His last record — 'Sitting On The Dock Of The Bay' — was his biggest seller ever.

Otis was a giant, the big boss soul man from the deep south who, more than any of his contemporaries, extended the appeal of his music to the white audience. At the Monterey Free Festival in 1967, he was the only soul artist to turn up, and he shimmied and shoved his 200 lbs of mohaired blackness all over the stage, to show the white hippy tribes that he too was a 'Love Man'.

Perhaps the Monterey and similar audiences — already shuffling their feet for acid rock and a ride on the Jefferson Starship — would have tired of Otis as quickly as they seemed to tire of other soul artists who had for a while been popular with them. Or perhaps Otis, like Aretha Franklin, would have managed to keep a following who were happy to let him stay within the confines of his own musical style. That he was among the very best soul performers — some could say he was *the* best — remains undeniable. His contribution was enormous.

Otis Redding was born in 1941, in Dawson, Georgia, one of the so-called 'slave' states of America, where whites are white and blacks *is* nigras, and never the two shall meet. At an early age the Redding family moved to nearby Macon City, and it was there, while still in his late teens, that Otis first joined a group. As vocalist with Johnny Jenkins and the Pinetoppers he gained valuable experience working the southern college circuit, and at 19 he made his first record, 'Shout Bamalama', for the small southern label of Bethlehem. In style,

'Shout Bamalama' was strongly influenced by the crude blues 'shout' style of Little Richard, another native son of Macon, whose success over the previous years would obviously have impressed the young Redding. His other idol at this time was Sam Cooke, another black artist who had been scoring consistently in the pop charts since his first release in 1957. Cooke's soft intimate style and distinctive phrasing were an example to almost every emergent soul singer, and while Otis was to soon outgrow the influence of Little Richard, the impression made by Sam Cooke remained to the last.

In 1962, Johnny Jenkins was scheduled to record for Atlantic Records (though without Otis), and he asked Otis to drive him to the studios in Memphis. When the recording session had finished, there were 40 minutes of studio time left, so Otis got permission to cut a song that he had written called 'These Arms Of Mine'. It was a simple tune, using minimal accompaniment, but Otis turned in a moving

73

delivery that completely transformed the song. It was obvious to those present that here was a fine and unacknowledged talent — if still a little raw and 'country' in their eyes — and Otis was promptly asked to sign with Volt records, the newly formed subsidiary of Stax Records, itself only a year old. For all intents and purposes, Volt was synonymous with Stax, using the same studios, session musicians, and producers, and for the rest of his life Otis would use on his records the talents of the wonderful musicians who had played on 'These Arms Of Mine'; Booker T and the MGs, who together with the Memphis Horns made up the Markeys.

'These Arms Of Mine' became Otis's first single, with the 'B' side 'Hey Hey Hey', a rough shouter which still showed the Little Richard influence. Possibly it surprised the organisation at Stax when it was a hit in the R&B charts. In any case, over the next couple of years Otis recorded a series of love ballads in a similar vein, most of them self-penned, and all of them big hits in the R&B charts, though among the pop audience they mostly fell on deaf ears. Success here was not to come for some years. These songs — 'Pain In My Heart', 'That's How Strong My Love Is', 'I've Been Loving You Too Long', and later 'Lover's Prayer' — exploited a similar vein to 'These Arms' with increasing confidence and artistry. Their lyrics were unashamedly sentimental, their tone confessional and imploring, their arrangements and tunes deceptively simple.

Counterpoise

The Stax houseband of the Markeys played an important role on all of Otis's recordings, and on these early hits they established the tender mood the songs needed — reinforcing the gradual build-up of the songs with smooth, sweeping horn riffs, while guitarist Steve Cropper chimed in as a counterpoise to Otis vocals. Part of Otis's greatness was that he could combine tenderness with forcefulness, and he rarely bettered his early performances in this respect. His voice often had a husky, smoky quality which could change abruptly into a hard, anguished tone, swapping its quavering emotional uncertainty for conviction. 'That's How Strong My Love Is' illustrates this process.

This was only one side of Otis Redding. In 1964, he released an uptempo number for his next single — 'Mr. Pitiful'. It was an altogether different style. For one thing, the Markeys blew harder, punchier, more insistent riffs, while bassist 'Duck' Dunn ran long loping bass figures beneath the beat. Otis himself did full justice to the title in his agonised vocals, running each line into inconclusion, like a man so overcome with the tribulations of romance that he could no longer fully control his verbal faculties. As a song it was quite ingenious.

It was the following year, 1965, that saw Otis's style reach fruition. Already renowned as a master of the soul ballad, and with 'Mr. Pitiful' as one of his nicknames, he released one of his greatest

Above: A shot of Otis Redding from the film 'Monterey Pop', where he produced such good vibes as the only soul performer.

singles, 'Respect'. In sound and tempo it was even more ferocious than 'Mr. Pitiful', while Otis shifted his persona from that of the tired, careworn lover to that of proud, uptight, and defiant main-man. 'Respect' was in fact an aggressively sexual song, while its demands for respect could also be extended to a wider social situation. In some ways it was Otis's equivalent to the Stones' 'Satisfaction', and it was to that hymn, to frustration, that Otis now turned for a follow-up.

Despite their brilliance, none of Otis' early records had made a sizeable impression on the pop charts. The (white) pop audience, soul freaks apart, simply wasn't ready for the raw aggression and emotionalism of black soul music. Now they began to show interest, partly because of the cover versions by groups like the Stones (who had covered 'That's How Strong' for example). Otis knew that it was the uptempo dance numbers like Wilson Pickett's 'Midnight Hour' and James Brown's 'Papa's Got A Brand New Bag' that were grabbing radio airspace and hence the chart success; now, on Steve Cropper's suggestion, he cut 'Satisfaction' to grab him some of the same.

Though the record had the desired effect of spreading Otis' reputation, it was nonetheless an inferior recording. Otis himself was alleged to have disliked it. His records until then had carried the ring of sincerity, 'Satisfaction' had artifice — Otis's heart was not in it. One has only to listen to the two superlative albums that he subsequently released to understand this. 'Dictionary Of Soul' and 'Otis Blue' both defined the Redding style, and gave proof to his growth into a creative force in his own right.

Otis rarely received adequate credit as a writer, yet the vast majority of his hits were self-penned, and on songs like

'Ole Man Trouble', and 'Sittin' On The Dock Of The Bay' he was beginning to show personal vision that went beyond the confines of love and romance. Like Sam Cooke, he was just finding his true ability as a writer when his life was cut off tragically (Sam Cooke died three years before Otis almost to the day).

Elsewhere, he co-wrote 'Sweet Soul Music' with Arthur Conley, perhaps the most joyful celebration of soul music among a number of songs on that theme. He also produced Arthur's records — another facet of his talent that was only just beginning to be explored. Otis loved to work, which is partly the reason why there is so much material by him available on record. He was always writing, touring, and recording, and still finding time to spend with his wife Zelma and their three children at his home — a 300 acre farm in Round Oak, Georgia.

Otis loved success and fame — few stars do not — but his concern always seemed to be to reach as many people as possible. Communication was a vital concern to Otis: "Basically I like music that is simple," he said, "and I feel that this is the formula that has made soul music a success."

Simplicity, though, did not mean lack of skill. It was as rare for the Markeys to overplay their parts as it was for Otis to overstate or overload his lines. Steve Cropper, shortly before Otis's death, remarked that:

"He gets over to the people what he's talking about, and he does so in so few words, that if you saw them written down on a piece of paper they might not make any sense. But when you hear the way he sings them, you know exactly what he's talking about."

Sometimes, of course, his attempts failed. He had his lapses of taste, his

Record Mirror

SKR

failures, his excesses. On 'Daytripper' and 'I Can't Turn You Loose' for example, his non-stop verbal barrage and repeated interjections are not warranted, though on stage he could get away with the same technique; in fact it was infectious, as the several live versions of 'Sad Song' show only too well. His biggest hit while he was alive — 'Tramp', a novelty number he recorded with Carla Thomas — is also one of his lamest offerings, far from the funky finesse of something like 'Down In The Valley'. In fact, 'Tramp' is stacked with stale old soul riffs that someone found lying about on the studio floor, and, like some others, say 'Chain Gang', it plods.

Throat Operation

For a while, it did seem like Otis was losing some of his magic. Like other soul artists, he had hit a rut, his style was becoming clichéd. 'Tramp' was indicative of what was happening to the music as a whole — though its commercial success had never been greater, and most artists were at last receiving recognition; among them Aretha Franklin with her version of 'Respect'. Otis had to have a throat operation, which put him out of action for a time, unable to make a record at a time when one was most badly needed. But on stage he never lost any of his charisma, quite the opposite, and in 1967, his appearance at the Monterey Festival was an enormous success. What he lacked in stage style and movement he made up for in delivery and feeling. It was shortly after his Monterey appearance that he wrote 'Sittin' On The Dock Of The Bay', which he recorded complete with sound effects of seagulls and lapping waves. It was a tribute to the Monterey audience and his best work for some time.

It was on December 10th, 1967, that Otis Redding died; when his private plane, not long acquired, crashed into a fog-shrouded lake near Madison, Wisconsin, while on a flight to Cleveland, Ohio. Seven others were killed as the plane plunged into the icy waters, among them four members of his backing group the Markeys, all of them under 20.

Otis Redding was 26 when they buried him at his home town of Macon, with a congregation of 4,500, who had come to pay their respects, including many of soul's top artists. The loss was enormous. Otis was one of the few soul artists who showed signs of coming to terms with the stagnation of soul, and though his cover versions of other people's songs were invariably more than adequate, he had his own lyrical voice which would undoubtedly have developed in the years to come. Ultimately, he managed to step outside the stage suit of 'soul man' and reach his audience as a real person.

A hick southern boy, a 'tramp' maybe, but he looked good out there on the boards, just singing his sad sad songs, still inviting the audience to shake; being brash, introvert, confused, and self-assured all in one set. There is no need for us to doubt how strong his love was.

75

Diana Ross Star Supreme

Rex Features

The jazz pianist, Lennie Tristano, once wrote a letter to *Downbeat*, the American jazz journal, inquiring whether anyone but he, had noticed that the logical heir to Billie Holiday's mantle as the greatest jazz singer was . . . Diana Ross.

That is something of an overstatement, but it is nonetheless true that, with Aretha Franklin and Dionne Warwick, Ross possesses one of the best female voices in rock, pop, jazz or soul.

She has come a long way for a girl who began life as a ghetto child, in Detroit's 'Black Bottom'. She grew up in a housing project — a comfortable American term for governmentally subsidised slums. Among her girlhood friends were Mary Wilson and Florence Ballard, and while at high school the three of them were inspired — by a group called the Primes, who later became the Temptations — to form a singing group called the Primettes. 'For almost two years', say the liner notes to their first US album, 'Meet the Supremes', 'they sang at schools, churches and civic affairs. . . . Then one night while attending a local record 'hop' as spectators, Diana, Mary and Florence met an A&R man from Motown, told him that they sang, and were invited down for a routine audition.'

Years later, Diana told the story much differently, on the five-volume, 'The Motown Story':

"I moved to a street on the north side of Detroit, and Smokey lived about four or five doors away from me . . . I used to sit and watch them rehearse on their basement steps. I told him that I had a group and any time he could listen to my group, I would really appreciate it. And he did set up an audition for us. The only reason Berry Gordy saw us or heard us was that he happened to be passing through the streets at the time we were singing.

"Finally, they decided that they might sign us if we would go back and finish high school . . . I needed a job, to help my family out and also for the car-fare to go back and forth from the studio to try to do some background sessions. (Gordy) gave me a job and it was about three months I worked there. I didn't do a thing except straighten off his desk. But it wasn't a real office, anyway, because at that time Berry used the whole building and everyone would gather in this one little room. I think he gave me about 20 dollars."

Even in the beginning, Diana stood out from the other girls. First, because of her beauty, which was great even then, and also because her voice was so clear, trilling out the soprano notes with an edge of profound despair.

Success Formula

Of the first three Supremes singles, only 'Buttered Popcorn' was very good, and it was uncharacteristically *risqué* for an early Motown recording: 'Nice and greasy and sticky and gooey and softly. I said what do you like, he said you know what I like: buttered popcorn.'

Their fourth single, 'Where Did Our Love Go?', catapulted the Supremes to the front ranks of girl groups. It was 1964, and British rock was sweeping the world. About the only competition, in fact, was Motown. Though Elton John claims in the liner notes to 'Touch', that 'Where Did Our Love Go?'

never became a hit in Britain, it did in fact reach no.3 after 10 weeks.

In America, the Supremes followed this initial success with four no.1s in succession: 'Baby Love', 'Stop In The Name Of Love', 'Come See About Me', and 'Back In My Arms Again'. They had 15 successive Top 20 hits, beginning with 'Where Did Our Love Go?' and ending with 'In And Out Of Love'. In that time, there were a total of 10 no.1s, and only one of those 15 failed to reach Top 10 status: 'Nothing But Heartaches', which made no.11.

But the inevitable friction had begun. For one thing, some observers began to complain that the Supremes' songs were written to a formula. Others had the view that Diana's soprano had become a radio irritant, and that Motown was just a pop mill back in Detroit, grinding out mediocrity.

All of this looks pretty silly today, of course. Among those 15 records were classics like 'My World Is Empty', 'The Happening', 'You Can't Hurry Love' and 'You Keep Me Hangin' On', besides the songs already mentioned. Holland-Dozier-Holland, who wrote most of those supposedly trite melodies and lyrics, are today recognised as innovative pop geniuses.

Right: Diana Ross singing a Billie Holiday number in the film *Lady Sings The Blues*.

Top L.H. pic & bottom R.H. pic: Diana Ross has successfully survived the jump from the '60s to the '70s and comes across as a very talented, beautiful lady, who is now making a name for herself in films, as well as in the super-glitter world of the top cabaret circuit. Centre pic: A sexy, showbiz shot of Diana in Hollywood. Bottom L.H. pic: Florence, Mary and Diana were the hit-making Supremes.

Centre pic Rex Features

Jimi Hendrix Bold As Love

An early shot of the original Jimi Hendrix Experience, which featured, left to right, bassist Noel Redding, Hendrix, and drummer Mitch Mitchell.

Had Jimi Hendrix died two years earlier he would have gone down as the greatest star in the rock & roll galaxy. The timing of his death was as tragic and wasteful as his death itself. In 1970, people were saying that Jimi was over the hill, and he never got a chance to prove them wrong. Had he died on the way up the hill, imagination, myth and fact would have turned that hill into the Mount Everest of Rock. For, in those early years, Jimi Hendrix was just about perfect — as rock stars go. As it was, Jimi spent two years spoiling the picture and then broke the frame.

In his time he eclipsed both Eric Clapton and Mick Jagger, and made everyone else look old-fashioned. He single-handedly changed the actual *sound* of rock & roll, opening up an entirely new field of music for the guitar, and then almost exhausted the possibilities of that field before he died. On stage he looked amazing, full of that threatening sexuality that suits rock & roll best, and the music . . . well Jimi summed it up himself in 'Voodoo Chile':

'I have a humming bird and it plays so loud You'd think that you're losing your mind'

Jimi Hendrix was born in Seattle, Washington, on November 27th, 1942, as James Marshall Hendrix; His mother, Lucille, who was of Indian descent, didn't get on too well with his father, James Allen Hendrix, so Jimi was frequently sent off to stay with his grandmother, a full blooded Cherokee, in Canada. Lucille died when Jimi was 10, just about the same time as Jimi first showed an interest in playing the guitar. This strained home background was to leave its mark on Hendrix, who found it difficult to make real friends and trust people throughout his life. Jimi had a brother, Leon, five years younger, who also plays guitar, and two step-sisters from his father's second marriage.

His father bought him his first guitar when he was 11. Jimi learned so fast that his father sold his sax to buy him an electric guitar a year later. Because his father didn't earn very much as a gardener, Jimi left school at 16 — although the story goes that he was thrown out for holding a white girl's hand in class. He played in some teenage rock & roll bands, copying the Coasters amongst others — his first gig was at a National Guard armoury, for which the group got 35 cents each.

In 1963, Jimi joined the Army. He volunteered 'to get it over with', but typically he chose the paratroops, making 25 jumps before injuring an ankle on the 26th, when he was discharged. It was during this 14 month stint in the army that Jimi met Billy Cox who was later to replace Noel Redding on bass.

After the army, Jimi worked for a vast number of black R&B bands touring the States. Amongst others he backed Little Richard, the Isley Brothers, Wilson Pickett, Ike and Tina Turner and Joey Dee and the Starlighters. Little Richard put Jimi's back up by refusing to let Jimi wear a brightly coloured shirt. Jimi jumped from band to band pretty fast, hopping one tour into town and another one out. The discipline was a little too heavy for him too — a $50 fine for missing a step in the routine or a chord change — and the musicians often

got fired when the band leader owed them too much money.

In 1964, Jimi went to New York's Greenwich Village, where he recorded with the Isley Brothers and Lonnie Youngblood. Then in 1965, after recording with Curtis Knight he formed his first band — Jimmy James and the Blue Flames. While he was playing at the Café Wha, Jimi was seen by the white blues singer, John Hammond Jnr, who moved Jimi to the classier Café A Go Go and played with him there for a month. It was here that Jimi was first seen by the stars of the day, Bob Dylan, the Beatles and the Stones among them, and the word started to spread round — as far as Chas Chandler.

Chandler had been the bass player with the original Animals, who, in 1966 were breaking up, and Chandler had decided to become a record producer and manager — not too many people gave much for his chances. Keith Richard's girlfriend, Linda Keith, told Chandler about this 'great guitar player' in the 'Village', and took Chas to see him at the Café Wha. They talked together and Chandler was impressed enough to be ready to take Jimi back to England before he heard him play. Hendrix wasn't so sure and asked a lot of questions about English equipment and musicians, but the clinch came with a promise of a meeting with Eric Clapton,

and asked if Jimi could provide the support band for his next tour of France.

Last Bass Guitar

On his return, things were fairly slow for Hendrix in Britain and Chas Chandler's money was running low. Chas sold six bass guitars to pay for a reception at the Bag 'O Nails and invited some promoters he knew. The result was a £25 booking as support group to the New Animals. For the second gig at the Chalk Farm Roundhouse, Jimi had had his guitar stolen, so Chandler sold his last bass to get Jimi a replacement. Two days later 'Hey Joe' climbed into the UK singles chart . . . 'We did it by the skin of our teeth', said Chandler.

'Hey Joe' launched the Experience onto a quick tour of London's top clubs, ('Purple Haze' was written in the dressing-room at the Upper Cut, in the East End). Then came national exposure on a 'package' tour with the Walker Brothers, Cat Stevens and Engelbert Humperdinck. Chandler knew that the Walker Brothers, who were the big sex idols at the time, were going to split after the tour, so the Experience worked out a very sexy act to 'cop all their reputation'. Jimi's upstaging of the big stars was not taken quietly, as Chandler recalled:

'There was a lot of ill feeling backstage, and they would screw up the lights, or put the house lights up on the audience during his act. It was quite a tour. There were no barriers in pop then, no pseudo hippies. It was all entertainment and a great tour for the audiences.'

(Jimi Hendrix by Chris Welch)

82

Then came the Monterey Pop Festival. Paul McCartney who had been helping to organise the festival had said that it wouldn't be a real festival without Jimi, and Brian Jones flew over specially to introduce him to the American audience. The Experience looked and sounded light years ahead of the competition and it took 30 minutes to quieten the audience down when Jimi had finished — waving his burning guitar above his head as a sacrifice to the occasion. On the strength of this Bill Graham booked the Experience for the Fillmore West to play with the Jefferson Airplane. Chas Chandler:

'We played the Fillmore and Bill Graham gave us $2,000 each as a bonus when the Airplane cried off the rest of the gigs after our first night. Bill also gave us antique engraved watches. Bill has had a lot of mud thrown at him, but he's a gas.' *(Jimi Hendrix by Chris Welch)*

In the meantime, Chandler's partner Mike Jeffery had signed the Experience for a tour of the States with the Monkees. This was not appreciated by Chandler and the rest of the group. Jimi died a death in front of the Monkees' 12-year-old audience, so promoter Dick Clark and Chandler dreamed up the story that the Daughters Of The American Revolution had waged a campaign to get Jimi banned for his obscene act. Jimi did several more gigs in the States; saw 'Are You Experienced' go up the American charts, and returned to England.

No Burning Guitars

While 1967 was Jimi's year with four singles and two albums in the British charts and two albums in the American charts, 1968 saw the first signs of that all was not well with the Experience. On tour in the States, Jimi was blowing amplifiers and walking off stage after only four numbers. Gone too was the dramatic showmanship — no dancing or burning guitars. Jimi was becoming bored with his image. Back in 1967 Jeff Beck had said:

'Jimi's only trouble will come when he wants to get himself off the nail he has hung himself on. The public will want something different, and Jimi has so established himself in one bag that he'll find it difficult to get anyone to accept him in another.' *(New Musical Express)*

And that's what happened. Jimi found audiences ready to cheer him even if he played badly — provided he threw himself around a bit and smashed a guitar. Quite a spot for a musician who wants to retain some self respect to find himself in. Jimi Hendrix was already a very lonely man, even those who knew him for years never felt that they really *knew* him. As Chas Chandler said in Chris Welch's book *Jimi Hendrix:*

'Jimi lived with me for two years and I would never presume to say I knew him. Nobody knew him. He never seemed to confide in anybody'.

Now he was cut off from his audience and rigours of touring were taking their toll. There were a few violent incidents with girls that were suitably hushed up and, on a three day tour of Sweden in 1968, Hendrix was jailed for smashing up a hotel room. But the music was still there, on record at least. 'Are You Experienced' and 'Axis: Bold As Love' still stand almost untouched by the passage of time. When they were released in 1967 they were so far ahead of the field, so different and strange that the rock & roll industry was just stunned at first. This was obviously the next craze/direction but no one had the faintest idea how to play it, for Jimi was doing things on the guitar that just seemed impossible. He would hold two strings feeding back while he played a melody line on the others and sang at the same time. His years on the road backing Little Richard and the rest had given him a firm mastery of rock & roll, blues and R&B; Jimi was a brilliant guitarist without any electronic gimickry. Given his head and musicians who could keep up with him, Jimi stretched his equipment to the limits, exploring every possibility that his guitar and amplifier could offer. Above all else, Jimi was an inventive flowing musician who put more ideas into a two minute guitar solo than most rock bands used in a whole album.

Dangerous But Desirable

He was also a much better songwriter than he was ever given credit for, largely because not many people saw the songs as anything more than pegs on which to hang that amazing guitar-work. 'Are You Experienced' contains some very strong songs, from the opening track 'Foxy Lady', which has Hendrix playing up his role as a dangerous but desirable sexual threat; through 'Manic Depression', one of the best pieces of heavy rock ever recorded; and 'Love Or Confusion' which has a stunningly fluid guitar solo; to the strange alienated world of 'I Don't Live Today'.

'Will I live tomorrow?
Well I just can't say
But I know for sure
I don't live today'

Jimi's lyrics often had this air of defiant but dejected loneliness about them. On 'Axis: Bold As Love', side one ends with 'If Six Was Nine' (a reference to the Chinese Oracle, the *I Ching* or *Book Of Changes).*

'If the mountains fall in the sea
Let it be, it ain't me
Got my own world to live through
And I ain't gonna talk to you'

Then, spoken over the long freak-out ending, Jimi makes one of the many references he made to his death:
'I'm the one who's got to die when it's time for me to die — so let me live my life the way I want to.'
'Axis' is probably the most poetic album that Hendrix made, and the guitar work throughout is particularly fluid and lyrical.

The guitar introduction to 'Little Wing' is a work of pure genius, as is Jimi's playing on 'Castles Made Of Sand'. 'Up From The Skies' features some beautifully laid-back wah-wah guitar and some strangely off-hand 'social comment' type lyrics:

'I heard some you got your famlies
Living in cages dark and cold
Some just stay there and dust away
Past the age of old.'

High Point of Experience

1968 saw the last album from the Experience as such — 'Electric Ladyland'. This double-album was not so well received by the rock critics and was dismissed as a collection of 'over indulgent blowing sessions'. In reality, 'Ladyland' was the high point of Jimi's recording career, but at the time people were looking for something more flashy and dramatic. As the Melody Maker's Chris Welch admits in his biography of Jimi Hendrix:
'Hearing the album again after an interval of a few years, it sounds infinitely better than it did on release to ears thirsting for a new 'Hey Joe' or 'Foxy Lady'.'
It's hard to think of an album as broad, witty and strong as 'Electric Ladyland' receiving a luke-warm response but that's what happened. This response was probably influenced by the performances the Experience were giving on stage at the time — they had never exactly been over-rehearsed but now they looked like three strangers playing together, and Mitch Mitchell was beginning to take drum solos on every number. Rows developed in the studio, and Chas Chandler decided that he was wasting his time:
'There were so many people hanging around him, (Hendrix) he couldn't be himself. We had an argument about it, and he said, "OK, no more." Then someone would turn up at the studio with a bag of goodies and pour some more down his throat. Mike Jeffery turned up at the studio as well and stuck his oar in. Things began to deteriorate. And there was a big row about the cover which Mike said was a piece of crap.
'There was a dreadful atmosphere in the studio, which was full of hangers-on. We did six tracks for the 'Electric Ladyland' album, and nobody was ready to compromise anymore. All I was doing was sitting there collecting a percentage. So I said, "Let's call it a day."' *(Jimi Hendrix by Chris Welch)*
Despite this, 'Ladyland' is probably the most successful, in musical terms, double album ever released, full of amazing guitar work and Jimi's vividly colourful lyrics:

'I'm not the only soul
To be accused of hit and run
Tyre tracks across your back
I can see you've had your fun'
(Cross-town Traffic)

And the bluesy but menacing 'Voodoo Chile' — a long studio jam with Jimi playing a heavily echoed guitar against Steve Winwood's hammond organ:

'Well the night I was born
I swear the moon turned a fire-red
Well my poor mother cried out
'Lord the gipsy was right''

There is a second version with just Redding and Mitchell ('Voodoo Chile: A Slight Return') which has Jimi playing wah-wah guitar as strong as the lyrics:

'Well, I'm standing next to a mountain
Chop it down with the edge of my hand'

After 'Electric Ladyland', the Experience broke up as such, when Noel Redding left to devote more time to his own Band, Fat Matress. For Jimi's appearance at Woodstock, Noel was replaced by Billy Cox, whom Hendrix had played with in his army days. They did two numbers and walked off stage because Jimi felt 'it's not coming together' — something that happened several times in the next year or so.

Black Power

There were no further albums until 'Band Of Gipsies' in 1970. Jimi spent most of 1969 hiding out in New York with some friends; flirting briefly with the Black Power Movement. The 'Band Of Gipsies' had Buddy Miles on drums and Billy Cox on bass. The album, recorded 'live' at the Fillmore East in New York is strangely flat and boring, and Jimi rarely gets into full flight. He would not have released it but he 'owed the record company an album'. Buddy Miles wasn't quite right for the band and when Jimi returned to Britain in August 1970, Mitch Mitchell was behind the drums again. At the third Isle of Wight festival Jimi was not at his very best, having just flown from a party in New York to celebrate the opening of the Electric Ladyland recording studios — yet he did manage to show a little of his old fire, in spite of the under-rehearsed band. They then embarked on a European tour but Billy Cox became ill so they returned to Britain. In September, Jimi gave an optimistic interview to the Melody Maker:
"I've turned full circle — I'm right back where I started. I've given this era of music everything, but I still sound the same. My music's the same, and I can't think of anything new to add to it in its present state.
"When the last American tour finished, I just wanted to go away and forget everything. I just wanted to record and see if I could write something. Then I started thinking. Thinking about the future. Thinking that this era of music, sparked off by the Beatles, had come to an end. Something new has to come and Jimi Hendrix will be there."
But Jimi Hendrix died on September 18th, 1970. That Friday morning his girl-

Mike Hope

friend, Monika Danneman, left Jimi sleeping to get some cigarettes. When she returned, Jimi had been sick in his sleep. She couldn't wake him and realised that he had taken some sleeping tablets. She phoned for an ambulance:

'The men said he was okay and sat him in the ambulance. I found out later they should have laid him down flat to breathe. But they put him on a chair with his head back. He did not die from the sleeping tablets because he had not taken enough to be an overdose. It was not fatal. The reason he died was because he couldn't get air. He suffocated on his own vomit.'

(Jimi Hendrix by Chris Welch)

The Coroner recorded an open verdict and said that there was no evidence to show that Hendrix intended to commit suicide, 'The question why he took so many sleeping tablets cannot be safely answered'. Apart from Eric Burdon, most of those who knew or worked with Jimi felt that his death was a tragic accident. Chas Chandler:

'I don't believe for one minute he killed himself. That was out of the question. But something had to happen and there was no way of stopping it. You just get a feeling sometimes. It was as if the last couple of years had prepared us for it. It was like the message I'd been waiting for.' *(Jimi Hendrix by Chris Welch)*

Last Of The Giants

Jimi Hendrix left behind several filmed performances and his records. The best of the films is *Jimi Plays Berkley* — a beautifully shot record of an entire show when Jimi was at his very best, musically and visually, moving at that intense emotional pitch that only he seemed to be able to sustain over a whole act. Second best is the Warner Brother's documentary *Jimi Hendrix* which contains some unique footage of Jimi playing a 12-string acoustic guitar.

'Cry Of Love' was released after Jimi's death and is an indecisive album, certainly nowhere as good as the first three, 'Are You Experienced', 'Axis: Bold As Love' and 'Electric Ladyland'. 'War Heroes' is merely a collection of odd bits and pieces they had lying around the studio.

It seems strange that such a major figure in rock & roll should recieve such shabby 'cash-in' treatment from his record company after his death. The only memorial album worthy of the name was issued by accident before he died — someone decided to issue an album called 'Historic Performances', with one side Jimi Hendrix and the other Otis Redding, live at Monterey — both artists subsequently died.

Be that as it may, when Don McClean wrote a song about the Altamont festival he got one thing wrong — the day the music died was Friday, the 18th of September. Jimi Hendrix may well be the last of the giant rock heroes, for rock has now become too safe, too socially acceptable, and too diverse, to fall under the spell of just one man again.

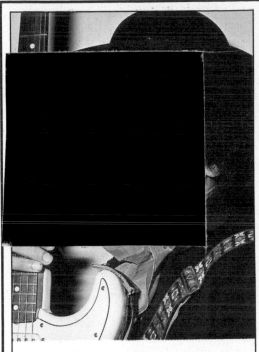

SKR

BACK TRACK

Born in Seattle, Washington, on November 27th, 1942.

1964: 'Jimi Hendrix and the Isley Brothers' album recorded in New York, (Buddah). Also 'Jimi Hendrix and Lonnie Youngblood' album (Platinum).

1965: 'Jimi Hendrix and Curtis Knight' album recorded in New York (London).

1966: Comes to England with Chas Chandler in September. Forms the Jimi Hendrix Experience with Noel Redding (bass) and Mitch Mitchell (drums).

1967: January: 'Hey Joe' makes the British charts. March: 'Purple Haze'. May: 'The Wind Cries Mary' and 'Are You Experienced' album. June: Monterey Pop Festival. September: 'The Burning Of The Midnight Lamp'. November: 'Axis: Bold As Love' album.

1968: January: Three day tour of Sweden. Jimi jailed for wrecking hotel room — fined all his earnings in Sweden. March: Tour of USA. May: 'Electric Ladyland' double album. July: Noel Redding leaves the Experience. November: the Experience officially disbanded, 'All Along The Watchtower' released in Britain.

1969: February: Concert at the Albert Hall in London with Mitchell and Redding filmed and recorded (album — 'Experience: Original Soundtrack' on Ember label). June: Woodstock Festival.

1970: January: 'Band Of Gipsies' recorded live at the Fillmore East — Buddy Miles, drums; Billy Cox, bass. August: Isle Of Wight Festival, with Cox and Mitchell. European tour abandoned because Cox becomes ill. September 18th. Jimi Hendrix dies.

1971: 'Cry Of Love' album.

1972: 'War Heroes' album.

1973: 'Jimi Hendrix' double album of live recordings from the Warner Brothers' film of the same name.

Britain [blacked out] the rock revolution [blacked out] in the '50s. A decade [blacked out] suddenly shifted across [blacked out] of four young Liverp[blacked out] the youth business, s[blacked out]d thing, quickly made [blacked out]ging image, not only in [blacked out]d pop art as well.
The [blacked out] American artists

and the few true home-grown stars who had achieved any sort of international success — like Cliff Richard — started as imitators of the US rock & roll stars. The year 1962 saw the Beatles emerge from obscurity to become first national, then international and then truly global stars. They changed so much, and in their wake came others — the Rolling Stones, the Animals and the Who and many more — each making their contribution. The second wave was also centred on

Syndication International

Keystone Press

BACK TRACK

1962: October, 'Love Me Do' released. December, 'Love Me Do' enters UK charts; highest position 17.
1963: January, 'Please Please Me' released; reaches no. 1. April, 'From Me To You' no. 1. 'Please Please Me' first album released. June, 'Twist And Shout' EP reaches no. 1. August, 'She Loves You' no. 1. November, 'With The

Beatles' album released. 'I Want To Hold Your Hand' released; direct to no. 1, advance orders of one million.
1964: January, 'I Want To Hold Your Hand' top in US charts. February, 'All My Loving' EP makes no. 13. March, 'Can't Buy Me Love' released; an instant no. 1 in UK and US. Summer, 'Long Tall Sally' EP makes no. 11. July, *A Hard Day's Night* premiered in London. 'A Hard Day's

Night' makes no. 1. 'A Hard Day's Night' album reaches no. 22. November, 'I Feel Fine' makes no. 1. December, 'Beatles For Sale' album released.
1965: April, 'Ticket To Ride' reaches no. 1. July, 'Help' single. August, 'Help' movie and album released. December, 'Day Tripper'/ 'We Can Work It Out', tenth consecutive hit to be instant no. 1 in UK. 'Rubber Soul' album released.

Britain but was slightly different. Tom Jones was the more traditional balladeer who stormed the American showbiz strongholds and conquered them; the Bee-Gees moved from Australia to find great success — based out of London. Then came the supergroups whose appeal was almost instantly international and who worked for a greater part of the year in America than their home country — Cream and Led Zeppelin became part of a transatlantic élite.

The break-up of the Beatles meant not so much the losing of a great group but, for their fans, the gaining of four new and individual superstars as John, George, Paul and Ringo cut their own separate careers. In the meantime Cliff Richard who, in a way, had started the whole British boom, continued, adapting to new times, broadening his appeal and surviving to become one of the world's most enduring pop stars.

London Features

Kobal Collection

Camera Press

1966: June, 'Paperback Writer' is the first single in over two years not to jump straight to the top of the British charts. It did eventually reach no. 1 position. August, 'Yellow Submarine'/'Eleanor Rigby' released. 'Revolver' album released.
1967: February, 'Penny Lane'/'Strawberry Fields Forever' released; first single since 'Love Me Do' to fail to reach no. 1. June, 'Sgt Pepper's Lonely Hearts Club Band' album released. July, 'All You Need Is Love'/'I Am The Walrus' released as single and makes no. 1. November, 'Hello Goodbye' released. December, *Magical Mystery Tour* T.V. film. 'Magical Mystery Tour' double EP released, and makes no. 2.
1968: March, 'Lady Madonna' released (no. 1). July, The cartoon film *Yellow Submarine* is premiered. September, 'Hey Jude', the Beatles' first release on the new Apple label (no. 1). November, 'The Beatles' white album released. December, 'Yellow Submarine' album released.
1969: April, 'Get Back' topped the charts. June, 'Ballad of John and Yoko'. August, 'Abbey Road', the Beatles' last album, recorded. October, 'Something' makes no. 2.
1970: May, *Let It Be* film première. 'Let It Be' album released.

Cliff Richard

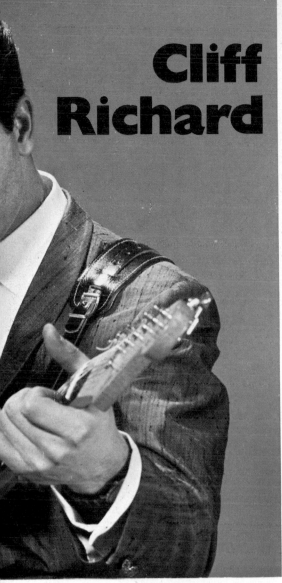

Top left: Cliff Richard in *Expresso Bongo*. Centre top: A scene from *Young Love*. Centre: Cliff in variety. Top right: The moody singer. Bottom left: An early serious portrait. Centre bottom: The laughing pirate in *Wonderful Life*.

Cliff Richard must have been swigging elixir three times a day for the last 15 years; certainly his looks dispute memories of his first hit in 1958. But that's when it was. 'Move It' entered the charts in September of that year. Almost as surprising, in retrospect, is the fact that he started so *late*, since he was cast as Britain's answer to Presley — and by 1958 Elvis had been going strong for more than two years.

Before Cliff (formerly Harold Webb) went professional he was a number one Elvis fan: he wanted to dress like Elvis, he greased his hair back the way Elvis did, grew his sideburns long like Elvis, slung his guitar from his shoulder like Elvis, tried to look exactly like Elvis and sing like Elvis. In truth he worshipped Elvis. Then Jack Good saw him and, as Cliff recalls, "the first thing he said to me was: 'You look too much like Elvis. Cut your sideburns off and throw away the guitar'." Still, even without the guitar and sideburns Cliff did pretty

well. He had a useful sneer (though it turns out that was because he had a bad tooth in front and was embarrassed to smile — he had it capped eventually) and, dressed in dark shirt and white tie, with his hair just breaking its greased formation, he could look good and moody.

'Move It', a no. 2 hit, was a wild enough rocker — 'C'mon Pretty baby, let's move it and groove it' — but hardly a trailer for his future career. Less than a year later, he recorded a song which was a model for the style he was to retain thereafter.

It happened like this. A film was to be made about a kindly vicar's attempts to win the respect of local juvenile delinquents. Someone in the production office had the smart idea of casting an up-and-coming young pop singer as one of the youths to boost the box-office appeal. The character naturally would turn out good. How else? Cliff got the part and a song to sing on the soundtrack.

A Rocker At Heart

The film was *Serious Charge*, the song 'Living Doll'. It wiped the sneer off Cliff's face. "I did 'Living Doll' under duress, and it was released because the film was out. And it absolutely took off. It was the first time I'd ever had a chart entry as high as 14 after five days' release. (It rapidly went on up to no. 1.) I didn't even like the song very much at first, but it changed the whole course of my career. Before, I was a rocker, only acceptable to kids; 'Living Doll' brought me an audience that was far more family, it brought mums and dads along to see what the apparition was on about. I was still a rocker at heart and remained a rocker for years, but from then on I had the best success with ballads."

The importance of 'Living Doll' in Cliff's career is beyond doubt, and it also had a crucial influence on British pop music in general. Nik Cohn overrated it when he called it 'by far the most influential British single of the whole decade', but he wasn't far off the mark, for many of the lightweight, tuneful pop ballads of the next years owed their style and success to 'Living Doll', and their domination of the charts remained unbroken until the later arrival of the Beatles.

Cliff himself, perhaps more through modesty than insight, is less sure of the song's influence: "At the time I was too selfish to think about anything else but the effect on myself. I always feel that 'Living Doll' happened only for me. I suppose it did lead the way, but not by itself. There were other tuneful things happening. I don't think I started a great fad for melodic music. I think it had been growing for quite a while. In those days there were hits in the charts that would be considered nonsensical now, but they were melodic. All I know is that it brought a fantastic new audience to me, and the chance to sing songs that I would have liked to have sung, but wouldn't have perhaps if I hadn't sung 'Living Doll' — things like 'Twelfth Of Never', 'Constantly' and 'It's All In The Game', which still remain the bigger ones

of my records. I have had hits since with out-and-out rock things, but 'Living Doll' changed my career."

If 'Living Doll' drew the mums and dads in alongside the kids, it was a film, *The Young Ones*, which brought along the rest of the relations. It was his third, as he had followed *Serious Charge* with another straight role in *Expresso Bongo*, playing an up-and-coming young pop singer. He did well even though he wasn't the star, and he didn't at all mind playing support to Laurence Harvey, because he wanted to be a serious actor.

In those days it seemed as soon as anyone made no. 1 in the charts he wasn't content to be just a pop singer anymore, he wanted to be a film star too. Presley, of course, set the style by visiting Hollywood every few months to rush off another box-office smash, so the rest wanted to do the same. In Britain Tommy Steele was the first — he made it easy on himself and starred in *The Tommy Steele Story* — then Cliff, then Adam Faith (*Beat Girl* and *Mix Me A Person*), then Billy Fury (*Play It Cool*) — and John Leyton took it so seriously that he gave up pop altogether.

With *Expresso Bongo* Cliff was luckier than most, and he knew it: "It was the first and only acting I did for years. I really had high ideas. I thought, 'I'm not going to star in a film for at least nine or ten years, because it's too much responsibility; let someone else do it and I'll just appear in them.' That was my little dream world. Then someone came up to me with this *Young Ones* idea and talked me into it — very easily. It sounded fun, so I thought I'd give it a try, but it was really an accident. After about three weeks of shooting it was obvious we had something. The whole studio was abuzz. Whenever our gang appeared people would nudge each other and say, 'They're making a great musical'. It was really nice. I enjoyed it."

Good Clean Kids

The Young Ones, made in 1961, established an ideal formula for commercial success — good clean kids having good clean fun, plus pop music, dancing, and a happy ending. It was followed by *Summer Holiday* (1962), *Wonderful Life* (1964), and *Finders Keepers* (1966). Then the formula wore thin, however, and the fun wasn't fun anymore. People still queued to see them, and put the soundtrack singles into the Top 10, but for Cliff they became a major drag. "They were all the same. And every time I got offered another film, it was always: 'Got a wonderful idea, chaps. Let's get a bus, paint it red, and let's go to Greece, huh?' So I cut out." But *The Young Ones* had served him proud, for by endorsing the wholly acceptable image first presented by 'Living Doll', and carrying it to an ageless and nationwide audience, it established him for keeps as the British Champion of Pop (Lightweight Division). All he had to do was stay fit and no one could touch him.

The year which began with the title song of *The Young Ones* topping the charts —

1962 — was just about Cliff's best. He released three other singles that year, two of which made no. 2, and the third no. 1. But a more remarkable demonstration of his consistency and the strength of his following lies in the fact that 1963 was almost as good, because 1963 was the year of the Beatles and the groups' boom. Only two other solo singers approached his success that year — Frank Ifield and Billy Fury, neither of whom had much further success. Elvis Presley reached the Top 10 just once in 1963, Adam Faith had only three Top 20 hits altogether after 1962, Bobby Vee had one, while neither Marty Wilde nor Craig Douglas nor Lonnie Donegan had any hits at all. Cliff hung on. Even when the Beatles knocked him he took it, didn't fight back — just kept the hits coming.

I Can't Sing Heavy

By then he had it figured out. As long as he continued to make good straight pop records, he would go on racking up hits. He was fortunate in that he never had a hot run of no. 1's to follow — in his total career he has only twice managed successive chart toppers — so he was never so high that he fell when innovation hit the scene. Apart from the loyalty of his fans, his consistent success has been due to his ability to change, to adjust his material to the climate of the charts. "That's what I like about my career. Every now and again I've come up with something that is of the time, so that I've been in it, but not on the bandwagon. I've never consciously cashed in and said, 'It's getting a bit heavy now — I can't really sing heavy, but we'll put a few fuzz guitars in.' I've done it if it fits the thing, without going out of my way to do it." The clearest example of this adaptability is also his classic song: 'The Day I Met Marie'.

It was recorded in 1967 and written (like 'Throw Down A Line' and 'The Joy Of Living' — both similarly attuned to their time) by Hank Marvin — who by then had outgrown his role as lead guitarist of Cliff's back-up band, the Shadows, and even that of front man on the band's own instrumental hits. (The Shadows had in fact become increasingly less important for Cliff, who almost from the start had displayed an equal liking, if not a preference, for studio orchestral instrumentation behind his voice. When the band finally broke up, he was personally sorry, but professionally unaffected: "People kept saying to me, 'What are you going to do now?' I said, 'What I've been doing for the last twelve years'.")

'The Day I Met Marie' entered the Top 20 on the same day as the Flowerpot Men's 'Let's Go To San Francisco'. Whereas the Flowerpot Men (sic) and their song typified the pop industry's crass bandwagon mentality, 'The Day I Met Marie' fitted that summer's mood without banal references to bells, beads or flowers. The fact that it was not one of Cliff's most successful songs was a considerable disappointment. "It's my favourite recording. It was one of the best

constructed songs I'd had given to me, up until that point, and I still do it on stage because it's such a good song to sing."

Six months later, though, Cliff was back at the top with a song that could only really beat 'Marie' in terms of popularity. In every other respect 'Congratulations' was a lesser song. In fairness to Cliff, it was not a song of his own choosing, although he did choose to enter the Eurovision Song Contest, for which it was the British entry. The fact that it reached no. 1, when better songs had failed, must have convinced him of the enormous effectiveness of television as a stage on which to sing — since both the contest itself and the original selection of 'Congratulations' (by viewers) took place on television.

In Britain, the notion of the television performer as pop star (and vice versa) plays an important part in both television entertainment and pop music. In recent years not only have pop singers swapped 'live' public appearances for the television screen — not surprisingly — but television entertainers, notably Ken Dodd, Rolf Harris, and Des O'Connor, have enjoyed success as pop singers. The conclusion to be drawn is obvious: television pushes the size of an audience into many millions.

Cliff took the point and joined the team. He had the right qualities — a pleasant appearance, an air of youthful maturity, an excellent voice, an easy manner — and found it easy to establish a powerful rapport with his vast unseen audience. Thus television became the pivot of his success.

Nevertheless, he still feels the need each year to reaffirm more personal contact and confirm the impression he gets from fan mail and viewing figures, (that his fans are still all there), by doing his own head count. "I go on tour every year and every year I expect it to be different. But it isn't and I'm amazed. The best test of the strength of one's popularity is if one can get people to come out from their television sets on a cold winter's night."

Not A Natural Guitarist

Despite the obvious and constant signs that his popularity is as great as ever, he doesn't feel he can ease back and simply coast on 15 years' momentum. He's been working hard at his guitar playing recently, for although he was strumming one even before he was 'discovered', he admits that "in the early days I played it like everyone else did — badly — and I do still really. But what I do is learn it now, and I play a lot more than I used to. I'm not a natural guitarist, so when I appear onstage playing nonchalantly it's taken months, but in my new act I'll do maybe five songs with a guitar, and a quiet section by myself with my guitar and strings, doing a couple of songs that I've written recently."

In 1973 he made Take Me High, which was his first film for quite a number of years, and more importantly, pumped greater energy into the soundtrack singing sessions than on any previous recording: "I felt they were the best sessions I'd done for yonks. Vocally, for me, they were the

best because they demanded so much. People say to me, 'Isn't it difficult being a singer?' and I say, 'No, I've been singing since I was six — in the bath, anywhere — it's easy. I open my mouth and sing'. Not everybody likes it, but that's the way it goes. It's just natural, there's no work involved at all . . . until that session, where I really had to think about opening my mouth a bit and bellowing."

Paul McCartney: The Wing Commander

Reference to the *Concise Oxford Dictionary* gives the meaning of 'super' as: 'exceeding, going beyond, more than, too exalted for contract and beyond the norm'. Turning the pages reveals the meaning of the word 'star' as: 'principal item in a performance or an entertainment, brilliant or prominent person, such a body that appears in groups of two, four or six'.

Having determined the literal meaning of 'superstar', it's easy to appreciate how all of these meanings can apply to Paul McCartney; and easy to understand exactly why he is often classed as such.

Trumpeting Start

For someone who showed little interest in music as a child, Paul must have surprised everyone when he persuaded an uncle to loan him a trumpet so he could pick out little tunes on it. Then, after acquiring a taste for the trumpet, Paul started doodling about with the family piano situated in the living-room. But it was only with the arrival of rock & roll that Paul's interest in music proper was aroused. Having witnessed a concert by Lonnie Donegan at the Liverpool Empire, Paul persuaded his father to buy him a guitar. His father, himself a keen musician, purchased a second-hand six-string for £15, and Paul's assault on pop music — a lot of which he was to change — had begun.

He began listening to records and the radio as much as possible. His favourite listening was Elvis, Little Richard and all the other American rock & rollers. Having listened to 'All Shook Up' over and over again, he began to pick out the chords on his guitar — which by this time he had converted into a left-handed model — and having learnt the chords, he started trying vocal imitations of Elvis' voice.

The next song he learnt came easier than the first, and the one after that, easier

Joseph Stevens

still. Paul began to realise that playing the guitar wasn't as difficult as it first looked; so, with a miniature repertoire of his own, he went out in search of other musicians who shared his devotion to rock & roll.

He didn't have to look very far. One afternoon a close friend dragged Paul along to the local parish church to listen to a group that he sometimes played with. Paul listened to the group and criticised them harshly — which for someone who'd never played out in front of an audience was a bit of a cheek. He did, however, remember that the lead guitarist was quite good (meaning by his own standards) . . . and that was the first meeting of Paul McCartney and John Lennon.

Paul Joins John

Having exchanged mutual likes and dislikes, Paul told John that he too could play a guitar. John showed typical Lennon-esque interest, and invited Paul along to the group's next rehearsal which was to be later that week. At the rehearsal Paul, armed with guitar, showed John all the chords he knew; and John in return did the same for Paul. Paul couldn't help noticing that John played all his chords in banjo structures, and later learned that this was because John had learned the guitar via the banjo. Nonetheless, Paul was invited to take part in the rehearsal — he was the most fluent player of them all — and immediately afterwards John asked Paul to join the group.

After John and Paul had been playing together for some months, they decided to expand their repertoire. The only songs they knew, though, were either the ones they had heard on the radio, or ones which either of them had on record. John explained to Paul that he had written a few little songs that maybe they could include in their act. Paul listened attentively, and liked what he heard. It had never occurred to Paul McCartney that songs had to be written in order to be performed, and for the first time in his 16-year-old life he considered the possibilities of writing some of his own. Little did he know that in his field he possessed the talent of the supernatural.

The first few songs he wrote were not very good. He found that he was able to write so much, but that when, for example, he got to the middle, he was lost. At this point he turned to his friend and, in his eyes, 'experienced' songwriter, John Lennon. John willingly helped Paul over the hump by writing in chords that had never before occurred to Paul. The result(?) . . . the first Lennon/McCartney compositions.

By this time the group had undergone major changes. The other original members had left, and a new guitarist — George Harrison — had joined. They also had Stu Sutcliffe on bass and, later, Pete Best on drums. They were playing raucous rock & roll with all the venom and drive of enthusiastic youngsters having a good laugh. But this group meant more than a good laugh to these 'kids'; they were serious,

they believed that they could make it big. All they needed, so they thought, was a good image, the right music and a lot of luck . . . and they could be as big as Elvis. But we all have our dreams!

The band, with Paul and John very much the leaders, moved on from clubs in and around Liverpool to Hamburg. The apprenticeship was taking place. Working long hours and, when not on stage, sitting in their room writing, they polished up their stage act. Furthermore, they were by now building up a fan following. Nobody, but nobody, and this included even Paul's parents, was going to tell them that they couldn't make it.

When, as the Beatles, they did begin to break the ice, it was Paul who acted as the group's go-between to the general public that wanted to get to them. Paul was, unofficially, the Beatles' public relations man: he did most of the talking during interviews, answering the serious questions seriously, and always managing to appear in spontaneous photographs as though he had spent at least three hours preparing for them.

Everyone had their particular favourite Beatle, but most people seemed to harbour a kind of affection for Paul. Perhaps it was because of his boy-next-door look, or perhaps that he never seemed too exalted for contact, but most probably it was because of the songs he wrote.

Parent Appeal

Paul seemed to have the uncanny knack of being able to write songs aimed directly at the hearts of his audience . . . a talent he doesn't appear to have lost. John, on the other hand, was even then writing far more about his inner self, and the fans found it just a little bit too difficult to associate his stuff with themselves. But this is generalising of course. Paul's songs also had, it appears, far more meaning for the Mums and Dads, and it was, after all, once the Mums and Dads started taking an interest in the Beatles that the affair blew up out of all proportion.

How easily a married couple of 50, for example, could identify with 'When I'm 64', 'She's Leaving Home', 'Honey Pie' and 'Here, There And Everywhere'. Because Paul sang them with great care and flavour these people made Paul, in their minds at least, a superstar. Like Frank Sinatra before him — and Tom Jones after — Paul had the charisma that makes people of all ages, colours, and sexes, warm to him. He appears to say in his music what everyone would like to say to each other, but can never find the words to express.

Then, when Brian Epstein died in 1967, the Beatles unconsciously became Paul McCartney's group. It was Paul who took over the running and musical direction of the group, and in many ways this signalled the beginning of the end for the Beatles. All four of them were by then writing in different directions, and it was plainly obvious that it wouldn't be long before the party was over.

But in order to keep the party going,

DACK TRACK

Born on June 18th, 1940, at Walton Hospital, Liverpool.
1969, Paul and Linda Eastman marry at Marylebone Registry Office, London.
1970, April: Paul's first solo album 'McCartney' released. December: the Beatles split up and Paul issues a court suit in order to get the Beatles dissolved.
1971, February: Paul & Linda release

their first single entitled 'Another Day', making the UK Top 10. May: Paul and Linda release first album together entitled 'Ram'. From this album 'Back Seat Of My Car' on single, flopped. December: Wings' first album released entitled 'Wild Life'.

1972, February: Wings release 'Give Ireland Back To The Irish' which is immediately banned by the BBC. Start of 'Wings Over Europe' tour. May: 'Mary Had A Little Lamb' single which

climbs into the UK Top 10. December: Wings release 'Hi, Hi, Hi' which again is banned by the BBC, this time for sexual references.

1973, May: Paul plays to a British audience for the first time since 1966 at Bristol Hippodrome, beginning a UK tour, followed by a UK TV spectacular. Wings' second album 'Red Rose Speedway' and from it a single 'My Love' is released. June: Paul writes music for James Bond film 'Live and Let Die'. The

song is also released as a single. October: 'Helen Wheels' released as single. November: Wings' third album 'Band On The Run' released and highly acclaimed by the press. Denny Seiwell and Henry McCullough leave Wings. December: McCartney family compère the Christmas Walt Disney TV show. 1974. Paul's US visa is granted by Home Office and he is able to reunite with John Lennon. February: single 'Jet' (no. 7).

Main picture: Wings, featuring Paul McCartney in the foreground and in the background, Linda McCartney and Denny Laine. Insert, L.H. pic: Linda, Paul and Denny in a London recording studio late in 1973. R.H. pic: The McCartney family (Mary and baby Stella) are definitely 'on the bus'. Here, they cuddle up together as they wing their way round Europe for their 1973 tour; only big sister Heather is missing.

Paul decided to make a film based on a magical mystery tour that he would plan, organise and see through. While the others were all doing their own things, Paul was busy working on — what was for him — his first major venture not directly linked with the other three. Unfortunately, press-wise, the project failed; or if it didn't fail, it failed to reach the required standards. But then, it was the Beatles who had set these standards.

Even though the TV film didn't do as well as everyone would have liked, Paul nevertheless came up with two classic songs: 'Your Mother Should Know' and 'Fool On The Hill'. These, like others before them, hit right upon the heart-strings of people all over the world.

Beatles Split Up

George, meanwhile, had gone into meditation and mysticism, John had met up with a Japanese avant-garde artist who was leading him into sacks, brown paper bags and a wild life-style, Ringo had left the limelight, and — to the people who make or break superstars — Paul was the only one who seemed to have retained any sanity.

Eventually, as all had expected, the Beatles split up. It was Paul who filed a court suit demanding the dissolution of the group, and just after he filed it he said: "For me I want to get out of the contract, I think the group is finished. We have split, and everything we have ever earned or that we were ever in should be divided equally. But the others don't agree. They think it should continue exactly as it was. If the three of them wanted to they could sit down today and write on a little piece of paper and I would be released. That is all I want."

The suit passed through court and Paul McCartney became detached from Ringo, John and George . . . free to do as he wished. Whether he would disappear into retirement or form himself another group, nobody was sure. But one thing that had sadly ended for good was the writing partnership of John Lennon and Paul, a partnership that had written so many classic hit tunes.

Much of the initial 'split-up' problem came from the fact that Paul, so typically, had made a solo album which he wanted to release at the same time as 'Let It Be'. The administrative king at Apple, Allan Klein, was worried that this solo effort from McCartney would offset the sales of 'Let It Be', a venture in which Mr Klein had a possible large financial return. 'McCartney' was, nevertheless, released, and it sold well without noticeably offsetting the sales of the group effort.

For people who had been saying that McCartney without Lennon just wasn't going to work, the release of this solo effort must have come as a great surprise. 'Maybe I'm Amazed' was a classic McCartney song, and in silent ways made it clear that Paul was quite content not only to work on his own, but also to write.

The press, though, were having their usual dig at Paul. It seemed that they just couldn't get used to the idea that one Beatle could do anything without the others. Paul just ignored all these journalistic put-downs and got down to the job at hand which was doing the thing that he did best: playing and composing music.

By this time Paul the superstar had married Linda Eastman the camp follower, and between them they set about the mammoth task of forming another group to follow in the Beatles' footsteps. Eventually they managed it and, as everyone knows, the new group was called Wings. Henry McCullough had been recruited from the Grease Band, Denny Seiwell from a couple of sessions he had done with the McCartneys in New York, and Denny Laine – an absolute Beatle freak – had been recruited on the telephone. These three, plus Mr and Mrs McCartney, made up the new band. The most incredible thing about Wings is the fact that they have found an audience. No, they're not Beatle leftover audiences either, they are a new breed of pop fans. Many of them have never seen or heard the Beatles, they are prepared to accept Wings for what they play, and the past counts for virtually nothing.

Paul – by now an old pro to the game – decided that he wasn't going to unleash the band on the world (waiting in the wings in anticipation) before he had broken them in. He did this with a couple of unannounced college gigs and a tour of Europe, visiting such remote places as the South of France, little villages in Germany, and hamlets up in the Swiss alps. Paul, in other words, left absolutely nothing to chance. The press reviews, for all this effort, were no more than lukewarm, but despite some criticism, the crowds still came out in their masses to see the new band – or at least to see Paul.

Ready In The Wings

After returning from Europe and following a short holiday, Wings were ready to play to the ever-waiting British audiences. Everyone, it appeared, wanted to see Paul on stage once again. Undoubtedly most people would rather have seen him alongside John, George and Ringo, but they were nonetheless perfectly willing to pay their money to settle for second-best.

It only took one song, 'Big Barn Bed', for Paul's new audiences to realise that they hadn't wasted their money. Paul had lost none of his glittering charisma – he walked on the stage like the return of the Messiah – and the fans went wild. Alright, there *were* four others in the band, but it was Paul they came to watch. It was like the Beatle days all over again. The only difference being there wasn't any screaming – you could actually hear the fullness of his voice, the beauty of his lyrics and the instant charm of his melodies.

Wings' repertoire is based on out and out rock music, with dashes of sentimentality thrown in for good measure. Denny Laine, formerly with the Moody Blues, is a better-than-average songwriter whose contribution to the Wings repertoire is increasing. When Paul moves over to piano, Denny plays bass. When Paul plays lead, Denny plays piano, and when Paul plays bass, Denny plays lead. The two of them complement each other perfectly, and although Linda is always being put down by the press, her harmonies are improving record by record. Perhaps she isn't a marvellous musician, but who needs to be when you have the qualities of Paul and Denny around you. Singles and albums came from Wings at regular intervals, some were mediocre, some were great; but more than anything else, all featured Paul McCartney, and that in a nutshell meant guaranteed sales figures. Sales figures, however, aren't solely dependent on Paul's charisma, his band Wings are very competent. If anything, the musicians within it are more fluent than those of the Beatles.

Search For Musicians

Unfortunately, though, in November, 1973, Denny Seiwell and Henry McCullough left the group after a disagreement with Paul. As though nothing had happened, Paul, Linda and Denny Laine went off to Lagos to record 'Band On The Run'. In the end, what Henry and Denny Seiwell had done, so Paul did – as well, if not better. But that was only in the studio. On returning to London it became obvious that the multi-talented McCartney was not going to be able to do all these chores on stage, and so since that moment in time he has been in search of two musicians who will be able to complement his band as well as just play along.

The word superstar is nowadays attached to almost anyone who is lucky enough to get a few singles into the charts. Then, if a successful album should follow, the whole world seems to stand agog. But superstars aren't made from singles or albums, it's all down to charisma. What is it the *Concise Oxford Dictionary* says: 'brilliant or prominent person', or 'too exalted for contact and beyond the norm'?

These are the qualities that make a superstar, and a lot of thought should be put into it before someone is so called. Paul McCartney, though, has earned it, and earned it well. From the very early days of the Beatles, Paul was destined to become a star. Maybe he wasn't as super then as he has since become, but all the ingredients were there, it was just a matter of stirring well and then bringing to the boil.

Paul's attitude and secret ingredient to his life and music is simplicity. He is automatically the leader of all around him. Show a photograph of the Beatles taken in about 1969–70 to anyone over 35 and then ask them which is their favourite and the answer is more often than not Paul. People follow him like children after the Pied Piper of Hamelin. Paul has shown the music world that simplicity is the mother of invention. In such a fickle world, there can't be very many people in pop who have made it twice over *and* be able to retain their strength of personality and quality of music.

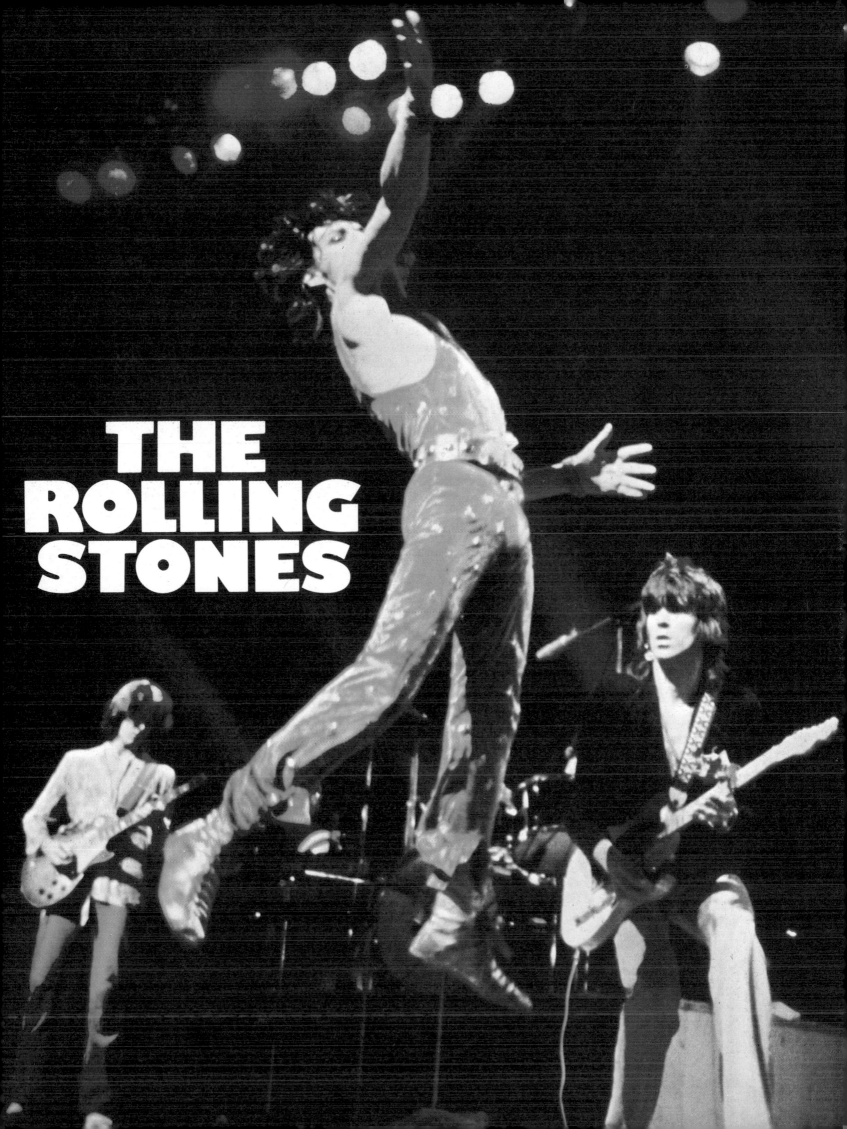

THE ROLLING STONES

So you wanna be a rock & roll star? Well, if you want to do it properly then the people you'll most likely choose as your models will be the (one and only) Rolling Stones. As the Stones themselves say in 'Live With Me' on their 'Let It Bleed' album:

'They got ear-phone heads,
They got dirty necks,
They're so twentieth century'

A grinding, tingling, and sometimes chilling R&B band, the Stones encourage aggravation, and their teasing attitudes and ambisexuality have gone a long way to concreting the generation gap into unbending slabs. The Stones were purposefully rough and rude, as they smashed out raw R&B and scowled up the establishment's nose. They challenged society's rules, laws, standards and values as they postured and pranced to the worried cries of 'decadence' and 'debauchery'.

We all need someone we can bleed on, and the Stones laid themselves out for the parents to do just that. They psyched the daddies of teenage daughters out of their closed-in minds. They shit-stirred the square world as they threw the Pill right back into the mothers' laps with their 'Mother's Little Helper' ditty – it wasn't just pill-popping teenager ravers bent on staying awake the weekend through, it was the housewives and tailored executives too. The Stones were deliberate and bloody-minded as they axed away at the social niceties, and started the fight for the young to live as they pleased, with a smirk on their faces. The Stones' scowl became as tantalising as the Beatles' grin.

Black Man's Sound

The Stones began as they really were: tough, defiant cynics beating out a harsh, cruel music without frilly trimmings or any sop to female romanticism. Their lead singer was Mick Jagger, whose surly, petulant lips made a black man's sound. The rest of the line-up was Brian Jones (guitar), Bill Wyman (bass), Keith Richard (guitar), and Charlie Watts on drums. They started in the middle-class West London suburb of Richmond, playing Sunday R&B nights at the local pubs and clubs. Soon the Stones found a manager in Andrew Loog Oldham, a 19-year-old ex-Brian Epstein office boy. They outraged and they flaunted, and Oldham encouraged them. He set them up to score with the resentful teenagers – and they succeeded. Oldham had no money and neither did they, so he encouraged them to dress just how they were – this at a time when all pop groups were wearing neat and tidy stage uniforms. (The Kinks, for example, wore hunting-pink jackets and frilly lace shirts.) Oldham allowed their hatred of conformity to have full sway, and pretty soon the rich elite were prepared to overlook the unkempt hair and the grubby jeans. But it was still a world of ties and suits, and the Stones were constantly in the news for being ordered out of bars and restaurants for not being properly dressed. Throughout it all though, they retained a certain sour honesty and refused to compromise. They were educated pretend-morons masquerading as oafs, and they committed themselves to pleasure and the present.

They admired the post-war urban blues of Muddy Waters, Bo Diddley and Chuck Berry, because the pre-war blues had just been for other Negroes. But now these

Gered Mankowitz, SKR, Conway Picture Library, Syndication International

blues were being shouted out into the big, white world – grind, roll, rock and ride all night long. And the suburban Stones heard the message and zeroed in.

From the beginning their records had a roughness to them, which was partly because at the outset Oldham could not afford expensive studios. This part of their musical history is best summed up in their second record to make the charts, 'Not Fade Away', which had been a previous success for the late Buddy Holly. The Stones' version was recorded at Regent Sound in London, the epitome, at the time, of the rawness of small studio sound.

'Not Fade Away' contained everything that the Stones represented musically at that moment, in early 1964. It was a period when pill taking among young people was on the increase, and 'Not Fade Away' sounds like the ultimate song to speed to – a rhythmic clap on the beat, Jagger's voice recorded almost in the background, and the driving guitar riffs of Brian Jones and Keith Richards reflected by the grating harmonica. It was also a significant record in the Stones' history for more than these musical reasons. It was their first record to enter the American

charts, albeit rising to no. 44 at its height, but it meant that at last America too was getting to know about the Stones.

The Beatles helped them, and mentioned them wherever they could. They were musical and at the time social opposites, but the Beatles were fascinated by them, and as a result the Stones made their first visit to America that same year in June. When they got back they were mobbed at London airport.

Gambling On Hits

As happened with the Beatles, they were at the stage where they had to pay for their sudden success. In those days promoters bought 'futures' in groups and booked them at low fees months ahead while they were unknown, gambling on the fact that they would have a hit before they were due to appear. It's well known that the Beatles had to honour many gigs for £50 to £100 a night under this system even when they had a no. 1, and so did the Stones. It just happened that one of the gigs they had agreed to play was at Magdalen College, Oxford, for £100. This gig fell during their American tour

so, contrary to the hard, careless press image they had collected, the Stones agreed to fly in and out of Britain to honour the one date.

'Not Fade Away' reached no. 3 in the British charts besides breaking the group in America, but it wasn't until June of 1964 that they got their first no. 1 with 'It's All Over Now'. Despite their new-found success however, the Stones didn't alter their image or life-style to suit the wider audience.

That same year, 1964, it seemed that Stones concerts always ended in riots – more particularly on the Continent. For example, a performance at The Hague in Holland was stopped after only 10 minutes, when teenagers threw bottles and chairs towards the stage. Jagger pouted and teased his audiences while the rest of the group remained stonily apart from it all. When they appeared at the famed Olympia Theatre in Paris, the management reported that £1,400 of damage was done and 150 young people were arrested. At home in Britain things were no more peaceful. In Blackpool, when Keith Richard aimed a kick at a young person who ran on stage, there was a riot which ended with £2,000

99

of damage and a grand piano wrecked in the orchestra pit. In Belfast such was the effect of their performance on the audience that several teenagers were carried out in straitjackets by ambulancemen. Watching them in the mid-'70s, all this is hard to imagine; their audiences have grown older with the group and, having miraculously obtained a ticket to a Stones concert, they are almost content to sit back and watch the pyrotechnics on stage.

Challenging The Beatles

In 1964 they recorded four consecutive no. 1s. After 'It's All Over Now' came 'Little Red Rooster', 'The Last Time' and then, one of the all-time classics of rock, 'Satisfaction'. Again the opening statement from Jagger 'I can't get no satisfaction. . .' expressed the view of a generation. After 'Satisfaction' came another no. 1 in 1965: 'Get Off Of My Cloud'. There was no doubt the Stones were now quite capable of challenging the immense success of the Beatles. It perhaps seems slightly ironic that the Beatles, who had been the foremost originators in British rock, have individually moved ever nearer to the musical freeness of the Stones, than the Stones have ever moved towards the Beatles' highly commercial sound of the early '60s.

As much as they were successful in the charts, the Stones showed no signs of being embraced, or indeed willing to be embraced, by the British Establishment, as were the Beatles. Not for them the MBE, awarded to each one of the Beatles for their musical services to the country. Not for the Stones an appearance at the *Royal Command Performance,* the annual charity show held in London before royalty. The Stones' appeal was to that part of the youth culture who were eventually to form the so-called Alternative Society — which is why, to this day, the group are still embraced by the underground press despite their change in private lifestyle.

In fact their superbly rhythmic drummer, Charlie Watts, was the first Stone to do what is now expected of the successful rock star and buy himself a country mansion. Poignantly, his was a 16th century house in Sussex, which had belonged to Lord Shawcross, the one-time Attorney General in the British Labour Government. Perhaps it was appropriate that for once the Left wing should sell out to the Stones.

Despite this elegant background, the group continued to make headlines by defying authority. In July, 1965, there was the infamous case of Wyman, Jagger and Jones urinating in the forecourt of a petrol station. What may now seem a small detail is in fact an integral part of the Stones' social history, for which they were severely censured and fined. It was around this time that the group's personal life became for the world public perhaps even more fascinating than their music. Even middle-aged people, who had not seen or even heard their records, knew about them because of their challenging life-style

which, because they were a hit-making group, they had to conduct in the public eye. Andrew Oldham at this point opted out of his co-management deal, but continued as the group's producer. He had decided he wanted to discover other talent, and one of the first singers he found was a blonde 17-year-old called Marianne Faithfull, who instantly became Mick Jagger's much-publicised girlfriend.

In January 1965 the Stones made their first recordings outside London when they flew to Los Angeles prior to an Australian tour. Back in London they finally gave in to demands to appear on the then prestigious TV show *Sunday Night At The London Palladium.* They had previously turned the show down five times, and even when they appeared there was trouble. They had refused to stand with the rest of the stars and go around on the traditional revolve at the end of the show; and the result was more front page news in Britain's popular press.

It was in 1965 too that the group caused a sensation on American TV by being allowed to do three numbers on the *Ed Sullivan Show* to the delight of their fans, and the despair of Middle American parents who wrote in to complain in their thousands. This tour was their turning point in America, where they outsold even the Beach Boys. By mid-'66 they were suing 14 New York hotels for refusing to house them. Things had changed: their records continued to be successful, but it was to be two years — until 1968 — before they had another no. 1 in Britain. This slight dip in their musical acceptance was accompanied by the release in 1966 of their album 'Their Satanic Majesties Request', which in the long-run may turn out to be one of their most underrated albums. It was in fact to be two years before they released another album, 'Beggars' Banquet', which was much more readily received — having as it did titles like 'Sympathy For The Devil' and 'Street Fighting Man'. This then really was the period of change in the Stones' career. There had been internal arguments within the group because Brian Jones felt that Mick Jagger and Keith Richard were monopolising the writing, when he felt some more of his own work should be used.

Brian Jones Dead

In June 1969 the difference reached an impasse, and Jones announced he was leaving the group. He was replaced by Mick Taylor who had been with the John Mayall band, as had many good musicians in Britain including Eric Clapton. But Brian Jones had been much more than just a good guitarist in the group: he was essentially one of the Rolling Stones, and it was his look, and impassive girl-like face, more than anything that contributed to their overall image. Anyhow, before the Stones fans had time to really argue about the decision, Jones died face down in the swimming pool of his house in the Sussex countryside — once lived in by A. A. Milne,

writer of the *Winnie The Pooh* books.

The date was July 3rd, 1969, two days before the Stones were due to give a massive free concert in London's Hyde Park. They decided to turn the concert into a memorial for Jones, Jagger reading a dedication to him from the poet Shelley, and thousands of white butterflies being released above the heads of the 200,000-strong crowd. It was a stunning and memorable event and was, by the way, responsible for launching two other groups now well known: King Crimson and Family.

Soon after the Hyde Park concert, Mick Jagger flew to Australia to play the title part of Ned Kelly in the Tony Richardson film; with him went Marianne Faithfull, but their relationship was obviously cooling off and she was taken ill. When released, the film was neither a critical nor box-office success. After the film was completed Jagger met up with the rest of the group in America for a major tour. On December 6th they played the now notorious open-air concert at Altamont. Notorious because the event was filmed and culminated in the historic onstage murder of a youth who tried to rush on to the stage. It was a concert that was to haunt them for sometime, and one that has since been seen by many as a turning point in the youth culture.

Performance

During 1970, there was the release of a much more interesting film starring Jagger, called *Performance*. The theme returned to that social affront at the beginning of the Stones' career: sexual doubt. The film appeared almost surreal, and just one of its delights was that Jagger appeared at times with make-up like a woman. The film was again not a commercial success, but in retrospect it might appear more important than it did at the time.

It now seemed that the Stones would probably never take to the road again, but a phone conversation between Jagger and Pete Townshend of the Who — who had never really given up going on the road in Britain — started off the great Stones comeback tour of the spring of 1971. It opened in Newcastle, showing that the group were still not very confident to be appearing again; whereas when it came to the 1973 tour they opened before 10,500 people at the Empire Pool, Wembley.

This tour marked the first public inclusion of session musicians on stage, augmenting the Stones' sound compared with their last performance in London as a group at the Saville Theatre in December, 1969. Now Nicky Hopkins, on piano, Jim Price, trumpet, and Bobby Keyes, saxophone, filled out the group's sound just as they were doing on their albums, and somehow retained the Stones' original raunch while at the same time adding further layers to it. As Jagger said in 1973: "It was all right in the old days when we only appeared on stage for half an hour at a time, but I think nowadays when we're on stage for an hour and a half people

might get a bit fed up with just us . . . you need to add something to it.''

On May 12th, 1971 Mick Jagger married Bianca Perez Morena de Macias in the Town Hall at St. Tropez in the South of France. The Stones had by this time moved to France because of increasing intricacies in their tax situation — only to suffer culture shock in a spate of particular police dynamism.

Playboy Party

The Stones' tour of America in 1972 was a staggering success. It quickly took on circus proportions, with people sleeping on the pavements all night for tickets, and when they came to play in Los Angeles the whole area around the stadium was cordoned off. They had in fact been lionised by American society, and the one-time rebels became social baubles. They had Truman Capote reporting their tour, and Princess Lee Radziwill in the wings during their shows saying that she was one of their greatest fans. Hugh Heffner even hosted a party for them at the Playboy mansion in Chicago. Jagger says about this situation: ''It was the same in 1965 when there were people like Baby Jane Holzer around. It doesn't affect us or our music. If they want to come along they come along, some of them are nice and some of them aren't.''

Yet just at the moment when there was a thought that the Stones might soften their musical approach, they put a track called 'Star, Star' on their 'Goat's Head Soup' album of autumn 1973. Based on the rock-word 'starfucker' it was immediately banned from airplay in most places in the world.

The '73 Stones Show at the Empire Pool in London completely dazzled and delighted the 10,500 dedicated fans who attended it. There are two inter-twining parts to a Stones Show these days — the music and the lighting. Their lighting spectaculars are unsurpassed by any previous visual stage show to date. The lighting doesn't go from dark to light; it goes from very light to incredibly light. The stage is always saturated with light. Their low lighting is like everyone else's high lighting; and when they turn it on full it becomes almost unbearable. This feat is the work of one of Chip Monck's protégés Brian Croft, and is essentially still a Chip Monck show. His trademark of rich light abounds in plentiful evidence.

He has eight enormous follow spots at the back of the stage (they strongly resemble navy search lights). Above their heads, supported by a hydraulic ram on each side, there are what appear to be rows of lights; but they are in fact a bunch of Q I's, thickly clustered together like grapes — six deep, in tight bunches. And finally, along the front of the stage, are two brilliant columns of light.

Because of the loss of light entailed in the long throw required at Wembley, the most incredible high-flying mirrors were rigged up, at the cost of £1,200. The mirrors shortened this long throw and enabled the intensity of the light to be utilised and were something Brian Croft had dreamed up and perfected for their last American tour.

The next thing the Stones had going for them was, the perfect timing of the lighting technicians — they were like musicians themselves, they were so beautifully harmonised. There was an operator for each of the eight follow spots, and they all had to operate together — and they never missed a beat. All the time, there was smoke swirling from two clear perspex columns that rose from the sides of the stage, a steady trickle of carbon dioxide until the end, when it belched out all over the audience.

Explosive Signal

For yet further effect, there was smoke rising from the paraffin generator at the front of the stage, and when Richard gave Jagger a cool-nodded signal, and Mick stepped on a little button, there were even explosive smoke flares shooting around.

Their ending was more than superb. Mick sprinkled flower petals around and poured water over himself, and did likewise to his happily receptive audience. Then he crouched on the stage and tore the audience apart with 'Sympathy For

Roger Morton

Roger Morton

Roger Morton

The Devil', all the time slamming his belt on the floor as the whole of the stage flooded with blood-red light. Amazing. And Jagger whanged his belt again and again, until it seemed unbelievable that the audience could cope with this load of rich red colour, or their senses with this rich rock music.

Jagger and Richard are the two extroverts of the band, with Jagger high-assing it for them all. A wild untamed beauty is a term usually reserved for the women of this world – but it describes Jagger well. He's a nipple flashing, lip-pouting, bum-pushing, juices-flowing he-star. He's a tongue-lapping, lean streak of power, a '70s tearaway – and in stoned splendour he gets his people off. In the guise of a bacchus-like Pan with all-embracing moist red lips, he turns on to his audience. He pulls the blokes and the chicks right down into his performance. He licks and slips them right into his mood. He's a mean master of compromise; a funk-eyed and flash jack-knifing body of rock. He moves and he grinds, and drives them in tight where he's at.

Who could fail to get off on Jagger? Though few can fail to get off on Jagger, a lot of people have been positively heart-less in their attacks on Keith Richard. He always seemed to lose out, first to beautiful Brian Jones, and always to sensual Mick Jagger. Nobody seemed ready to concede any glory and favours to the bony-faced crim with the gypsy

diffidence and raggle-taggle hair who smacked of drugs and sinister magical doings, and wore a bone earring as visual proof of his corrupted soul. This was someone they didn't want to recognise, let alone get off on. The public seemed prepared to persecute Richard to the extent that they almost seemed to will their own perverse death-wish fantasies on him.

Definitive Wild Ones

They made hay with his wasted features, and seemed determined to label him an incoherent zombie; while, in fact, his stoned drawl rarely lapses into inco-herence. As he was quoted in an interview with Nick Kent of *NME:*
"Right now, I'm sticking pretty much to playing rhythm onstage. It depends on the number usually, but since Brian died I've had to pay more attention to rhythm guitar anyway. I move more now, simply because, back when we were playing old halls, I had to stand next to Charlie's drums in order to catch the beat, the sound was always so bad.

"I like numbers to be organised – my thing is organisation, I suppose – kicking the number off, pacing it and ending it." Despite this musical penchant for organ-isation, Richard and his girlfriend Anita Pallenberg remain as the definitive 'Wild Ones', in a way that Mick and Bianca Jagger could never be.

So where can the Stones go after that? Jagger feels that they are free to work on their own as long as it does not affect the recording schedules of the group as a whole. "I've already worked in the studios with several of my friends and I'd like to work on stage with them as well but I don't because then immediately everyone would say I was going solo, which I'm not." Just as long as the group carries on recording and performing, the Stones will no doubt remain, what for a decade they have been, 'the world's greatest rock band'.

Syndication International

103

Robert Ellis

SKR

MICK JAGGER: Born 26th July, 1943. Father was senior lecturer in physical education. Attended Maypole County Primary School, London School of Economics. Worked as a sort of physical education counsellor, games and sports instructor on a U.S. service base at 18. His first stage work was with Alexis Korner.

BRIAN JONES: Born 28th February, 1942. Mother was a piano teacher. Attended Dean Close Public School, Cheltenham Grammar School. Among other things he worked as an assistant in the electrical department of Whiteley's department store. His first stage work was playing alto in Cheltenham with a group called 'The Ramrods'.

KEITH RICHARD: Born 18th December, 1943. Father was electrical engineer. Attended Westhill Infants' School, Wentworth County Primary School, Dartford Technical School, Sidcup Art School. Was a postman for four days during 1961 Christmas season. His first stage appearance was with a country & western band while in art school.

SKR

SKR

Robert Ellis

BILL WYMAN: Born 24th October, 1941. Father was a bricklayer. Attended Oakfield Junior School in Penge and Beckenham Grammar School. He worked as a bookmaker's clerk in London before joining the Air Force, then did engineering with a firm in Streatham.

MICK TAYLOR: Born 17th January, 1948. Father was an aircraft worker. Attended Onslow Secondary Modern, Hatfield. Worked as a commercial artist engraver for a few months. Played with John Mayall before joining the Stones.

CHARLIE WATTS: Born 2nd June, 1941. Father was a lorry driver for British rail. Attended Tylers Croft Secondary Modern, Harrow Art School. He was working a club called the Troubador with a group called Blues By Five when he met Alexis Korner. Played with him before joining the Stones.

1962: Brian, Keith, Mick and Ian Stewart get together for the general purpose of playing at Bricklayers Arms. On 26th December, the Rolling Stones (as yet unnamed) have a disastrous booking in the Piccadilly Club.

Early in 1963 they deputise for Alexis Korner at the Marquee Club. Following this they have semi regular gigs at the Marquee, Eel Pie Island, Ealing Club. They record at I.B.C. Studios. In February the Rolling Stones begin an eight month residency at the Crawdaddy, Station Road, Richmond, Georgio Gomelski calls Peter Jones of Record Mirror, who tells Andrew Oldham about the Rolling Stones.

1963: April. Andrew Oldham and Eric Easton see Stones at Richmond. Signed management deal next day. May. First Official recording session at Olympic Studios. Oldham produced. June. 'Come On'. September. Start of first English tour with Everly Brothers and Bo Diddley. November. 'I Wanna Be Your Man' released.

1964: January. The Rolling Stones start tour, topping the bill for the first time, with the Ronettes. February. 'Not Fade Away'. April. LP 'The Rolling Stones'. June. 'It's All Over Now'. November. 'Little Red Rooster'.

1965: January. Release of LP 'The Rolling Stones No 2'. August. 'Satisfaction'. Andrew Oldham and Allen Klein to co-manage the Rolling Stones, new contract signed with Decca for five years. October. LP 'Out Of Our Heads'. 'Get Off Of My Cloud'.

1966: February. '19th Nervous Breakdown'. April. LP 'Aftermath'. May. 'Paint It Black'. September. 'Have You Seen Your Mother Baby'. November. LP 'Big Hits (High Tide and Green Grass)'.

1967: January. 'Let's Spend The Night Together'/'Ruby Tuesday'. August. 'We Love You'/'Dandelion'. December. LP 'Their Satanic Majesties'.

1968: May. Release of 'Jumpin' Jack Flash'. December. Rolling Stones *Rock 'n' Roll Circus* filmed at Wembley studios for TV. LP 'Beggars' Banquet'.

1969: June. Brian Jones leaves the Rolling Stones. Mick Taylor to replace him. July. Brian Jones dies at his home near Hartfield (Cotchford Farm). Free concert by the Rolling Stones in Hyde Park. 'Honky Tonk Women'/'You Can't Always Get What You Want'. September. LP 'Through The Past Darkly'.

1970: January. LP 'Let It Bleed'. July. Break with Klein. LP 'Get Yer Ya Yas Out!'. November. 'Memo To Turner' — Mick Jagger solo, from *Performance*.

1971: April. Release of 'Brown Sugar'/'Bitch'/'Let It Rock' — a maxi single, the first release on Rolling Stones Records label. LP 'Sticky Fingers'. May. Mick Jagger marries Bianca Perez Morena de Macias in St. Tropez. August. Decca Records release 'Gimme Shelter' LP which is a collection of oldies mainly taken from live concerts.

1972: April. 'Tumblin' Dice'/'Sweet Black Angel'. May. LP 'Exile On Main Street'. June. Decca release a maxi single — 'Street Fighting Man'/'Surprise Surprise'/'Everybody Needs Somebody To Love'.

1973: August. 'Angie'/'Silver Train'. LP 'Goat's Head Soup'.

John Lennon:
A Man Who Cares

When the Beatles sang for the Queen and Prince Philip at the annual Royal Variety Show in London in 1963, it was John Lennon who invited the audience to join in with the words . . . "Those of you in the cheaper seats — clap your hands, and those of you in the more expensive seats — just rattle your jewellery." Like a court jester, Lennon was taking the opportunity to lay down some hard social truths from behind a joker's mask.

Right from the Beatles' first public appearances John Lennon had been type-cast as the aggressive intellectual of the group. Stories abounded of his art college days in Liverpool, when he would roam around town 'like a wounded buffalo', getting drunk and having heavy arguments. Later, Brian Epstein might have made the Beatles wash their hair more often, wear suits, and stop swearing in front of their audience, but he could never completely stop Lennon from shooting his mouth off.

In 1966 however, John found himself in deep water when he told a London newspaper that the Beatles were more popular than Jesus. In Britain, no one

Top left-hand picture: Lennon, with the Plastic Ono Band on British TV in 1969. Below: John and Yoko in various stages of undress, as they try to show the press how sincere they are.

seemed to even blink at the remark, but in the southern states of the US such words were taken as blasphemy. In Alabama, Beatles' records and effigies were burnt in public and their songs were banned by several radio stations — all this on the eve of their final American tour. Brian Epstein hurriedly issued a statement watering down Lennon's remark, apologies were made, and the Beatles survived the tour without being burnt as heretics. In fact, the tour was their most profitable of all, but by then they had had enough. They decided to give up performing as a live band in order to concentrate on their recordings, and pursue their separate interests. This decision was quickly justified by the brilliant 'Sgt. Pepper' album in 1967, and the lavish critical praise it collected. Then, in August of that year, while the Beatles were meditating with the Maharishi in India, the world was shocked to hear of the death of Brian Epstein.

Separate Superstars

In quick succession the Beatles had both given up the gruelling tours which had cemented them together, and lost the man who had protected their clean, innocent image from the sarcasm of the press. Four very different minds, previously concealed under 'Mop-Top' haircuts, went their separate ways. As a result, 'The Beatles' double-album, 'Let It Be' and 'Abbey Road' contain simply Lennon songs, McCartney songs, and Harrison songs, played with great skill, but without the alchemy that had previously blended their four minds into one. The Beatles disintegrated into four separate superstars who continued to pool their backing roles — drums, bass, rhythm and lead guitars — but stopped sharing their identity.

While Paul McCartney took on Brian Epstein's job of being tactful to the press and thinking up new Beatles' enterprises, and George Harrison retreated from the limelight to concentrate on his music and religion, John Lennon's identity quickly developed along the lines of the angry artist.

John had always been the Beatle with whom intellectuals loved to flirt and had published two slim volumes of drawings and verse that had drawn critical comparison with James Joyce and Lewis Carroll. Now, though, he was going far beyond the role of the pop poet. His marriage to Cynthia broke down in 1968 and John met Yoko Ono — a veteran of the New York experimental art world who created events and art happenings designed to disturb people or make them question the way in which they saw the world. John and Yoko were married in Gibraltar in March 1969, and then flew to Vienna, where they invented a new form of

C. Walters

BAGISM

Keystone

106

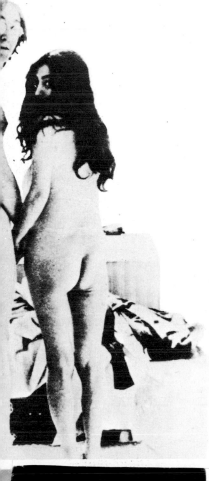

communication by holding a press conference from inside a gigantic bag, which John later commented on:

"The reporters all stood back saying 'Is it really John and Yoko?' and 'What are you wearing and why are you doing this?' We said, 'This is total communication with no prejudice'."

John then started supporting every unpopular cause he came across, outraging public opinion and doing the unexpected. To announce his love for Yoko, they made a record together of sound experiments, put it inside a sleeve showing John and Yoko holding hands, stark naked, and called it 'Two Virgins', released in November 1968. Instead of communicating the love they had found together, John and Yoko made themselves vulnerable to every accusation from childishness to obscenity, and Lennon looked like becoming the first pop star to be destroyed by public ridicule . . .

*'The way things are going
They're gonna crucify me'*

. . . he sang hopefully on 'The Ballad Of John And Yoko' in May 1969, the last single that John and Paul recorded together. Then, in November 1969, John took another step towards martyrdom when he returned his MBE award to the Queen, accompanied by a note explaining that he was protesting against British involvement in the wars in Biafra and Vietnam, and protesting against 'Cold Turkey' slipping down the charts.

Bed-In For Peace

'Cold Turkey' was a single that John and Yoko had recorded with the Plastic Ono Band in October '69 — a group of musical friends whose membership changed with every recording that they made. John started the group at a time when differences of opinion between the Beatles were increasing as he kept coming up with songs that the other Beatles showed little enthusiasm for. The Plastic Ono Band's first single was 'Give Peace A Chance', a repetitive rock mantra recorded in the Queen Elizabeth Hotel in Montreal. John and Yoko had arrived in Montreal after flying round the world campaigning for peace by lying in bed for a week in various hotels. They called the campaign a 'Bed-In,' and when they reached Montreal, John and Yoko and various friends in the hotel room, including Timothy Leary and the Radha Krishna Temple, recorded this new anthem for the peace movement.

The second Plastic Ono single, 'Cold Turkey', was a much more frightening record, featuring Eric Clapton's howling lead guitar and lyrics that screamed of the pain of heroin withdrawal. Of course, John Lennon's pain went a lot deeper than taking a few drugs. The public were becoming more and more confused and alienated by John and Yoko's antics. Everything they did seemed to land them in the headlines or in the courtroom, and

C. Walter

Ono Band singles, used an hypnotic, constantly changing rock & roll rhythm to sing about the light that lay at the end of the tunnel:

'Instant Karma's gonna get you
Gonna look you right in the face
You better get yourself together darlin'
Join the human race'

'Instant Karma' was the first single that Phil Spector produced for Lennon, and out of the simplest ingredients they created a classic for the '70s. The lyrics summoned up instant enlightenment in the same way that the 20th Century has already given us instant coffee and instant pain-killers and Alan White's brilliant drumming drove the message home with a strangely fractured dance rhythm. But most of all it was Lennon's voice, multiplied into an entire choir by Spector's subtle use of echo, that transformed the song into something both magical and desperate.

Raw Emotion

Magic and desperation. Those two qualities have always been present in Lennon's work, and his greatest songs happened when the two became fused into one, as in 'Strawberry Fields Forever' or 'I Am The Walrus'. Lennon always used more raw emotion in his songs than Paul McCartney, who tended to create short stories or cameo portraits in song form. Many of John's Beatle songs, such as 'I'm A Loser' and 'Help!', had worked on two different levels. To the public they appeared to be good, bouncy songs in the boy-loses-girl tradition. You could tap your feet to the rhythm and the tune stayed in your head forever. But inside these songs, John was also screaming that his Beatle image was suffocating him. The Beatles seemed to be four cuddly boys-on-the-block, lively but harmless, and Lennon felt stifled:

'Although I laugh and I act like a clown
Beneath this mask I am wearing a frown'

('I'm A Loser')

The antics of John and Yoko were confusing, and sometimes pathetic, but it was a stage Lennon had to go through to tear up his old image in full public view, so that he could start again as John Lennon rather than John the Beatle.

The final ███████████████
when John ███████████████
from the ra███████████████
Dr. Arthur Ja███████████████
or therapy is███████████████
but Janov bel███████████████
selves from th███████████████
decisive bre███████████████
patients to r███████████████
difficult expe███████████████
patient would███████████████
liberation: a 'p███████████████

John Lenn███████████████
home. He ha███████████████
Aunt Mimi, who disapproved of his

BACK TRACK

1968, June: John's marriage to Cynthia breaks down. John and Yoko become good friends. October: John arrested for possession of cannabis in his Marylebone flat. November: John and Yoko release 'Two Virgins' album with cover photo of themselves naked.

1969, March: John marries Yoko in Gibraltar. They fly to Amsterdam for first 'Bed-In' for peace. July: John releases his first non-Beatle single 'Give Peace A Chance', recorded in Montreal. October: 'Cold Turkey' single released by Plastic Ono Band with Eric Clapton. November: John returns his MBE to protest against British involvement in Vietnam and Biafra wars. December: 'Live Peace In Toronto' album of Plastic Ono Band (with Clapton) performing at Toronto Rock & Roll Festival.

1970, February: John releases 'Instant Karma' single produced by Phil Spector.

March: Exhibition of John's lithographs seized by police on grounds of indecency. Summer: John and Yoko receive 'primal scream' therapy from Dr. Janov in Los Angeles. December: Paul files suit demanding dissolution of the Beatles. John releases 'John Lennon/Plastic Ono Band', announcing 'The dream is over'.

1971, March: 'Power To The People' single from John & POB. September: John releases 'Imagine' album. December: 'Happy Xmas (War Is Over)' single from John & POB & Harlem Community Choir.

1972, September: 'Some Time In New York City' (plus Live Jam) album by John and Yoko and Plastic Ono Band and Elephant's Memory.

1973, March: US Immigration Department order Lennon's deportation (because of 1968 drug conviction). Mayor of New York and *Wall Street Journal* protest decision. 'Pardon Lennon' movement launched. November: John releases 'Mind Games' album and single.

when a London art gallery exhibited John's drawings, they were — predictably — visited by the police and charged with displaying obscene art. At the same time, Lennon had a short haircut and auctioned off his long tresses to raise money for the Black Panthers. John and Yoko, meanwhile, were periodically climbing back into their bags and announcing that Hanratty, the last man to be executed in Britain, was really innocent and should be posthumously pardoned.

None of this endeared them to the

public. Vicious remarks were made against Yoko Ono, partly because she was a woman with a mind of her own, partly because she was Japanese; but also because people were puzzled and frightened by the games that she and John were playing in public. If you believed what the papers were saying, it was as though Lennon was determined to destroy what was left of his mass popularity. And yet, among all this pain and confusion, he was still making great music.

'Instant Karma', the best of the Plastic

Teddy-Boy looks and obsession with pop music, and when he was 18, his mother had been killed in a car crash. All this had left a deep scar on his mind, and then he had been catapulted into world-wide fame. For five Beatlemaniac years he had been struggling to keep his own personality together, while the world tried to turn him into a cuddly Mop Top.

Plastic Pop Idol

So John went through Janov's treatment, and out of his experiences he created the 'John Lennon/Plastic Ono Band' album, on which he sang about losing his mother, about being a plastic pop idol, and about a world that was ruled by greed and prejudice. The album was everything the Beatles weren't – it was hysterical, it was violent, it was politically committed – and it worked brilliantly. In the hands of a lesser artist these ideas might have been embarrassing or simply bizarre. Lennon made them work by using three separate areas of his life. He used the rawest form of rock music and screaming vocals – the same scream he had used on 'Twist And Shout' and 'Help!' – but now he screamed something real and personal, instead of an imaginary boy-loses-girl misery. He used his experience as a Beatle to explain, in 'Working-Class Hero', that although the world had made him an idol and a millionaire, he felt neither free nor happy, because he had been used. The Beatles, he was saying, had been played up as heroes and success stories to distract people from their own problems:

'Keep you doped with religion and sex
    and TV
And you think you're so clever and
    classless and free
But you're still . . . peasants as far as
    I can see'

He used the loss of his mother to describe a pain that every one of his audience had felt: the pain of separating from home and family, the pain of experiencing the world as a lonely and competitive place. And Lennon balanced all this pain against the love he had found with Yoko: the belief that people *could* reach each other and help each other, when free from illusions. Lennon was saying that the Beatles had been a beautiful dream, and it was now time to wake up.

It was a powerful statement, and for some it was too raw and aggressive to swallow easily. So Lennon's next album, 'Imagine' in October '71, repeated these beliefs, but phrased them in music that had more traditional beauty: lush strings and haunting melodies. The title song suggested discarding all the illusions which got in the way of world unity:

'Imagine there's no countries
It isn't hard to do
Nothing to kill or die for
And no religion too'

. . . but the words were set in a sensuously beautiful tune and cushioned by banks of violins, so it was hard to resist the spell of the music. 'Imagine' also contained the sinister 'How Do You Sleep?' – the most controversial song written by an ex-Beatle. To the average listener it amounted to a violent and sneering attack on Paul McCartney, who was criticised for making vacuous muzak, obeying all his wife's whims (something which Lennon had often been criticised for), and being a washed-out talent. The song even began with audience noises and violins tuning up – just like the beginning of 'Sgt. Pepper', the album on which the Beatles had pooled their personalities and musical talents most successfully.

The song seemed impossible to justify. It was John Lennon's carefully calculated attempt to hurt his former best friend as deeply as possible, and it made nonsense of Lennon's preaching about love and harmony. Yet for two reasons, it worked. Musically it was brilliant, regardless of what it was saying. The eerie violin riffs, one of George Harrison's most menacing guitar solos, Nicky Hopkins' funky piano, and Lennon's sneering vocal, were combined by Spector's adroit production into an elegant musical nightmare. More importantly, the song was Lennon's way of pointing out he was still human, and could still be overwhelmed by irrational and spiteful emotions. John Lennon still contained a mass of contradictions, and he tried to understand them by exposing them – rather than coming on like a glib salesman for peace and love.

Musical Godfather

After 'Imagine', John and Yoko settled down in Greenwich Village as permanent members of the New York scene, and in many ways John created an American version of his life as a Beatle. Allen Klein was his financial adviser, doing Brian Epstein's old job. Phil Spector was his producer and musical godfather, the part once played by George Martin. And his constant companion and collaborator was Yoko, instead of Paul. Lennon wanted to experience a different scene, and he and Yoko were also trying to find Kyoko, Yoko's daughter from her first marriage who had been brought up by Yoko's divorced husband. They dedicated several songs to the lost child, and the search caused them a lot of pain and frustration.

Out of their new life, John and Yoko created 'Some Time In New York City' released in September '72, a musical diary about the people they met and the issues they were involved with. The album cover resembled the front page of the *New York Times,* and John and Yoko attempted to write an anthem for every radical cause that caught their eye. Women's Lib, Angela Davies, the Attica Prison shooting, the British troops in Northern Ireland – everyone got a song, and yet the total effect was curiously empty. 'John Lennon/Plastic Ono Band' and 'Imagine' had

worked because the politics and the ideas had flowed from John's personal experiences, never sounding like a newspaper headline or a glib slogan. But on 'Some Time In New York City', John and Yoko seemed to be echoing every liberal slogan they had heard in New York's radical-chic penthouses. It was hard to believe they knew or cared much about their subjects, especially since their lyrics were so facile and they managed to somehow preach passionate support for at least 10 different causes at once.

Lennon seemed to realise this, for 'Mind Games', his next album released in November '73, concentrated again on his own thoughts and emotions. Compared with his first post-Beatle recording, 'Mind Games' was a very mellow piece of work. Instead of screams or musical hysteria, Lennon used a more delicate approach to instrumentation, and the lyrics dissolved political struggles and the fight to preserve one's balance into images of continual cosmic evolution:

'So keep on playing those mind games
    forever
Doing the ritual dance in the sun
Millions of mind guerillas
Putting their soul power to the karmic
    wheel'

Pushing Forward Boundaries

A handful of innovators have made the story of pop music something more important than a list of hit parades and a museum of teenage fashions. By pushing forward the boundaries of what could be expressed in song, how it could be said in music, and the relationship between songs and society, they have made pop chronicle the anger, the ambitions, and the fantasies of millions of young people.

On these counts it is arguable that John Lennon was the most important innovator of the late '60s and early '70s. He explored whole areas of psychology, politics, and personal fantasy, without losing contact with the roots of pop or with his audience. And he backed up everything he sang with the way he lived. His voice remained as earthy and exciting as when he sang 'Twist And Shout', and he has created hundreds of good tunes, from 'Please Please Me' to 'Mind Games'.

Since the break-up of the Beatles, Paul, George and Ringo have all continued making fine records – but within a narrow range of music and emotions. They've given their followers a lot of pleasure, but few surprises. John has been the most ambitious, the most unstable, and the most interesting. A clear thread of anger, idealism, and rock & roll has run right through his antics and his different albums. As he summed it all up on the single 'Instant Karma':

'Why in the world are we here?
Surely not to live in pain and fear
Why on earth are you there?
When you're everywhere
Come and get your share!'

THE ANIMALS

Dezzo Hoffman

The Beatles' meteoric rise to fame just over 10 years ago ushered in a new era for British pop music. Out went Cliff Richard, Hank B. Marvin, the Shadows, Billy Fury, Marty Wilde and their many rather feeble imitators. In came the Mersey Sound and, hot on its heels, rhythm & blues — English-style. Looking back, it's hard not to be amazed by the excesses and world-wide trends inspired by this sudden change in musical fashions.

Following his successes with the Beatles, manager Brian Epstein quickly got most of the top-line Liverpool bands under contract — well before the London promoters and record company executives had really begun to grasp what was going on. The only potential challengers to the Beatles at that time were the London-based, blues-orientated Rolling Stones, and the promoters' initial reaction was to rush out and start signing up any bunch of young hopefuls that could fumble their way through a 12-bar blues and pronounce a few revered names like Muddy Waters and Howlin' Wolf.

Virtually overnight, hundreds of so-called 'blues' bands sprang up. Partly, it was an attempt by the powers-that-be in the music industry to cash in on the phenomenal success of the Rolling Stones, but it was also a genuine recognition of the sudden awakening of interest in the black musical styles that had launched the whole rock & roll explosion 10 years earlier.

Syndication International

Predictably enough, many of the bands that flourished briefly in this hot-house atmosphere were pretty dire. Some, like the Kinks and the Who (both initially promoted as R&B bands), were very good indeed, but had little or nothing to do with any part of the blues tradition. But the British blues boom was never a total fraud, because among the many promoters and musicians busily jumping on the bandwagon there were at least a handful of musicians who did have a very real love for the blues — and also had the considerable musical talents necessary to do any real justice to one of the most disciplined and demanding forms of music. The London suburbs, with their curious blend of sophistication and provincial funk, produced the Rolling Stones and the Yardbirds (then featuring Eric Clapton), two of the bands that went on to dominate the British R&B movement. Only one other band came anywhere near them. They were called the Animals, and they came from Newcastle upon Tyne.

Wild Stage Act

Like the Stones and the Yardbirds, the Animals came up the hard way. They started out as the Alan Price Combo, playing a ramshackle Newcastle club called the Downbeat. Gradually they built up a fanatical local following, and moved to the larger and plushier Club A Go Go. The wildness of their stage act prompted the nickname 'Animals' and, by the time they came down to try and make it in London in January 1964, the name had stuck. In those days the band was a five-man outfit, with Eric Burdon's vocals backed up by Alan Price on keyboards,

111

Bryan 'Chas' Chandler on bass, Hilton Valentine on guitar, and John Steel on drums. All five were Newcastle born and bred, and their Northern working-class background helped add the conviction that so many of their middle-class Southern rivals sadly lacked.

Inverted Snobbery

There was always something intrinsically phoney and ridiculous about the attempts made by so many financially secure, white, English, middle-class kids to reproduce the music that had been born out of the poverty, despair and alienation of the American negroes. After 13 years of uninterrupted Conservative government Britain was stagnating, and the kids were heartily bored. The middle-class dream was rapidly going sour, and there was a lot of inverted snobbery in the air. Youngsters with impeccable grammar school and college backgrounds, who'd never seen the inside of a terraced house, suddenly developed working-class accents and ritualistically adopted a number of anti middle-class attitudes. But the Animals never had to fake it. They knew what it was like to be on the bottom looking up. More importantly, they really cared about the music. Their enthusiasm and their understanding gave them an emotional feel for the blues that was totally convincing.

Like most other R&B bands at the time, the Animals built their repertoire around re-workings of songs by black American artists like Chuck Berry, Bo Diddley, Ray Charles, John Lee Hooker, Jimmy Reed and Slim Harpo — all of whom had become immensely fashionable in the cellar-clubs of Britain. But the Animals were far more eclectic in their approach than most of their contemporaries, and never subscribed to the grotesque purism that was so common at that time. Their first single, 'Baby Let Me Take You Home', was a re-working of a traditional blues number called 'Baby Don't You Tear My Clothes' but, as they freely admitted at the time, their direct inspiration was a version called 'Baby Let Me Follow You Down', recorded by a then unknown white folk singer named Bob Dylan. The single was moderately successful, and in July 1964 they followed it with another old blues tune that Dylan had already recorded, 'The House Of The Rising Sun'. The record got to no. 1 on both sides of the Atlantic, and is reputed to have sold over four million copies. If it didn't, it certainly deserved to. Burdon's aggressively emotional vocal backed up by Alan Price's driving organ had in fact produced one of the greatest singles ever to come out of Britain. As the story goes this version of the song was so stunning that it provided Dylan himself with all he needed to move into rock music.

Now established as a top-line national band, the Animals embarked on a series of successful tours, both in Britain and abroad, and 'The House Of The Rising Sun' was followed, over the next two years, by a string of singles hits: 'I'm Crying' (September, 1964); 'Don't Let Me Be Misunderstood' (February, 1965); 'Bring It On Home To Me' (April, 1965); 'We Got To Get Out Of This Place' (July, 1965); 'It's My Life' (November, 1965); 'Inside Looking Out' (February, 1966) and 'Don't Bring Me Down' (June, 1966). None of these records reached no. 1 in Britain, and their much underrated second album, 'Animal Tracks' (1965), was ignored. In 1965 Alan Price left the group to pursue a solo career and was replaced by Dave Rowberry. In 1966, by which time John Steel had also left, Eric Burdon disbanded the group much to everyone's amazement.

New Animals

At the end of 1966, Burdon reappeared with a totally new line-up under the name 'Eric Burdon and the Animals'. The new band enjoyed some measure of chart success in Britain with 'Help Me Girl' (November, 1966), 'Good Times' (September, 1967), and 'San Franciscan Nights' (November, 1967); but the aggressive energy of the old Animals was gone for good. Burdon himself had undergone a complete change of attitude —

Rex Features

S.K.R. Photos

his old love for the blues was now over-shadowed by his adoption of flower power's peace and love credo. In December 1968, after producing 'Love Is' (ironically one of the best albums to emerge from the flower power era) Burdon announced his intention of forsaking music for a career in films. He resurfaced briefly in 1970 backed up by War (a funky black band that has since pursued a successful 'solo' career), and in 1971 recorded a rather patchy album with Jimmy Wither-spoon. In August 1973 he reappeared for three sensational nights at London's Marquee Club with an unnamed three-piece backing group — and what the future holds for him is anybody's guess. Certainly, he seems to have no intention of remaining idle, and with several projects he wants to follow up, he could well re-emerge as a star again in the '70s.

Driving Excitement

During their comparatively brief career the Animals were enormously influential. They were as good a live band in their time as the Stones, and in the studio they had Mickie Most's inspired pro-duction to help them reproduce the driving excitement of their stage act. Eric Burdon was (and, judging by his recent appearances, still is) the greatest interpretative singer England has pro-duced. Rod Stewart is the only other British singer who rivals Burdon's amazing ability to take other people's material and mold it into something com-pletely original. Unfortunately Burdon, Price, and the other members of the group lacked the songwriting talents of noted contemporaries like Lennon/McCartney and Jagger/Richard, and Burdon's efforts as a songwriter after the group's split in 1966 only served to emphasise his limitations in that field.

Unlike the Stones, the Animals never managed to move away from their blues roots and establish some sort of personal identity for themselves. First and last they were *the* great British blues band, but as the Beatles, Dylan and the Stones pushed pop music into an era of greater intellectual complexity, the blues boom died and the Animals died with it. Eric Burdon and Alan Price, though, have both kept trucking on with their respective solo careers. Chas Chandler (who managed Hendrix and now manages Slade) has been a major behind-the-scenes influence on pop music's development in recent years.

But to most young people today the Animals are just history — one of the many bands that never quite managed to achieve lasting success. The Animals deserve more than that. Without their talent and their integrity, the R&B move-ment in this country would have been a much shabbier affair. They had a lot of guts and a lot of soul, and there are plenty of people around who still remember them with affection and respect. Maybe they weren't 'superstars', but the '60s would never have been the same without them.

THE KINKS: Suburban Lads Make Good

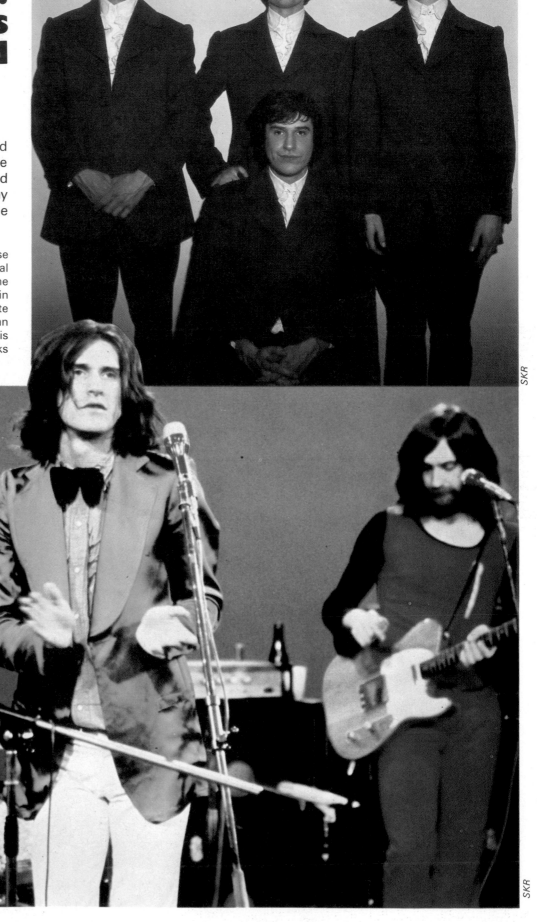

From 'Louie Louie' to 'Celluloid Heroes' by way of 'The Village Green Preservation Society' and 'Lola' is a strange journey for any group, let alone one with the unlikely name of the Kinks.

A further irony is that for a group whose material is so defiantly English, critical success came first in America, despite the fact that, apart from an abortive tour in 1965, they didn't perform there until late in 1969. One result of their American reputation is that a lot of Kinks' material is only available in America. So are the Kinks

SKR

SKR

114

Redferns

The original line-up of the Kinks, above, from left to right, Ray Davies, Pete Quaife, Mick Avory and Dave Davies, looks a lot different from their recent line-up on the right.

a recording group rather than a performing group? In part yes, though their live performances do have a certain charm.

The reason for the long interval between tours in the States was a ban by the American Federation of Musicians on the Kinks for 'unprofessional conduct'. By all accounts the standards of their American tours since then haven't been noticeably any higher: the much repeated — and reported — highlight of their '71 tour was an apparently drunk Ray Davies giving up even attempting to remember the words of songs he'd written, in order to concentrate on falling over as many amplifiers as possible.

But if the Kinks' reputation isn't based upon their live performances (unless you want to take 'the Kinks-ought-to-be-sloppy-performers' line) their recordings show a marked contrast, John Mendelsohn, an American critic, has acclaimed Ray Davies' 'unique comic/humanist vision', while his colleague Ken Emerson points out that 'from the beginning in 1963, the

SKR

Kinks have relied on the most worn out rock & roll clichés.' Two critics who obviously disagree. But no, for Emerson ends up by pointing out that their albums include some of the most consistently earthy numbers in rock music.

Leader Of The Kinks

At the centre of this mass of contradictions is Ray Davies — songwriter, singer and leader of the Kinks — the man whose obsessions have charted the course the Kinks have followed since the days when they were the Ravens, a well-dressed, if musically inept R&B group on the deb circuit in 1963. The Kinks' career is as strange as their reputation. Like a lot of the R&B groups, they started out at art school playing a mixture of Sonny Terry and Chuck Berry-type numbers. Their first record, a very Beatles-influenced version of Little Richard's 'Long Tall Sally' failed miserably, as did their second, 'You Do Something To Me'. However, their third single, 'You Really Got Me', marked the beginning of Ray Davies' songwriting career and the Kinks' prominence in the British (and world) charts for a couple of years.

The Kinks, it seemed, had it made. If only Mick Avory, Peter Quaife, Dave Davies and brother Ray could keep cool and churn out those chunka-chunka-chunk songs, everything would be alright. However, after seven hits from the same mould – as Ray laconically put it, 'Those three chords are part of my life, G, F, Bb; G, F, Bb' – the Kinks, and Ray in particular wanted to develop.

In 1966 came the first indication of the group's change of direction. At a time when the rest of the world was glorying in the idea of 'Swinging London', and Britain was smugly recognising her lead in fashion and pop music, the Kinks with 'Well Respected Man' and 'Dedicated Follower Of Fashion' chose to question the whole giddy scene.

Amazing though they were at the time, these songs, and others, like 'House In The Country', 'Session Man' and 'Exclusive Residence For Sale' (from 'Face To Face', their first concept album) can in retrospect be seen only as transitional. They showed that Ray Davies was quite sure of what he *didn't* like but, as yet, in a superficial and negative way. It wasn't until 'Sunny Afternoon', 'Dead End Street' and the glorious 'Waterloo Sunset' of May, 1967, that Ray Davies began to examine the world around him in depth.

For a while the change in direction seemed a smart move, the hits kept coming, although at a slower rate. But 'Days', a hit in September 1968, was to mark the group's end as consistent hitmakers. In part the reason was that Ray Davies was into other projects as well. 'Face To Face', 'Live At Kelvin Hall' and 'Something Else' (not released in Britain), the three albums of the period '66–'68, found the Kinks still writing three-minute songs, but they were no longer purely aimed at specific audiences, either

in the Hit Parade or the underground, as the live album demonstrated. It consisted not of lengthy solos by the group but of one long 30-minute scream of applause by the audience, over which the Kinks could barely be heard. And it wasn't an accident, as the note 'produced under the musical direction of Ray Davies' made clear.

Also around this time Davies was writing music for the film *The Virgin Soldiers* and as the Kinks were no longer performing very frequently, Ray's brother Dave decided to branch out on his own as well. His first single, 'Death Of A Clown' (on which he was backed by the Kinks) was a successful no. 3 in Britain. He planned a solo album but when the follow-up singles flopped, as did the Kinks' of this period, the album was scrapped.

'Something Else'

By late '68, despite their absence from the charts for some time, the Kinks had amassed a lot of material similar to the 'Something Else' album. It wasn't released at the time because their recording company was still primarily interested in singles; the theory being that if they couldn't sell singles they certainly couldn't sell albums.

The songs on 'Face To Face' and 'Something Else' had mostly been topical. On '(The Kinks Are) The Village Green Preservation Society', their next album, Ray Davies began his long, nostalgic look back at a make-believe, Edwardian Britain when life was comfortable — if you were middle class that is. 'Village Green' was a combination of a search for personal security in the past and a suggestion that all was peace and paradise around the village greens of England. Its follow-up, 'Arthur (Or The Decline Of The British Empire)' was again a look back, but this time the past was seen not as a haven but as a burden on the present, like the bric-a-brac that fills the houses — the 'Shangri Las' — of the nation.

Having summed up the pressures of the past, the Kinks next moved to a description of their own situation as pop stars in 'Lola Versus The Powermen And The Moneygo-round'. This album was produced when the group were preparing to leave the Pye label and their old managers. The old theme of 'why are they doing this to me?' reappears but is more objective. There is a much broader view of people's problems in 'Lola' than in 'I'm Not Like Everybody Else' for instance, which tended to be very personal. The songs paint complex and more ambiguous pictures, like 'Lola' of whom Ray finally sings 'I'm glad I'm a man and so is Lola'. Just quite what that means belongs in the mind of the listener. In career terms, however, the album and its hit single marked a new lease of life for the group.

The Kinks' last album for Pye was a soundtrack for the film *Percy*, but it was very much of a stop-gap and hardly met up to the group's usual standards. It wasn't until 'Muswell Hillbillies', the group's first RCA album that they moved forward again.

By this time John Dalton had replaced Peter Quaife, and John Gosling had joined on piano. The group's sound was by now much fuller but their lyrics continued to focus on social problems. Whereas 'Arthur' had been about the burdens of the past; 'Muswell Hillbillies' was about the burdens of the present. The villains were the property developers and 'The People In Gray' who Davies accuses of destroying working-class values; the only defence left being traditional — 'whatever the situation . . . have a cuppa tea'. He sings hopefully and (very ambiguously) to the possibility of retreating into fantasies of living 'In Oklahoma USA with Shirley Jones and Gordon McRae'.

'Everybody In Showbiz', the latest Kinks' album to date is an uneasy marriage of the themes of the 'Lola' album and 'Muswell Hillbillies'. It deals with a pop group's life on the road for the most part, but only in 'Celluloid Heroes' do the lyrics get a lift from the drudgery of the situation, into an escapist look at a fantasy world with a need for some kind of release from monotony and routine. A quote from the album: 'If life's for living, what's living for?'

In 'Celluloid Heroes' he describes 'the fantasy world of celluloid heroes and villains who never really die', and at the same time he reminds us that 'Everybody's a dreamer, everybody's a star, and everybody's in movies, it doesn't matter who you are'. As usual the song is very ambiguous; Ray Davies both describes the need for fantasy that entertainment provides for all of us and at the same time suggests that we are all stars in our own right, or could be if we could discover what living is all about and put that into practice.

These later albums which oscillate between bitterness and bitchiness, attempt to contextualise the situation in which Ray Davies sees the Kinks and their audience. However, they fail to come over as much as the earlier singles 'You Really Got Me' and 'All Of The Day And All Of The Night' and the mellow songs of the 'Waterloo Sunset' period.

Melodramatic Performances

Like John Lennon, Ray Davies has a need for his audience to identify with his pain. Thus the Kinks' live performances (and even their records at times) are often rather melodramatic. There's an over-riding feeling that the audience is expected to adore and admire, regardless of the performance given. This image is a difficult one to sustain and the Kinks, as they are now, are not an easy group to like or respect. But our memories serve us well and it's easy to remember them for their great songs, and in his own way, Ray Davies lists with Lennon and Townshend, as an equally important critic of past, present and future who still manages to inject a bitter-sweet humour into the Kinks' music. The group has always been more of a vehicle for Ray Davies than anything else, but the Kinks have carved themselves a niche as the most 'English' of rock bands.

George Harrison:
The Mystic Maestro

Neither baby-faced beauty nor arrogant sex symbol, George was just the quiet one in the middle . . . playing in the spaces left by two giant egos.

In the touring days of the Beatles, George used to stand half-way between John and Paul and get on with playing his guitar. Then one of them would end the verse and George would stride over to join the other one for the chorus. He'd walk purposefully backwards, playing an economical guitar solo and perhaps throwing in a couple of dance steps. And then he started to write the occasional song for their albums. At first they were run-of-the-mill love songs that the others did better, but then he started turning out strange songs. On first hearing they often sounded normal enough, but . . . whoever started a song with 'If I needed someone to love you're the one that I'd be thinking of'? Soon after this, the Beatles' music became more complex, and as if on cue, out stepped the quiet one to show them the way. George had become interested in Eastern religion, and the next album, 'Revolver', duly marked a watershed in the Beatles' career. 'Revolver' was the only album on which the Beatles ever managed group unity in a serious way, before it they were fun, after it they were each on their own.

George's interest in the East had been a major influence in this shake-up. He was introduced to it by his wife Patti and the two of them went into it seriously. They read and they talked and they meditated, and then they started to spread the word among their friends. Lennon had got really caught up in it, and even Paul's contributions on 'Revolver' had a mystical aura

George Harrison with his wife, ex-actress and model Patti Boyd.

during the filming of *Let It Be* after a huge row with Paul. And although he came back again the problems were not resolved. Basically these centred on George's feeling that he wasn't sufficiently recognised as a writer and musician by Paul. George had just come back from the States, where he had been jamming with many musicians just for the fun of it. The co-operation of these musicians, George said, "contrasted dramatically with the superior attitude which for years Paul had shown towards me musically. In normal circumstances I had not let this attitude bother me and to get a peaceful life I had always let him have his own way, even when this meant that songs which I had composed were not being recorded. When I came back from the States . . . I was in a very happy frame of mind, but I quickly discovered that I was up against the same old Paul . . . In front of the cameras, as we were actually being filmed, Paul started to 'get at' me about the way I was playing."

An Equal Songwriter

This ill-feeling between George and Paul was preserved on the film. At one point Paul says "I always seem to be annoying you." George replies, "All right I'll play whatever you want me to play, or I won't play at all if you don't want me to play." The Beatles' old friend in Hamburg, Astrid Kemp, perhaps put her finger on the background to all this when she observed that George was younger than the others and it took him longer to grow up. Paul had always been something of a father-figure to George and George found it difficult to escape some sort of inferiority complex without over-reacting. Paul, on the other hand, found it difficult to accept that George was by this time his equal as a musician. George was writing as many if not more songs than John and Paul but he wasn't getting an equal share of the cake.

The songs he *was* allowed to record on the Apple albums definitely showed that he was flowering as a songwriter.

His two main themes — love and society — were the usual ones, but what made his contributions different was approaching the subjects from a radically new angle.

The love songs on the Apple albums differ appreciably in feel from any others written at the time. George was not only concerned with the complexity of hang-ups created by Western views of *time* and *change*: loving forever, possessiveness, the inability to communicate. He was also concerned with getting across a simple statement of what he was feeling, of saying, in effect, that if *he* opened himself, then that at least was a start:

> *'You're asking me, will my love grow?*
> *I don't know, I don't know . . .'*

('Something' from 'Abbey Road')

. . . there was no truth in anything else, no need to invoke the past or future to satisfy the present. This notion relates directly to the central reference point of George's Eastern vision: the crucial need

that he never again tried to capture. George's three songs on 'Revolver' marked his emergence as a definite third force, a factor — given the already strained, creative relationship between John and Paul — that was bound to loosen and eventually break up the group.

For a time though, everything went well. Lennon was heavily into acid, George into his enlightenment. For a short time, Paul and George Martin had the group and its talents more or less at their disposal. So arrived 'Sgt. Pepper'. On that album, George had just the one song, 'Within You Without You', which lyrically defined his general position:

> *'When you've seen beyond yourself*
> *Then you may find, peace of mind,*
> *is waiting there'*

Musically, it was George's last attempt at full-scale Indian music. From then on he

began to lyrically explore Western themes through an Eastern-mediated world-view; and in the process create a rock music heavily influenced by Indian moods and tones. 'Within You Without You' had a George Harrison stamp on it, as did John Lennon's contributions. It had become clear that the two of them would not be content to follow Paul's ideas as to the group's direction.

As George's own musical ideas took shape, the last years with the Beatles must have become increasingly frustrating for him; for no matter how friendly members of a group are, there's only so much space on an album. The chance to create tension between songs, to create interacting moods, is something that can't easily be shared. The Beatle albums became less than the sum of their parts; a series of conflicting tracks.

George in fact walked out of the Beatles

Camera Press

BACK TRACK

Born February 25th, 1943.
1966, January: Marries Patti Boyd.
1967, February: George and Patti's first contact with the Maharishi.

1968, February: Studies with the Maharishi in India. November: 'Wonderwall' album.
1969, June: 'Electronic Sounds' album.
1970, September: 'All Things Must Pass' album.
1971, January: 'My Sweet Lord' single. April: Co-writes Ringo's single 'It Don't Come Easy'. July: 'Bangla Desh' single.

August: Organised concert for Bangla Desh in Madison Square Garden, NY.
1972, January: 'Bangla Desh' concert album.
1973, May: 'Give Me Love' single. June: 'Living In The Material World' album. George helps out Ringo on his album 'Ringo' and co-writes the single 'Photograph'.

Left: George Harrison was the only Beatle to attend the opening party for Apple Studios. Right: George and sundry other musicians playing at the Bangla Desh concert in Madison Square Garden, New York, in August of '71.

to escape the self. Thus the lament to our society in 'I Me Mine':

*'All through the day
I me mine I me mine I me mine
All through the night
I me mine I me mine I me mine'*

The sentiments here are spelt out less abstractly in songs like 'Piggies' and 'Savoy Truffle', which remind the listener that George's 'vision' indicates only *two* ways. One way, and 'the sweat will fill your head'; the other way, and 'little darling, the smile's returning to the faces . . . here comes the sun'. Through this period it became apparent that George's voice and his style of guitar-playing perfectly matched his subject-matter. The voice is thin, lacks arrogance, and can float high above the musical ground, forever seeming to reach forward. The guitar-style is similar; long, keening notes hanging in the air — sad rather than painful — above the rhythms flowing beneath.

Shot In The Arm

In May 1970, the Beatles became independent of each other musically and George went solo at a time when the idea-content of rock music clearly needed a positive shot in the arm. The essentially negative business of clearing the ground, dynamiting illusions and generally painting pictures of a world gone mad, had been done in the great creative breakthrough of the mid-'60s. Now, the positive side needed a helping hand — but where was the positive side to be found? The Beatles themselves had always been about enthusiasm and infinite possibilities, all the way from Lennon's sick humour to 'tomorrow never knows'. Now, George in particular seemed to have worked out for himself a way to approach reality through his music that neither contradicted the earlier dreams nor ignored them.

The first evidence of this was the single 'My Sweet Lord', which swept to the top of the charts on both sides of the Atlantic. The album, 'All Things Must Pass', was released a few months later in September 1970. George had spent a lot of time and money on it, using many of the best musicians around and Phil Spector as co-producer. Clapton and Dave Mason helped out on guitar, Bobby Whitlock, Billy Preston and others on keyboards — the list is a long one. The result was a technically flawless record, faultlessly performed. Ultimately though, it would stand or fall on the songs, and, with one exception, these were George's sole responsibility. Those who thought he could only manage two or three good songs a year got a surprise. The 16 on 'All Things Must Pass' were almost uniformly good, melodic and interesting.

This album alone would have been enough to establish George on a level with John and Paul as solo performers, but the underlying philosophic vision took him one step higher, making the album one of the rock masterpieces of the '70s. This vision

is so consistent within itself that it comes almost as a surprise to find it consistent with little else. It's like living in an upside-down room — it doesn't seem strange until you look out of the window. Then suddenly everything in the room acquires a new significance. You begin to wonder how the table doesn't fall off the ceiling, and why people come through the door backwards with their feet in the air. You begin to wonder what, in fact, is reality.

His love-songs on side 2 of the album emphasise his strong feelings about the individuality of people and free will, even though the two do merge into one. On 'Run Of The Mill' George states:

*'No one around you will carry the blame
for you
No one around you will love you today
and throw it all away'*

. . . for ultimately

*'Only you'll arrive at your own made end
With no one but yourself to be offended
It's you that decides . . .'*

Not that George himself is that strong. In 'Let It Down' he worries all the time about other people's opinions of him. But he knows his feelings and recognises his weaknesses, hoping that sharing them will eliminate them to a degree. Compassion is at the heart of his songs.

Love between two people is also part of something wider to George, part of the way of approaching living here in the material world. The rest of 'All Things Must Pass' illustrates both this wider vision and the control George has over all the components of his music. The basic philosophic vision underpins it all, expressed not as philosophy but as a series of 'moods' occasionally illuminated by flashes of lyrical insight.

To have found strength in the truth that nothing is certain and that nothing survives, a truth that is central to all Eastern ways and so foreign to the West, is a measure of the distance George has travelled spiritually. That he can convincingly communicate that strength in the rock idiom is a mark of the distance he has travelled as a musician.

Occasionally, on 'All Things Must Pass', the underlying Hindu world-view breaks surface, almost as a preface to his second album, 'Living In The Material World'. 'The Art Of Dying', for instance, deals with re-incarnation in words that make little allowance for Western sensibilities.

'Do you believe me?', George sings hopefully. The final track, 'Hear Me Lord' is a straight-ahead prayer, not a multi-religious pop anthem like 'My Sweet Lord', but an act of devotion, of total commitment:

*'Help me Lord please to rise a little
higher
Help me Lord please to burn out this
desire'*

In a society bombarded with sexual aspirations, that plea is likely to find few sympathetic ears. As a song though, 'Hear Me Lord' succeeds because it conveys in

the music a mood far wider than the lyrics suggest. The old Harrison-Spector formula of the relentless flow cascading down to flow yet again, has never been done better.

Then, in the summer of 1973, came another carefully structured album. 'Living In The Material World' had taken two and a half years to make, and this time offered a specifically Hindu view of the world. Once again though, the music transcends the particular. It charts George's journey of self-discovery, starting with the simple invocation: 'give me love, give me peace on earth'. From there George works his way through illuminations and limitations, Beatle hassles and drug hassles, to a calm acceptance of what he thinks life in the material world must be all about.

Rolling Majesty

Musically, the album sounds like a river, from the tumbling stream of 'Give Me Love' through free-flow and rolling majesty and down to the oceanic serenity of 'That Is All'. The music and the vision once again fit each other perfectly. At the time of its release, in fact, many critics were prompted to suggest that George had at last made a real connection between rock music and social commitment.

George has always been stereotyped as the Beatle who was most concerned with money, but an early anecdote of the Cavern days tends to undermine this. A girl waiting outside didn't have the money to get in. George slipped a few shillings to the Cavern bouncer, saying ''give'er this and don't tell'er I gave it to yer''.

In the later days of success he has given away money to what he thinks worthy causes, less perhaps than Lennon but with rather more care and with less publicity.

But the most obvious thing has been his organisation of the Concert for Bangla Desh, which began with a visit from his old friend Ravi Shankar —

*'My friend came to me with sadness
in his eyes
Said he wanted help before his
country died'*

George spent a long time getting the concert together. He knew it was important. Rock had made a lot of noise about the way things were going, but how much had it done? The sale of tickets for the concert and the subsequent record and film receipts raised vital funds for war-torn Bangla Desh.

For the concert George coaxed both Eric Clapton and Bob Dylan out of their semi-retirement. The music was an amazing success due to George's insistence on proper rehearsals, but the concert was much more than that. It was described in a music paper as 'a brief incandescent revival of all that was best about the '60s . . . the magnificence of the music and the selflessness of the motives were proof that the art and the spirit are still alive. And the audience and the musicians and the producers were respectful.'

And George was still the quiet one in the middle.

This Is...
TOM JONES

Fleetway Publications

It's ironic that Tom Jones' career should have begun with an appearance on British television's *Ready Steady Go!,* for he was the antithesis of everything the programme represented to most of its viewers.

By 1965 *Ready Steady Go!* was at its peak, and for countless kids the weekend really *did* start there. School and work were over, and while they dried their hair, pressed their clothes, and checked out their new shoes on the latest dance steps, they'd keep one eye on the TV screen to make sure they weren't shaping their hair into last week's style, wearing last week's colour, or tracing out last week's dance in the wrong shoes. *Ready, Steady Go!* belonged to the Mods.

So what was Tom Jones doing up there on a tiny stage surrounded by these snappy kids who wanted to see Georgie Fame or the Who? Mods were neat, mostly tiny it seemed, and very cool. Jones was a hefty brute who threw himself about and worked up a sweat that stained his shirt. He must've disliked the kids just about as much as they loathed him, but he had a couple of things going for him: a great voice and a good song — and three weeks after it entered the charts, 'It's Not Unusual' was at no. 1.

Tom Jones' success with that song at that time is indicative of two things: the decline of the record buying public's interest in groups, and his manager's sharpness in spotting this trend. In 1964 only three solo performers had made no. 1 in the British charts: Cilla Black (twice), Roy Orbison (three times) and Sandie Shaw (once). The Top 20 was dominated by groups, 13 of which topped the charts at least once. 1965, though, was different. In April, Cliff Richard returned to the top for the first time in over two years, to be followed by singers such as Roger Miller, Jackie Trent, Sandie Shaw, Elvis Presley, Ken Dodd, Sonny and Cher, the Seekers, and even the Walker Brothers . . . all emphasising the enormous changes from only the year before.

The Beatles, and the group boom of the early '60s, had wrecked the careers — or at least broken the chart success — of most of Britain's male pop singers. Adam Faith only made the Top 20 three times after 1962, Mark Wynter twice, Eden Kane once, and Marty Wilde, Craig Douglas,

Lonnie Donegan, Jimmy Justice, John Leyton had no further hits. Only Cliff Richard survived and, for another three years, Billy Fury. So once the public's overwhelming infatuation with groups had subsided, there wasn't much left to offer as an alternative . . . which is where Gordon Mills comes in, with Tom Jones.

Jones had been around for a long time — in Wales, that is. Born in Tretorest, Glamorganshire, in 1940, he was still hanging out in pubs drinking under age when rock & roll hit the valleys in 1956. His 'career' started with bar-room singing — and enough brawling to break his nose a few times — and he'd give everything that was popular from the big throat — first for beer, then pound notes. Since Welshmen, especially in groups, probably make up the greatest nation of amateur singers in the world, Jones must have had something powerful going for him to get the rest of the boozers to shut up enough to join in at the right places, if not just listen.

Tommy Woodward

At that time he was calling himself Tommy Scott. Tommy was real enough, but Scott was just what he figured to be a good name for a rock & roller. Not that his real name was Jones — like half the families in his street it was Woodward. The Jones bit came later, an invention of Gordon Mills (who subsequently transformed Gerry Dorsey into Engelbert Humperdinck), and it wasn't chosen to go down well with the folks back home, but to exploit the enormous success of the film of the same name.

Scott, however, was stuck in Pontypridd bars and working mens' clubs until long after rock & roll died. He sang on through the early '60s — switching from the Top 10 to old rockers, and then to even older songs. In those days though, neither his repertoire, his voice, nor the extravagant movements he began to jerk and bump together, were enough to make him a living — especially with the wife and kid he'd had with him since he was 16. So he worked as a casual labourer during the day, and later when he was a star and people said he looked more like a hod-carrier than anything else, that was the reason why . . . he *was* a hod-carrier.

When the groups broke out of Liverpool in 1963, and every town with more than three strummers and a fourth inhabitant

who could keep time threw up its own pop group, it didn't make a whole lot of difference to Tom's music. All he did was pull a few locals together to back him, and carry right on singing the way he always had done. He knew it made one difference, though: it made it harder to sell himself outside his home town — and that was the only way he was ever going to make it.

Gordon Mills, meanwhile, had been playing with a couple of groups. First, the Morton Frazer Harmonica Gang — Larry Adler with laughs — and later the Viscounts, who had had two small hits in 1960 and '61 with 'Shortnin' Bread' and a cover of 'Who Put The Bomp?'. By 1964, though, he'd given up performing to try his hand at songwriting, and during this phase he went to see Mandy Rice-Davies' act at a club in Pontypridd, but she didn't show. However, Tommy Scott did, knocked Mills out, and believed enough of what Mills told him after the show to move up to London with him. He'd been there before the big break, and had even made some tapes for Joe Meek, with his group the Senators, in 1963. But afterwards Meek hadn't called.

At first, the A&R men that saw Jones didn't display the same foresight as Mills had done. They wanted groups, and Tom Jones and the Squires didn't count. Besides this his image was all wrong – he was too old at 24, his face was battered and he was altogether the wrong size and shape: 'It's not that I don't like his voice, it's just that . . . Next please.' Eventually, however, Mills managed to get him a contract with Decca. Jones recorded 'Chills And Fever', it was released as his first single, and it bombed.

During this period Jones stayed alive by running up Mills' overdraft and making demos. Naturally he made demos of Mills' own songs, so when Mills wrote 'It's Not Unusual' with Les Reed – hoping to place it with an already established female singer and thus stand a good chance of making it a hit – Tom sang it for the demo. His instant liking for the song was clear in the way he performed it. All a demo requires is competence, and after that it's the song that's being sold – not the singer – but Tom wanted 'It's Not Unusual' for himself, wanted it bad, and he got it.

The first no. 1 by a new singer is often described as a surprise hit, especially when the singer has no form at all. The term, though, is often a cover-up for the promoters who neglected to plug it, the journalists who didn't review it, and the DJs who didn't get around to playing it. In fact, 'It's Not Unusual' wasn't any kind of a surprise hit. It had a strong melody, a neat catch-phrase, and an exhilarating tempo; it was arranged brilliantly, and sung with more muscle than anyone had heard in ages. Knock the Seekers off the top? Easy. It was, quite simply, a natural.

Classic Pop Song

Here, maybe, is the only time Gordon Mills played Tom Jones wrong. The kids who saw Tom on *Ready, Steady Go!*, or heard the record on the radio and went out and bought it, weren't buying Tom Jones, they were buying 'It's Not Unusual'. They didn't buy it because they were attached to the way he looked, but because they were suckers for a classic pop song. What happened next was a failure to follow it. His next release, 'Once Upon A Time', which was supposed to push up through the charts when 'It's Not Unusual' dropped out in April, did nothing. It was a weak follow-up, but Tom's chances with it were killed stone dead when Joe Meek looked out those old 1963 Tommy Scott tapes and cut 'Little Lonely One'. Tom made statements in the press disassociating himself from its 'dated' sound, but Joe Meek insisted it was a good record and Tom should be proud of it. Whatever its merits though, it split the buyers and smothered what small life there was in 'Once Upon A Time'.

In July, an old Billy Eckstine number, 'With These Hands', reached no. 13 and

Syndication International. All other pics. Rex Features.

showed they were still plugging the voice. Then, in September, 'What's New Pussycat', a bizarre film title-song written by Burt Bacharach and performed in monstro bravura style by Jones did slightly better and reached no. 11. On the strength of these songs Jones was voted fifth in the British Male Singer category of *Melody Maker's* 1965 popularity poll, but after that . . . nothing. 'This And That', 'Stop Breaking My Heart', 'Thunderball', all got nowhere. Apart from 'Not Responsible', which scraped in to the Top 20 at no. 18, he didn't have a hit in Britain between September 1965 and November 1966. What he did have was a car smash and his tonsils out.

But the message had got through to Mills. Tom wasn't for the kids. That was the bad news. The good news was that if the kids didn't like him, another generation would. So he quit one-nighters that the pop stars and the groups did, put on a tuxedo, and moved into the cabaret circuit. There he cleaned up.

The cabaret audiences weren't all middle-aged, many were in their 20s, but they weren't young at heart. They were steady company men who wore suits and short hair and drove company cars. Maybe they'd been a bit wild in their teens — pulling girls, getting drunk, punching heads — but then they'd got married and settled down. If you were a junior company man you couldn't have long hair even if you wanted it and anyway, when you got married you had to smarten up a bit. Stands to reason. So they probably didn't like the long-haired groups — disapproved or envied the way they carried on — and their wives didn't like them either.

A Real Man

Now, Tom Jones was different: he was clean, he was smart, he didn't have long hair. More than that, he was a real man. You could tell the difference between him and a girl without any trouble, and what's more he sang loud and clear and didn't mumble beneath the clangour of loud guitars. Here was a man's man — and a woman's man.

Tom really played up to them. He didn't find it difficult because he felt exactly the same way. After all, he'd cut loose as a kid, then settled down in marriage, and in Pontypridd people had strong and traditional ideas about what was what. In interviews he invariably said all the right things: how, when he was a teenager, if he tried to tell his old man what to do he'd feel the backside of a hand across his face; how he hated the protest movement; how anyone could take drugs, but it took a man to hold his drink; and even sometimes felt like crying when he sang 'My Yiddisha Momma' or 'My Mother's Eyes'; how he loved his mother; and how he phoned his wife every day he was away. Naturally he was the champion of male chauvinism. He once said: ''I think a woman's job is to serve her man,'' and pronounced, ''a woman may like to think she's equal, but she's not.'' His fans loved it. The men respected the way he handled himself and the women wished he was their bread-winner. Tom had it made from there on in. When he sang the manfully maudlin 'Green Green Grass Of Home' late in 1966, it went straight to no. 1 and stayed there for seven weeks.

During this period he also conquered the States, where the rift between the over-25s and pop music was even greater — they didn't just have the longhairs, there they had the Monkees as well. Also, they didn't really have Elvis any more since he'd become a recluse in Memphis, unseen in years apart from his movies. So Tom moved in and took over his live audience. On stage, in fact, Tom resembled the early Presley in the uninhibited movements of his body. Off stage his views were pretty popular as well, especially when he said he thought you should fight for your country. He became the hard hats' hero, and the fantasy of the blue-rinsed matrons.

Eventually he took the Copacabana in New York, the Flamingo and Caesar's Palace in Las Vegas. Elvis Presley went to watch his act, and Frank Sinatra said he was Tom's number one fan. His British-made TV series showed weekly to enormous ratings, and the stars queued up to be his special guests. These days, as a result, he spends six months of every year in the States. Not bad going for a hod-carrier from the valleys.

Popperfoto

BACK TRACK

Born 1940 in Glamorganshire; real name Thomas Woodward. He married at 16, and supported his wife and child working as casual building labourer. He sang in pubs as Tommy Scott.
1963: Formed a backing group, the Senators, went to London to audition for Joe Meek — turned down.
1964: Gordon Mills 'discovers' Scott in Pontypridd — changes name to Tom Jones and the Squires. Eventually signs with Decca.
Singles, all with Decca:
1964: 'Chills And Fever' (miss).
1965: 'It's Not Unusual', 'Once Upon A Time', 'With These Hands', 'What's New Pussycat', 'Not Responsible', 'Thunderball'.
1966: 'Green Green Grass Of Home'.
1967: 'Detroit City', 'Funny Familiar Forgotten Feeling', 'I'll Never Fall In Love Again', 'I'm Coming Home'.
1968: 'Delilah', 'Help Yourself', 'A Minute Of Your Time'.
1969: 'Love Me Tonight', 'Without Love'.
1970: 'Daughter Of Darkness', 'I Who Have Nothing'.
1971: 'She's A Lady', 'Puppet Man', 'Till'.
1972: 'The Young New Mexican Puppeteer'.
1973: 'Letter To Lucille', 'Golden Days'.
1974: 'La-La-La'.
Albums:
1965: 'Along Came Jones'.
1966: 'A-tomic Jones', 'From The Heart'.
1967: 'Green Green Grass of Home', 'Tom Jones ''Live'' At The Talk Of The Town', 'Thirteen Smash Hits'.
1968: 'Help Yourself'.
1969: 'This Is Tom Jones', 'Tom Jones ''Live'' In Las Vegas'.
1970: 'Tom', 'I Who Have Nothing'.
1971: 'Tom Jones Sings She's A Lady', 'Tom Jones ''Live'' At Caesar's Palace, Las Vegas'.
1972: 'Close Up'.
1973: 'Body And Soul', 'Tom Jones Greatest Hits'.

SKR

Top: The Who as pin-ups in the late '60s. Above: The Who on stage in France with their thunder-wall of speakers behind them.

words and music, they took the act a stage further — to actual physical violence, and into the realms of what was being called auto-destructive art. Anyway, that was the intellectual interpretation of Pete Townshend's guitar-smashing on stage. It had all started perfectly naturally, he insisted — one night he'd bashed his guitar's neck off at the climax of the act, there was no premeditation — but he started to do it every night and, of course, it was all very good publicity. Was he making a protest against materialistic society? Was it a deeply philosophical statement? Did it just look good? And anyway, did it matter?

The Who had always looked like the sort of blokes you'd try to avoid on a Saturday night — they looked, in a word, *mean*. Pete would glare at the audience, swinging his arm across his guitar in great sweeping arcs; Roger swung the microphone round his head like a lasso and barked out his words like bullets, while Keith went storming berserk behind his enormous drum kit. Only John, usually dressed in black with a supercilious half-smile of considerable threat, stood still. Smoke bombs exploded, drums were sent crashing over, and the stage was invariably left looking like the aftermath of World War Three. No encores: the band would suddenly vanish from the stage, maybe Keith staying a little longer to see if there was anything else to destroy, while the amplifiers and guitars buzzed and shrieked in abandoned agony.

Backlog Of Debts

The Who were the first to do it. Later on, the Move tried a similar trick, which involved attacking TV sets with hatchets, and Jimi Hendrix (unwillingly) tried to set light to his guitar with some lighter fluid. The Who remained the only ones to do it convincingly; though it became a standard feature of their act. Pete said he only smashed guitars when he felt like it, but few were the occasions when he didn't.

Each time a couple of hundred pounds' worth of guitar went, and the group built up a vast backlog of debts to guitar shops.

'My Generation', their first album, was released in 1965 — showing the group in best natty gear. It wasn't an enormous seller, and is now unobtainable. 'It's A Legal Matter' and 'La-La-Lies' were probably the most effective tracks despite the fairly dismal recording quality. After this they changed labels, joining Reaction, on which they released their next three hits: 'Substitute' in March 1966, 'I'm A Boy' in October, and 'Happy Jack' at Christmas. All reached the Top 5, though they never had a no. 1. All three featured typical Townshend freak characters — the Substitute 'was born with a plastic spoon in my mouth' — looked all white but his dad was black; in 'I'm A Boy', his mother wouldn't admit it and treated him like a girl; and Happy Jack lived in the sand in the Isle of Man. All featured that same unique Who style of thudding, over-crowded bass lines, that occasionally took on the role of lead guitar, a welter of drums leaving no part of the kit unhammered, great slashing crescendoes of guitar chords and high harmonies in a style reminiscent of the Beach Boys — strangely smooth in comparison with the

129

BACK TRACK

Fleetway Studio

1964 The High Numbers, having been turned down by EMI, released their first and only single on Fontana, 'I'm The Face'/'Zoot Suit'.

1965 Reverting to their original name, the Who reached no. 8 in the charts with a Pete Townshend composition, 'I Can't Explain', on Brunswick. 'Anyway, Anyhow, Anywhere' and 'My Generation' followed during the same year.

1966 The group signed to the Reaction label. 'Substitute', 'I'm A Boy' and 'Happy Jack' all reached the Top 5.

1967 Now released on Track, 'Pictures Of Lilly' and 'I'm A Boy' reached the Top 10. 'The Last Time'/'Under My Thumb' released in support of Mick Jagger and Keith Richard during their controversial trial for drug offences — but failed to make the Top 10.

1968 Townshend's long-promised rock opera, 'Tommy', released to great critical acclaim.

1969 The band played at the Woodstock Festival, N.Y.

1970 'Live At Leeds' released; included a revival of Johnny Kidd's 'Shaking All Over' and Eddie Cochran's 'Summertime Blues'.

1971 John Entwistle released his first solo album, 'Smash Your Head Against The Wall'.

1972 Pete Townshend released 'Who Came First', a solo album dedicated to Meher Baba.

1973 Roger Daltrey released his solo album, produced by Adam Faith. 'Giving It All Away', a single from the album, reached the Top 10. The Who release 'Quadrophenia', double album; '5:15' single (no. 19).

uproar of the backing. No group ever got more variety, more meat, into a three-piece instrument line-up.

Townshend was by now being recognised as something of an expert on pop, and was frequently quoted as a sort of ambassador from the teenage wasteland. He was getting credit for his songwriting, and he was talking about moving on to bigger things than the pop single. An album released on Reaction, 'A Quick One', was his first move towards the pop opera he kept on talking about. Nobody believed that rock — and, least of all, an uncouth bunch like the Who — could come up with a major work. 'A Quick One' was a short domestic drama, featuring such unlikely characters as Ivor The Engine Driver. And more singles came along, now on the newly-formed Track label, which was run by Lambert and Stamp, the group's managers. 'Pictures Of Lilly' was the first, in May 1967, and was followed by what is often considered the finest Who single, 'I Can See For Miles'. Strangely enough, this cataclysm of a record only just made it into the Top 10. Like 'Anyway, Anyhow, Anywhere', it seemed that pure and total Who music was a bit too strong for the majority of record buyers to take. Also, the group had failed to make much impact in the States. Whereas the Beatles, Stones, even the Dave Clark Five and Herman's Hermits had had the nation's teenagers entranced, the Who — and the Kinks — weren't making it.

Two events won America over to the Who — both in 1969. One was their appearance at the Woodstock Festival, which finally put the seal on their slowly growing fortunes. The other was 'Tommy'.

Townshend had finally done what he said he would for so long, and written the first successful pop opera, the beautifully-packaged story of the deaf, dumb and blind boy Tommy. The form was traditional opera — it had an overture, giving a glimpse of all the main themes and of various characters — Uncle Ernie, Cousin Kevin, Sally Simpson and the Acid Queen — but this was fused with a formidable mixture of religion, drugs, the business of pop stardom, metaphysics and pinball. (Oddly enough, Ray Davies had written his pop opera shortly before. His was called 'Arthur', but it slipped by largely unnoticed. The Kinks, at the time, were not a very fashionable band.)

Pretty Sick Of Tommy

The floodgates of America had opened, once and for all, and after 'Tommy' the Who were vying with the Rolling Stones for the honour of being called the 'Best Rock Band In The World'. 'Tommy' was performed by the band at the Metropolitan Opera House in New York. Critics said it was the first complete rock work on a large scale, and the band survived with 'Tommy' as the centrepiece of their stage act for three years after, by which time they were pretty sick of playing it.

As if exhausted by the gargantuan effort of getting 'Tommy' out, the Who went through a relatively quiet patch in the early '70s. They continued to do tours, they put out the occasional single, but there was a gap of almost two years between 'Tommy' and their next 'Who's Next', studio album. 'Live At Leeds' came out the year before, a rough and ready counterpart to the polished studio work of the opera, it was notable for a documentary history of the group provided through copies of early contracts, accounts, letters and pictures. Creatively though, the band were marking time. 'Who's Next', in 1971, was nothing like the band had ever done before. Townshend's writing had become smoother and more abstract, and he'd also, more importantly, discovered the synthesiser, which set the keynote of the album. It was a big step forward, but was it pop? At any rate, things have been relatively quiet for the Who since 'Who's Next'.

All the members of the group have had time to get out and do their own things. Entwistle has made a couple of albums under his own name which have sold very well in the States. Daltrey has had a couple of big single hits, and made an excellent solo album under the direction of Adam Faith which bears little relation to his work with the Who. Moon has acted in *That'll Be The Day*, become a DJ, and a leading contender for the British hovercraft racing championship. Meanwhile, Townshend has put out his own solo album, and there's been the glossy all-star stage production of 'Tommy', starring Rod Stewart, Maggie Bell and others. The Who are to appear in yet another version of 'Tommy' — this time a film which is to be directed by Ken Russell.

Keith Moon said in a recent interview that the group are more united than ever. They've all been doing their various individual projects, but the biggest thing in their lives is still, 10 years later, the Who. Among all the bands, who else has managed to keep the same line-up through such a long and pioneering career?

Ringo

As John Lennon once affirmed in an interview, "The Beatles would *probably not* have been as successful without Ringo." To think that anyone could have asked such a question, and especially at a time when the standard Beatles answer to any interviewer's question was to be found somewhere in among a flood of Liverpudlian wisecracks and private jokes, itself testifies to the low profile that Ringo maintained during those heady years of the '60s.

Nevertheless, while there were always conflicting reports about the identity of the *fifth* Beatle — Brian Epstein, George Martin and Pete Best all rated — it was always well understood that Ringo was well-and-truly a Beatle.

Ringo's story is well-known. While John, Paul, George and Pete Best sweated through their apprenticeship in Hamburg and Liverpool, Ringo learned his trade around the coasts of Britain working in summer holiday camps. He didn't play on the first single, 'Love Me Do', or on any of the early demo tapes. When the cover photograph for 'Please Please Me' was taken, he still hadn't got his hair straightened out, Beatle-style. Yet, after a childhood of persistent illness, the tide turned for him and he signed on the dotted line at the exact moment of Beatle take-off.

Many people have claimed, cynically, that Ringo was the luckiest person of the decade, and certainly he received more than his share of malevolent criticism; but all that ignores the very real contribution that he was able to make to the success of the Fab Four.

Ringo may indeed have been — as *A Hard Day's Night* suggested — the fall guy, but equally he was always able to command the loyalty and deep affection of the others. (Indeed, he has since become the first Beatle to engage the services of all the others for a solo album.) Equally, while it was left to the others to chart new musical directions, Ringo always seemed to move comfortably in their wake, content every now and again to bash out old C&W numbers like Buck Owens' 'Act Naturally' or

131

Carl Perkins' 'Matchbox' and 'Honey, Don't'.

Ringo was the first to settle down to a happy family life, and where John eventually married a Japanese-American avant-garde culture-freak, George a top British model, and Paul an American photographer, Ringo opted for a hairdresser from Liverpool — Maureen — whom he'd known from the early days and has stayed with ever since — still holding her hand. He quickly got down to the business of raising a family — Zak was born in 1965 and Jason in 1967 — and affirmed his intention of opening a chain of hairdressing shops. In other words, Ringo has never pretended to be anything other than a home-lovin', law-abidin' man. He is the only one of the four never to have been convicted of drug offences; and when the Beatles were all performing their spiritual exercises with the Maharishi in Wales, Ringo, down-to-earth as ever, said it all reminded him of the holiday camps . . . and came home early.

The Sweetest Of Them All

Ringo, said Hunter Davies in his official biography of the Beatles, was 'the sweetest of them all really', and that's probably his raison d'être: Ringo, the nice guy. It's both unnecessary and facile to observe that the Beatles couldn't have been the force they were without each member taking a distinct part that fitted perfectly into the whole. Therefore, Ringo's contribution to the group was as essential as anyone else's.

Even having said all this, the fact remains that most people thought when the four Beatles went their separate ways, Ringo would be the one who would first sink to the bottom. In the years since, however, Ringo has remained as much in the public eye as ever.

On the surface, Ringo never had too much going for him. He, after all, was the one who played drums. "He's very touchy about his drums," George had said in *A Hard Day's Night*, "they loom large in his legend." His playing though was never particularly outstanding: he could never do a roll, and in the beginning was restricted to occasional elaborations on thump-thump-bang-thump. But he persisted, and showed continuous improvement — his playing on the 'White Album' and 'Abbey Road' is particularly good — in the process developing a recognisable style.

Of his vocal abilities, there's not much to say, save that he's certainly no Caruso. His voice is a flat, pleasant monotone for which John and Paul used to write special songs. The first was 'I Wanna Be Your Man', from 'With The Beatles', though on the first album he had delivered 'Boys', an old Shirelles' number, with characteristic enthusiasm. The songs that were subsequently written for him, 'Yellow Submarine' for example, always seemed to emphasise the affection which the others felt for him. 'With A Little Help From My Friends' may have been composed with deliberate irony, but anyway it was the quintessential Ringo song. John and Paul

had got Ringo down to a 'T' — he had such a winning, affable personality, and so many friends that his own failings were irrelevant, since he never needed to do anything on his own.

In the Beatles' feature films too, it was lovable Ringo who was singled out for special treatment; he was the thinker, the loner. In *A Hard Day's Night* (the title of which he had thought of) he was the butt of everyone's jokes, the one who was mocked and treated unfairly. He was rewarded with a scene to himself, walking dolefully along the bank of the Thames. It was a scene which provided the film with some of its more wistful moments, and won Ringo much critical acclaim. Afterwards, though, he claimed that he had been drunk at the time, and that the success of the scene was a fluke. Then, in *Help!*, he was Ringo with one enormous ring too many, and that was the core of the plot, such as it was. "Why do you wear so many rings on your fingers?" he was once asked. "Because I can't get them all through my nose," he retorted.

Finally, it should be mentioned that the complete works of Ringo Starr, up to the dissolution of the group, amounted to just two songs — 'Don't Pass Me By', from the 'White Album', and 'Octopus's Garden' on 'Abbey Road' — and even then a scene from *Let It Be* showed George helping him to write it.

When the time eventually came for them all to stand or fall on their individual reputations, Ringo quickly surprised everyone. For a start, he already had two solo film roles behind him (a bit-part in *Candy*, and an outstanding leading role in *The Magic Christian*), and when the Beatle break-up became inevitable, he was quickly out of his starting-gates with two solo albums by September 1970.

Pub Songs

Both of these albums were special projects that came into the 'things-to-get-off-your-chest' category. The first one, 'Sentimental Journey' was something of a joke, and failed on every conceivable level except the all-important one of providing Ringo himself with some satisfaction. It was an album of standards that Ringo remembered hearing heartily sung in his local pubs back home in Liverpool when he was a kid. A sentimental journey, right; also, one would have thought, a rather private one, and many people still believe he should have left it on his own tapes at home.

Ringo nevertheless entered the project whole-heartedly, and, characteristically, had no trouble in persuading various first-class reputations to come along and produce one track each. It's difficult to imagine, for instance, that Quincy Jones, Johnny Dankworth and Elmer Bernstein would have done the favour for anyone else. The idea of having a different producer for each track (Paul McCartney, for example, directed 'Star Dust' in a super-schmaltzy manner) was to acquire a different 'feel' to each number — but this was

SKR

Ringo Starr, the slicked-back greaser in his rocker gear, and wife Maureen. He is no longer instantly recognisable as the wholesome, cuddly Beatle he once was.

BACK TRACK

1968: October, had a cameo part in *Candy*.

1970: April, *The Magic Christian* opens in London – Ringo in star part. 'Sentimental Journey' released. June, flies to Nashville to record 'Beaucoups Of Blues'. September, 'Beaucoups Of Blues' released. December, Paul files suit for dissolution of Beatles.

1971: February, Ringo said in High Court that McCartney acting like a 'spoilt child'. April, 'It Don't Come Easy'

released (reached no. 5 in Britain; no. 1 in US). July, filming *Blindman* on location in Spain, and also writing the score (which never materialised). August 1st, appears at Madison Square Garden with George Harrison *et al* in Concert for Bangla Desh. December, *200 Motels* opens with Ringo in lead role.

1972: January, 'Bangla Desh' LP package released. March, 'Back Off Boogaloo' released (reaches no. 2 in Britain; no. 10 in US). T. Rex concert at Empire Pool, London, which Ringo filmed for *Born To Boogie*. August, filming *Son Of Dracula* with Nilsson.

October, *Born To Boogie* opens in London. *That'll Be The Day* goes into production, shooting on the Isle of Wight. December, agrees to take part of Uncle Ernie in Lou Reizner's *Tommy* production at London Rainbow, but pulls out of show and is heard only on the album.

1973: April, *That'll Be The Day* opens. November, 'Photograph' released (reaches no. 8 in Britain, no. 1 in US). December, 'Ringo' released. *Blindman* opens in London.

1974: January, 'You're Sixteen' released in US – reaches no. 1.

Top pic.: Ringo Starr, as Mike, in a scene from *That'll Be The Day*, the film that portrays the '50s beautifully. Below, L.H. pic.: Harry Nilsson played the Son Of Dracula in the film of the same name. Ringo, plus beard and whiskers played Merlin the Magician. Above: Maureen and Ringo and friends. Main pic.: Ringo as a Mexican bandit in the film, *Blindman*.

never satisfactorily achieved. The major problem was that Ringo's voice and swing standards like 'Night And Day' and 'Love Is A Many Splendoured Thing' were never meant to come within a hundred miles of each other. 'Bye Bye Blackbird' was really the only song that worked well, and that's jokey anyway.

It Came Easy

The second album, later that same year, was a different matter entirely. Ringo had always liked C&W music, as his choice of songs from early Beatle days had indicated. This time, however, he was invited by steel-guitarist Pete Drake to record a complete album in Nashville, and was granted the services of the cream of local studio musicians – from Jerry Reed right through to the Jordanaires. Since Pete Drake had also obligingly commissioned all the songs from top country writers, this was one time it did come easy for Ringo.

The album was engineered by Elvis' old guitarist, Scotty Moore, and the company was in fact so distinguished and talented that Ringo didn't even have to play drums – what everyone had always thought he did. In the end it was Ringo's album only in so far as he sang the lead vocals on it; but who else could have assembled such an army of respected talents?

Ringo's contributions left the spirit of Nashville intact, and the album was accurately titled 'Beaucoups Of Blues' (he pronounced it 'boo-coos'), and contained many maudlin songs of love and death which Ringo delivered in his usual carefree manner:

'. . . Found her with another man
In a fit of anger he took her life and the
   stranger's
Then he took his own
Um . . . love don't last long'

Still, Ringo sounded quite cheerful about it all; even so, there's a natural dolefulness about him – 'If I talked about the good times/there wouldn't be much to say'. It's perhaps as well Ringo doesn't get taken that seriously.

Needless to say, the production made use of every trick in the book. 'Beaucoups Of Blues' might easily have been a classic C&W album had the vocals been of a different ilk, but then that was never the point . . . was it?

'It Don't Come Easy' was an archetypal Ringo record, and his first single. It was written by himself and George Harrison, who produced it in a sort of sub-Spector fashion; but it was a belting, driving song that was perfect for Ringo's voice. The lyrics were plain and typical – 'got to sing the blues, if you wanna sing the blues/ but you know it don't come easy'. In the States, it provided Ringo with his first Gold Disc, whereas 'Back Off Boogaloo', his only other real single, was not quite as powerful and not quite as successful.

With these projects out of the way, and

with the exception of his appearance at the Bangla Desh concert at Madison Square Garden, Ringo otherwise diverted his attention from making what he off-handedly describes as 'pieces of plastic'. Each of the Beatles had had individual film work before Ringo, but ultimately it was he who was more attracted to the cinema.

In *Candy* he had portrayed a lecherous Mexican gardener, and in *The Magic Christian* – also taken from an original work by Terry Southern – he played the unruly nephew of Peter Sellers. If he wasn't entirely successful, it wasn't so much his fault as the film's, since his part had been invented for him as there was no such character in the original novel. He wasn't then a great actor, but he did provide occasional moments of humour, and was emphatically not the embarrassment that many unkind people had suggested he would be.

Blindman was a bloody Western, made on location in Spain, in which Ringo played a passable Mexican bandit. Even so, it appeared an ill-judged attempt by Ringo to broaden his acting experience by playing a dramatic role in a film that took over two years to open in Britain, and was instantly forgettable at a time when violent, neo-Peckinpah Westerns were two-a-penny.

His next film was *200 Motels*, written and conceived by Frank Zappa, in which Ringo played the part of Frank Zappa(!). The film was made by Tony Palmer, although long before it opened he had publically dissociated himself from it. While embodying a certain anarchic quality, the film was nevertheless moderately disastrous. Made in the post-*Tommy* era, when rock stars liked to think themselves masters of several art forms, *200 Motels* was one of the events that proved conclusively that few of them were.

Crazy Ideas

During 1972 Ringo himself took up directing. However crazy the idea might have sounded, he was in a position to indulge his craziness, and anyway the Beatles had already made their own film – *Magical Mystery Tour* – although that had given them their first-ever taste of artistic failure. Ringo had several projects in mind, but only two he carried to fruition. The first one was a documentary about Marc Bolan, who was then at the zenith of his career, called *Born To Boogie*. Much of the film surrounded a T. Rex concert at London's Empire Pool in April, 1972. If it proved anything it was perhaps that Ringo could occasionally point a camera in the right direction, and that Marc Bolan was considerably out of his depth as 'superstar' material, as he didn't have the character to carry a whole film – something which the Beatles themselves had once done so successfully.

The other film, *Son Of Dracula*, starring Harry Nilsson – another of Ringo's show-biz friends – had a soundtrack by an ad-hoc grouping of Ringo, Nilsson, Klaus Voorman, Peter Frampton and John Bonham, but for some reason its release just

didn't follow. Then, towards the end of 1972, Ringo eagerly accepted the opportunity to play the part of a philosophising Teddy Boy in a film designed to catch the vogue for '50s nostalgia, *That'll Be The Day*.

The film was, as expected, an enormous success, and Ringo played his part superbly. All he had to do was act naturally, and – whether working on a fairground, as a holiday camp barmaid, or wising-up inexperienced David Essex to the best way to lay girls – he was entirely at home in the part, infusing it with his own irresistible sense of humour. Ringo was brilliant – easily the most authentic thing in the film, which collapsed two-thirds of the way through when he was written out.

Helping Out

That'll Be The Day was given a general release in Easter 1973, and in December Ringo crowned a personally successful year by releasing his first solo rock album which, as though to emphasise that, was called simply 'Ringo'. Once again, even if Ringo *isn't* a reincarnation of the Great Caruso, his voice – if not melodic – has a warm and friendly quality that is perfectly suited to many of the songs on 'Ringo'. Once again many eminent rock musicians turned up to help out, and the production – by Richard Perry – was quite magnificent. With a fine collection of material, the album is one of the most rewarding of the Beatle solo ventures, though its release was at the time overshadowed by Paul's 'Band On The Run'.

What was especially triumphant about 'Ringo' was that here Ringo had established a precedent for the eventual reunion of the Beatles. All the others had written songs for the album; John's song, 'I'm The Greatest', displayed a welcome return to his tongue-in-cheek humour, and 'Six O'Clock' was one of the most appealing tunes that even McCartney has ever written. The Harrison-Starkey composition, 'Photograph', released as a single, hinted at that old, romantic flavour:

'Every time I see your face it reminds me
   of the place we used to go.
But all I've got is a photograph and I feel
   like you're not gonna be back anymore'

It did well in America, and his next release, 'You're Sixteen', provided him with yet another no. 1.

If the Beatles should ever get back together again, Ringo may well have been a prime agent in the business. Even so he has admirably proved his ability to come from the Beatle shadows and achieve things for himself. In his spare time, he's even been busy designing furniture.

The three songs that best define Ringo are 'It Don't Come Easy', 'Act Naturally' and 'With A Little Help From My Friends'. So it hasn't been easy, but in films he's acted naturally, and in music he's got by, as few others ever could, with a little help from his friends.

Bee Gees
Brothers in Pop

In 1956 a Manchester cinema stage saw the appearance of a group called the Blue Cats. They comprised nine-year-old Barry Gibb and his seven-year-old twin brothers Robin and Maurice. Even in those days of skiffle they were singing harmonies.

Their precocious talent survived the family emigration to Australia in 1958, and by 1960 the brothers had their own TV series in Brisbane. Rules about minors cut down the TV though, and the trio performed in gambling clubs and on speedway tracks. As the Bee Gees, they made a number of records, and by the time they left Australia they had scored several no. 1 smashes.

An album of these hits had been sent to Brian Epstein, Beatle manager and head of NEMS, by their father before they set sail. While Brian was pondering their salability, the family arrived in London in February 1967. About a week later, after a day of being told how impossible it was for a new group to break into the scene, they arrived home to find that the new NEMS whizzkid, Robert Stigwood, had been phoning up all day. They met him and the breakthrough was made. 'Spicks And Specks', a song recorded in Australia, was rushed out, making little impact but enough for Stigwood.

In April they released 'New York Mining Disaster 1941', accompanied by advertising that claimed them as 'the most significant talent to emerge in 1967'. This incredible claim wasn't taken too seriously at the time. They were accused of copying the Beatles and the record only reached the wrong end of the Top 20.

It was a remarkable song though, displaying an originality that promised much for the future. A frantically slow rhythm perfectly complements the story of a miner trapped underground waiting for an escape he really knows won't come. Doom-laden harmonies intone the key lines — 'have you seen my wife Mr Jones? Do you know what it's like on the outside?' The whole song is a masterpiece of imagination.

During these first few months they signed two Australians, Vince Melouney and Colin Peterson, to play guitar and drums, and they were receiving requests from all sorts of big names for their songs. Even the inexplicable failure of their second single, 'To Love Somebody' — a song since recorded by over 200 people — failed to stop the ball rolling. In May they

From left to right: Robin, Barry and Maurice Gibb.

were approached by US Atlantic Records and offered an £80,000 record deal over five years, the largest amount ever offered to a new group. 'New York Mining Disaster' made the US Top 20, as did 'To Love Somebody'. In July they went across on a promotional visit.

By mid-summer, a well-known TV producer was calling them 'the best song-writing talent in Britain after the Beatles and the biggest influence on the pop scene at the moment'. And this with only one minor hit and a flop! As if to justify this high praise they proceeded to produce their most commercial song to date, 'Massachusetts'. Another doom-laden piece of imagination, it shot to no. 1 in both Britain and the US, selling over five million copies. It was one of those few songs that are instantly hummable until you reach the high note, which only Robin Gibb could scale with ease.

This hit, and the release earlier of their first album, seemed to confirm that the Bee Gees were capable of writing an endless series of good songs. They were obviously here to stay. The magazines interviewed them and found that they were all Christians, that none of them were interested in politics, and that they all liked steak best but with different drinks. Robin was afraid of loneliness, poverty and darkness; Maurice had apparently always dreamed of having a round bed. Then Robin was in a train crash which killed over fifty people; he was hurt but pulled several people to safety.

Romance With Lulu

The work permit problems with Colin and Vince were solved in November, and the same month saw Stigwood leaving NEMS and taking the Bee Gees with him; the beginning of Maurice's much publicised romance with Lulu, and the making of a film called 'Cucumber Castle' with Spike Milligan. The group played at London theatres to scenes of BeeGeemania and secured a £130,000 contract to tour the States in early '68. The world was opening up for them, with older brother Barry barely out of his teens.

But the music scene was in some ways closing in on them. Stigwood's other main group, sold to Atlantic as a makeshift in the Bee Gees deal, were the Cream, and their success was to mirror the growing distance between pop and rock. The Bee Gees' next single, 'World', perhaps failed to appreciate this distance. It was by any standards a great record, superbly conceived, arranged and performed. Yet it was a little too elusive for the straight pop market, and the lads were not endearing themselves to the growing rock market. A fairly typical quote from Barry around this time was – "Thank goodness the hippy gear is going out of pop. I've talked to pop fans and they simply hate these hippy scruffy groups. They'd rather see Cliff Richard or Scott Walker looking smart in their suits. It's so much more healthy." Hardly the way to win the audience their music at this time deserved.

'World', selling in the wake of 'Massachusetts', reached only no. 9.

But at the time they still seemed on the crest of the wave. In April '68 they became the first group to take a full orchestra out with them on tour, a breakthrough for which they deserve great credit. The tour ended at London's Albert Hall amid scenes of fanmania that completely drowned orchestra and group, leaving velvet-clad Robin and shot-silk, jump-suited Barry gesturing like silent movie idols.

They went to the States in the summer and received tumultous receptions everywhere – a little less mania but a lot more attention and applause. They seemed to have been taken more seriously there, and well they should – in the 18 months since their arrival in Britain they had sold a staggering 10 million singles and 3 million albums, and in the process lived up to Stigwood's extravagant hype. This indeed proved the crest, for on their return Robin collapsed from nervous exhaustion and Barry, doubtless in a moment of weariness, announced that he intended to leave the group when their commitments had all been fulfilled. This would admittedly take two years, but the breach had been made. From then on the group seemed dogged by internal strain, appearing in the press, so it seemed, merely to insult each other.

The music of those first 18 months was basically an original synthesis of two existing themes. One was the ballad form, using guitar and piano as rhythm and strings as a lifter and 'romanticiser'. The other was the bizarre lyrics of the post-Pepper period, which the Bee Gees took further than anyone else. They seemed to write lyrics in a trance, fashioning songs from whatever occurred to them, songs that could not be understood in any logical way but which communicated a definite feeling of outer madness and a broken heart. Barry specialised in love songs littered with strange objects and twisted phrases, Robin in a melodramatic paranoia – 'Til I finally died which started the whole world living' – brought back to earth by powerfully simple hook lines.

Soaring Harmony

Their other great asset was the possession of two voices that sounded devastating either solo or in harmony. As one sung one verse and then the other followed, as in 'World' or 'Let There Be Love', – the transition produced a remarkable effect, like changing gear upwards. Then they'd go a notch higher into a soaring harmony. All of this might have been in vain had they not had the supreme attribute – an ability to write melodies both instant and lasting.

But this ability has also proved double-edged. Already in 1969 the spotlight in rock was turning to a combination of imagination and an intensely personal self-expression. But the Bee Gees never wrote about themselves in that way. The ballad form of which they were masters was to be left in its pre-Beatle state of moons and Junes, and the Bee Gees marooned

with it in the straight pop category.

For the next six months there was no new single. Then, eventually in February 1969 'First Of May' was released, one of Barry's songs, which he sang with no assistance from Robin. Robin apparently wanted the other side as the 'A'-side. In March he announced his decision to go solo, and his wife told the press that he had never been given enough credit for the group's successes. Barry said that it would all blow over, and Dad said that Robin needed the others, but Robin apparently didn't think so. A US tour was looming up and Barry said that they'd do it 'with or without Robin'. Gradually the split began to look permanent.

By the end of May, Barry was saying, "I don't think I could work with him again even if I wanted to. He has said such hurtful things about Maurice and I and our manager." Stigwood was himself threatening Robin with legal action, but eventually managed to create a compromise whereby Robin would play with the group for a few months each year. But Barry wouldn't have him back anyway.

A Bee Gees' single was released without Robin. It didn't do too well, and as Robin's solo 'Saved By The Bell' (which Barry had thought uncommercial) shot past them to no. 2, the boys seemed far from brothers.

The rot had really set in for the group. A year earlier, Vince had left to play his beloved blues – electric guitar was rarely to be heard again on a Bee Gees single. Now in August '69 Colin departed too, leaving just the two of them. They continued as a duo for a while but then Barry quit both Maurice and Stigwood. Two and a half years after their formation the group was no more.

Brothers Together

Robin failed with his follow-up and by mid '70 the brothers were back together again. But it wasn't the same. Somehow in the interval they had lost track of where rock was going, and chose or were forced to confine themselves to churning out superior ballads. Their most creative period was behind them. Still the hits came, still they produced albums of a remarkable quality, showing all their flair for arranging, performing, and imaginative subject-matter. But their audience was now more restricted. The 'Trafalgar' album was at least the musical equal of their albums of four years before, but whereas the latter received lead reviews in all the papers, 'Trafalgar' received just a few lines at the bottom of a page. But their talent for melody has not deserted them; their rather simplistic words presumably a matter of choice rather than necessity. Stigwood once said that he thought Robin had one of the finest pop voices ever and cited 'Odessa' as one of the greatest songs ever written. Extravagant as these claims are, they are not totally ridiculous. The Bee Gees of 1967–69 were a great deal better than either they or the rock audience now gives them credit for. They might just turn round and show us in the future.

S.J.

CHAPTER 4
Dylan & American Rock

The history of rock music has thrown up three dominant influences – Presley, The Beatles, Bob Dylan. Each of them has helped to change the progress of the music significantly. During the Beatles' period as the most important stars in the world interest was drawn away from America but activity — almost unnoticed at the time — was centred around Greenwich Village in New York where folk artists gathered. In their midst a young man with a rasping voice, a battered cap and some astonishing songs emerged to give the music a new literacy, even a poetry, that had been thought impossible in so popular a medium. When Dylan wedded his amazing writing ability to the hard forms of electric music, rock found a whole new mode of expression.

After the Beatles' first wave, the Beach Boys were probably the only American rock group that could hope to compete; then came a 'protest' boom spearheaded by Dylan. The West Coast then threw up the Byrds who took Dylan's plaintive songs and rocked them. This seemingly simple progression wrought untold changes. Dylan first met hostility and then great acclaim with his heavy rock songs; he showed newly formed groups what could be done; that songs need no longer be two and a half minutes long and about love. Allied to the drug experimentation in California this produced an astonishing flowering of talent. Drugs, the Beatles, and the desire for an alternative to accepted life-style led to 'Flower Power' and the San Francisco summer of 1967. It led to Jefferson Airplane, to Janis Joplin and later still to the supergroup syndrome that reached its brief peak with Crosby, Stills, Nash and Young.

These few years of the '60s saw so many changes that by the '70s the need was felt for greater simplicity, but through the American scene of the time Bob Dylan stood head and shoulders above anyone else. To him must go the accolade of bringing the music into the realms of commitment, literacy and meaning. Alone, he brought a culture to maturity.

THE BEACH BOYS A DECADE OF PET SOUNDS

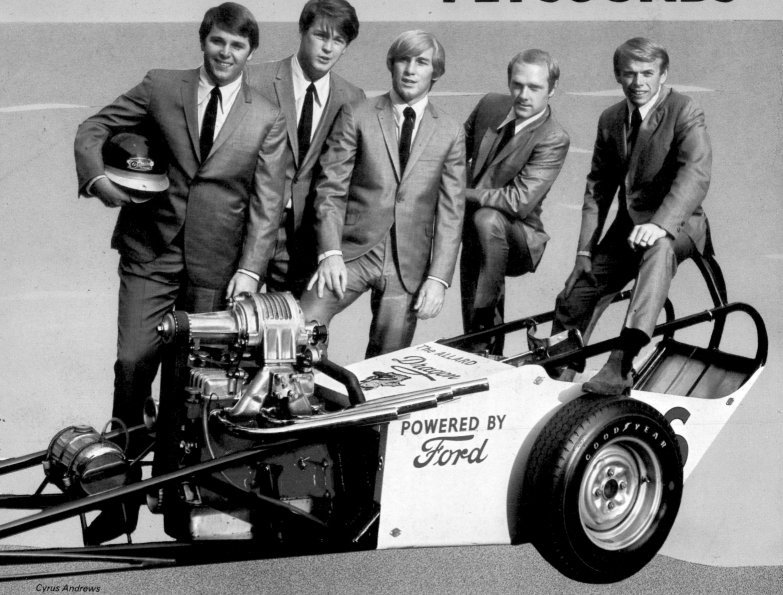

Cyrus Andrews

'Dennis Wilson, toenails tough like brazil nuts, has been surfing for 13 years. It was Dennis Wilson who came out of the water and told Brian what it was like out there. It was Brian who fooled the world.'

(Tom Nolan, *Rolling Stone*, October 71)

The Beach Boys are one of the true enigmas of rock. The 'Surf's Up' album, released in October 1971, completed a 10-year cycle for the group ('Surfin'', their first record, was released in October 1961); a 10-year cycle which had seen a somewhat chequered career. The group rose to fame on the wave of enthusiasm for surfing and drag-racing; managed to outlive those crazes by shifting the emphasis of their music to the American/

Californian teenage good life in general; produced one of the most remarkable albums in rock, 'Pet Sounds', only to fall victim to intellectual pretensions. Experimentation with psychedelic drugs, obscure religious sects, the Maharishi and transcendental meditation, health foods, and even an oblique flirtation with Charles Manson, all failed to produce music which would recapture the glory of older days. It took the simple re-discovering of their very life-blood, water, to do that.

The Wilson brothers, Brian, Dennis and Carl, their cousin Mike Love and friend Alan Jardine, all attended high school in Hawthorne, a suburb of San Francisco just five miles from the Pacific Ocean rollers. While Dennis was out surfing, the other four would sit around the house running through Four Freshmen songs. Dennis

loved surfing so much that he persuaded them to form a group together to play music which would be a celebration of the sport. He even came up with the name of the group – Carl and the Passions.

Brian and Mike Love wrote 'Surfin' for brother Dennis; a simple twelve-bar rock & roll beat. Murry Wilson, the boys' father, was also something of a songwriter himself, and it was his publisher, Hite Morgan, who put the boys on to vinyl. On October 8th, 1971, 'Surfin'' was released on the local Candix label under the name the Beach Boys.

'Surfin'' became quite a sizeable local hit, pushed up to no. 76 in the national Hot 100, and the Beach Boys made their concert debut at the New Year's Eve *Ritchie Valens Memorial Concert* at the Long Beach Municipal Auditorium. The

144

London Features International

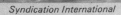

Syndication International

London Features International

Left: The Beach Boys on their first visit to the U.K. From left to right: Carl, Brian and Dennis Wilson, Mike Love and Al Jardine. Top and top right: The Beach Boys on stage. Above: A Beach Boys line-up with Bruce Johnston. Right: An early Beach Boy Concert at the Civic Auditorium, Sacramento, California on August 1st, 1964. Below: The Beach Boy line-up in 1973 playing with Elton John.

Capitol Records

Reprise Records

145

whole music scene at that time was dominated by the East Coast, and Dick Clark's thin-tied Italian singers from Philadelphia and Brooklyn. So, instead of angling the record solely on surfing (a then purely Californian obsession), the Beach Boys tried to cover themselves by introducing a dance into it (Dick Clark's national TV show, *Bandstand*, promoted dances as much as it did Clearasil and Dentyne):

> *From the early early morning,*
> *To the middle of the night*
> *Anytime the surf is up,*
> *The time is right*
> *And when the surf is down,*
> *To take its place*
> *We'll do the surfers' stomp*
> *It's the latest craze.*

Candix thought that the Beach Boys, like 'the surfers' stomp', were simply another craze, a one-hit wonder. Al Jardine did too, and left the group to pursue dentistry. He was replaced by Dave Marks, but returned when the summer, and success, came along. The Candix label itself failed to outlive 'the surfers stomp', and folded, but the group had managed to put down a few more sides including 'Surfin' Safari', 'Surfin' USA' and '409'. Murry Wilson took these around the major record labels without success until he met Nick Venet of Capitol Records, who bought the masters for $300.

In June, 1962, Capitol released 'Surfin' Safari' as the 'B' side to '409' — a song written by Brian Wilson and Gary Usher about Usher's Chevrolet 409. But the American public preferred surfing, even if they were completely land-locked (it says something for its appeal that the record broke first in Phoenix, in the deserts of Arizona). Surfing swept through the nation, and surfing groups sprang up everywhere, even, according to Nick Venet's sleeve notes to 'Surfin' USA', 'in places where the nearest thing to surf is the froth on a chocolate milk shake.'

California Dreaming

After 'Surfin' Safari'/'409' made the Top 10 lists nationally, the Beach Boys clung on to the formula of surfing b/w cars, and five months later 'Surfin' USA'/'Shut Down' repeated the success. 'Surfer Girl'/'Little Deuce Coupe', in August, firmly established the phenomenon of California Dreaming, and the Beach Boys as its leading exponents. At this time the Beach Boys were unashamedly using Chuck Berry's music. Carl Wilson was undoubtedly the best Berry imitator in the business — witness his introduction to 'Fun, Fun, Fun' and his countless guitar breaks, pure Berry. But the Beach Boys weren't content simply to rip off Chuck Berry's riffs, they also borrowed entire songs, particularly 'Sweet Little Sixteen', which was imperceptibly changed to 'Surfin' USA'.

'Surfer Girl'/'Little Deuce Coupe' was the Beach Boys' third national surfing/drag-car hit, after which they wisely abandoned such close identification with

so narrow a life-style. While still retaining the California backdrop of surf, sand, sun and cars, they widened their lyric content to encompass the teenage 'good-life' in general. 'Fun, Fun, Fun' and 'I Get Around' were transition records into the celebration of this American Dream of good times; of school and friend loyalty, of kissing for the first time, of dancing, of girls in general, and of course the hang-ups and heartaches they can bring.

From 1963–65, the Beach Boys poured out hit after hit that paid homage to this life-style: 'Be True To Your School', 'In My Room', 'Don't Worry Baby', 'Barbara Ann', 'All Summer Long', 'Dance, Dance, Dance', 'Do You Want To Dance?', 'Help Me Rhonda', and 'California Girls'. This simple, undemanding music evoked images of the summer sun, waves and girls, open roads and cars; which altogether spelled 'freedom'. The person responsible for all this was Beach Boy Brian Wilson, the oldest of the three brothers. In this period there are two things which mark the music of the Beach Boys: the incredible harmonies of their voices, and the production of the records. Brian Wilson sang lead, arranged all the other voices, and produced their records. Without meaning to demean the talents of the others, during this period he *was* the Beach Boys.

Freedom

Capitol Records, to their credit, recognised the talent that lay within him, and allowed him to produce the group's records — at a time when it was unheard of for a performer to produce himself. When he couldn't find satisfaction within Capitol's own studios, Brian simply used studios, musicians and technicians of his own choice — another unheard of move. At these sessions Brian, who could play almost every instrument himself, would show each session musician what to play. In the process he wasn't only singing about freedom, but actually giving it to musicians in California, and subsequently the whole of the rock industry. The more he worked, the more sophisticated Brian became in his production techniques. The progression can be seen simply enough from 'Don't Worry Baby', through 'Help Me Rhonda' and 'Do You Want To Dance?' to the brilliant 'California Girls' — which used brass and organ prominently for the first time. This increasing sophistication of production techniques was paralleled by Brian's increased dissatisfaction with the lyric content and style of their records. His ideas were not being adequately expressed in either his own lyrics or those of the lyricists he used. It was time to put away the surfboard wax — the wave had been ridden long enough.

Because of several nervous breakdowns caused through over-work, Brian Wilson decided to stop touring with the group. "I used to be Mr. Everything", he explained, "I felt I had no choice. I was run down mentally and emotionally because I was running around jumping on jets from one

city to another on one-night stands, also producing, writing, arranging, singing, planning, teaching — to the point where I had no peace of mind, and no chance to actually sit down and think or even rest."

Death Blow

Naturally enough, the other guys in the group — and indeed the world — saw this as the death-blow to the Beach Boys. But Brian had it all worked out, and he convinced the rest of the group that he would still carry on working and singing with them . . . he just wouldn't, *couldn't*, go on those energy-sapping tours. Reconciled to his decision, the group took on a local studio musician by the name of Glenn Campbell, as Brian's touring substitute. But he didn't work out so well, and after about four months Mike Love brought in Bruce Johnston. They'd known Bruce for a couple of years, since the days when he was producing over at Columbia, and had been the 'Bruce' in another California surfing group Bruce and Terry — the 'Terry' being Terry Melcher of Byrds, Raiders, Doris Day and Charles Manson fame. Bruce fitted in perfectly, and was to stay with them through to 1972 and just after 'Surf's Up'.

While the others were touring Brian wasn't wasting his time, and the year's breathing space it had given him enabled him to develop so much that with their next album they produced one of the milestones of rock music, 'Pet Sounds'. Brian had always been a devotee of Phil Spector, and the progression through 'Don't Worry Baby', 'Help Me Rhonda' and 'California Girls' had been a process of synthesising Spector's production techniques with the raunchy rock music of the Beach Boys. With 'Pet Sounds' this synthesis was complete.

'Pet Sounds' marked a complete abandonment of the Beach Boys' music (1962–65). No longer was it enough to be concerned only with the next wave or the new set of tyres or even the problems of adolescent love; the world had far wider horizons, and far more meaningful relationships (the opening track, 'Wouldn't It Be Nice?' explicitly extolled the simple pleasures of sleeping together). 'Pet Sounds' retained all those intricate vocal harmonies, but matched them with more ambitious structures — not too ambitious, but a decided advance on the 'two-verse/chorus/instrumental-break/chorus' formula of the past. The instrumentation was more advanced, and used a much wider range of instruments and styles and sound effects. The album even had two orchestrated tracks, and overlooking Brian's tendency to overdo the lush production, the album was near-faultless. Brian himself wrote all 13 tracks, collaborating on 8 of them with Tony Asher. It was to be the maturation of not only the Beach Boys, but the whole American rock movement.

Capitol Records, however, didn't want the Beach Boys to mature into the Beach Men; after all, as boys they'd been turning out hit after predictable hit, so why change? At first they even refused to issue it, and it was only after a long-protracted battle that they did eventually release it — while at the same time re-issuing their old hits on 'The Best Of The Beach Boys', and giving it a preferential promotion.

Brian Wilson is a very sensitive guy, prone to nervous breakdowns. He'd worked on the album for almost a year, so when Capitol rejected it he was deeply affected, and its eventual release didn't do much to alter that. 'Pet Sounds' was a critical success, but not (understandably in the circumstances) a commercial one, although three of the tracks became big singles hits: 'Wouldn't It Be Nice?', 'Sloop John B' and 'God Only Knows'.

Own Label

The rift with Capitol and the subsequent critical acclaim of 'Pet Sounds' had two important consequences. The group decided to form their own record label, and to leave Capitol. They wanted to do so immediately, but after some strong legal words they agreed to work out their contract, but no more. (Their following album, 'Smiley Smile', was on their Brother Records label, but distributed through Capitol. They had to give up three more albums before they could go fully independent, which they did with the 'Sunflower' album).

Critics began to acclaim Brian as a genius, but this was something which disturbed him. He had always been 'eccentric', to say the least, and when he received the blessing of the nascent underground/flower movement in California, he started to go through all the many different trips and crazes they embraced — but at super-speed. Brian Wilson has often been described as a 'total' person, meaning that when he commits himself, he goes the whole way. The first four years of the Beach Boys had given him the money to indulge in anything that took his fancy; so, when he suddenly had a craze on basketball, the main room in his house was converted into a gymnasium; when he wanted to play the piano with his feet in the sand, the room was filled up with sand. The stories of Brian's eccentricity just go on and on — living in a tent in the living room, holding business meetings in his outdoor swimming pool, at night, wanting to open a 24-hour table tennis shop because he found he couldn't buy equipment at three in the morning . . .

Brian also went through the more serious eccentricities of the time, LSD and other drugs. He enlisted the help of Van Dyke Parks during this period, and they began work on an album which was to be called 'Smile'. In November of 1966, while deeply immersed in the album, 'Good Vibrations' was released. It had taken six months to make (at one point Brian decided not to release it) and cost $16,000. It was the Beach Boys' biggest hit of all time, and their first million-seller. The laurels marked 'genius' started piling up outside Brian's door, unnerving him in his current project.

While he and Van Dyke Parks were making the album in the studios, the Beach Boys were out touring Europe. When they returned they were astounded by the sounds they heard, and rejected it. They couldn't comprehend the Van Dyke Parks lyrics, they argued that such studio-based music with orchestras and all couldn't be reproduced on stage, and they couldn't relate to the very advanced studio techniques and use of effects — this in pre-'Sgt. Pepper' days.

This rift within the group hampered the completion of the album, and when Brian was forced to concentrate on 'Heroes And Villains' — one of the 'Smile' tracks — as the single follow-up to 'Good Vibrations', things began to disintegrate. Van Dyke Parks left, and the release of 'Sgt. Pepper' sealed the project's fate. But the 'Smile' music wasn't all lost, and most of it has turned up on various post-'Pet Sounds' albums: 'Surf's Up' on the album of the same name; 'Cabinessence' '20/20'; and the bulk of it, including 'Heroes And Villains', 'Vegetables', 'Wonderful' and 'Wind Chimes', on the 'Smiley Smile' album.

Warmth And Humour

At the insistence of Capitol, 'Good Vibrations' was also included on 'Smiley Smile', which turned out to be a very under-rated album. It has a high critical reputation now, and is used by some drug-therapy clinics in the States. The making of 'Smiley Smile' as a good album was not so much the individually brilliant tracks such as 'Good Vibrations' and 'Heroes And Villains', as the general warmth and humour which came through as a result of those unique Beach Boy harmonies. Much of the album is purely vocal with the very minimum of instrumentation, and it was a high-point in Brian Wilson's use of the voice as an instrument.

In the meantime, Brian had moved into his Bel-Air Mansion with its own studio. The first album to come out of it was 'Wild Honey', released only two months after 'Smiley Smile'. 'Wild Honey' seemed in many ways to be an album aimed at patching up the damaged relations within the group itself, with its deceptively simple music firmly back in the rhythm & blues vein and several of the tracks co-written by Brian and Mike Love, who had been his sternest critic as regards the 'new music'. In fact Wilson Love wrote 10 of the 11 tracks on 'Wild Honey', including the album's two masterpieces, 'Wild Honey' and 'Country Air'. In many ways 'Country Air' is the perfect Beach Boys track of all-time in both style and content. The merciless singing of their voices blends superbly with their own instrumentation, while still retaining the orchestral 'wave' and mixing in the lone sound effect of a cock crowing.

The brief lyrics too are simple but evocative:

Capitol Records

Reprise Records

Get a breath of that country air
Breathe the beauty of the everywhere
Get a look at that clear blue sky

But 'Wild Honey' failed to lift them back into the 'Good Vibrations' league of popularity, as did their subsequent albums 'Friends' (Brian's personal favourite album and their first stereo one), '20/20' and 'Sunflower' (which was their first after breaking away from Capitol). Perhaps a reason was the lack of a distinct image for the group, which had by now completely lost its surfing label, but had simply replaced it with a succession of others, each changing from album to album. "They've been trying to get away from the beach, you know?" said Van Dyke Parks: "They don't like their image. Even when I first ran into them I could never figure out why. What's wrong with it? Get them down to the beach. Put them into trunks. The beach ain't so bad. The ocean is the repository of the entire human condition – the pollution, the solution . . . "

Pollution

Van Dyke Parks was shown to be right. 'Sunflower' ended on the right note with 'Cool Cool Water' and the 'Surf's Up' album, which followed it, started with 'Don't Go Near The Water' (by Al Jardine). Much of the 'Surf's Up' album dealt with water and environmental pollution in general. And it was this album which lifted them back into cult status of the 'Good Vibrations' order. The Beach Boys re-discovered water, and the rock movement re-discovered them. Perhaps the attraction to the album was the inclusion of the title track, a song by Brian and Van Dyke Parks from the ill-fated 'Smile' album; or perhaps it was simply the

brilliant album cover that sold the record.

In the event, 'Surf's Up' proved to be a very important album for several reasons. First, it saw the first collaborations of Brian (and the others) with Jack Rieley, a former reporter for NBC news, former producer for Pacifica Radio, who had become something nebulous in their management, co-ordinator of the press office and, of course, lyricist. Rieley even sang lead vocal on one of the tracks, 'A Day In The Life Of A Tree', which he had written with Brian. Secondly, the album saw the demise of Brian's influence as major songwriter and producer. Only the last three songs on the album were by him, two very short and the last one, 'Surf's Up' quite a few years old. All the other Beach Boys had songs on it, even Carl who had never written before. Most of the songs by the other Beach Boys were successful, notably Bruce Johnston's 'Disney Girls (1957)', and Mike Love's 'Student Demonstration Time' (a re-wording of Leiber and Stoller's 'Riot In Cell Block Number 9'), in which his voice was distorted to give a 'megaphone' effect, and police sirens were, with amazing success, used as instruments. But the attention of the album centred on Carl, his successful tracks, particularly 'Feel Flows', and his emerging talents as a producer.

'Surf's Up' was to be effectively the last 'Beach Boys' album. While everyone had had his own songs, the production and performance seemed to still unify the group. But after the release of the album Bruce Johnston (the only one not into transcendental meditation and health foods) left and Ricky Fataar and Blondie Chaplin from Flame, a South African group the Beach Boys had signed, came in. Dennis' right hand was badly cut in an

accident, and he couldn't drum or contribute very effectively any longer.

With these changes, the internal structure of the Beach Boys broke down. The first album of this radically new line-up was the very disappointing 'Carl And The Passions: So Tough'. The superb art-work and titling on the cover gave the impression of consolidating the return to earlier sentiments, as did the title, which was their original name. But the whole album was the worst for a long time, and clearly showed the fate of Brian's producing. Only one track stood out above the mediocrity, and that was Dennis Wilson and Jack Rieley's 'Marcella' – but even its brilliance couldn't carry so much dead wood.

Return To Their Roots

The group moved away to Amsterdam for a while and recorded their 'Holland' album there. It was a great improvement on 'Carl And The Passions', and Alan Jardine's 'California Saga: California' particularly was heralded as a return to their roots. Again Brian Wilson's role was cut back, to just two tracks – 'Sail On Sailor' (another Van Dyke Parks collaboration) and 'Funky Pretty' – and to the 7-inch record enclosed, which was a fairy tale called 'Mount Vernon And Fairway'. Suffice it to say it was in between this dialogue on this little throwaway record that the best music was to be heard. In fact it will probably need a fairy tale to save the Beach Boys from disintegrating completely into just a collection of very talented people. Sadly, it is a case of them not recognising that the sum of the individual parts can never equal the quality of the whole – such has been the fate of too many of rock's heroes.

Bob Dylan

Elvis Presley; the Beatles; and Bob Dylan. That wraps up the true super-greats — the people who came along and changed the music forever. Of the three, Bob Dylan has sold the least records and made the most changes. Elvis started it all off; the Beatles gave it a new lease of life when it was sagging into a rut. But Bob Dylan took on all the rules and all the restrictions, and broke them down single-handed.

He wrote songs that were 5, 9, 12 minutes long when the old showbiz rule-book said 3 minutes, kid. He refused to answer stupid questions politely, when the rule-book said always be nice to the press. He never lent his name to adverts for Coca-Cola, or allowed his tunes to be turned into TV jingles. He refused to have an official fan club because 'to call someone a fan is an insult'. He was prepared to stand up in front of audiences, who yelled abuse and slow handclapped when he sang the things he believed in, rather than bow down to the rule that says always-give-the-public-what-it-wants. And when the rules said stick to 'I-love-you-please-be-true', Bob Dylan wrote honest, powerful songs about the real world outside.

And all this in 13 years — a career that spans traditional folk music, modern folk, country music, the blues, protest-singing, folk-rock, acid rock, rock & roll and cowboy-movie music. The lot.

It was in 1965, to the boos and cat-calls of folk fans and politicos who thought he'd betrayed them, that Dylan picked up an electric guitar for the first time. But by then he'd already made himself a legend. This is the story of those stunning pre-rock years.

In The Beginning

Bob Dylan, born Robert Zimmerman, in Minnesota, was indeed a boy from the north country. The climate and the times were fierce, the countryside long-since stripped of its forests and then raped by the mining companies.

Late in 1960 Dylan left Minnesota, and in early '61 arrived in freezing New York City — in the depths of the coldest winter for 17 years. He made straight for the folk haven of Greenwich Village, and spent his time sleeping on people's floors, playing at any of the coffee-houses and clubs that would let him, and getting to know all the big-wheels on the scene. By this time, Woody Guthrie was very much Bob's idol, and eventually Dylan met Guthrie, both in the hospital where Guthrie had been since 1958, and later at the home of friends.

Guthrie was impressed. "Pete Seeger's a singer of folk-songs," said Guthrie, "and Jack Elliott's a singer of folk-songs. But Bobby Dylan's a folk-singer. Oh Christ he's folk-singer all right." There could have been no higher tribute.

When Dylan first made the kind of impact that Guthrie's compliment suggests, it was as a *performer*, not a writer. He bowled people over as a shy kid with a funny Huck Finn cap (much copied later by mid-'60s folk-rockers like Donovan) and a Charlie Chaplinish style of stage movement. He might have looked very young and waif-like, but he *sounded* like some octogenarian black guy singing the distilled experience of a lifetime's hardship and regret — or, one song later, like an equally time-battered old Calvinist from the rugged communities of the Appalachian mountains. And what was especially amazing about all this was that everyone else around — all the other middle-class whites emerging on the same folk circuits — *sounded* white, and middle-class, and *nice.*

When Dylan put one of his earliest compositions on his first album, 'Bob Dylan', a song called 'Talking New York', he made out that people's reactions to his arrival had been hostile:

*'You sound like a hillbilly
We want folk singers here . . .'*

The point, as Guthrie had already settled, was that of course Dylan *was* a folk-singer, a genuine folk-singer, and a truly exceptional one.

By the time his first album came out in March, 1962, it was already much less than a representative sample of his talent, for by then Dylan *was* writing. He was turning out songs in an incredible torrent — five or six a day, at times — and all seeming to pin down in a new and original way some challenging subject or important cause . . . within the framework of American folk-song structures.

Shining Contrast

The album had, apart from 'Talking New York', one other Dylan composition — the beautiful, understated tribute of the young man for his idol, 'Song To Woody'. Beyond that, it was a breathless race through the songs of old bluesmen, like Blind Lemon Jefferson's formidable 'See That My Grave Is Kept Clean', Bukka White's 'Fixing To Die' and C. Jones' 'Highway 51' Blues' — all of which underlined the stunning contrast between Dylan's youthfulness and his Ancient's voice. The preoccupation in the songs with dying and the decay of death — plus torrid re-workings of purely traditional material ('House Of The Rising Sun', 'Man Of Constant Sorrow'), of one man-band Vesse Fuller's medicine-show hurly-burly ('You're No Good'), of modern folk material like young Rick Von Schmidt's 'Baby Let Me Follow You Down', and old Roy Acuff's 'Freight Train Blues' was heady stuff. This was rough, rugged, raunchy material soaked in a sense of the traditions of others and the freshness of the moment; and it makes for an album that crackles with an overload of nervous energy, and tugs with the remorseless pulse of the blues.

'Bob Dylan' was cut in 12 hours at Columbia's New York Studios at the cost of just $402, with Dylan's girl Suze Rotolo watching and Bob using her lipstick holder to fret his guitar.

The second album, 'The Freewheelin' Bob Dylan', with Suze Rotolo on the front cover, came out less than a year later and demonstrated the leaps Dylan had made. Though several of the songs were, as before, based on traditional material, they were all Dylan compositions, and ran with an unfailingly abrasive edge through a whole welter of those social and political subjects with which the young radical New Left was becoming preoccupied.

There was 'Blowing In The Wind' which stated, in a kind of abstract call to arms, the general outlines of this new socially-conscious thinking that was infiltrating the brash, materially acquisitive insularity of American life in the '50s. It was a precursor of 'The Times They Are-A-Changing' — an anthem — and it touched a chord in the hearts of many thousands of people . . . so much so that around 80 different artist from *outside* the folk arena rushed into studios to cut their own sugar-sweet versions of the song.

Cuttin' Through

There was 'Masters Of War', with all the structural strength of the English folk ballad transmuted into the Yankee American tradition, and with all the unflinching venom of a lyric attacking the faceless merchandiser of war . . . though this was before the real escalation in Vietnam, in which those masters of war were to supply 6,000,000 tons of bombs.

There was 'Oxford Town', a barbed satiric attack on the racial segregation that, not long before, James Meredith had tried to challenge in Oxford, Mississippi. There was the black humour of 'Talkin' World War III Blues', with its chilling portrayal of the all-American survivor of a nuclear decimation — the spectre of which had been raised by Kennedy's brinkmanship in the 1962 Cuban Crisis — still gleefully playing with his big flashy cars on desolate New York streets.

And the nuclear theme was employed most successfully in 'A Hard Rain's A-Gonna Fall', a song of extraordinary achievement. No wonder Dylan disliked the term 'protest song', with its implication of a crude polemic process, for 'A Hard Rain's A-Gonna Fall' is the result of a very different process — the paring down and distillation of language into a bare elemental structure that has the penetration, economy, and undeflected purpose of great art. As we listen, 'we are beseiged with images of dead and dying life . . . the vision at the brink' (as David Horowitz put it). Line upon line the pictures are piled up; direct moral diagrams rolling past as if on and then off a screen, without opportunity of recall:

*'I met a young woman whose body was
    burning . . .'
'I saw a highway of diamonds with nobody
    on it . . .'
'Heard the song of a poet who died in the
    gutter . . .'*

Yet there is not one single redundant syllable in the song — and it is with the confidence of knowing himself that Dylan ends up a song with a theme as apocalyptic as this, on the lines:

*'And it's a hard, it's a hard, it's a hard,
    it's a hard,
It's a hard rain's a-gonna fall.'*

In addition, the album looked both back towards the first, in having another travelling blues number, 'Down The Highway', though this time the song was by Dylan himself instead of an older black artist from the past; and forward to the albums that were to come after, with the first of Dylan's extraordinarily powerful and unconventional love songs, 'Girl From The North Country' (based on 'Scarborough Fair'), and the classic 'Don't Think Twice, It's All Right'.

By now he was getting known, though only to the outside world as a writer of unusual, controversial songs. In the Village he was big as a performer in his own right, but across the rest of America 'Bob Dylan' was only the name in tiny print under the song-titles when people bought 'Blowing In The Wind' by Peter, Paul and Mary.

But Dylan couldn't be held back long.

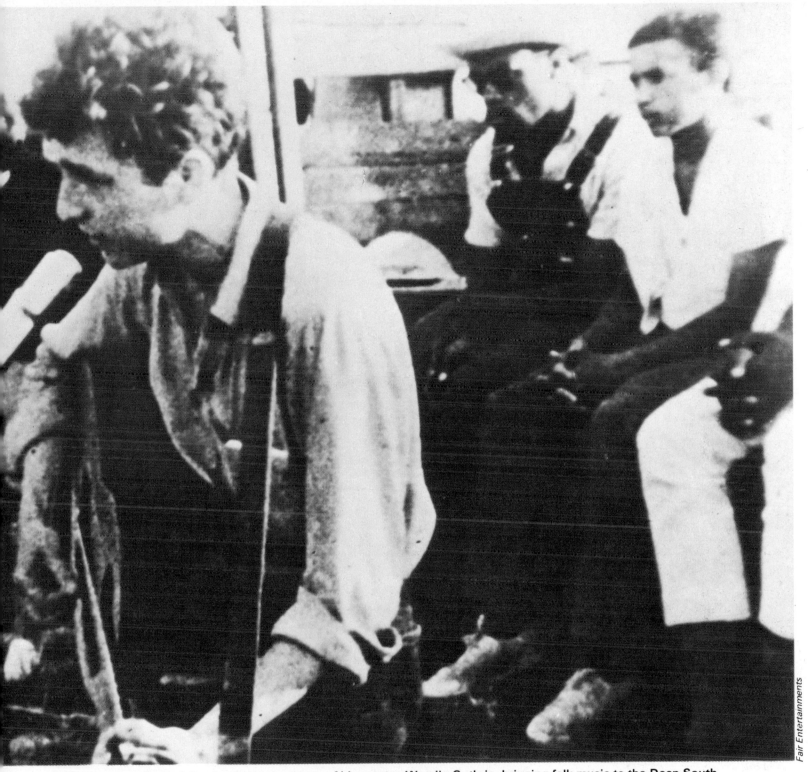

The young Bob Dylan following in the footsteps of his mentor, Woodie Guthrie, bringing folk music to the Deep South.

At first he held himself back, by telling his manager he didn't want to perform, he wanted to get on with his songwriting. Then, Dylan appeared in front of a national audience at last, at the Newport Folk Festival of 1963. He came to the Festival as a minor artist way down on the bill underneath the big names — Pete Seeger, Peter, Paul and Mary, and Joan Baez. By the end of the three-day event, he had (as they say) stolen the show. Bob Dylan emerged from Newport as the unchallenged spokesman of the new youth/folk movement.

His second album, full of his own material, was a far bigger seller, and by the time of his third album, 'The Times They Are A-Changin' ', he was established as an artist in every sense: he was a singer/songwriter now, and not just a composer in the background; and he had won himself a national, even an international, audience. His own rough-edged single of 'The Times They Are A-Changin' ' was played on pop radio stations — hitting millions of listeners more accustomed to the dulcet tones of Roy Orbison and Ricky Nelson like a bombshell.

Meanwhile, every other established folk-singer had long been obliged to include Dylan's songs in their repertoires; and the thinking of a whole generation of

college kids and other young people was finding not only a voice, but a direction, through Dylan himself. A new consciousness was awakened — an awareness that America wasn't the glorious Land of the Free, that there were many, many things to stand up and fight for, and that an increasing affluence wasn't enough. Young people began to make it plain that life was about more important things than hot dogs and drive-in movies, and that love needed a more complex and honest expression than Moon-and-June lyrics gave it.

Dylan was saying it all in his songs, and not even the hysteria of Beatlemania

Top/Camera Press, London Features   *Pictorial Press*

Above. Top from left to right: Maybe pondering the 'Blonde On Blonde' album; Pre-electric in 1965; Backstage at the Isle of Wight. Bottom: The King and Queen of Folk in 1965; Shades of 1966, not long before the crash. Opposite page. Top from left to right: Dylan at the Isle of Wight; Bangla Desh concert. Bottom: 1973, plays Alias in Sam Peckinpah's film, *Pat Garrett & Billy The Kid.*

in America could squash the new movement which Dylan had led. And in time the Beatles themselves, and all those other bright new groups who led the 'British invasion' of 1964–5, were strongly under the influence of Dylan's work. They were influenced by his revivals of older, traditional folk material (so that the first two singles by the Animals were songs from Dylan's first album, the second — 'House Of The Rising Sun' — using the same arrangement except that Alan Price's organ took over from the guitar-part). They were influenced by his protest songs (so that Manfred Mann, for instance, recorded

'God On Our Side'). And they were influenced by the intelligent, honest lyrics which Dylan was putting into the increasing number of personal, as against political, songs he was writing (so that the earlier Beatles lyrics seemed strangely out-of-date, and the newer ones got more and more thoughtful and articulate).

Eventually, in 1965, it erupted into a whole 'protest craze'. Barry McGuire got a Gold Record for 'Eve Of Destruction', which protested against almost everything you could possibly think of; the Hollies made a record about nuclear war solving the over-population problem; Sonny, of

Sonny and Cher, had a hit that protested about people telling him to cut his hair.

In other words, it had become silly. It had become vulgarised and commercialised as a pop music trend; but behind that, as a genuine movement, as a consciousness and an awareness and an ability to question all the tired old assumptions and rules by which people were supposed to live — as all that, it was unstoppable.

Chained Down

Dylan himself, in any case, had moved away from 'protest' long before it became

152

Top, Rex Features

MGM/EMI

a craze. He had resented being made to feel chained down to singing 'Blowing' In The Wind' for the rest of his life; he felt he had already said it all (as indeed he had); and he wanted to explore more personal, introspective realities. All through his concert schedule in 1964, he was cutting down the number of openly political songs in his repertoire, and was writing instead love songs and songs of personal perception. A lot of his oldest admirers attacked him viciously for making this shift — yet these new compositions were just as revolutionary in their own way as the old. And their impact was as great.

But by the time pop fans were adjusting themselves to that, Dylan was moving on — fast. In August 1964 he came out with the 'Another Side Of Bob Dylan' album, which shook a lot of the folk fans rigid. Why? Because Dylan seemed to have deserted politics and protest. True, the album included another anthem, 'Chimes Of Freedom', but it was mostly filled with personal songs — love songs — and it also included 'My Back Pages', a song that showed a new Dylan: a new Dylan who was actually lamming into the old Dylan for the protest songs and describing them as 'lies that life was black and white'. It had an almost singalong chorus:

'Ah! but I was so much older then,
I'm younger than that now.'

Talk about being ahead of everyone — Dylan was about three jumps ahead. The pop fans were only just waking up to the fact that you could sing songs that were thoughtful and critical of the society around you; the folk fans were quaking in their duffel coats at this sudden about-turn from their spokesman-idol; and on top of that, Dylan's new *personal* songs were about to set off two further explosions.

153

First, Dylan had reappeared, the month before the album came out, at the Newport Folk Festival, and had sung there a magnificent, beautiful and lengthy song which celebrated freedom of the spirit in general, but which in particular celebrated the effects of drug trips: 'Mr. Tambourine Man'. A drug song! Of course, the old blues singers had had repertoires soaked in narcotic imagery — but this was different: this was getting through to a mass audience . . . explosion number one.

Number two was set off by those other personal songs, the love songs, on the 'Another Side Of Bob Dylan' album. These were far from being the love songs that pop records provided. In pop, it was 'She Loves You', 'I Wanna Hold Your Hand'; or it was 'You're So Fine You Gotta Be Mine'; or it was 'I Cried A Million Tears Cos You Left Me Blue'. In other words, boy always wanted to own girl; love had to last forever and was the ultimate achievement in life; and if you didn't have eternal love you died of a broken heart.

Plastic Goo Of Pop

Dylan's love songs simply said look, let's cut out the hype and get down to reality: nobody owns anybody — and shouldn't want to or try to; love needn't last forever, rarely does, and it's a waste of energy trying to make it happen; and people do have other aims besides being someone's eternal love. If all that seems basic and pretty obvious today, that simply demonstrates how enormous Dylan's influence has been — because at the time Dylan first came out and said it, it was like a great blast of fresh air and honesty blowing a hole in all the plastic goo of pop romance. Back then, the Beatles' lyrics, like everybody else's, were still inside this old pop straitjacket — still saying that to be somebody's life-long lover was the peak of ambition; but Dylan, with that simple guitar and harmonica backing and that remorselessly steady down-to-earth beat, was singing 'All I Really Want To Do Is Baby Be Friends With You' and:

'You say you're lookin' for someone
Who'll pick you up each time you fall . . .
A lover for your life an' nothing more —
It aint me, babe . . .'

('It Ain't Me, Babe')

A lover for your life and nothing more! Again, after the shock, it made sense. It touched a chord — it expressed, as Dylan had done before, what people were feeling but unable to express.

The people who wanted to just churn out bubblegum music carried on, of course — they ignored all the changes Bob Dylan was introducing, though as time went on and Dylan's impact got through even to the 14-year-olds that the pop business had always assumed were stupid, the bubblegum brigade had to find younger and younger audiences. But everyone who wanted to improve the quality and honesty of their music caught on to what Dylan was declaring. The Beatles started thinking

about their lyrics, instead of just their chord sequences. It began to happen — a real revolution in pop.

At this point in time, however, despite the enormous impact that Dylan was having on the pop world, his own career still seemed set in the folk mould, at least in the sense that he was a solo performer using only acoustic guitar and harmonica. But changes here were coming too.

Return To Rock

When the 'Another Side Of' album had been recorded, Dylan had amazed producer Tom Wilson by using a piano in the studio and revealing his ability as a pianist: Dylan had never told anyone he could play keyboards. Yet rock piano, as we've noted, was actually how he'd begun in the music world, and rock music wasn't as foreign to him as the folk fans assumed.

He very soon returned to it. He'd been knocked out by hearing the Animals' recording of 'House Of The Rising Sun' a song he'd [ ]
album. [ ]
when he [ ]
from som [ ]
hear wha [ ]
Burdon [ ]
Rising Su [ ]
Later, wh [ ]
copy of t [ ]
that clinch [ ]

By the [ ]
May 196 [ ]
before, [ ]
'Bringing [ ]
one side [ ]
side of n [ ]
side of th [ ]
'Subterranean Homesick Blues' as a single, and while Dylan was touring the country, giving what were to be among his last solo performances, this amazing rock record was hitting the British Top 10.

Dylan had given his imprimatur to this mixing of folk and rock, and the famous 'folk-rock' label was stuck onto it. It was a misleading term, however, because what Dylan had done was to marry rock not to old folk songs or his own earlier love songs, as the Animals and the Byrds had done; Dylan had married rock to new, urban poetry with harsh, effervescent lyrics and moods that fitted the electricity in the music.

Few people caught on to what he had done at that time. Dylan returned to the States, and in July appeared once again at the Newport Folk Festival — this time carrying his electric guitar and backed by part of the Paul Butterfield Blues Band. He was booed off the stage. If the non-protest solo album 'Another Side Of' had been seen as a betrayal by some of Dylan's audience, this new stuff was nothing less than blasphemy. There were still, back then in 1965, an awful lot of college kids, as well as older folk-music followers, who regarded pop music as just a commercial rip-off which could have no real value.

And for a while — if you went by what happened in the charts — it looked as if

those people were right: because the first effect of Dylan 'going electric' was a sudden Protest Craze. It seemed as if every group in Britain and America suddenly decided to cash in on the new fashion for anti-war songs, anti-anti-long-hair songs, anti-everything songs.

As usual, Dylan was miles away. Not only was he totally uninterested in Protest, but his new rock music was genuinely new. His old stuff bored him stiff, despite how much other non-rip-off artists were learning from it, and he was getting into a more prolific, creative phase of composing than ever, despite the boos and despite all the abuses which Tin Pan Alley was churning out. In August, just one month after Newport, he released an incredible new album, 'Highway 61 Revisited', which contained the epic 12-minute 'Desolation Row', the astonishing 'Ballad Of A Thin Man', and, among much else of real originality and power, the masterpiece 'Like A Rolling Stone'.

Dylan was jubilant — and the fact that he could feel jubilant in the face of the howls and boos of his old audience and the general non-comprehension of a newer pop audience, illustrates another of his pioneering battles: alone in the music world, he had the resilience and integrity to stick to what he believed in doing regardless of public opinion. That was absolutely the opposite of the usual showbiz maxim, 'Give The Public What It Wants, Son', which everyone else bowed down to, right from Bing Crosby to the Beatles.

First Breakthrough

It was obvious to Dylan that what he was doing was right, and important, and he could only hope that once again, as with all his innovations of the past, people would eventually catch on.

They did; 'Like A Rolling Stone' was perhaps the first breakthrough. It was so plainly a major accomplishment, it so obviously opened the door for rock music to realise unlimited new potential, that at least some of those previously hostile did begin to see that rock could be used for communicating reality instead of just grinding out unreal artifacts whose only purpose was to make money.

Dylan was working hard. He launched into a massive international tour, this time taking a rock group with him culled from Levon and the Hawks, who had been back-up band for Ronnie Hawkins, an Arkansas singer who'd found relative fame and fortune in Canada in the early '60s. The tour went all over the States, to a very mixed reception, and in 1966 it took in Australia, then Scandinavia, then Eire, Britain, France, and Britain again. Dylan got a vicious hammering from the press in Australia, and hoped for a better time in the UK. He didn't get it. People walked out of every concert he did, from Liverpool to Sheffield, to Birmingham, to Bristol — everywhere. At the first of his two Albert Hall concerts in London it was the same. Dylan flew from London to Paris and played

154

Photo: Fair Enterprises

at the Olympia Theatre there on his birthday, May 24th. The French, alone, loved his new music; but from the Olympia, it was back to the Albert Hall and the same old barrage of hostility.

Judas!

'Judas!' someone screamed out at him just before the last number. Dylan stepped up to the microphone for almost the first time in the 1½-hour show, and said "I don't believe you!" The opening notes of the last song came thundering out of the amps, and then Dylan added, shouting, "You're a liar!" . . . then crashed into the opening of the song — it was 'Like A Rolling Stone' — hurling the words at the audience:

'How does it feel? How does it feel?
To be on your own . . .'

It was an incredible atmosphere, and an incredible achievement. There was Dylan on his own, in total conflict with large sections of his audience, but with the power of conviction never wavering that it was *them* who were wrong, *them* who were behind the times.

The month after that, with Dylan back in the States, his next album, 'Blonde On Blonde', was issued — and yet again, it established that Dylan was light years ahead of the field. It was an ornate concept-album, an all-embracing world of its own, flowing with surrealist chaos and turmoil, yet soaked in a breathtaking poetic vision and an enfolding sensuality. It showed up very clearly indeed just how right Dylan had been all along, and just how far the Beatles, the Stones and the rest had been left behind.

As they listened, keeled over, and began to pick themselves up to start following this incredible artist into yet further new pastures, there came the news that with a further 67 concert dates to fulfil (an indication of how hard Dylan's manager, Albert Grossman — since dumped — was driving him) Dylan had crashed badly on his motorcycle in upstate New York, and was in hospital with a broken neck.

Death rumours abounded, and matching them even more gruesome rumours of the damage a wrecked but still alive Bob Dylan had sustained. The rumours were not damped down by the long, long silence that ensued from Dylan himself. The accident happened in July 1966, and it was not until January 1968 that Dylan re-appeared. He came back to appear at a Woody Guthrie Memorial Concert at Carnegie Hall; and later in the same month a new album was released, 'John Wesley Harding'.

What had happened on the rock scene in the intervening period was a massive pick-up on all that Dylan had previously been pioneering and asserting. Rock broke up clearly into two factions — the bubblegum brigade, and The Rest: and The Rest was full of new names, new talent, new directions. The label 'progressive music' emerged — and at first it was accurate

enough. For an awful lot of people, the pennies had, at long last, dropped. There were a thousand offshoots from the harsh new urban rock-poetry that Dylan had produced with 'Highway 61 Revisited', from the druggy surrealist achievement of 'Blonde On Blonde', and from the unflinchingly honest love songs that Dylan had earlier hurled in the face of all the Tin Pan Alley clichés. Commercial fads like the Protest Craze were as dead as the Twist. A lot of people were really trying to achieve music and artistry of real significance, and there was no longer any question of college audiences being able to feel that pop was all beneath them. In short, there was an exciting and at first genuinely exploratory rushing in through all the doors that Dylan had opened. Perhaps in particular, the Beatles finally got there, with the 'Sgt. Pepper' album.

But as usual, fame and money and the process of becoming cut off from all ordinary life soon came wading in to drown much of this new real progress in hype and nonsense; and by the end of 1967, though no one would admit it, the brave new world of 'progressive' music was getting tatty and cliché-ridden and pretentious.

Dylan's comeback album punctured it all. 'John Wesley Harding' was a direct challenge to the whole ornate superstructure: it was a devastatingly simple album both musically and lyrically, and though it was far from simple it was remorselessly pared-down. Far from abounding in the druggy, impressionistic self-indulgences that were currently in fashion, 'John Wesley Harding' didn't have a single word more than necessary, and the insistent economy of the songs was matched by a new, thin, urgent voice from Dylan as performer.

Pure Country

Once again, Dylan had unilaterally taken a fresh direction — and again, once taken, the falsehoods and cul-de-sacs of the rest of the music scene were laid bare. Perhaps most challenging of all, the last two songs on the album were pure country music, unadulterated by any clever-cleverness, or 'progressive' gimmicks.

Country music! Nothing, then, could have been less hip, or seemed to make so little sense. Country music was a complete contradiction of all the radicalism, all the trendiness, and all the complexity that everyone was trying to include in their music. Yet once more . . . they followed. The back-to-the-roots, back-to-simplicity movement was well under way, if tentatively, when Dylan came along in 1969 with the album that was to crystallise it all, 'Nashville Skyline'. A totally country album — even a duet with Johnny Cash — and for Dylan, another about-face. Now he could sing, as if it now could be simple and honest and not just gooey pop-romance, lines like:

'It's love and love alone
It makes the world go round . . .'

Dylan taking a break during his British tour, when he filmed *Don't Look Back*.

What Dylan was doing, however, was much more than another re-sculpturing of our music. By re-alerting our generation to the strengths of country music — a music that registered with ordinary Americans, good and bad, whose lives were traditional at base, changed more by technology than by post-adolescent radical ideas — Dylan was also dismantling his own myth.

His long silence, enforced by the motorcycle crash and the need to recuperate, cool down and sort himself out, had left Dylan with a very clear and pessimistic feeling that when people followed him it was at best unproductive, and at worst just the compulsion to be hip — and that people demanded that he take on his shoulders the crippling weight of deciding their life-styles and futures and philosophies for them. For Dylan had become not merely a superstar in the usual sense — not merely a celebrity of special magic, style and success, like an Elvis Presley or a Rod Stewart — but, for thousands upon countless thousands of people, a full-time *Messiah*.

Shedding The Messiah Role

It was too much to ask. There was no way that Dylan could take all that on any longer. When he'd been out of it all, right through half of 1966 and all of 1967, it hadn't eased off one bit. Quite the contrary — the intensity of fervour with which people looked towards Dylan for answers and leadership had increased in his absence. So it was obvious that shedding the Messiah role had to be done another way.

'Nashville Skyline' was a start: with this album there would be many people who wouldn't be able to accept that kind of music and the kind of political stance that it suggested. It seemed on the surface that here was either a deliberate move towards the reactionary redneck politics associated with country music audiences,

Bob Dylan, Judy Collins and Arlo Guthrie were but a few of the artists who all played Woodie Guthrie material at the Carnegie Hall, Jan. '68, as a tribute to a great man.

or else a stepping back from politics as politics altogether, in favour of a simple countryman's let-it-be position.

A lot of people didn't accept it; and when, four months later, Dylan appeared at the Isle of Wight Festival, where 200,000 people spent three days waiting in the mud for their Moses to finally come down from the Mount, he disappointed them again. Gone without trace was the bone-thin, mystic/revolutionary genius. In his place was a rich-looking, chubby-faced man in a well-tailored suit, saying 'Thank you, thank you very much' between numbers, and singing both the new bland songs and the old songs in a maddeningly bland new way. And he sang only for an hour. And he reportedly walked off with £35,000.

Topping that, months later, came the double-album 'Self Portrait'. 'What is this shit?', Greil Marcus began his *Rolling Stone* review. The old familiar howls and boos were ringing around Dylan's ears once again, and 'Self Portrait' seemed designed to provoke them — full, as it was, of songs like 'Blue Moon', violin orchestrations, and the whole paraphernalia of Tin Pan Alley show-biz.

Even Dylan was alarmed by all these signs of contempt. He dashed back to the studio (while suffering from a cold which gave his voice the cracked quality of his early recordings) and only four months later, in October 1970, released a new album. It was called 'New Morning' — to re-assure everyone that he'd woken up — and it featured one song guaranteed to curl the toes of every 'radical' rock critic: 'Day Of The Locusts', which described a college graduation ceremony reeking of violence and decay. Dylan was trying to re-visit Highway 61 yet again:

'The man standing next to me
His head was exploding

Well I was prayin' the pieces wouldn't
fall on me'

'We've got Dylan back,' said *Rolling Stone* ecstatically.

Sentimental Charm

It would appear today that there was much more pleasure to be found in 'Self Portrait' than anyone would allow back in 1970, and a lot less to 'New Morning'. While some of 'Self Portrait' remains puzzling or painful (particularly the Isle of Wight recordings), the album as a whole was Dylan's way of acknowledging some of his roots and influences, including Hit Parade material and the sentimental charm of commercial country music.

As in 'Nashville Skyline', it was musicianship that made the album work: the way in which Dylan's voice wrung new twists out of such old lyrics as 'Days Of '49' and 'Copper Kettle', or the way in which the backing group revitalized the Everly Brothers' 'Take A Message To Mary'. Dylan's very first album had been an eclectic collection of blues, gospel and Nashville songs, but then he had emphasised songs about death, isolation and travelling. It was Dylan's romantic image of himself riding a hard road to an early grave. 'Self Portrait' repeated the process, but this time Dylan acknowledged friendship ('It Hurts Me Too') and the joys of getting paralytically drunk ('Copper Kettle'). When he sang about himself as an outlaw ('Little Sadie') or a lonesome traveller ('Early Morning Rain') he gave the song a rather corny treatment, admitting it was far removed from his then-present station.

'Self Portrait' was Dylan melodramatically abandoning himself to being old, commercial, married and drunk. 'New Morning' saw him attempting to be alert and energetic; thinking about Elvis Presley

('Went To See The Gypsy'), joylessness ('Three Angels') and imprisonment ('If Dogs Run Free'). But the music and lyrics didn't quite have the energy to carry it off. He sounded as though he'd been told what topics to write about and he was trying hard. More convincing was 'Time Passes Slowly', which sang of marriage and living in the country as though poised half-way between pure joy and pure boredom. Or 'Sign On The Window', which suggested the possessiveness which can creep into any relationship:

'Sign on the window says ''Lonely''
Sign on the door said ''No Company
* Allowed''*
Sign on the street says ''Y'Don't Own Me''
Sign on the porch says ''Three's A
* Crowd'' '*

Through 1971, Dylan continued to flirt with his past. He performed at George Harrison's Concert for Bangla Desh and astonished the audience by singing 'A Hard Rain's A-Gonna Fall' and 'Blowin' In The Wind', reminding them that the songs expressed far more than the naïve idealism of the early '60s. To follow this apparent return to commitment, he released a single commemorating George Jackson, a black convict imprisoned for a $70 robbery who had educated himself and written a powerful series of letters from prison, and who was finally killed by prison guards 'while attempting to escape'. One side of the single featured just Dylan and his acoustic guitar sounding much as he did on 'Freewheelin''; the other side contained the same song, but with girls' voices singing along on the chorus turning the song into a gospel-style celebration of death. It was one of Dylan's most imaginative recording ideas to use a gospel sound on a requiem for a black radical: conveying the tragedy and the triumph of his death. It wasn't George Jackson, the symbol of oppressed blacks, Dylan was commemorating, but the triumph of a spirit that could not be forced to bow down to authority. In one haunting phrase, Dylan describes the guards as fearing Jackson because he was too *real*, and being frightened of his *love*.

Powerful Song

Through 1972 and '73, Dylan maintained his low profile. He played the part of Alias (''Alias what?'' . . . ''Alias whatever you like.'') in Peckinpah's film *Pat Garrett and Billy the Kid*. He also composed the music for the film, including one very powerful song, 'Knockin' On Heaven's Door', which climbed the singles' charts in both Britain and America. Dylan also did session work on a few friends' albums, but as a public figure he had virtually ceased to exist: since his crash he had appeared in concert only five times in seven years, and by the end of 1973 it was three years since Dylan had released an album of new songs.

The second phase of Bob Dylan's career, which had begun so triumphantly with 'John Wesley Harding' and the Woody

Guthrie Concert, ended not with a bang (like the '66 crash) but a whimper:

'Go take this badge off of me
I can't use it any more
It's getting dark — too dark to see
Feels like I'm knockin' on heaven's door'

After the critical mauling of 'Self Portrait', and the strange *volte-face* of 'New Morning', it is easy to understand why Dylan lost interest in an audience obsessed with idolizing him or destroying him. So at this stage Dylan collected all his songs, sleeve notes, poems and a few doodles into a fat book, and published it with a dedication to Robert Johnson and Woody Guthrie; it felt like his last testimony, and scribbled in the corner of the first page were a few words expressing his mood: 'If I can't please everybody/I might as well please nobody at all/But there's so many people/I just can't please them all.'

Kind Of Flattered

And then, lo and behold, Dylan decided to get up and do it all over again. Not just appear in concerts, but sign a new recording contract and undertake a massive tour with the Band, playing 39 concerts in 21 cities in front of a total of 700,000 people. News of the tour triggered off an estimated 20,000,000 applications for tickets, enclosing $92 million in cash. To put it mildly, Dylan was in a class of his own: and was reported to be *kind of flattered* by the reaction.

Dylan and the Band played their first date in Chicago on January 3rd, 1974, and the critics all agreed they carried it off very well. They mixed together rock & roll arrangements and acoustic solos, playing a song from practically every one of his albums. And it was uncanny how Dylan's songs kept striking sparks off contemporary America, years after he had written them. For 18 months America had been reading bizarre news stories about Watergate and White House Enemy Lists and groups of 'Plumbers' and Cuban exiles and ex-CIA agents performing strange operations 'in the interests of national security'. When Dylan sang 'It's Alright Ma (I'm Only Bleeding)' he paused at the line:

'But even the President of the United
States
Sometimes must have to stand naked'

. . . and the audience exploded.

At the start of the tour Dylan's new record label, Asylum, released 'Planet Waves', a studio album he'd recorded with the Band in November, 1973. Musically it was Dylan's best album since 'Blonde On Blonde'. The Band's music combined strength with relaxation in a way no other group could match. After the sparseness of 'John Wesley Harding', the almost camp country sound of 'Nashville Skyline', and the false start of 'New Morning', 'Planet Waves' came like a wave of warm, confident music. Garth Hudson's organ and Robbie Robertson's guitar provided just the

right degree of embellishment for Dylan's voice and, although the lyrics sometimes sank into sentimentality on love songs like 'Something There Is About You', there still remained the indefinable feeling that once again, with the help of the Band, Dylan had found his edge.

On 'Forever Young', two versions of which appear on the album, Dylan wished young people the dubious joy of staying cocooned in youth. On the second take Dylan sneered the words out of the corner of his mouth, as though sending it up in an old familiar way; but if the song *was* a joke, it was a joke without a punch-line. Like 'If Dogs Run Free' on 'New Morning', 'Forever Young' verged on self-parody, but never settled for it. 'On A Night Like This', and 'Tough Mama', however, were more successful at conveying affection mixed with humour, but the heaviest of the love-songs, 'Wedding Song', sang about a love so total that it turned into near-paranoid fanaticism:

'Eye for an eye and tooth for tooth
Your love cuts like a knife
But I'd sacrifice the world for you
And watch my senses die'

. . . and Dylan's voice ground out the litany with bitter clarity, lacking any trace of humour or tenderness. It was a new style of song for Dylan, and one of his most disturbing. 'Going Going Gone', was refreshing as a song that used the spaces between the words to convey something supernatural and desperate: 'I've just reached a place where the willows don't bend' — the song of a man preparing to break loose. Most sinister of all was 'Dirge', a bitter song of broken promises which becomes a hymn of hopelessness:

'So sing your songs of progress
And other doom machines
The naked truth is still taboo
Wherever it is seen.'

. . . sung to a superb acoustic guitar accompaniment that recalled the flamenco patterns of 'Desolation Row'.

Perfect Partnership

Predictably, critics greeted 'Planet Waves' as they had greeted 'New Morning' — instantly acclaiming it as a triumph and welcoming Dylan back again. 'Planet Waves', though, had too many soft spots to be a work of genius, but it showed Dylan beginning to marshall words and music with some of his former power. And once again it proved that the Band were the perfect foil for Dylan's performances.

Dylan's art has always been profoundly split, because Dylan could never do anything half-heartedly. His electric songs explored extremes of chaos and self-destruction. His post-crash work explored extremes of cosiness and complacency. 'Planet Waves'' real achievement was in the way that Dylan had begun to build a bridge between these two halves of his mind — a bridge across his 'lost years'.

The Byrds West Coast High Flyers

*'Won't you pay for your riches and
 fame?
Was it all a strange game? You're a
 little insane,
Money that came and the public
 acclaim
Don't forget what you are, you're
 a rock'n'roll star.'*

('So You Wanna Be A Rock'n'Roll Star?')

So sang the Byrds in 1967 in a song
riddled with irony. After two years of
success, a year as international chart
toppers and a year as an 'established'
group, 1967 saw the Byrds as has-beens.
The dubbed-on screams were real, but
they came from a 1965 concert; no one
was screaming at the Byrds in '67.

A further level of irony is that back in the
early '60s, when the various soon-to-be-
Byrds were making their first tentative
steps in the music business, rock & roll
stardom was the last thing that they
sought. For Jim (later Roger) McGuinn,
Dave Crosby, Chris Hillman, Gene Clark
and Michael Clarke — in common with
many others — rock & roll was dead. It
was in folk that most of the Byrds began

their musical careers. McGuinn, the only
one with a musical education, started
backing the Limeliters, joined the Chad
Mitchell Trio, and then in 1962 began
doing folk music session work and
supporting Bobby Darin, who had introduced a folk spot into his night-club act.
Similarly, Gene Clark did a stint with the
New Christy Minstrels, and Crosby was a
Les Baxter Balladeer for a while (Baxter
was a big-time American band leader, who
in the wake of the folk boom, like Darin,
quickly inserted a folk slot in his show).
Hillman, like McGuinn, began playing folk
in local coffee houses, then temporarily
left folk for bluegrass, first with the
Scottsville Squirell Breakers and then
with his own group, the Hillmen, as a joint

S.I./Peter Owen

Above: Byrds 1965 — Chris Hillman, David Crosby, Gene Clark, Jim McGuinn, Mike Clarke (unseen). Centre picture: Byrds 1965 again — Mike Clarke, Jim McGuinn, Chris Hillman, David Crosby, Gene Clark — and Bob Dylan, whose songs the Byrds remade, adding their own distinct formula at that time.

CBS Records

folk and bluegrass venture of some merit.

By 1964, the Byrds as individuals were almost old troupers on the folk scene. Like rock & roll before it, folk was being swallowed up by the record industry. In McGuinn's words: "It was getting very commercial and plastic packaged in cellophane . . . a low quality product . . . I wanted to get into something else."

The opportunity to form a group came when McGuinn played the Troubadour in L.A. in the summer of 1964. Gene Clark saw him, and suggested they form a group — 24 hours later Crosby joined them and they began rehearsing as the Jet Set. Stuck in L.A. on their own, they turned for help to Jim Dickson, who had tried recording Crosby as a solo singer and was also trying to sell an album he'd produced for the Hillmen. When it became apparent that the Jet Set wouldn't make it as a trio, Dickson asked Hillman to join. He did, and so all that was needed now was a drummer — enter Mike Clarke, a conga-playing acquaintance of Crosby's.

Songs On Tape

The next step was to get some material together and go looking for a recording contract. Since Dickson had the run of World Pacific studios they decided to make a tape of their songs. McGuinn later described their early music as a synthesis of Dylan and the Beatles:

"In the spectrum of music at the time . . .

I saw this gap, with Dylan and the Beatles leaning towards each other in concept. That's where we aimed."

But when the tapes were eventually released as 'Preflyte', the lame 'Little Drummer Boy' version of 'Mr. Tambourine Man' notwithstanding, it was the Beatles influence, not to mention imitation, that stood out.

On the basis of this tape Dickson got them a 'one record and option' deal with Elektra for which, billed as the Beefeaters ("I plead guilty . . . but there had been such a run of British groups," Jac Holzman, then president of Elektra) they put out a very Beatlish single 'Please Let Me Love You' in the autumn of 1964. The record failed, and the band, now officially the Byrds, switched to Columbia (CBS). Once again the search for a single began. Earlier that year the Animals had had hits with 'Baby Let Me Take You Down' and 'House Of The Rising Sun', which were rocked-up Dylan material, if not Dylan compositions, so Dickson suggested they remake 'Mr. Tambourine Man'. They did (with the help of session-men Hal Blaine, Leon Russell and Larry Knetchel), and after a six-month wait for it to be released it soared to the top of both the US and British charts.

Like 'Satisfaction', 'Like A Rolling Stone' and 'She Loves You', 'Mr. Tambourine Man' is one of rock's great singles, but in 1965, its significance lay more in what it represented: the arrival of folk rock and the

stemming of the tide of the British Invasion. Though the Byrds rose to success with the song and the freaky image they projected, they faded quickly. Their second record, 'All I Really Want To Do', was beaten to the top by a Sonny and Cher cover version, and, though their next, 'Turn! Turn! Turn!'; made no. 1 in October 1965, from then on they were always struggling for chart success.

Diamonds Of Perfection

In the two years between 'Mr. Tambourine Man' and 'Eight Miles High' the Byrds changed a lot. After their first success Columbia allowed the band to play on the follow-up album, which was the expected synthesis of Dylan, 'folk' songs and their own compositions. But if the material was straight folk-rock, their performance of it showed the first real signs that 'Mr. Tambourine Man' was no accident. On all the songs the Byrds made an attempt to stylise and Byrdise the material. By the next album, 'Turn! Turn! Turn!', the Byrds had got folk-rock down pat: out of songs like Gene Clark's 'Set You Free This Time', Dylan's 'Lay Down Your Weary Tune' and the traditional title song, the Byrds created little diamonds of formal perfection. All that was missing was a sense of excitement.

The next album, 'SD', demonstrated that the Byrds were certainly weary of folk-rock. In between it and 'Turn', Gene

Above: Byrds in 1966 – from left to right: Chris Hillman, Mike Clarke, Jim McGuinn, David Crosby, Gene Clark.

Clark had quit to pursue a solo career, thus causing McGuinn and Crosby to either write more songs (Clark had been the group's major songwriter) or look further outside the group than Dylan for material. Strangely, the result was the first Byrds album without any Dylan songs. In their place were very traditional folk songs ('Wild Mountain Tyme'), and the beginnings of McGuinn's personal space odyssey in which science and mysticism were equally mixed ('Mr. Spaceman', '5D'). '5D', which was issued as a single and bombed completely, made explicit the gap between the group's concerns and those of their audience:

'Oh how is it that I could come out to here
And be still floating,
And never hit bottom and keep falling
    through
Just relaxed and paying attention?'

At a time when 'Eight Days A Week' was a surrealist idea for most record buyers, McGuinn wanted his fans to understand and *buy* a record that he later explained '. . . as an ethereal trip into metaphysics . . .'

On the singles McGuinn *was* the Byrds: it was his voice and distinctive guitar that were the group's trademarks. On the albums however, McGuinn was merely one of the group. 'Younger Than Yesterday', the fourth album, saw Hillman and Crosby step forward. The album was released just after 'Sgt. Pepper', and was wholly overshadowed by it. Moreover it was made at the time when the Byrds were at their lowest ebb. As Crosby explained:

"The Byrds would come out there and be a mechanical wind-up-doll. . . . We would get through a set, forty minutes long – just barely – of material that we had done so many times we were ready to throw up with it. We were bored we were uptight."

Baroque Rock

Yet, following up their tradition of capping each album with the next one, 'Younger' saw the electronic experimentation of '5D' brought to absolute perfection: 'CTA 102', a McGuinn space-song about a quasar, caught the sounds of space to a T, 'Have You Seen Her Face?', and 'Time Between' saw Hillman out-do the Beatles, while Crosby on 'Everybody's Been Burned' and 'Renaissance Fair' proved himself a master of baroque rock and, of course, there was 'So You Want To Be A Rock'n'Roll Star'.

Crosby, by this time fed up with the bad gigs and bad feeling inside the group, was forever threatening to leave and showing his feelings by gigging with Buffalo Springfield when they opened the show for the Byrds – a very unprofessional thing to do.

The crisis came to a head in late 1967, during the recording of the next album, 'The Notorious Byrd Brothers'. Crosby refused to sing Goffin King 'pop' songs – 'Goin' Back' and 'Wasn't Born To Follow' – demanded more political songs, and then finally quit for a cash settlement to join Crosby, Stills and Nash – leaving the group with a half-completed album. Somehow the Byrds managed to finish it as a trio, and again somehow it was superb. More importantly, for the Byrds at least, the group had a lucky break. Classified as a singles group by the new rock audience that had suddenly appeared in 1967, 'Younger Than Yesterday' had been neglected as an album. But by the time of 'The Notorious Byrd Brothers' in 1968, the growing number of rock *critics* had begun to re-appraise the Byrds, and thus gave the album a good reception and it sold fairly well. Moreover, the same audience that couldn't understand 'Eight Miles High' would quite happily accept 'Change Is Now'.

By now the Byrds had a growing cult following, though the larger audience raised on San Francisco music still eluded the band. To capture that audience another 'Notorious' was required. Instead, the Byrds added Gram Parsons and replaced Mike Clarke with Kevin Kelley and headed up country with 'Sweetheart Of The Rodeo'. The Byrds just couldn't stand still for long enough to collect an audience around them. Later, 'Sweetheart' would be seen as enormously influential,

Whatever the line-up, the Byrds and their longest lasting member, Roger McGuinn, are part of our established music scene.

but in 1968, no one in either the States or Britain was willing to accept any rock group, let alone the Byrds, singing Merle Haggard redneck songs.

But if 'Sweetheart Of The Rodeo' lost the Byrds the progressive album audience, it also more or less destroyed the band. The next time the group came to record, McGuinn would be the only original member left. First Gram Parsons left when the Byrds agreed to do a tour of South Africa, and then on their return, when McGuinn wanted out of the country trip, Hillman, who's idea it had been, left to form the Flying Burritto Brothers with . . . Gram Parsons. McGuinn had always been the group's front-man but, never very good at handling break-ups, he seemed about to lose all credibility as Crosby sneered at him from the safety of CSN: ''As far as I'm concerned there were only five Byrds ever. Period.'' Leaving Hillman to deal the killing blow: ''All McGuinn's doing now is riding it out till it ends, just for the money.''

Easy Rider

The new, new Byrds' album, 'Dr. Byrds And Mr. Hyde', with Gene Parsons (no relation) on drums, Clarence White on guitar and John York on bass, didn't help McGuinn much: first it was pretty bad, and second he seemed unable to get away from country musicians. Henceforth, like it or not, there would always be a country tinge to the Byrds' music. At this low point luck entered the picture again in the

form of the film *Easy Rider,* which used a few of their songs on the soundtrack. The Byrds were almost respectable again. The album that quickly followed, 'Ballad Of Easy Rider', was better than average and against all predictions, the Byrds seemed to be on the way up again.

By 1970, Skip Battin (of Skip and Flip, an early '60s imitation Everly Brothers) had replaced John York, and after some hard touring the group even began to earn a reputation as a live band. Indeed, they seemed so sure of themselves that half of the double-album 'Untitled' was a recording of a live performance. As if that wasn't amazing enough, the other half saw McGuinn back on form as a songwriter. He'd been commissioned, with Jaques Levy, to write a musical version of Ibsen's *Peer Gynt: Gene Tryp.* The musical fell through, but out of it came a batch of fine McGuinn/Levy songs, all of which slotted into the classic Byrds mould of weary resignation. In 'Chestnut Mare', McGuinn sings of 'Catch(ing) that horse if I can', knowing that when he does he'll lose it again, and soon. 'Just A Season' offers a bleaker and sadder version of 'Change Is Now':

> 'If all my days were hills to climb,
> And circles without reason,
> If all I was was passing time,
> My life was just a reason.'

Change seemed impossible for the Byrds and, just as McGuinn's philosophy was becoming stuck in a rut, all that was

left for the group was to continue in the hope that something would turn up. In 1972, after another two albums — 'Byrdmaniax' and 'Farther Along' — McGuinn gave in and folded the Byrds to, of all things, reform the original five Byrds. The idea was to see if in an atmosphere of revived 45s, the group could take off yet again. The album, 'Byrds', was a failure: there was nothing to return to, there weren't even any worthwhile little-known Dylan songs for them to do!

Solo Album

But if 'Byrds' managed to demonstrate that there wasn't any magic left in the original Byrds by 1973, it helped lay the ghost of the Byrds for McGuinn. Quickly after 'Byrds' came McGuinn's solo album, 'Roger McGuinn'. It was this album rather than 'Byrds' that was in the tradition of the Byrds: Hillman, Clarke, Crosby and even Dylan were all in there helping out as McGuinn re-worked his old themes of space, technology, and of course helpless weariness . . . but this time with a spark of optimism:

> 'The water is wide, I cannot cross over
> And neither have I wings to fly.
> Build me a boat that I can carry two
> And both shall roam my love and I.'

McGuinn may not ever have been the Byrds, but he has certainly outlasted all the members of the group.

Valerie Wilmer

Lovin' Spoonful

Likened at the time to a carton of ping-pong balls on their way to some great party somewhere, the Lovin' Spoonful bounced into the US pop scene in the summer of 1965 with enough style, colour and image to fill the role of America's very own Beatles. And, for a while, they were just that. They came along just one year after the so-called British invasion of beat groups, and at a time when everything seemed to be 'England' — music, fashion, culture.

The Spoonful looked the part: they were New York boys, and they dressed in the striped sweatshirts and faded denims that were the standard outfit of every Greenwich Village kid. What was more, they obviously had talent — the talent, in fact, to produce the loveliest, cleanest, most American sound yet heard

in the '60s. The pop industry, because of the group's Greenwich Village beginnings, immediately classed them as folk-rock, but in fact the Spoonful never confined themselves to any particular style or even a synthesis of styles. They played blues, folk, country and straight commercial pop with equal enthusiasm and competence.

The musical mainstay of the group was John Sebastian, son of a classical harmonica player, and former guitarist and singer with the Even Dozen Jug Band — the first New York group of any importance in the early '60s. Sebastian's background was in folk music but he'd spent some of his teens in Nashville, Tennessee, and there soaked up both country & western influences and the earliest Southern rock & roll. Zal Yankovsky, a Jewish-Canadian émigré who had come to the village with some vague idea of becoming a folk singer, was the Spoonful's lead guitarist. His roots were in blues and rock, and he started playing electric rather than acoustic guitar because, as he put it, "it's loud,

and people dance to it." Completing the line-up were bassist Steve Boone, who had played in a swing band in North Carolina, and drummer Joe Butler, whose musical roots were in rock — and more particularly in the early '60s pop scene on the East Coast of the States.

The Lovin' Spoonful's status as a folk-rock group was as much due to their look of naturalness and their folksy image generally as to the actual style of music they played. Basically, the Spoonful were a second generation rock & roll harmony group with an exceptionally broad stylistic range. Unlike other contemporary harmony groups like the Beach Boys and the Mamas and Papas, the instrumentation on the Spoonful's recordings was given as much emphasis as their vocal harmony patterns, which were less involved, if somewhat less innovative.

Spoonful music was dance music, and, 'Do You Believe In Magic?', their first hit single, was altogether the most joyful and succinct evocation of the very power of

163

pop music and dance since Chuck Berry's 'Rock 'n' Roll Music':

'Do you believe in magic in a young girl's heart
And the music can free her whenever it starts
And it's magic if the music is groovy
And makes you feel happy like an old-time movie'

To attempt to explain that 'magic', the Spoonful sang, was as difficult as trying to tell a stranger about rock & roll.

'Do You Believe In Magic?' was written by John Sebastian, who was responsible for most of the material that the Spoonful recorded during their career. Although he had come from a folk music background, and was influenced as much by traditional American musical elements as by rock & roll, his lyric writing was very much in the mainstream of American pop music. Instead of concerning himself with writing songs of social or political significance, as many of his Greenwich Village contemporaries were doing, Sebastian wrote about far happier things. His songs were about the ups and downs of teenage love — dating, dancing, and simple joys like going fishing . . . standard pop situations. What distinguished Sebastian's work from that of the average pop songwriter was his ability to describe these situations without resorting to the use of cliché or false poeticism. Sebastian's approach was fresher, more alive, more natural than that of the Tin Pan Alley writers whose work consistently topped the charts. Sebastian was an artist as well as a supreme craftsman but, more than this, he was able to relate and express the feelings of teenagers in as precise and as humorous a way as Chuck Berry had done for his teenage audience in the '50s.

'Did You Ever Have To Make Up Your Mind?' used the classic Berry technique of inviting the listener to relate his own experience of a particular situation to that the song was describing, encouraging the listener to respond with a 'yeah, I've been through this too'.

Adolescent Emotions

Sebastian was at his best writing love songs because he was, on his own admission, an incurable romantic. Two of his most outstanding love songs were 'Younger Girl' and 'Didn't Want To Have To Do It', which, though never issued by the Spoonfuls as singles, were hits for other artists (the Critters and Georgie Fame respectively). Both songs presented situations that, while familiar to teenagers of any generation, had rarely been dealt with before in song. Infatuation with someone older is one of the most fickle adolescent emotions of all, and there were a glut of songs during pop's 'high school' period that exploited it: 'Diana', 'Born Too Late', 'Johnny Angel'.

But 'Younger Girl' approached the problems of age difference and infatuation from a different standpoint: in this song

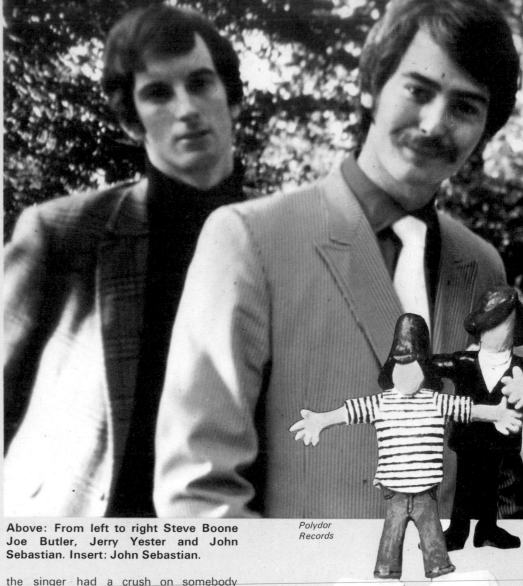

Above: From left to right Steve Boone Joe Butler, Jerry Yester and John Sebastian. Insert: John Sebastian.

Polydor Records

the singer had a crush on somebody younger, in fact too young to be accessible to him. Not only was the song remarkable for breaking new ground lyrically, but it also heralded a new maturity in pop songwriting generally. The boy (or man) in 'Younger Girl' actually understands his feelings, and accepts the fact that he must live with them:

'And should I hang around acting like her brother
In a few more years they'd call us right for each other
But why, if I wait I'll just die'

. . . unlike the girl in, say, 'Born Too Late', who drowns her feelings in pools of adolescent tears. We know that she'll get over it, probably very quickly, but the hero of Sebastian's song leaves us wondering. Almost for the first time, teenage emotion was presented in song as something genuine.

'Didn't Want To Have To Do It' also took a situation long familiar in pop music and looked at it from a new angle. Breaking up with one's partner is pop music's most favourite situation of all, but songwriters have always tended to view it through the eyes of the partner who is hurt, the guy or girl who is put down, two-timed or simply unloved. The other partner is seen as a brute or a coward although, of course, the injured party still loves him despite every-

thing. But Sebastian's lyric deals with this situation far more realistically. He takes the side of the partner who brings the relationship to an end, and expresses this side of the story — sad enough in itself:

'Didn't want to have to do it
Didn't want to have to break your heart
I kept hoping from the very start
But you kept on trying
Then I knew you'd end up crying
Then I knew I didn't want to have to do it at all'

In expressing the heartbreak of that side of Jew's harp, scratchy violin and off-key new ground.

Musically, too, the Spoonful broke new ground with each album. Their most accomplished album was 'Hums', released in mid-1966 with other musicians augmenting their line-up for the first time. Each track represented a different musical style; from primitive jazz ('Bes' Friends'), to country rock ('Darlin' Companion', which Johnny Cash later recorded), the album was a deliberate exercise in experimentation rather than the loose collection of styles that the previous albums had been. 'Lovin' You' was Fats

London Features International   Pictorial Press

album called 'Everything Playing'. It had some charming songs on it like 'Six O'Clock', 'She Is Still A Mystery' and 'Boredom', and included the funniest line Sebastian had ever written:

*'So here we are together, machines and me
I feel about as local as a fish in a tree'*

. . . but the single taken from the album, 'Money', failed to achieve even a chart placing. Eventually and inevitably, Sebastian left, to go back to New York, he said, to write Broadway musicals. Shortly afterwards Steve Boone followed suit, to be replaced by a returning Zal, whose solo career had never really even got started, and John Stewart, ex-member of the Kingston Trio. A while later Gary Bonner, songwriter for the Turtles, joined them, and the group made one last album, 'Revelation, Revolution', which consisted almost entirely of Stewart and Bonner songs. Then, in the summer of 1969, the Spoonful finally folded.

Sebastian meanwhile wrote the score for one unsuccessful Broadway show and promptly returned to California. In 1969, just as the final chapter of the Spoonful's career was drawing to a close, he re-emerged, quite unexpectedly, at the Woodstock rock festival. This time he was alone and had only guitar and harmonica to accompany himself with, but he won the crowd over and in the space of an afternoon re-established himself on the rock scene. There was talk of him joining Crosby, Stills, Nash and Young, but this never materialised, and he made a couple of albums on which a lot of his former folkie friends from Greenwich Village, friends who were now superstars in their own right, participated. The old Spoonful sound was missing, but his new songs contained flashes of the old wit and were of sufficient quality to sustain his new-found popularity.

Reunion Unlikely

At his best, Sebastian touched on the emotional consciousness of the American teenager far more cogently than any of his mid-'60s contemporaries, and it is as a spokesman for that particular generation, or mini-generation, that he should be remembered. Inevitably, there has been talk of bringing the Lovin' Spoonful back together again perhaps for just the one final tour, but Sebastian has been cagey, and rightly so, about such a project. As he wrote in his song 'Six O'Clock' in 1967:

*'If we go back to where we parted
Could it ever be like that again'*

The answer is no. The Spoonful belonged too much to the 1965–67 period — post-Beatles but pre-acid revolution — and too much has changed, in both the social and the musical climate, for them ever to regain the 'magic' that Sebastian once described so appropriately.

Waller revisited; 'Coconut Grove' was softened rock & roll; 'Henry Thomas' had words that were difficult to determine even by listening closely, but the mixture of Jew's harp, scratchy violin and off-key penny-whistle chorus proved funny enough in itself, and predated the popular interest in bluegrass music by several years. Two tracks on the album were released as singles:, 'Nashville Cats' and 'Summer In The City'. The former was an amusing, affectionate tribute to the musicians of Nashville, and told of Sebastian's own introduction to country music. 'Summer In The City' was another Spoonful 'first', this time in the field of record production: it was one of the first ever singles to use sound effects.

In 1966 Sebastian was commissioned to write, and the Spoonful to perform, the music for two motion pictures: *What's Up Tiger Lily?*, directed by Woody Allen, and *You're A Big Boy Now*, directed by Francis Ford Coppola. For *Tiger Lily* all they had to do was go into a recording studio and put down whatever they liked, but in *Big Boy* they had to work to a more rigid concept. Asked to simulate a discotheque sound for one sequence, they placed four microphones in four corners of a studio and proceeded to play — and scream — as loud as they could. The effect was shattering, to the ears at least, but brilliant.

Their film work won them critical plaudits, and everything seemed to be going well when, suddenly, in early 1967, Zal Yankovsky left the group to go solo. His reasons for doing so were not made clear at the time, but emerged soon after. By all accounts, in late '66 the group had been the victim of a drug bust in San Francisco, and Yankovsky had been threatened with deportation if he did not reveal the source of his hash supply. A deal was made with the police and Yankovsky was let free, but the source was subsequently arrested, tried and convicted, purely on Zal's evidence.

The Spoonful carried on as best it could without him and Jerry Yester, former producer of the Association, took Zal's place. There was a change of producer and, for the first time, the group started using orchestral arrangements on their albums. The stage act fell apart without Yankovsky's clowning to hold it together, and Yester was too serious a musician to worry about trying to project an image. The musical climate, too, had changed. Folk-rock was passé, and flower power was just around the corner. Indeed, too much had changed for the Lovin' Spoonful to continue as the force they once had been in American pop music. Everybody lost interest, including, so it seemed, the Spoonful themselves. They put out an

SIMON & GARFUNKEL

Roy Carr

Soon after Paul Simon and Art Garfunkel decided to go their separate ways, it is alleged that Clive Davis pulled the somewhat introverted songwriting half of the duo to one side to voice his displeasure. ''Simon and Garfunkel,'' he growled, ''is a household word. So no matter how successful you'll be, you'll never be as successful as Simon and Garfunkel.''

A statement like this must surely go down in music annals as being the most tactless gesture of goodwill and encouragement ever to have been uttered by the head of a record company to a contracted artist. Especially when one takes into consideration that Paul Simon and Art Garfunkel had just presented the label with its biggest-ever selling album, 'Bridge Over Troubled Water', and, after much preparation were about to embark on solo careers. Perhaps the now deposed Davis was motivated by the fact that with Dylan having gone to ground, CBS did not look favourably upon the demise of

166

its most lucrative investment at the peak of their popularity. It was therefore up to Davis to discourage, the best way he could, any solo ventures which might render the duo's split final.

As a result, such childish snides as: 'Paul has got to get this out of his system', were leaked to the trade press; or worse still, when Simon set foot on CBS soil, he would be greeted with such seemingly off-the-cuff digs as: 'Say Paul, when do you think you'll do the next Simon and Garfunkel album'.

Company Pawn

It seems almost irrational that someone of the stature of Paul Simon – an intelligent artist who has had some of his finest work seriously compared to that of T. S. Eliot – should be subjected to such abuse, let alone used as a pawn in petty company politics. For without doubt, Paul Simon has emerged as one of the few artists of his own generation to have refined his natural talent to such a level of creativity that, within its particular genre, it is almost exempt from adverse criticism. As Paul Simon declared on the self-penned

sleeve note of his first solo album which he cut in London in the spring of 1965:

''I start with the knowledge that everything I write will turn and laugh at me. Still, you never get used to mocking laughter. I am forever withdrawn and shuffling before my own words. I do have some feeble phrases that I put forward to excuse myself: 'But that's the way I felt at the time'. But I can barely hear them for the ringing of laughter in my ears. You see, I know that in one year's time (did I say a year?) I'll read these scribbled notes and think 'Oh no, did I write this junk?''

Whether this was a concerted attempt by Simon to adopt an 'intellectual' stance, at a time when the sheer presence of Bob Dylan had prompted almost everyone who took up a guitar to display an attitude of false modesty and deep concern, or whether in fact he felt this of his own work, only Paul Simon can answer.

Setting aside whatever motives lay behind Paul's handful of words, it was, nonetheless, an album which revealed a vast and untapped potential through such perceptive little vignettes as 'I Am A Rock', 'The Sound Of Silence' and 'A Most

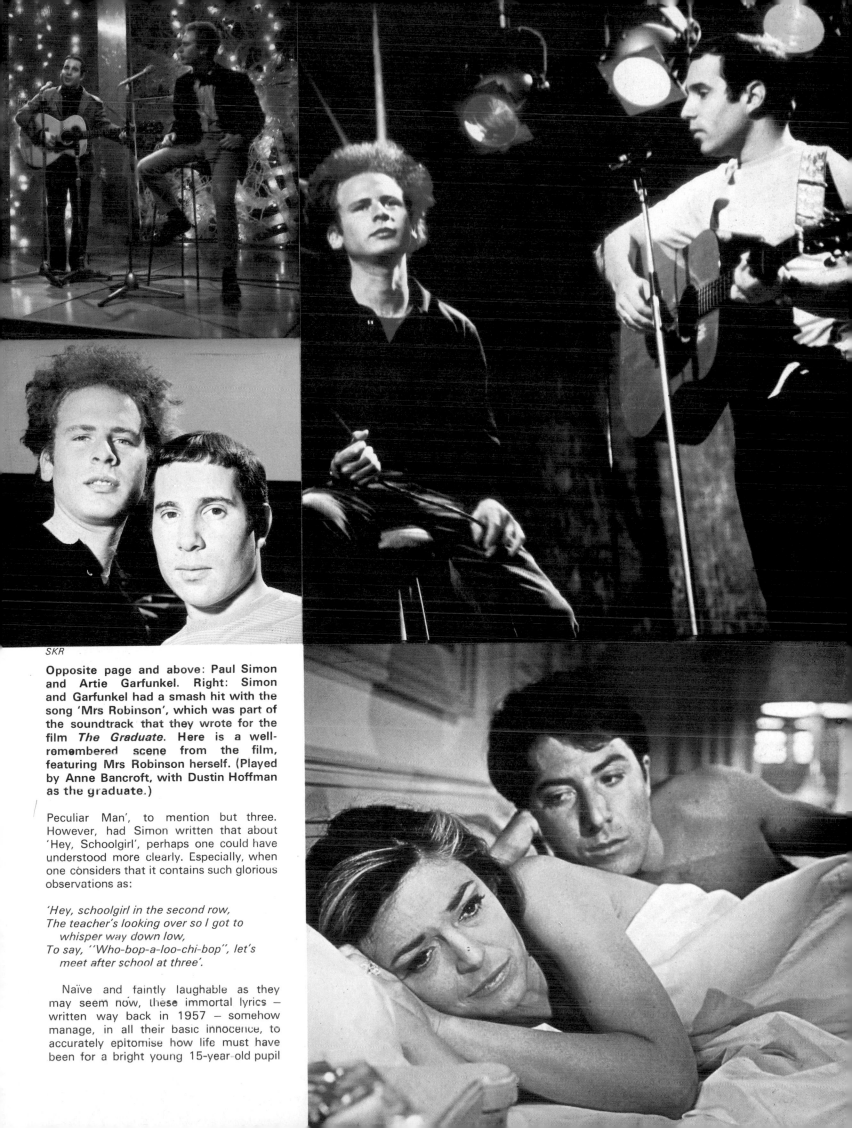

Opposite page and above: Paul Simon and Artie Garfunkel. Right: Simon and Garfunkel had a smash hit with the song 'Mrs Robinson', which was part of the soundtrack that they wrote for the film *The Graduate*. Here is a well-remembered scene from the film, featuring Mrs Robinson herself. (Played by Anne Bancroft, with Dustin Hoffman as the graduate.)

Peculiar Man', to mention but three. However, had Simon written that about 'Hey, Schoolgirl', perhaps one could have understood more clearly. Especially, when one considers that it contains such glorious observations as:

*'Hey, schoolgirl in the second row,
The teacher's looking over so I got to
   whisper way down low,
To say, ''Who-bop-a-loo-chi-bop'', let's
   meet after school at three'.*

Naïve and faintly laughable as they may seem now, these immortal lyrics — written way back in 1957 — somehow manage, in all their basic innocence, to accurately epitomise how life must have been for a bright young 15-year-old pupil

Rex Features

From left to right: A boyish portrait of Paul Simon and Artie Garfunkel; Paul Simon in concert.

at Forest Hills High School in a suburb of New York City.

They were conceived by a chubby-faced, flat-topped kid from out of Queens, trading under the nom de plume of Paul Kane. An average sort of Jewish adolescent who wanted to be as sexually dangerous as Elvis, with the killer tactics of Chuck Berry. But at 15 it was not to be, so as a consolation he settled for Phil Everly — with his sidekick eager to act out the role of brother Don. He may have been short on talent and animalistic charisma at that time, but just the same Paul (Kane) Simon sure knew how to rock & roll.

Tom And Jerry

Under yet another pseudonym — Jerry Landis — and with some help from his trusty schoolchum Tom Graph, 'Hey, Schoolgirl' was soon to be transferred on to seven inches of shining black plastic under the patronage of Big Records. Surnames, however, were dispensed with, and the label proclaimed them simply as 'Tom and Jerry'.

This record made the US Top 40, and sold 100,000 copies — making them the toast of the neighbourhood burger joint and corner soda shop. They even managed to get around to singing their hit on the Thanksgiving Day edition of Dick Clark's *American Bandstand* in November, 1957, along with Jerry Lee Lewis — who was strafing the charts all the time with 'Great Balls Of Fire'. And look good they sure did, as they cut-the-mustard in their brand new draped sports coats, snazzy bow-ties, super-cool pegged pants and the inevitable white bucks. Yep, Tom and Jerry — or should we say Paul Simon and Artie Garfunkel — sure looked a couple of smoothies.

But, like innumerable other acts of the first rock & roll era, their fame was to be short-lived. By the time they were 16, Tom and Jerry were 'has-beens'. A follow-up single 'Dancin' Wild' had flopped miserably, and so did their third attempt; so when Big Records went bankrupt, there was no alternative for them but to go

slightly saddened no doubt, back to school.

Though Paul and Artie were washed up as Tom and Jerry — Garfunkel moving to Columbia University to study mathematics, and Simon majoring in English literature at Queen's University — the ghost of Jerry Landis refused to lie down. "In those days," Simon recalls, "you could earn money making masters or demos, so that's what I did. I can remember being paid $15 a time cutting Burt Bacharach's demos." He also has a vague recollection of receiving $100 for singing lead with Tico and the Triumphs on 'Motorcycle'/ 'Lisa' which came out on Amy in 1962, and eventually accounted for 100,000 sales.

In the meantime, Artie Garfunkel attempted an unsuccessful comeback in 1961–62 by recording under the name of Arty Garr for both the Octavia and Warwick labels. But in no way was he as committed as Simon to establishing himself as a professional musician. "Around the time I was making those demos for Bacharach," admits Simon, "I teamed up briefly with this young girl called Carole Klein." Paul would play guitar and bass, Carole would handle piano and drums, and together they sang in close harmony. The subsequent demos were then despatched to artists like Frankie Avalon and the Fleetwoods, but without too much response.

One of their demos, 'Just To Be With You', proved to be a chart entry for the Passions. Carole was elated by this, but, Paul was cautious and did everything in his power to talk Carole out of quitting Queens and becoming a professional songwriter. He failed. Carole Klein (King) notched up 10 big hits that same year.

After a stint at Queen's College, Simon also quit — this time to enrol in Law School. But his rock & roll shoes made his feet itch, and on two separate occasions he cut classes, determined to make it as a musician. The second time Simon dropped out, he popped up in London. The year was 1964 and, still retaining the name Jerry Landis, he somehow managed to cut 'Carlos Dominguez'/ 'He Was My Brother' for Oriole. It dis-

appeared without trace or mention.

Prior to his arrival in London, Simon had been peddling songs for a New York publisher, and he arranged an audition for both Artie and himself with Tom Wilson at CBS, with the result that an album 'Wednesday Morning, 3 a.m.' materialised, and for a time nearly became billed as 'Simon And Garfield'. "I was frightened they might think we were comedians or something," Simon said at the time, "but at least we were honest, I always thought it was a big shock to people when Bob Dylan turned out to be Bob Zimmerman".

Garfield or Garfunkel, honest or not, 'Wednesday Morning, 3 a.m.' was yet another non-starter, so Simon once again packed his bags and came to London, where he spent the next few months working folk clubs and pubs all over the British Isles, doing some radio and TV work, and cutting 'The Paul Simon Song Book'. Artie had now joined Paul in London, and though he was on vacation undertook a couple of local gigs. It was 1965, and 'folk rock' was becoming a tag with which to sell records. After hearing Simon and Garfunkel's acoustic version of 'Sound Of Silence' on the radio, producer Tom Wilson — who was very big at the time with Dylan — dashed round to the CBS studios and proceeded to over-dub both a rock and string section on the existing master-tracks.

Breakthrough

It was goodbye Tom and Jerry, welcome Simon and Garfunkel. They were still in London when the record broke big and the paradox was that after struggling for years to attain this breakthrough, Simon was in no hurry to return to the States to capitalize on his success.

There were a number of reasons why Simon was reticent about returning to the States. Perhaps his prime one stemmed from his bitter experiences the previous year. In no way was New York City 1964 conducive to the emergent talent of young Paul Simon. Materialistic, insensitive, this cold metropolis of 10 million souls was at

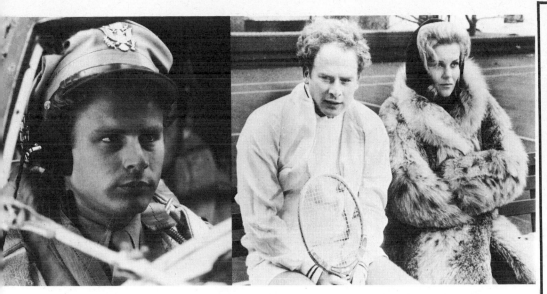

Arthur Garfunkel, as he appeared in the film, *Catch-22*, and *Carnal Knowledge*.

that time no place for Simon's sensitive artistry. He was rejected, dejected, and struck with complete apathy.

At the same time, New York City's anonymous, obese mobile cigars were desperately trying to instigate an effective counter-attack to the British Beat invasion. It desperately needed hordes of mop-topped Beatles plagiarists, and raunchy, dirtier-than-thou Stones alternatives. So up against all this, here was a stocky, short-haired kid singing and pickin' his acoustic guitar with his lanky, fuzzy-haired friend peering over his shoulder. Forget it . . . they'd never sell records. It seemed to Paul and Artie that in New York every back was turned, every door was closed.

"We just couldn't get a job," Simon remembers, "Artie and I auditioned at a lot of clubs in the States, but absolutely nobody showed any interest in either us or the music. We received absolutely no encouragement or acceptance whatso-ever." And so, disillusioned, he packed his guitar and a few clothes, and with just enough money to buy some food and a bed arrived in London where, within weeks, he became a familiar face around Soho's smoky cellar clubs, East End laundrettes and working-class pubs. Not for one minute did Simon harbour any real aspirations of stardom. It was just a nice way to travel around the British Isles.

By delaying his return to America, Simon figured he was putting off any sickening let-down. However, upon Simon and Garfunkel's arrival in New York City, they found 'Sound Of Silence' resting at no. 2 on the nation's chart, and contracts whereby they could pick up $13,000 for a weekend's work. Success and record releases came fast and often furious. 'Homeward Bound', 'I Am A Rock', 'The Dangling Conversation' and 'A Hazy Shade Of Winter' kept them on the best-selling charts for most of 1966. By the same token, their albums 'Sounds Of Silence' and 'Parsley, Sage, Rosemary And Thyme' rapidly accumulated millions of dollars and fans all at the same time.

It appeared that when Simon and Garfunkel sang, an entire generation listened. But the pressure was on, the demand for anything emblazoned with 'Simon and Garfunkel' was enormous, and in no way conducive to creativity. Simon was something of a perfectionist. He was far more interested in quality, as opposed to the industry's plea for quantity. If a recorded performance didn't measure up to the set of standards he'd long ago set himself then it wasn't made public.

Alienation And Isolation

In fact, for a brief period Simon was forced to backtrack in an attempt to catch a second breath. In doing so, two songs from off his 'Song Book' portfolio, 'Flowers Never Bend With The Rain' and 'A Simple Desultory (Or How I Was Robert McNamara'd Into Submission)', reappeared with added trimmings on 'Parsley, Sage, Rosemary And Thyme'. Up to and including this album, much of Paul Simon's work dealt with the connecting subjects of alienation and isolation. The top side of their next album was, in some ways, to take it a step further with its complex theme of growing old. The flip side was an assortment of singles. It is an album of which both artists are exceedingly proud.

"I rate it just below the 'Bridge' album," states Simon. "I rate each album as being better than the last one. With 'Bookends' we started taking much more time with the singing and the overall production. In many ways, I thought that it was the logical extension of our recording career, which in my opinion didn't really start until we recorded 'Parsley, Sage, Rosemary And Thyme." Garfunkel has also gone on record as stating: "With 'Bookends' we got around to making records the way we wanted to."

Around the same time, the soundtrack of *The Graduate* was released and 'Mrs. Robinson', the main song, became an immediate smash. Simon and Garfunkel were now nearly as hot as John, Paul, George and Ringo. For the week of June 15th, 1968, 'Mrs. Robinson' was sitting at no. 1 on the US singles chart; while on

the album charts, 'The Graduate', 'Bookends' and 'Parsley, Sage, Rosemary And Thyme' were at nos. 1, 2, and 3 respectively. 'Sounds Of Silence' rested at no. 27, while 'Wednesday Morning, 3 a.m.' stood at no. 163.

'Bridge Over Troubled Water'

It seemed that Simon and Garfunkel couldn't get any bigger. But there was one more album to come. A collection of 11 immaculate tracks, which has since become one of the three biggest-ever selling albums in history. Figures of between 7 and 10 million copies have been mentioned, and it's still selling. 'Bridge Over Troubled Water' was something of an artistic phenomenon, though of course the duo were not aware of this at the time of conception — as it transpires, it wasn't even cut under the best conditions.

"Recording that album was hard work. Artie was already away filming *Catch-22,* so I wouldn't see him for say three months at a time, with the result that I did most of that album on my own. In fact on some tracks Artie doesn't even sing.'' 'Baby Driver' is just a multi-tracked Simon, while on 'The Only Living Boy In New York' Artie appeared somewhere in the background. "He'd come back and I'd say, 'I wrote the lyrics to 'El Condor Pasa', or I've already finished 'Baby Driver' and 'The Boxer'. So to a degree there was this separation without there being a lessening of musical quality.''

On one such reunion in the studio, when Simon gave his partner 'Bridge Over Troubled Water' to sing, he wasn't all that enthusiastic. It was only after much persuasion that he relented and sang it as a solo showcase, but his heart wasn't really in it.

The 'Bridge' album was originally

scheduled as a 12-song set, but hassles erupted as to which song would round off the collection. Simon had plans for a song entitled 'Cuba Si, Nixon No', while it is alleged that Artie had ideas concerning a Bach chorale. With the duo totally exhausted by recording, filming, touring and a two month TV commitment, the final song was scrapped and the album put out in its familiar form. As Simon has said in his own words:

"At the time of recording, we both had it in our minds that this would be the last one together. What I think we actually said was something to the effect that we'll finish the album and that will be it. We hadn't any plans to do anything together after that. I planned to do an album by myself, and Artie went off to commence filming on the set of *Carnal Knowledge*. First off, the reason why Artie and I stopped touring was simple. We had both agreed that we had reached a logical conclusion to our constantly going out on the road. You've got to remember that we were locked into the same material each and every night. We were obligated to sing the required Simon and Garfunkel hits, which realistically speaking the audiences had come along to hear. I mean, we just couldn't say 'I can't sing 'Bridge Over Troubled Water' again because we've sung it so many times'. People want to hear it, and if you're going out on stage you've got to give the public what it wants.''

"Therefore, when you are in that situation there are a lot of pressures forced on an act. So it was the logical end to the act. Also, having a track record to live up to and a string of successful records eventually becomes a hindrance. It becomes increasingly difficult to break away from what people naturally expect from you. From this point of view, I'm delighted that I didn't have to write a

Simon and Garfunkel follow-up to 'Bridge Over Troubled Water' for, to be honest, I think that it would have been a let-down for everyone concerned.''

While most of his contemporaries have truly blown their integrity, Paul Simon has retained his equilibrium — his new material is as good, if not better, than anything he's put down in the past. Even the unparalleled success of the 'Bridge' album, and his split with Artie, didn't in any way impair his direction or judgement.

Better Writer

It is futile to even begin to compare one collection of Simon's songs with its predecessor. They are complete entities. As Paul Simon has put it:

"You can't ever write the same thing twice. I know some people try to, but that's silly because it just doesn't work. I'm aware that success often satiates an artist's hunger to succeed further, but personally I don't think it's the hunger that is dimmed . . . it's their drive. I don't know if I have as much drive to be successful as I did when I first started out, but I still have the desire to be good. It's very embarrassing to be bad. But if I'm going to be totally realistic, I honestly don't think I will ever repeat the success of Simon *and* Garfunkel, but I hope to prove myself to be a much better writer than I was when I wrote for Simon and Garfunkel. And it's only this which keeps the game alive for me. You see, I still have a healthy enough ego to want to do things well, and for people to say that I'm good. But I was only prepared to go back on the road once I was ready and I'm ready now.''

From the response to his brace of solo albums, it appears that Simon, even without Garfunkel, is still one of the most respected and popular performers today.

Pictorial Press

Jefferson Airplane

'Hey people now smile on your
  brother
Let me see you get together
Love one another right now'

The anthem of the 'love generation', 'Get Together', was a hit for the Young-bloods in the summer of 1967, just about the same time that the Beatles' 'All You Need Is Love' was released. It was the song of the moment, the expression of everything that the 'summer of love and peace' was supposed to be about. And, if there was one group who represented San Francisco, summer 1967, it was the Jefferson Airplane. It comes as no surprise that the Airplane recorded 'Get Together' for a track on their very first album, 'Jefferson Airplane Takes Off', released in August, 1966; and yet the Airplane had not written the song. It was in fact written by Chester Powers, better known as Dino Valenti, who didn't release his own album until 1968, and played along with San Francisco's Quicksilver Messenger Service from the end of 1969. Valenti is something of a strange starting point for the story of Jefferson Airplane, and yet to start with him actually makes two important things about the Airplane clear.

Like Valenti, the Airplane's roots are in the mid-'60s revival of folk and folk-style music; and their declared aim was to develop a style they called 'folk rock'. Secondly, the Airplane and the whole San Francisco scene, which included Valenti, were connected by almost familial ties. It

is impossible to talk about one San Francisco performer, promoter or manager without bringing in most of the other local figures in the music scene.

In March, 1965, Dylan's electric (in all senses of the word) 'Bringing It All Back Home' was released, and the idea of electrified 'folk' music took root and blossomed with the Byrds' version of Dylan's 'Mr Tambourine Man'.

The Byrds originally came from Los Angeles, and their sound was typical of the place — disciplined yet relaxed, so that the instruments were all clear and distinct, like the geography and architecture of the city. Even before the Byrds had started as a group, though, the connections between L.A. and 'Frisco were being made. David Crosby, for example, would often play (folk) on the same bill as Valenti when both were itinerant musicians. Paul Kantner, Airplane guitarist and songwriter, met Crosby in L.A., and the two of them, along with David Freiberg, lived together in Venice, California, when they were all trying to make a living out of coffee-house performances. Freiberg was a founder member of Quicksilver, and joined the Airplane around the beginning of 1972 after an enforced absence from Quicksilver due to a drugs charge.

It has often been said that the Airplane was the first San Francisco group. 'Only the Charlatans and Mystery Trend pre-date them', according to one writer. Whether or not they were the *first*, though, is not important. What is important is that the Airplane 'was the first of the big San

Francisco bands *to make it*, the first to snap up a big contract, the first to get big national promotion, the first with a big national hit . . .', as Lillian Roxon put it. In 1966, the Airplane signed a contract with RCA Victor guaranteeing them a $20,000 advance.

Marty Balin was the group's founder. He was born Martyn Jerel Buchwald, the son of a lithographer and himself a designer and painter. In 1964, Balin was with a folk group called the Town Criers. He saw the Beatles on the *Ed Sullivan Show* in February of that year and decided, there and then, to get 'involved with the rock & roll thing'. Previously he had met Dylan in New York, and when Dylan 'started getting popular and the Byrds went to L.A. and started . . . the folk rock line', Balin decided to go to San Francisco and start a group there. He didn't exactly audition people, but got the band together through asking friends.

After Kantner left the Los Angeles area he moved to San José. By then he'd listened to the Beatles and started playing around casually with Roger McGuinn and stated: "The Byrds were the first American group that really turned me on." In San José he played and helped run a folk club. In Santa Cruz he lived in a proto-type commune and met Jorma Kaukonen — still at college in Santa Clara — who became the Airplane's lead guitarist. When Kantner eventually returned home to San Francisco, he began playing at the Drinking Gourd, a local folk club. It was here that Marty Balin met him, after a fruitless

171

search for musicians to build up the group. Balin describes his intuitive recognition that Kantner, with "a 12-string and a banjo, and . . . hair down to here and an old cap," was the man for the group: "I had never heard of him, but I *knew* he was good."

Kaukonen joined as a favour to Kantner — he was, at the time, 'a Bay Area folk figure'. Among the people Kaukonen had already played with was Janis Joplin, and it was the strength of Janis' vocals that made him buy his first electric guitar: ". . . she was so loud it was just impossible for an acoustic guitar player to compete with her." While at school in Washington, Kaukonen had also played casually with Jack Casady. It was through that connection that Casady came to San Francisco to play bass with the newly formed Airplane.

Musical Centre

In the spring of 1965, Marty Balin took over the Matrix club. The Matrix had been a folk and jazz club under the name of the Honeybucket. Balin had the idea of turning it from a quiet, almost underground club, into a centre of musical activity in the town. He decorated the place, put in a stage, and — in August, 1965 — the Airplane opened there as a semi-resident group. The two members, apart from Balin, Kantner, Kaukonen and Casady, were the girl singer Signe Tolne Anderson, and Skip Spence on drums. Interestingly, at the time Balin caught Spence, he was on his way to audition for the Quicksilver people, who were also starting their band. Skip Spence had never played drums before, and pretty soon after the first album had been recorded in the early autumn of 1966, he left, to eventually form another San Francisco group, Moby Grape, with whom he sang and played guitar. Spence was replaced by Spencer Dryden, an experienced jazz drummer; and it was Kaukonen, Casady and Dryden who provided the essentials of the Airplane's musical excitement during their best period.

Signe Anderson also left after the first album due to pregnancy and Casady recruited a girl singer to replace her from a group that had started in the Airplane's wake. She was called Grace Slick, and the group she had formed with her husband and brother-in-law was called the Great Society. Her voice, much more raucous and rough than Signe Anderson's, was the perfect complement to Balin's sweetness. She also happened to bring with her the two songs which were to become the Airplane's only two real hit singles: 'Somebody To Love' and 'White Rabbit'.

By the time of 'Take Off', the Airplane had already changed direction considerably. The changes in personnel had something to do with it, but perhaps the two most important factors were acid and amplification. Grace Slick brought with her a harsher vocal style, but she also brought a drug song ('White Rabbit'). The lyric field open to rock had been started by Dylan and his successors, but the particular

concern with psychedelia and 'mind expanding' drugs was almost completely restricted to San Francisco in those early days. Even the Berkeley groups from across the Bay, like Country Joe and the Fish, were involved in it — whereas their previous involvement with music had always been far more overtly political.

In November, 1965, yet another California group with a folk-singing background became involved with the 'Acid Set' — a group of people focused on ex-beatnik Ken Kesey and his Merry Pranksters, and Augustus Owsley III, who made LSD in his house in Watts, Los Angeles. They were the Warlocks, who became the Grateful Dead around February, 1966. Kesey and Owsley held what they described as 'Acid Tests' around the beginning of 1966, and the Dead provided the music. In June, 1966, the Dead moved to San Francisco, and LSD began to hit the Bay Area in a big way — furthered by the rapidly growing number of large dance/concert halls that were springing up all over the city. The Airplane, the Marbles, the Great Society and the Charlatans played at the first of these to be organized in San Francisco. It was held at the Longshoreman's Hall on October 16th, 1965. The promoters were the original Family Dog — a group of young people who were probably the first hippie communards. Marty Balin designed the posters, and the Airplane topped the bill.

The unexpected popularity of that event led others like Bill Graham and Chet Helms to organize follow-ups. Light-shows and gaudy clothes blossomed; people came in their thousands to celebrate and to dance, or simply to observe. The Fillmore Auditorium and the Avalon Ballroom became Meccas for the young people of San Francisco, goldmines for the owners and promoters . . . and potential threats to the moral order for the police. Jefferson Airplane were usually there, the doyens of San Francisco's own music; and as the audiences got larger and more eager to dance, through acid or simple excitement, the need for more and more amplification and more and more free expression in the music increased.

The Airplane's early sound was dominated by Marty Balin. His voice was smooth and rich, his songs mainly love songs. Signe Anderson had merely supplemented him, but Grace Slick began to complement him. Eventually, Marty Balin gave up playing guitar, and Grace Slick, who had come in on keyboards and recorder, gave up her instruments. The amplified guitars took over, especially Kaukonen's beautifully clear and aggressive playing, and a vocal style depending on anything from two to four-part harmony developed — Balin usually singing on top with Slick cutting through like a flint wheel. The folksy, acoustic sound began to give way to a harsher, electric and freer approach. This trend can be detected on 'Surrealistic Pillow', their second album, which, although containing two of Balin's finest love songs, 'Today' and 'Comin' Back To Me', also has the more energetic 'Some-

body To Love' (by Grace's husband Jerry), Balin's angry '⅗ Of A Mile In 10 Seconds', and 'White Rabbit' (on the American version of the album only — the British version is a combination of the first two American albums).

The Airplane's music began to reflect the functions it performed. Very often it was simply a question of stance-taking. But outrageousness for its own sake fitted in well with the newly awakening hippie consciousness. Like their name (from an imaginary blues singer, 'Blind Jefferson Airplane'), much of what they did was, at worst, a joke and, at best, simply a response to the question 'Why not?'. 'Crown Of Creation', their fourth album, had Paul Kantner stealing the lyrics of the title song almost verbatim from John Wyndham's *The Chrysalids*: 'The Old People are determined still that there is a final form to defend: soon they will attain the stability they strive for, in the only form it is granted — a place among the fossils'.

Love too became a stance, and on '⅗ Of A Mile In 10 Seconds', Balin points forward to the political stance he and Kantner would later take on 'Volunteers'. He writes: 'Do away with people frowning on my precious prayer/Do away with people laughing at my hair'. The huge Fillmore and Avalon dances, the almost instantaneous creation of a hippie lifestyle born largely of young dropouts, brought people suddenly together in shared experiences in which music played an important part. The music and its free-form dance approach became a major way in which people identified each other as belonging to their group. It is not surprising that some sort of political statement eventually grew out of it, and it is equally clear why it was later abandoned to things like Kantner's private science-fiction fantasies.

Mirrored Feelings

The Airplane quickly became reflectors of the feelings and ideas of their audiences. Kantner even admits this to be the case when questioned about his earlier political views: "It's like I'm a sort of news man. Like you, I write down what I see happening, but I don't have a paper. I use my songs as the vehicle. Everything that was in 'Volunteers' has happened, and is happening right now. I just saw it and wrote it down." The Airplane's politics, in other words, were just a reflection of the state of their audiences. And they were as short-lived and as superficial as most writers have observed, simply because the hippie rebellion itself was involved with superficiality.

An Airplane concert was certainly an experience not to be missed. Between August and September, 1968, they were in Britain to do the Isle of Wight festival, a free concert and two gigs at the Roundhouse — London's answer to the Avalon Ballroom. By this time they had a huge underground following on both sides of the Atlantic. They released plenty of singles,

but they never were a singles band. Only 'White Rabbit' and 'Somebody To Love' approached the kind of success most bands had previously been interested in. 'White Rabbit' reached no. 8 in the *Billboard* charts, and 'Somebody To Love' went up to no. 5.

In comparison to the success of 'Somebody To Love', which got to no. 22 in the *Cash Box* listing of top singles for 1967, nothing else the Airplane did in America and nothing they did in Britain had any impact. Yet their draw as a live band, and, to a lesser extent, their album sales, were remarkable. They made greater and more exciting use of light-shows than anyone around at the time, and would drift off into lengthy and meandering jams — very appropriate for the psychedelic mood of the moment. When they wanted to they could still be tight and heavy, but their involvement with acid and electronics made that less and less likely. These changes showed up on record too. 'After Bathing At Baxters', released in January, 1968, was recorded after the group's first big American tour. Balin, who couldn't write on tour, figures less on it than on any previous album, and it also features a nine-minute instrumental jam between Kaukonen and Casady called 'Spare Chaynge'.

The light-shows and the group's developing musical style were obviously attempts to superficially re-create the drug experience. But drugs changed perception rather than the reality underlying it, and psychedelic music and its off-shoots — light-shows and hippie dress — now appear as attempts to change certain objects of perception. The hippie rebellion was superficial, in this sense. The hippies only attacked certain areas of the cultural ways of expression — they dressed differently, looked different and spoke differently . . . but underneath, little had changed. Bill Graham, who used to manage the Airplane, was the first and most successful entrepreneur of the hippie world. He ran the biggest dances, managed groups and started a record label. He kept a careful watch on his world — he was involved with 'people dancing and having fun, that's all'. And, of course, making money. His comments to a young kid trying to get into the Fillmore for nothing sum up that whole side of things: "Forget love," he is reported to have said, "get in line!"

Water Brothers

The cult book of the time was Robert Heinlein's science-fiction fantasy *Stranger In A Strange Land,* about a Mars-born Earthman who brings with him from Mars to Earth a whole new code of morals and the beginnings of a new religion. Mars compares well with Southern California. The Martian culture values water above all else, because, like Southern California, it is a desert world. The highest compliment is to call someone a 'water brother', and the hero of the novel lives with two women in a happy threesome. He makes his appearance in David Crosby's song 'Triad' on 'Crown Of Creation':

'If you're crazy too
I don't really see
Why can't we go on as three'.

It was a very gentle rebellion. In contrast to the Doors — an L.A. group who shared the bill with the Airplane at their London Roundhouse gig — the Airplane only challenged society by default. Where the Doors demanded, 'We want the world, and we want it now!', the Airplane merely suggested, 'We can be together'. At their most extreme — as with Marty Balin's last work on an Airplane album, 'Volunteers' — they came out with: 'Got to revolution, Got a revolution'. In a confused way they expressed the idea that the revolution was already here: 'We are outlaws in the eyes of America' (from 'We Can Be Together' on 'Volunteers'); but they never really knew what they wanted . . . if they wanted anything at all. In that same song Grace Slick shouted 'Up against the wall', only to follow immediately with 'Tear down the wall'. No one ever knew what the wall was really for.

The Airplane, though, moved from success to success. Only Marty Balin seemed disaffected. He clearly didn't enjoy touring, and he wrote less and less. Kantner, who used to be Balin's co-writer, fell in with Grace Slick, and Kaukonen and Casady spent more time playing together. The group began to be dominated by Slick's harsh and meandering vocal style. The

Top insert: Pictorial Press. Bottom insert: L.F.I.

Against a background of the Jefferson Airplane group are pinpointed – Bottom L.H. insert: Papa John Creach on fiddle. Top L.H. insert:

Airplane had quickly become a lead-guitar based group, and that set them apart from the British-style rhythm-oriented bands. But it also meant that they became undisciplined and undirected. They lost their inherent sense of structure, and when Grace Slick began to dominate the group, their artistic decline became inevitable. Slick's voice has been described as 'I-am-a-background-instrument' in style, and her biggest contribution to the group was when she complemented Balin. Undoubtedly Grace has a way of moving, seemingly

without direction, sliding from phrase to phrase without giving the feeling of getting anywhere, but this is precisely what destroyed the Airplane. Not only her voice, but her lyrics too, shift from phrase to phrase without any overall sense. On 'Long John Silver', their eighth album as the Jefferson Airplane, she was able to write:

'You can't fly – human master
You can't fly – by yourself
You can't fly – dying master
Without a rifle on your shelf'.

The comparison between Slick's style and the light-shows they used is irresistible. The almost formless meanderings are fine for a light-show, but are a hopeless basis on which to build a growing, progressing music.

Between 'Volunteers' and 'Park', nearly two years elapsed without a single original Jefferson Airplane album. When Balin left in the summer of 1971, the group seemed to fall apart. They moved out of their communal house, set up their own label, Grunt, on a very good manufac-

Top insert: L.F.I. Bottom insert: Pictorial Press.

Grace Slick and Paul Kantner in concert. Centre insert: Grace Slick. Top R.H. insert: Paul Kantner, guitarist and science fiction addict.

turing and distribution deal with RCA, and each seemed to go their own way. Kantner and Slick had a child, who was to be named 'God' but got off with 'China', and Kantner — in the face of the failure of the hippie rebellion to actually change anything — went off into a fantasy world of giant starships, which he and David Crosby would pilot in a bid to escape the strife-torn planet Earth.

Balin ended up producing and singing with a Bay Area group called Grootna, and has since moved on to another called

Bodacious D. F. Kaukonen and Casady started Hot Tuna which was a part-time acoustic band. It later acquired additional members and made several albums. Joey Covington — Hot Tuna's first drummer — joined the Airplane when Dryden left, eventually to join the New Riders of the Purple Sage. He left to join Kaukonen's brother's group in 1972, and was replaced by John Barbata, from the Turtles and ex-CSN & Y session drummer. Covington brought old, black, fiddle player, Papa John Creach, into the fold, and all of them

— Creach included — have made individual solo albums exploring their own private obsessions. Since the late '60s they all became more and more involved in their own internal machinations, drifting away from real contact with their audiences. But the Airplane always did belong to a particular era, and the hopes and dreams of that time disappeared, living on only as a pleasant memory — the symbol of many people's awakening to a new experience and a new way of thinking.

175

Joe Stevens

L. Van Houten

Janis Joplin: Queen of the Blues

She was a real little earth-mama. A child-woman who sang black country blues gone electric. Her husky voice rasped out the notes and people said she was the greatest white female blues singer ever, and they always qualified it like that — 'white and female'.

Maybe, if she had lasted a few years more, Janis could have made it all the way to becoming *the* 'greatest blues singer'. Still, she *was* a legend in her own time. She zapped in at the end of the twin-set, pearls and brogues era — when girl singers were either wholesome and happy, or chirpily sexy — and showed that being a girl didn't automatically put you into one of those moulds . . . in fact, she showed you could be a girl *and* have soul.

Janis Joplin was an anachronism in her small hometown of Port Arthur in Texas. She was a beatnik weirdo who didn't fit into the routine of small-town life at all. Born there on January 19th, 1943, by the time she was 14, the locals — with their middle-class values and middle-income habits — had decided she was some kind of revolutionary. At high school she dressed differently and cared about different things, and as a result had few friends that she could relate to. At this stage though, neither she nor her family — younger brother Michael and younger sister Laura — had any great musical leanings, but, according to her father, she read, she painted and she thought.

By all accounts her teenage years were typical of the '50s — boring, stifling and endless. So, although it's difficult to believe, as a teenager Janis was quiet, introspective, lonely . . . and waiting.

Janis had pure animal grace as she moved. Insert: Janis and Tina Turner at a New York concert in November '69.

Texas isn't the place for outrageous people, and as Janis said, "they laughed me out of class, out of town and out of the state".

She also had to bear with the musical mish-mash of the '50s — the untainted petting of the high school jingles, those shallow old tunes that came floating out of every transistor in town, with no meaning, no guts, no bottom. She was 17 before she discovered the blues, in the form of Leadbelly and Bessie Smith, and for the next few years Bessie Smith was her idol. She played her music endlessly, and naturally she sang her songs . . . in an incredible blues moan that was light years away from anything that was happening musically in Texas at that time. Years later, when Janis spoke of Bessie Smith, she said, "she showed me the air and taught me how to fill it. She's the reason I started singing really". (Janis' feelings for this blues queen were so strong that she even organised a headstone for her grave.)

Free Beer And Hillbillies

When Janis finished high school, she began singing whenever she got the opportunity. Locally, she began to gain a reputation as a blues singer, mostly singing in a little bar outside of Austin, Texas. It was a Saturday night place, with bring-your-own guitars, free beer and real live hillbillies. Still, she hadn't yet escaped the conformity of her upbringing, and so enrolled at a college to study to be a teacher — giving up the coffee-bar circuit where she had been singing.

College life, however, was no more appetising than that of high school, and so when Chet Helms, an old friend of hers, appeared on the scene, she decided to drop out of college and head for San Francisco with him. She was only 18, and California was a whole new world. She stayed around there for five years, singing in the bars and folk clubs, playing auto-harp, and becoming a high-flying speed freak who didn't have too much going for her. But she *was* learning to be free, and no longer felt a monster in a world of goody-goods.

Then, in the mid-'60s, the 'underground' started to really happen strongly in California. The beards and hair flowed unshaped and untamed. The clothes were long, wild and spacey. They were improvised, colourful and precious. They were timeless in their non-adherence to a fashion format. The young lived in a charming mix-up of squalor and beauty — brown rice and black beans, chenille curtains, embroidered cushions, Spanish pots and Tibetan prints, broken toilets and bead curtains, blocked-up refrigerators, flax matting and scrubbed wooden tables. Wax-eyed friends flowed in and out, sipped camomile tea, and carried enamelled snuff boxes that belied the sagging ceilings above them. And in all this, Janis sowed her oats without a break, and in a spate of burnt-out tiredness, decided to return home and give the straight life one more chance.

She sang the blues in her rawest, most sensuous fashion, letting her tearaway voice out at full-throttle. This satin-shine, this tender tart, made them get up and move.

This was 1965, and it was the year that San Francisco finally came together, musically. Underground clubs started up, including the now legendary Fillmore Auditorium. The psychedelic rockers and the acid rockers came in the shape of Jefferson Airplane, the Grateful Dead, Captain Beefheart, the Doors, Moby Grape, Country Joe and the Fish, the Fugs and Velvet Underground. They were mostly community bands, friends who just happened to come together and play for fun. They were communal and tolerant, and they were rebelling against material-istic and bigoted repression — it was love versus violence.

The mid-'60s were a time of acid art, light shows — vibrating, merging splodges of colour that blended silkily and serenely, glowing milkily-pearlescent and translucent across the walls. And their music reflected this in intense details. Janis' Texan friend Chet Helms, who was organising the first hippie dances at the Avalon Ballroom (where Big Brother and the Holding Company eventually established themselves) became their manager. At the time, though, they needed another singer, and Chet persuaded them that Janis was the right one.

He drove to Texas to see her, and Janis threw in college for the final time. Janis and Big Brother — Sam Andrew and Jim Gurley on guitars, Peter Albin on bass and Dave Getz on drums — regularly worked the Avalon and other small gigs around the Bay. Janis learned to fuse her blues with the strength of Big Brother's power-ful amplifiers. She discovered that the only way to cope with an electric rock band was to explode. She sang wild and free. She screamed into that high-energy rock music, and the hippies couldn't get enough of her. Big Brother were fast moving into the top group ratings, along with the Grateful Dead and Jefferson Airplane. Janis was living with Country Joe at the time, and when their relationship ended he wrote a song about her, called 'Janis' in his album 'Fixin' To Die'.

She was singing wilder and louder than ever and her voice hid her youth. It was gravelly and gutsy, and it hollered, screeched and seduced everyone with its raw caresses. It didn't take long before Big Brother got an offer to record, from a small Chicago outfit called Mainstream. It was a disastrous liaison, and the album 'Big Brother And The Holding Company' wasn't released until after the Monterey Pop Festival, when the record company were absolutely certain that they would make a killing with it. Big Brother tried to prevent its release, as they had improved immensely in the interval, but the album nevertheless sold fantastically (this was still at a time when Janis was *in* the band, rather than *being* the band).

Monterey Pop

Big Brother continued to gig and rehearse three or four times a week, and Janis was by now ripping into the blues with a blown-out, earthy passion. The Monterey Pop Festival of June '67 was the big break for Janis and Big Brother, and after months of practising in the Haight, they were ready for it, and so were 50,000 love-freaks. It was their first real festival, and they turned on to the magic brew of love, flowers and music. From Otis Redding to Ravi Shankar the music was amazing, but no one had any expectations of Big Brother, who were relatively unknown outside San Francisco. They had to follow on from the Who and Hendrix . . . and they made it.

Janis' rendering of 'Big Mama' and 'Ball And Chain' broke the place apart, and they couldn't get enough of her. It all came out front — her tough, hooker voice tore at their insides. She was a mean blues singer with sex flowing out to the audience in a hot, full rush. It was crude and rough and tremendously important. Janis was the big discovery of the festival and the rock critics couldn't write enough about her. Her pure animal grace as she moved and stomped — letting her tearaway voice out at full-throttle — whipped her audience again and again into a frenzy of applause.

Big Brother had arrived, and Janis had made the transition from a street-singer to a rock star. By January '68, they had signed with Albert Grossman — then managing Bob Dylan — and were ready to start touring. By the end of August, their tours had included the Fillmore East and the Newport Folk Festival, and Janis had become a true, husky-voiced earth-mama yelling her aching hurt. She said, 'she'd rather not sing than sing quiet', and she flooded her fans with her deep anguish. Her whisky-soaked, Southern Comfort voice could touch on a tender quietness too, but it was her wailing and whoring moaning that plugged the audience into her.

Janis controlled the entire audience with her body. She tore right into them, with her breasts and hair and beads flying, her clothes the ultimate in extravagance:

'Are your clothes matching your soul? Your soul goes through changes, you're always feeling all things at once. So why not wear all things at once — its groovy, its real.'

Her spaced-out clothes amazed and delighted every male in the audience. She dripped feathers and bangles as her impassioned voice blasted the lids off their minds. Her satin and silk slipped tight over her heaving breasts as she groaned into the cold steel microphone.

In her no-faking, tender-tart clothes, she whipped herself into a lather of frenzied singing and boogying. It was a huge and raw performance, and gradually the band fell further and further behind her. However, when 'Cheap Thrills' came out in September '68, it earned a Gold Record almost immediately. The band had a full rock sound and Janis came across as a powerful, confident singer. Some of the best tracks were 'Summertime', 'Piece Of My Heart' and 'Turtle Blues', written by Janis herself:

'I once had a daddy,
He said he'd give me everything in sight.
So I said, honey, I want the sunshine,
   yeah,
An' take the stars out of the night.'

Soon after the success of 'Cheap Thrills', Janis and Big Brother split up. Their final concert together was appropriately enough with Chet Helms' Family Dogg. Janis antagonised a lot of her fans with the split, but there were too many tensions for the band to be able to hold together any longer.

She had difficulty choosing a new band, telling a good sax from a faker. She was doing a mammoth task, virtually carrying the whole band by herself. She wanted a thicker sound — a soul sound — and the final line-up was Sam Andrew (from Big Brother), lead guitar; Bill King, organ; Marcus Doubleday, trumpet; Terry Clements on alto sax (both formerly of the Electric Flag and Buddy Miles Express); Brad Campbell, bass; and Ron Markowtiz, drums. She toured with them until December '69, and although they never bombed out completely, they were never much more than a back-up band, and somehow never quite captured the magic of Big Brother. They had recorded an album called 'Kozmic Blues', which was released in November '69 and received very mixed reviews, although it was generally agreed that 'Work Me Lord', 'Try' and 'One Good Man', had all the tough, appealing essence of Janis in them. But for all that, her voice had not heightened its magic, and critics began to ask her if her voice was going. With her usual below-the-belt bounce, she replied: ''People like their blues singers dying; they don't like them rocking — I'm rocking, at least I think I am.''

She was right, she was first and foremost a blues singer, and there is a tradition attached to that tag, one of 'hardship, tragedy and early death'. Janis' answer to that was: ''Just have a good time. I juice up real good and that's what I have. Man, I'd rather have 10 years of superhypermost, than live to be 70 by sitting in some goddam chair watching TV. Right now is where you are, how can you wait?''

Full-Tilt Boogie Band

In mid-April, 1970, Janis re-appeared with Big Brother and the Holding Company (plus Nick Gravenites) at the Fillmore West. They played all their old numbers and everyone loved them. But everything really came together for Janis in May, when she formed her Full-Tilt Boogie Band. The five-piece band included John Till, lead guitar; Brad Campbell, bass; Richard Bell, piano; Ken Pearson, organ and Clark Pierson, drummer.

The group was on the same wavelength as Janis, and the effect was five really good musicians making a tight sound and playing as if they'd been together for years. Their first official gig was on June 12th 1970, at Freedom Hall in Louisville, and it was wilder and more magical than anything that had ever happened for Janis before. She sang the blues in her rawest, most jean-creaming fashion, and everyone rocked in their seats as her high energy poured over them in endless waves. Her voice blew the walls apart and this tender tart made them get up and move. She was a sensuous satin-shine, who would sing until she dropped.

By September, they had almost finished recording their album, with Paul Rothchild as producer. It included two tracks written by Janis, 'Mercedes Benz' and 'Move Over', Kris Kristofferson's memorable 'Me And Bobby McGee', and one that said everything there was to say about Janis, 'Get It While You Can'. They were mostly slower numbers than before, and when the album was posthumously released as 'Pearl', it played like a tribute to a great lady who had been buried alive in the blues.

Dual Deaths

She died on October 3rd, 1970, after accidentally injecting an overdose of heroin into her arm. Another death had been added to the toll of artists who had been at Monterey — Otis Redding, Brian Jones, Al Wilson, Hendrix and then Janis. Hendrix had died only three weeks before, and the similarity in both their lives and deaths was uncanny. They were both 27, and had both made it big at Monterey. They both poured out solid sexuality on the stage, and were both preparing new songs, with new bands to reinstate themselves as rock stars. Lastly, they both neutralised their lives with narcotics.

It seemed as though no one ever realised how lonely and insecure Janis was, or how much she depended on drugs. Yet she gave them a clue when she said, ''I'm going to write a song about making love to 25,000 people in a concert and then going back to my room alone.'' Her world was up onstage, and that was a reality that could only extend to a couple of hours a day. It was her high, her Nirvana, her pinnacle of pleasure. How then could the rest of the day match up? The surreal world of plastic planes, shiny-tiled motels, coffin-sized concrete dressing-rooms and pre-packaged food was too hard to take. It was inevitable that Southern Comfort would not always be enough. As Deborah Landau in her book *Janis Joplin — Her Life And Times* said:

'What more lonely way to die, than alone in a motel room in Los Angeles, feeling great and being that careless, blowing the whole thing, all alone, quietly before she was ready.'

Capitol

The Band
Big Sound from Big Pink

"I can't believe that people are so gullible to accept what they accept in art and in music. Nowadays they're playing jock-strap and feedback, and they knock them out . . . I think it's up to the individual to get himself to the place where he doesn't have to be that taken in by anything. Now people are saying, let's hear the truth; we haven't heard it in a long long time."

(Robbie Robertson, *Time* interview, 1970)

1968 was an important year. It was the year of the May Events in Paris; the year of the Chicago Democratic Convention; the year, in Britain, of the massive October 27th Vietnam demonstration in the streets of London. It was the year of 'Beggars Banquet', the summer of 'Street Fighting Man' and the Doors' 'Waiting For The Sun' album . . . including their frightening 'Five To One'; the time of 'Electric Lady-land', 'Cheap Thrills', and the Cream's 'Wheels On Fire'.

It was the year in which the frenetic energies of 1967 raced away into uncharted and unknown territories: the year in which acid consolidated its arrival of the year before. The lines were being drawn: 'Your ballroom days are over' . . . 'We are the people your parents warned you against' . . . 'They've got the guns but we've got the numbers' . . . 'I think the time is right for violent revolution' . . . 'Everywhere I hear the sound of marching, charging feet, boy'.

It was at this emotionally charged moment that the Band arrived. Their first album, 'Music From Big Pink', was released in the States in June 1968 – a month after the May Events and a couple of months before 'Street Fighting Man'. The Band themselves though, had been playing for a number of years: four of them had been brought up in Canada, and they had played together as far back as 1959. They had acted as the backing group for Canadian rock & roll singer Ronnie Hawkins, and had been known as the Hawks. Robbie Robertson, the lead guitarist of the group, had distinguished himself on many of Ronnie's rock records, in particular with a high-powered solo on 'Who Do You Love?' (1963). Levon Helm, the only American in the group, had sung a few times with Ronnie, and some of his early efforts had found their way on to recordings – usually blues standards like

179

The Band in 1970. Left to right: Levon Helm, Rick Danko, Robbie Robertson, Garth Hudson and Richard Manuel.

Bobby Bland's 'Further On Up The Road' and Muddy Waters' '19 Years Old'.

On tracks like these, we have the Band in embryo — Helm's rough, brutally honest vocals accentuated by his raunchy drumming, Robertson's precise but exciting guitar sound, and Rick Danko's Motowny bass lines. Ronnie Hawkins has always known how to pick sidemen, and the group sounded like a good one.

Good as they were, however, their sound was neither original nor truly creative. They were — as they would be the first to admit — their master's voice, and it wasn't until they broke with Ronnie and toured the southern states of the US, as Levon and the Hawks, that things began to happen. On tour they tightened up their sound considerably, and gained the confidence they could never have got as Ronnie's group — they even released a couple of singles, the most famous being 'Stones That I Throw', which was a landmark if only as a Robbie Robertson composition. Nevertheless, the records didn't sell and they still seemed to be getting nowhere fast. Levon Helm said: "We just played joints, just swinging and grooving the best we could. But after a while it got to be a drag. It was just reproduction. We'd do rhythm and blues like someone else because that's what the audience wanted to hear. But when you do that, you end up just being a house band. You either do that or you go home."

By some amazing quirk of fortune however, their music received just the jolt it needed when they were spotted by Bob Dylan in the summer of 1965. Dylan, shortly after the release of his rock & roll debut album 'Bringing It All Back Home', was looking for a rock group to back him on live appearances. Quite how he knew of the Hawks is one of *the* great mysteries

of rock — but his choice was a magnificent one. Dylan contacted the Hawks when they were playing in Atlanta City and, if we can believe them, they hadn't really heard much of his musical career. "We'd heard of him," admitted Robbie Robertson, "but we weren't into that kind of music, and I really didn't know who he was or that he was *that* famous." Nevertheless, a few months later, they were immersed in his kind of music and played behind him through the Fall of 1965 and until his motorbike smash in the summer of 1966.

Dylan provided the key to the Hawks' growth. Over the years they had become superb musicians technically, but on the ideas level their potential had been stultified by their situation: they had been expected to play traditional rock wherever they performed, and this continual repetition had put a stopper on any creative developments in their music. Dylan, though, would not tolerate this kind of stagnancy — his own career had been full of movement, full of a restless search for something quite indefinable. The effect on the Hawks was traumatic, with Robbie Robertson in particular being shaken out of his preconceptions by the continual state of musical flux that for Dylan was almost normal. "Dylan brought us into a whole new thing," Robbie said, "and I guess he got something from us."

The understanding that built up between Dylan and the Hawks was truly astonishing, as anyone who has heard them play together will attest to. It's one of the tragedies of rock that they made so few recordings together. Officially, we have only odd tracks from 'Blonde On Blonde' ('One Of Us Must Know'), the live version of 'Just Like Tom Thumbs Blues', released as the 'B' side to the 'I Want You' single, and the occasional live recording released

on the 'Self Portrait' album ('The Mighty Quinn', 'Like A Rolling Stone', 'She Belongs To Me' and 'Minstrel Boy'). The two most fruitful periods of their collaboration — the tours of 1965 and 1966, and the time of Dylan's recluse in 1967 — are simply ignored. We know that recordings were made due to the explosion of bootleg releases in 1969 and 1970, but — as of 1973 — it would appear that CBS have no plans to make the tracks legally available.

The Hawks stayed with Dylan throughout 1967, and it wasn't until the summer of 1968 that their first solo album was finally released. 'Music From Big Pink' was a massive, personal statement, and the influence of Dylan on their music is apparent in practically every line of every song. The album opened, appropriately enough, with a song jointly written by bassist Rick Danko and Bob Dylan — 'Tears Of Rage', a number written during the Haight-Ashbury happenings of 1967:

'We carried you in our arms
On Independence Day,
And now you'd throw us all aside
And put us on our way . . . '

The lyrics, presumably written by Dylan, were not just unusual in that summer of 1968 — they were a positive insult. The Hawks, now called the Band from Big Pink, launched straight into a head-on collision with the prevailing rock hegemony. While others were singing the praises of the imminent war of the generations, 'Big Pink' began with a picture from the other side of the conflict:

'Tears of rage, tears of grief,
Why must I always be the thief?'

'Music From Big Pink' acted, together with Dylan's 'John Wesley Harding', as a brake on the psychedelic momentum of 1967 and 1968 — they were both conscious acts of disassociation. 'Big Pink' played down electronics — you could hardly hear the wah-wah at all — and Robbie sought out the group's problems by looking into the past, searching among the forgotten areas of pop music. 'Strap yourself to a tree with roots' Dylan had sung, and Robbie agreed: "Your roots," he has said, "really are everything that has ever impressed you." It was this approach from the group, this tendency to eclecticism, that marked out 'Big Pink' as something special. The vocals, as an example, covered every conceivable influence from the soul-tinged bluesy sound of Richard Manuel on 'Tears Of Rage' and 'Lonesome Susie', to the raucous country sounds of Levon Helm on 'The Weight', taking in Rick Danko's great straight-pop vocals on 'Caledonia Mission' and 'In A Station' on the way.

But even this sort of catalogue leaves half the story unsaid, for the most remarkable achievement of the vocal sound of 'Big Pink' is the incredible ease with which the group manages to fuse all of these different influences together. This cohesion is brilliantly demonstrated on 'We Can Talk About It Now', where all three of the band's singers appear to be singing lead. The result is not the confusion you might expect, but a beautifully natural sound, with the harmonies emerging quite effortlessly and spontaneously. It was an amazing vocal sound to be confronted with in 1968, and even the best of the 'progressivists' like Clapton and Hendrix seemed to pall beside it.

'Jock-strap And Feedback'

Instrumentally, Robbie Robertson's guitar playing was a complete rebuff to the 'jock-strap and feedback' sounds of the late '60s — its total lack of showmanship was quite out of place in the heyday of Cream and Jeff Beck. The piano/organ combination was not new, but its use by the Band was Garth Hudson's organ was a Lowrey, and his sound added a cathedral quality to the Band's music, which merged in distinctively with Richard Manuel's rock piano. But, most important, was the Band's insistence on the *song* being the central hook-point of the music — everything else, including Robertson's complete mastery of his guitar, was secondary.

The Band's instrumental sound was *illustrative,* it created a mood in which the essence of the song could be adequately portrayed. It was an important lesson that they had picked up from Dylan. But if 'Big Pink' was a great album, it must be said that their follow-up, simply called 'The Band', was even greater. Dylan had dominated the first album, with even the group's own songs like 'The Weight' and 'Chest Fever' very much dependent on his inspiration. But the second album was Robertson's.

Robbie quite suddenly emerged as a

First column from top to bottom: Garth Hudson. The Band at Woodstock. Rick Danko. Second column from top to bottom: Robbie Robertson. Richard Manuel. Levon Helm. The Band during a performance at the Woodstock festival.

writer of major stature, with his lyrics revealing enormous hidden depths of wit, compassion and astuteness. 'The Band' is a musical merry-go-round of the US, an exploration of its moods and quirks, its legacies and attitudes. Most of the songs are written from the standpoint of the poor working-class Southerner, and one of them, 'The Night They Drove Old Dixie Down' has since become established as a Southern classic. On the album, this song acts as a superb vehicle for the voice of Levon Helm, for whom it had been written. Levon is the Southerner in the group, and the passions of the song and his treatment of it are the highlight of any concert given by the group.

'Dixie' might well remain the most famous of the album's songs, but none of the others fall short of this standard. Some are wryly funny and human ('Jaw-bone', 'Up On Cripple Creek'), some are devastatingly nostalgic and homely ('Rockin' Chair', 'When You Awake') and others are notable for their incisive intelligence ('King Harvest Has Surely Come', 'Look Out Cleveland'). And, right through the heart of the album, there is the stabbing economy of Robertson's guitar, the majestic, universal touch of Garth's organ, and the wistfulness of Richard Manuel's piano.

'Stage Fright', their third album, was patchy by comparison. The strength remains in certain songs, and odd moments of the record seize the imagination like their earlier work. 'All La Glory' — a characteristically sweet lullaby — and 'The Rumour' come over as well as anything they had done before, but much of the material sounds rather rushed and annoyingly messy. The group's sound had lost none of its impact, but Robbie's songs seemed to have suffered. This feeling — which remained just that on 'Stage Fright' — was confirmed by the release of 'Cahoots' in 1971. On 'Cahoots', Robertson's material sounds almost contrived, with none of the natural, easy flow of the songs from 'The Band'. It sounds, in a phrase, as if he's trying too hard, and the weakness of the material is underlined by the arrangements Robertson decided upon: they are clever, they are tight, but they are a far cry from the primitive ease of 'We Can Talk About It Now' and 'Across The Great Divide'.

Quite why this happened is anybody's guess. It may well be that the demands of the recording industry had put too much of a strain on Robertson, and the release of the live album in 1972, 'Rock Of Ages' was, in the negative sense, an admission of this failing. There had by then been no new songs from Robbie since 'Cahoots'.

But then, towards the end of 1973, the Band's period of apparent inactivity was uncompromisingly ended. First came 'Moondog Matinee', a musical *tour de force* featuring such rock & roll classics as 'Promised Land', 'The Great Pretender' and 'Mystery Train'. This was followed at the beginning of 1974 by Dylan's 'Planet Waves' (the first legal album to feature him backed by the Band throughout), and Dylan and the Band's sell-out tour of the States, from which a live album was recorded for release in mid-1974.

Meanwhile, having moved from the seclusion of Woodstock to California, they began to play on a surprising number of sessions with other musicians. Robertson in particular was featured on recordings by artists as various as Carly Simon, Joni Mitchell and Ringo Starr. The vigour and enthusiasm of their playing on all of these bodes well for the future. Certainly, if the results of their latest association with Dylan are as formidable as their own first albums, the Band are going to be a force to reckon with for a long time to come.

The Band's Robbie Robertson playing with Bob Dylan in Chicago, during their '74 six week, sell-out tour of the States.

L.F.I.

Creedence Clearwater Revival

Creedence Clearwater Revival were always something of an anachronism, a throwback, a band out of their real time. Coming to prominence in 1968, in an era of psychedelic, underground and increasingly complex 'progressive' rock, Creedence chose to base their own style very firmly and very obviously in the simple, direct and immediately accessible rock & roll of the mid-1950s.

In an era when — in the wake of the Beatles' 'Sgt. Pepper' — the *album* was widely held to be the only truly worthwhile rock commodity, Creedence embarked upon a string of classic hit *singles*. And in an era when most bands changed personnel nearly as often as they changed their socks, the members of Creedence had stuck together for almost 10 years before their first real breakthrough to national success.

But though old-fashioned and in many ways unfashionable, Creedence were also an enormously popular band, by a long way the most commercially successful white American act of their day: Gold Album followed Gold Single, and both followed sold-out tours apparently inexorably, until their final break-up in October 1972.

Creedence were a band out of time, who demonstrated that the times were to some degree out of joint. Then, despite psychedelia and drug-rock and the growth of a real or imagined counter-culture, Creedence made it clear that there were still millions of kids looking for the kind of music they could play on juke-boxes, cruise to on car radios, dance to at parties. That there was still a huge demand for fairly simple and straightforward rock & roll.

Unchallenged Mainstream Band

Creedence filled that demand, and were able to occupy the mainstream of American rock almost unchallenged for the better part of five years. Moreover, they were able to use their authority as a definitive mainstream band to promote ideas and attitudes some way outside the general rock mainstream.

Officially, Creedence Clearwater Revival came into existence on the first day of 1968. Before that, a long way before that, there were the Blue Velvets: Doug Clifford, Stu Cook and John Fogerty. Three 13-year-olds who got together in 1959 at El Cerrito High School in the then quiet (pre-Free Speech Movement) north Californian suburb of Berkeley, near San Francisco. It was John Fogerty's idea:

". . . one day I was listening to the Corvettes on the radio and boom! . . . I said to myself 'Gee, I could have thought of that name. Corvettes. Like the car . . . And gee, I could make a record like that.'"

The Blue Velvets played at the local school hops, often joined by John's elder brother Tom. Then Tom would sing lead and they would be billed as Tom Fogerty and the Blue Velvets. All four kids were Berkeley born and bred, middle-class and middle income, playing and imitating the music of poor white southerners and northern city ghetto blacks.

In 1964, the Blue Velvets moved up to semi-professional status, acquiring a recording contract with a local San Francisco label, Fantasy. Despite the group's strong objections, Fantasy insisted on a change of name. And so, in the wake of Beatlemania and the British Invasion —

a devastating experience for the native American recording industry – the Blue Velvets became the Golliwogs. It was under this unlikely name that they released a string of mostly unsuccessful singles between 1965 and 1967, all of them now long deleted and unavailable.

Music was still a hobby rather than a full-time occupation. The Golliwogs played primarily in bars in and around the Berkeley area, working very hard and to little appreciation. A very character-building experience, as John Fogerty would recall later in 'Lodi':

'If I only had a dollar, for every song I've sung
And every time I've had to play while people sat there drunk
You know I'd catch the next train back to where I live
Oh Lord, I'm stuck in Lodi again.'

During this period, the Golliwogs scored just one moderate-size regional hit single, 'Brown-Eyed Girl'. John Fogerty was now singing lead and Tom had stepped back, confining himself to rhythm guitar: "I could sing, but he had a *sound*." With Doug Clifford on drums and Stu Cook on bass, the line-up of the future Creedence was already fixed. And John Fogerty, lead singer, lead guitarist and soon to be the band's one and only songwriter, was now undisputed leader. If this caused any conflict between the brothers back then, it took a very long time to break the surface.

The Golliwogs Turn Professional

In 1967, control of the Fantasy label passed to one Saul Zaentz, a man with more imagination and more faith in the band. And so, after nearly 10 years without real success, the band decided on one last all-out effort to break through. They turned professional, devoted all their time to music, chose a new name, and made one more new start.

Myths cluster around that new name. The usual story is: they had a friend called Creedence, they saw a TV beer commercial about clear water, they knew there had to be a revival. Creedence Clearwater Revival. Anyway, it was a great name, and it somehow exactly represented the music upon which they would build their new career.

Under the nominal guidance of Saul Zaentz, Creedence went into the studio and cut a first album, titled simply 'Creedence Clearwater Revival'. That album, with its stereotyped Ralph J. Gleason, 'San Francisco Explosion' sleevenotes, undoubtedly profited from the then widespread interest in West Coast music. And yet, the music inside the sleeve actually bore very little relationship to the so-called 'San Francisco Sound'. It was mostly very tough, hard-edged rock & roll and blues, with a clean and relatively uncluttered production that often seemed to hark back to the two-track Memphis sound of Sam Phillips' old Sun studio rock & roll classics.

The usual San Francisco album of the period (Country Joe and the Fish, the Jefferson Airplane, the Grateful Dead, and so on) was cool, spacey and very cerebral, featuring lengthy and complex instrumental passages, much apparently directionless riffing, and lyrics concerning drugs, religious insights and universal love. The Creedence sound, and in particular Fogerty's singing, was hot, raucous and urgent. The songs were tightly arranged and performed, the instrumental passages kept neat and concise: only one track, the old Dale Hawkins rock & roll standard 'Susie Q', broke the five-minute barrier. The lyrics referred only to universal rock & roll and blues mythology: women, love, sex, poverty, misery. This was music that knew exactly where it was going. It was, predominantly, music to excite the body rather than the mind.

Standard R & R Numbers

Though John Fogerty had written five original songs for that album, it was the two rock & roll standards – 'Susie Q' and the old Screaming Jay Hawkins number 'I Put A Spell On You' – that stood out as the strongest cuts. Both were released, simultaneously, as singles, and both reached the US Top 10.

So Creedence began with an unusual name and a distinctly unusual image: that of a rock & roll revival band. Their next single, 'Proud Mary' – first in a long sequence of contemporary rock & roll classics written by John Fogerty – redefined and extended that image:

'Cleaned a lot of plates in Memphis
Pumped a lot of gas down in New Orleans
But I never saw the good side of the city
'Til I hitched a ride on a riverboat queen
Big wheel keeps on turning
Proud Mary keeps on burning
Rolling, rolling on the river . . .'

Raised and based in Berkeley, John Fogerty now led his band into a celebration of the mythology of the American South-West, producing something which the critics would immediately tag 'swamp rock'. Their second album, from which 'Proud Mary' was culled, was called 'Bayou Country', and included one song which advanced the claim to be 'Born On The Bayou'. Their third album was entitled 'Green River', and featured a cover photograph of the band apparently deep in that bayou country: the photograph was taken in Berkeley's Tilden Park.

Since John Fogerty was by now taking sole production credits for these albums, and writing nearly all the songs, one must assume that he was largely responsible for this exercise in image-building. And it was, indeed, a curious image for a north Californian band to adopt. But when Creedence sang those songs, they were somehow entirely convincing. John Fogerty managed to translate his obsession with the Old West – with a land of freedom and open spaces, where the catfish bite, the bootleg stills bubble, and barefoot girls

Chris Walter

From left to right: Stu Cook, John

dance in the moonlight – into compelling and authoritative music. For the city dwellers who largely made up Creedence's audience, these songs brought alive what was to them a dead and gone American landscape.

Co-existing with these swamp rock archetypes, a secondary theme begins to appear in Fogerty's songs, from the 'Green River' album on. Moving from a celebration of freedom in the American past, Fogerty arrived at a deeply pessimistic view of the American present. Creedence's big hit single of mid-1969, 'Bad Moon Rising', was a furiously energetic cry of despair: 'I hear the voice of rage and ruin', Fogerty rants like some Biblical prophet, 'One eye is taken for an eye'. The 'nasty weather' here, though outside of human control, isn't just some arbitrary whim of fate: it's very clearly seen as a punishment, something that we've brought upon ourselves.

Very cautiously at first, Creedence were beginning to use their authority as a mainstream good-time rock & roll band to put over messages distinct from the usual rock mainstream. These messages were, loosely speaking, 'political'. Not defiantly political, like the songs of the Jefferson Airplane of that period, nor obnoxiously

Fogerty, Tom Fogerty, Doug Clifford.

political, like the later John Lennon; but political all the same, in the sense that *any* comment about the way people live is political.

Another song on the 'Green River' album, 'Wrote A Song For Everyone', made the scope of John Fogerty's political vision a lot more clear. The song starts out as an apparent recollection of his short and disastrous enlistment in the US Army in 1967: 'Saw myself a goin'/Down to war in June'. Of that experience, Fogerty has recalled: "I had to convince myself I was a slave." The song then dives into apparent myth . . . 'Richmond's 'bout to blow up, communications failed'. Is that history, Civil War vintage? Is it a headline from yesterday's newspaper? Or is it a glimpse into the future?

'. . . If you see the answer, now's the time to say
All I want, all I want, is to get you down and pray'

Pray. Fogerty's Catholic upbringing continually breaks through into these political tracts, turning them into morality tales:

'. . . Saw the people standing, thousand years in chains

Somebody says, it's different now, look it's just the same

The music is as slow and turgid as 'Bad Moon Rising' is fast and urgent, and it creates a powerful mood of despair.

'. . . Wrote a song for everyone, wrote a song for truth
Wrote a song for everyone, and I couldn't even talk to you'

At no stage in their career did Creedence become a fully-fledged political-rock band. They played benefits when the cause seemed right, they gave financial support to the Indian occupation of Alcatraz, but they still made a great deal of money for themselves and were primarily a commercial rock & roll band. Essentially, Creedence were a band with a certain integrity. They tried to make music that was true to what they themselves believed, they tried to respond honestly to the needs of their audience. They tried, also, not to bore their audience to tears. Political songs were just one strand in their music, but an important and necessary strand. And Creedence would make some of the most moving and dignified political songs in the history of rock.

At most, in these songs, Creedence stood out against man's inhumanity to man, and for individual freedom. They stood for the kind of freedom that Fogerty glimpsed in the American past, for the kind of freedom that they found in rock & roll. In a period when American police and state agencies appeared to be doing their best to repeal the Bill of Rights, that was enough to make Creedence a dangerously revolutionary outfit.

Urban Landscape

With their fourth album, 'Willy And The Poorboys', Creedence largely abandoned swamp rock for a more urban landscape. The cover photograph has them playing skiffle-style out on the ghetto streets, playing for the poor black kids. The album itself kicks off with 'Down On The Corner', a tribute to street-corner rock & roll. It also contains several more 'political' songs: 'Fortunate Son' about the folks born with silver spoons and star-spangled eyes who send you off to fight their wars; 'Don't Look Now', about the real roots of middle-class affluence. But on the whole it was a much brighter and more optimistic album, and — many people thought — perhaps their most consistent to date.

Finally, though, Creedence music had developed around an ideological inconsistency that John Fogerty could never properly resolve. On the one hand, Creedence were a commercial rock & roll band, celebrating the social and emotional liberation that a whole generation of Americans had gained from rock & roll. But on the other hand, they were well aware of — and anxious to comment on — the desperate social/political situation in which that music was flourishing.

Balancing between these two obsessions, Creedence drifted into a kind of

schizophrenia. In early 1970, for example, they chose to issue two songs from their fifth album, 'Cosmo's Factory', as a double-sided single: 'Travellin' Band'/'Who'll Stop The Rain?' Both songs subsequently became US hits. Together, they made very clear the Creedence contradiction.

Golden Days Of Rock

'Travellin' Band' was simple enough — about a rock & roll band on the road and set to the tune of Little Richard's 'Good Golly Miss Molly'. It recalled those simple golden days when all a rock & roller had to worry about was getting to his next gig on time. The other side of the single, 'Who'll Stop The Rain?' — perhaps John Fogerty's best song ever — was a slow and deeply textured allegory:

'Long as I remember, the rain been coming down . . . .
Clouds of mystery pouring confusion on the ground'

Once again, bad weather fills in for the forces of destruction and decay. The second verse apparently recalls the biblical myth of the Tower of Babel. Corporate man has created an edifice to displease the gods:

'I went down to Virginia, seeking shelter from the storm
Caught up in the fable, I watched the tower grow
Five year plans and new deals, wrapped in golden chains
And I wonder, still I wonder
Who'll stop the rain?'

What was it, Fogerty seemed to be asking, that made rock & roll necessary? It was technology, bureaucracy, voluntary slavery, Five Year Plans and New Deals. Rock & roll was an escape from those golden chains, but — as the final verse points out — actually only a very frail and fragile substitute for real freedom and dignity and community. At best, a reminder of things lost:

'Heard the singers playing, how we cheered for more
The crowd had rushed together, trying to keep warm
Still the rain kept falling, falling on my ears
And I wonder, still I wonder,
Who'll stop the rain?'

The song was written after Woodstock, and enjoyed success after the Rolling Stones' catastrophic concert at Altamont. But its terms of reference are rather wider than that. Yet 'Who'll Stop The Rain?' has finally very little significance in the Creedence canon. It was just the hit record that came after 'Travellin' Band' and before 'Up Around The Bend' (a further celebration of the joys of rock & roll and the open country). On the 'Cosmo's Factory' album it's sandwiched between a redundant recapitulation of the early Elvis hit, 'My Baby Left Me', and an admittedly spectacular work-out on 'I Heard It Through The Grapevine'.

Both pictures: C. Walter

Undisputed leader of Creedence Clearwater, John Fogerty, plays lead guitar. Insert: Stu on bass and Doug on drums.

Finally, Creedence were just a little too shy about their political commitments, with the result that no one ever took the band particularly seriously in their political role. For every 'Who'll Stop The Rain?' there were two songs like 'Travellin' Band', affirming that everything was going to be alright if we kept on rocking.

The four-man Creedence made just one more album, 'Pendulum', released in 1971. A very stiff and processed-sounding album, with lots of overdubbed instruments and some good but by now over-familiar tunes. It seemed that John Fogerty was finally running out of ideas.

Creedence had scored no less than three double-sided hit singles from 'Cosmo's Factory'. They were the top-selling album artists of 1970 in the States, ahead of even the Beatles. Everything they touched seemed to turn to gold. And yet, remorseless tensions were building up inside the group. Resentment at John Fogerty's star role, long-suppressed rivalry between the older and younger brother. Something had to give. Tom Fogerty walked out.

'Creedence Clearwater Revival', Doug Clifford once affirmed, 'was definitely a fifth person outside of the four of us. The whole is bigger than any individual. Like a marriage . . .' The marriage had not yet broken down irretrievably, but it continued on very different terms. The three-man Creedence agreed to 'democratise' the band. Doug Clifford and Stu Cook were now to take an equal share of the responsibility for running the band, and assume an equal share of the songwriting and production duties. As for Tom Fogerty, he was happy to be out of it and going his own way.

A successful Creedence tour of Europe followed. But when they went into the studios to cut what would turn out to be the very last Creedence album, 'Mardi Gras', released in early 1972, the weakness of the new arrangement showed through. After nearly 15 years in the back line, Doug Clifford and Stu Cook had earned the right to try and sing their own songs. But when it came down to it, they appeared to be incapable of distinguishing between what was good and what was bad in their productions. The new democratic arrangement seemed to imply a complete absence of self-criticism or selectivity.

For every good song Cook or Clifford wrote, there seemed to be a total atrocity waiting to cancel it out. And meanwhile John Fogerty confined himself to just new songs, only one of which had any real substance: 'Someday Never Comes', the group's very last hit.

'Mardi Gras' took a pounding from the critical establishment. Jon Landau, elder statesman of rock, led the way in *Rolling Stone*, dismissing it as 'the worst album I have ever heard from a major rock band'. John Fogerty, he implied, was a genius entrapped by vicious mediocrity.

At any rate, the generally poor reception of 'Mardi Gras' meant the end of Creedence Clearwater Revival: they announced their decision to call it quits on October 16th, 1972. Doug Clifford made a solo album. John Fogerty formed the Blue Ridge Rangers, featuring himself on guitars, steel drums, fiddle, voices and everything else, and made an album of country standards. And then Tom Fogerty, Stu Cook and Doug Clifford teamed up yet again to make an album, 'Joyful Resurrection'.

We don't know, yet, the effect of all this on John Fogerty's music. Blue Ridge Rangers was an interesting project, but John Fogerty was always a better songwriter than arranger, singer or musician. Until we hear enough of his own new songs, we won't know what, if anything, he might have lost in the wreckage of Creedence. There were four individuals in Creedence Clearwater Revival, not just one. We may never hear their like again, for Creedence were something special.

186

CROSBY STILLS NASH & YOUNG

Top left: David Crosby with the Byrds. Top right: Stephen Stills and Neil Young with Buffalo Springfield. Bottom: Far left, Graham Nash with the Hollies.

Rex Features

Valerie Wilmer

"Hey man, I just gotta say that you people have gotta be the strongest buncha people I ever saw. Three days man! Three days! We just love yuh, we just love yuh . . . This is our second gig. This is the second time we've ever played in front of people man! We're scared shitless!"

Thus spake Stephen Stills and David Crosby to an audience of 500,000 at Woodstock, N.Y. in the summer of 1969. For their performance, Crosby, Stills, Nash and Young received $5,000, which made them in financial terms 13th on the bill, below such people as Canned Heat, Richie Havens, Blood, Sweat and Tears and Joan Baez. Just 12 months later, C.S.N.&Y., with two best-selling albums behind them, were drawing greater audiences and earning more money than nearly everyone else who had played at Woodstock.

They made it because they managed to capture something of the mood of young people like the Woodstock audience and the hundreds of thousands who were there in spirit. 1969–70 was a time when the earlier simplicities of 'Peace and Love' were crumbling as opposition to the war in South East Asia grew, resulting in events like the Kent State massacre, when National Guardsmen shot four student protesters.

The reaction of Crosby, Stills, Nash & Young to that event was to rush out 'Ohio', an angry song of protest which reflected the feelings of a generation.

The main feature of the sound of C.S.N.&Y. was their vocal harmonies which they brought close to clear-white perfection. Principally responsible for the incredibly tight singing were Graham Nash and David Crosby, each of whom had previously been in groups particularly noted for their harmonies.

Nash, formerly leader of the Hollies, one of Britain's most consistent pop groups in the '60s with 18 consecutive Top 20 records between 1963–68, had his head turned away from straight 'pop' by the philosophies and the sounds that came out of California in the wake of flower power and all that. He began to feel constricted within the Hollies, a prisoner of his early success with simplistic pop tunes, and so set out for the West Coast to hang out with David Crosby.

After three years with the Byrds, writing songs like 'Eight Miles High', Crosby had been sacked in October 1967. The immediate reason was a political comment he had made from the stage at the Monterey Pop Festival, but for some time it had been clear that he didn't fit the image the rest of the group had created for themselves – that of a hip, progressive band, but still safe enough for the AM (Top 40) radio stations. David Crosby was

too much of a hippie, too eager to propagate his new-found life-style.

Underpinning the harmonies created by Crosby and Nash was the playing and songwriting of Stephen Stills and later, Neil Young, former members of one of the most important American groups of the mid-'60s, the Buffalo Springfield. Like the Byrds and the Lovin' Spoonful, the Springfield contained musicians, who had first of all gone into the thriving folk scene of the early '60s because of the deadness of most pop music of the time, and then into rock when the Beatles showed that imaginative beat music was possible.

Stills and Young were the group's main writers, and while the former specialised in more up-tempo comments on love and life, Neil Young was the introvert of the group. Their first hit was the Steve Stills song, 'For What It's Worth', a response to the clashes between teenagers and police on Los Angeles' Sunset Strip in 1966. It started with a series of menacing guitar chords, and then came the opening lines:

'There's something happening here
What it is ain't exactly clear
There's a man with a gun over there
Telling me I've got to beware'

Young's best songs for Buffalo Springfield were mysterious evocations of states of mind, like 'Expecting To Fly' or

oblique sequences of poetic comments on the situation of the pop star, like the six-minute epic 'Broken Arrow', which foreshadowed some of his later songs on albums like 'After The Gold Rush'.

Buffalo Springfield dissolved for two main reasons. The first was the pressure (common to all four members of C.S.N.&Y.) of working within a straight pop context when your ambitions went beyond the hit single format. The second was the heavy tension within the group between its most creative members, notably Stills and Young, who felt frustrated by having to subordinate themselves to the group identity. The same problem arose, of course, within Crosby, Stills, Nash & Young itself, and though it was ultimately responsible for their breaking up too, it also generated much of the energy that C.S.N.&Y. projected in their live concerts.

To begin with, they were a trio: Crosby, Stills & Nash. In an interview with *Rolling Stone,* David Crosby described the moment it all began:

'We started singing together and one night we were at Joni Mitchell's – Ah,

there's a story. Cass (of the Mamas and Papas) was there. Stephen was there, me and Willie (Graham Nash), just us five hangin' out . . . What happened was we started singing a country song of Stephen's called 'Helplessly Hoping'. I had already worked out the third harmony and Stephen and I started singin' it. Willie looked at the rafters for about ten seconds, listened and started singin' the other part like he'd been singin' it all his life.'

'Captain Manyhands'

Nash went back to London with the Hollies, and various contractual negotiations allowed him to begin recording with Crosby and Stills. Finally the three went into the studio in Los Angeles with Dallas Taylor, the drummer from Buffalo Springfield. The result was the 'Crosby, Stills & Nash' album. Most of the instrumental work on this was done by Stills, who lived up to his nickname of 'Captain Manyhands'. Nash and Crosby strummed and sang.

Still a very attractive record, 'Crosby,

Stills & Nash' was however overshadowed by the more well-known 'Deja Vu'. This album's more forceful playing and singing showed clearly the impact of Neil Young on the group. Whereas the first album was mainly acoustic with gentle harmonies and, if at times the lyrics are overblown, there's a sense of group involvement in every track lacking in 'Deja Vu' where each of the four does his own songs, virtually using the others as a backing group.

Several songs on 'Crosby, Stills & Nash' had the familiar Californian style of romantic autobiography: bitter-sweet in Stills' superb tour-de-force 'Suite: Judy Blue Eyes' written about Judy Collins; lazily sensual in Nash's 'Lady Of The Island'. There were also songs evoking mythologies old and new: Crosby's 'Guinnevere', and 'Wooden Ships' which came out of a long science-fiction story he and Stills had constructed in the long, hot, Pacific summer. But most typical was Graham Nash's 'Marrakesh Express', with its evocation of the sights, smells and sounds of that hippie Shangri-La. It was the perfect laid-back song on a classic laid-back album.

The album completed, they were ready to get out on the road. Crosby and Nash were happy to play acoustic guitars and put all the weight of their performance on the singing. Stills wasn't so sure, he wanted a band that played some rock & roll. So they compromised. One half of each concert would be soft and acoustic, the other amplified with a rhythm section and rippling lead guitar.

Drive To The Sun

And so, enter Neil Young, the quiet, intense Canadian who a few years earlier had left Toronto to drive down to Los Angeles 'because that's where the sun was'. Since the break-up of Buffalo Springfield he'd made a much-acclaimed solo album, featuring more impassioned singing and biting guitar-work than he'd ever been able to do in a group format. Stills persuaded him to come to a rehearsal, and he liked what he heard. Greg Reeves was brought in to play bass, and soon after C.S.N.&Y. went out to play before live audiences.

It was the era of supergroups, but this one was a far cry from the daddy of them all, Cream. Clapton, Baker and Bruce had a well-organised, well-oiled act with nothing left to chance except the pre-planned places for improvised solos. But Crosby, Stills, Nash and Young took chances, relied on the chemistry of their relationships to spark off the highest points of their performance. Sometimes they didn't quite hit the harmonies, or Stills and Young would cancel each other out in frantic guitar battles. But mostly it was the way an American writer described their finale at the Big Sur Folk Festival:

'Finally they begin. Crosby is angry at the wait, and once into the song he tries to pull Young in by jamming on him but Young is still fiddling, tuning, and finally he turns his back on the whole thing, walks over to the amps, and begins re-stringing his guitar. Nash and Stills pull the song along, twisting it about until Young gets through and jumps in, licking and a-picking on his electric. The song goes on for 15 minutes with the best electric music ever made before an audience, but the concept is nowhere,

the refrain is ridiculous, 'I shot my baby—down by the river'.'

Much of the energy of those concerts is captured on the live double-album '4-Way Street', but by the time the band went into the studio to cut 'Deja Vu' it had begun to evaporate. Nevertheless, whatever criticism could be made of the record on *musical* grounds missed the main point: 'Deja Vu', like a very few albums before it, seemed for a moment to focus the feelings of every young American who went out and bought it — feelings about what their generation was and where it might be going.

Here were songs of hope for the new life-style, like Joni Mitchell's 'Woodstock' and Nash's 'Our House', and balanced against them the powerful sadness of Young's 'Helpless' and Stills' '4 + 20'. And in a weird way David Crosby's 'Almost Cut My Hair' seemed to sum up the confusions and paranoia of living in Nixon's America.

The End Of The Road

And that was it as far as Crosby, Stills, Nash, Young, Taylor and Reeves were concerned. For contractual reasons they had to make one more tour, but their hearts weren't really in it. ''It just wasn't fun any more, what with all the bickering and fighting that went on,'' Stills told an interviewer later. Ironically, a group which had come together to escape the pressures and limitations of the successful hit singles band found in its turn just the same problems as it rocketed to stardom in the album market. And the result was the same.

C.S.N.&Y. was never intended to be a band which demanded full-time commitment from each member, though at one euphoric moment one of them was quoted as saying that he could see them cutting an album a year for the next decade. And in fact even during the unit's active life, Neil Young was working with his own band Crazy Horse, and Stephen Stills was exercising his diverse talents in preparing a solo album.

Predictably enough, since the split those

two have been the most prolific in their recorded output. Graham Nash and David Crosby have each made a solo album and one joint record, all of them basically stretching out the amiable talent they showed on the 'Crosby, Stills & Nash' album, but stretching it thinly. Without the abrasive qualities of Stills and Young their gentleness always seems to be on the brink of mere blandness.

Search for Direction

While Crosby and Nash have been content to stay laid-back in California, Stills and Young have, in different ways, been moving out and away in their search for the musical means to express themselves. Stephen Stills has been the more eclectic and diverse in his projects. All four of his recent records use country music and latin rhythms, in addition to the familiar rock style he developed in Buffalo Springfield and C.S.N.&Y. Indeed, with his current band Manassas he seems almost to have come full circle since his second-in-command, Chris Hillman — as a member of the Byrds — helped to give the Springfield their start back in 1966.

In contrast, Neil Young has been refining his music down to its essence in a series of records which have simultaneously drawn more deeply on country music and established his as one of *the* voices of rock in the '70s. Like Rod Stewart, there is something about just the sound of his voice, apart from what he sings about, which seems to fit the times. It's a quality of anguish mixed with probing clarity, which linked to the poetic simplicity of the best of his lyrics ('Don't Let It Bring You Down', 'A Man Needs A Maid') has made him one of the most important performers around today.

Looking back, the most surprising thing about Crosby, Stills, Nash & Young was not the short space of time they stayed together, but the fact that such diverse personalities and musicians got together at all. In many ways, they were the first

example of the now common phenomenon of well-known musicians getting together to play on each others records. But unlike most of those records, at their best C.S.N.&Y. were able to spark each other off and create a fiery unity of almost frightening intensity.

If rumours which have circulated recently are true, then C.S.N.&Y. are once again heading towards the recording studio. This time though they come together not only as a band re-formed, but as a group of musicians who, over their years of separation, have each established themselves as outstanding talents in their own individual rights.

Neil Young, particularly, released 'Time Fades Away' in September, 1973, and showed a return to a harder, more electric sound that had been missing in his previous solo effort, 'Harvest'.

Like Steve Stills, Young has been on the road for some time with a hard rockin' band, and with Nash and Crosby having spent the time mooning around on the West Coast, it's hard to imagine that C.S.N.&Y. are going to find it any easier this time to work together as a unit — although the well-known rivalry between Steve Stills and Neil Young, dating from their days as alternate lead guitarists with the Buffalo Springfield, is what was supposed to have provided the special energy of that band.

A Mirror Of Moods

However, more than anyone else in 1969–70 they were a symbol for their audiences, singing and playing songs which mirrored a whole range of moods and reactions common to many thousands of young people. When they split up it was almost as if they broke in half, with Crosby and Nash taking the softer, more contented side, and Young and Stills the exploration and questioning. Even if they do get together again, they'll never quite recapture the magic they created when the two sides were united back in the '60s.

BACK TRACK

1968, Graham met David Crosby, an ex-Byrd, and Stephen Stills. Graham and David became close friends.
1969, January: 'Neil Young'. July: 'Crosby Stills & Nash'. September: 'Everybody Knows This Is Nowhere' by Neil Young.
1970, March: 'Deja Vu' by C.S,N. & Y. October: 'After The Goldrush' by Neil Young. December: 'Stephen Stills'.
1971, March: 'If Only I Could Remember My Name' by Dave Crosby. April: 'Four Way Street' by C.S.N. & Y. May: 'Songs For Beginners' by Graham Nash. June: 'Stephen Stills II'.

Chris Walter

CHAPTER 5
Rock in the Seventies

The great outpouring of social, religious, philosophical and political rock of the late '60s left many confused. Millions had no understanding of, or sympathy for, popular music used as propaganda. Others were far too young to consider it had any relevance. Many more were simply bored with groups who cared nothing for their audience and were self-indulgent in music and performance. The first stirrings of a backlash became apparent in the emergence of a new audience, younger by years than the traditional buyers of records. They were the teeny-boppers and, later, the weeny-boppers. They demanded their own simpler music and their own idols. They got them in the shape of David Cassidy, the Osmond Brothers and the Jackson 5.

The music was turning full circle. The old rock & rollers were being re-discovered, the old records re-released and some performers were hankering for the fun, glamour, the sheer theatrical entertainment and

excitement that characterised the first years of rock. Marc Bolan switched from being an underground 'poet' to a spangled rocker — and hit gold. Others quickly followed. Gary Glitter, Alice Cooper, The Sweet and, ultimately, David Bowie pushed the frontiers of outrageous performance, clothes and images farther and farther. The '70s found a style, but one that was based firmly in the music and the performances of the past. It came as no surprise that the decade should look back — millions of young fans had hardly heard of the Beatles, let alone Haley; the older fans looked back nostalgically to the glorious posturings of Little Richard and the songs of their youth.

The '70s became the decade of the star, the teen idol, of good dance music, easily assimilated beat and lyrics, of the trappings of fame. The stars of the '70s re-fashioned the styles of the '50s and added another chapter to the continuing, ever-changing history of rock.

Success and ROD STEWART
He wears it well

Back in 1971 rock had got very serious indeed. Many musicians were affecting an off-hand attitude by playing interminable guitar solos with their backs to the crowd. To show they were enjoying themselves on stage was most uncool. Then suddenly Rod Stewart bounced onto the scene with the Faces.

On stage Rod is dressed up to the eyeballs — but wearing an old scarf. He's dancing and prancing and joking with the group, hurling mike stands into the air and kicking footballs out into the audience. He has brought a much-needed sense of fun back into rock, and he deserves to be remembered for this above all else in years to come.

"We're always available for parties, weddings and funerals," he told the audience at the Reading Festival last year. A big part of Rod's success over the last two years, which has established him in the same bracket as Roger Daltry, Robert Plant and even Mick Jagger, comes from the way he puts over a totally extrovert show without being at all remote from his audience.

For Rod, the main thing is going out on stage and playing to people. He doesn't enjoy recording very much, and it shows in the way his solo albums and the Faces' releases have the very opposite of lavish production. In fact a lot of them have been pretty rough; as if Rod rushed in, knocked off the album in a day, and then drove off again at high speed. "If I couldn't perform I'd give up," Rod told *Rolling Stone* magazine. "The recording side bores me stiff. I hate studios. I hate record company business. I hate writing songs. The only thing I get a buzz from is getting up and playing. When that goes I'll go with it. Do like the professional footballers do — retire at the top."

Rod the Mod

But Rod hasn't always thrived on the buzz of a live performance. Not so long ago it was an extremely nervous young 'Rod the Mod' hiding behind the amplifiers who used to sing with the Jeff Beck Group. It's only since the Faces have come together that Rod has overcome his stage-fright and found the confidence to go out and win an audience. He himself credits the group, and Ron Wood especially, with the change; and he is adamant that he would never have made it without the band.

Rod had been singing for seven years before he found success with the Faces, and before that he seemed destined for a career as a professional footballer. He's fond of bringing up football when he's talking, and often compares his situation to that of a soccer star. "The best gig we ever did in Britain was in Glasgow," he once said. "I thought I was playing for Scotland in the World Cup."

Cleaning Boots

He was born Roderick David Stewart on January 10th, 1945, the youngest of five children in a family of football enthusiasts. His father wanted him to turn professional after he played as a wing-forward for his school team in Highgate (along with one Raymond Douglas Davies of Kink fame), and was picked for the England Schoolboy XI in an international. He did sign to the groundstaff of Brentford F.C., and after cleaning players' boots for a while made it onto the field for a few games before dropping the idea of a football career. He still plays the odd amateur game even now, and admits football is still a major interest with him. Audiences were quick to take up on this, and Rod gets the same terrace chant of *ROD-NEE* as footballer Rodney Marsh.

"My dad was a good footballer and my brothers were too," says Rod, "but I was the last hope in the family to make it big on the football field." Rod gives no particular reason for getting into music instead; "I just drifted into it. I don't know how it happened, I just started doing it."

Maybe another factor was the crowd he

got in with after leaving Brentford. He had a spell at Art School — the breeding ground for many rock musicians including John Lennon, Pete Townshend and Eric Clapton — and lived on a derelict houseboat at Shoreham in Sussex with some 20 other 'beat' characters. It was people like this who were the driving force behind the British blues boom of the early '60s in which Rod played his part.

Rod first started playing guitar and harmonica and singing for his own amusement. His two major influences were Sam Cooke and Al Jolson; his mother had always had piles of Jolson's 78s around the house, and took Rod to see all his films. Rod was bowled over by him and somehow the influence rubbed off. Then in the late '50s he first heard the black American singer Sam Cooke. "He was the first funky singer, and I've got every album he ever made," says Rod. "He really made a big change in my life." Such a change in fact that Rod closely modelled his style on Sam Cooke, and even imitated him to the extent of drinking Cognac before he went on stage because he heard that's what Cooke used to do. Sam Cooke still remains Rod's favourite singer, and he doesn't like other people, including himself, doing Cooke material. Eventually though he succumbed, and put 'Twistin' The Night Away' onto his 'Never A Dull Moment' album.

Early Days

It was with these influences that Rod toured Spain and the South of France with folk singer Wizz Jones. 'Tour' is a bit of an elevated work for this jaunt — the two of them slept on beaches and got deported from Spain for vagrancy. Legend has it that they slept under the arches of Barcelona football stadium while Rod turned down offers of professional football contracts.

Back in Britain he got his first job in rock as second singer and harmonica player with Jimmy Powell and the Five Dimensions, a group that was highly rated in the early '60s R&B boom on the club circuits, but which never got beyond that stage. The band had a residency at the Ken Colyer Club in London along with another group called the Rolling Stones. It was here that Rod got to know Mick Jagger — they are still friendly, and are glad to bump into each other on tour and have the chance to play together.

In 1966, three years after Rod joined Jimmy Powell, Mick Jagger produced a solo single for him. A Goffin/King song called 'Come Home Baby', it was released on Decca, but along with other singles including a version of 'Good Morning Little Schoolgirl' it passed unnoticed. By this time Rod was singing in Steam Packet, Long John Baldry's group that included Elton John, Brian Auger and Julie Driscoll. But when Baldry stopped singing blues, and found short-lived success as a singer of soft ballads, Rod joined Shotgun Express. This group included Beryl Marsden and Peter Green — who was later

to form Fleetwood Mac of 'Albatross' fame.

Shotgun Express didn't stay together long, and never recorded, but Rod made some solo recordings in 1967 including 'Little Miss Understood' for Immediate, and 'In A Broken Dream'. In 1972, re-released under the name of Python Lee Jackson, 'In A Broken Dream' eventually made the Top Ten.

Just a Lamborghini

With Shotgun Express Rod had learned what life on the road was like, and had built himself a reasonable reputation as a singer. His next move took him a stage further. In 1967, he joined the original Jeff Beck Group and found himself alongside Beck sidemen Viv Prince (ex-Pretty Things drummer), Jet Harris (ex-Shadows bassist), and Ron Wood (from the English group the Birds). This group didn't last long, and Beck reformed his band with Ron Wood switching from guitar to bass, and Mickey Waller coming in on drums. This band spent most of its time in America, where Beck was a huge name from his days in the Yardbirds, and Rod had his first taste of large concerts and fanmania. The group recorded two fine albums, 'Truth' and 'Beck-Ola', and Rod had by now established himself on the recording scene. Last but not least Rod struck up a close friendship with Ron Wood, and when Beck sacked Wood, Rod tried to get him back in the group. Ron did return when the replacement bassist didn't work out, but by this time Ron and Rod were both looking elsewhere.

Before the band finally split, Rod signed a solo contract with Lou Reizner of Mercury Records. There was no money involved in the deal, and Rod settled for a Lamborghini. Around the time Rod recorded his first album 'An Old Raincoat Won't Ever Let You Down' (released in the US as 'The Rod Stewart Album'), the Beck group split up. "Ronnie was really pissed-off," says Rod, "as he should have been, because he'd been sacked and it hurts the pride. He was looking for another group to play with and when the Faces opportunity came up he left. I was really close to him as I still am and I didn't want to be in the band if he wasn't — so I split."

Bunch of Losers

That opportunity arose after Small Faces singer and guitarist Steve Marriott left the group in 1969 to form Humble Pie. The Small Faces were unjustly looked down on as a 'mere' teenybopper pop group, and no one gave the remnants much chance of further success. But Kenny Jones, Ronnie Laine and Ian McLagan decided to stick together, and invited Ron Wood to join. Soon Rod came in as well and after some rehearsals at the Stones' studios in Bermondsey, the Small Faces were no more — and the Faces were in existence.

There wasn't much trumpeting about the birth of the new group, and few people

imagined that the Faces would become a bigger name than Humble Pie seemed likely to be. The popular feeling was that the Faces were a bunch of losers, and their first album, 'First Step', released in February 1970 at the same time as Rod's 'Raincoat', didn't do much to dispel that opinion — in Britain at any rate. It was on the college circuit in the States that the Faces first scored. They toured there three times in a year, breaking box-office records in the process, but it wasn't until 1971 that Britain woke up to the fact that Rod and the lads were a giant name across the Atlantic.

Rod had released his second album, 'Gasoline Alley', in September 1970, and the following spring the Faces came out with 'Long Player' which enhanced their reputation. But it was only when Rod released 'Every Picture Tells A Story' in the summer of 1971 that the Faces got their due recognition. Suddenly things changed. 'Maggie May' topped the singles charts across the world, and the Faces put on a knockout show at the Bangla Desh concert at the Oval cricket ground in September. They had at last made their mark in Britain, and went away the heroes of the hour.

Wreckers Extraordinary

But success brought problems for Rod. 'Maggie May' came from one of his albums not one of the Faces', and rumour had it that Rod was going to quit the Faces, who were seen as holding him back. It seems there was a crisis in the group at the time, but Rod sensibly reckoned that everyone had had a part in the success of 'Maggie May', and decided to stay put. Later he told a reporter, "I'd always said that I'd never be with another band and I meant it. I could have formed my own band — and I'd have been a total failure. Ninety per cent of the reason I've been successful is because of the band."

Anyway Rod's next single 'Stay With Me' came from the Faces' third album 'A Nod's As Good As A Wink To A Blind Horse'. From that point on he has successfully combined a solo and a group recording career, with his album 'Never A Dull Moment' released in August 1972, and the Faces 'Ooh La La' released at the beginning of 1973. He's had further hits with 'You Wear It Well' and 'What Made Milwaukee Famous' for himself, and 'Cindy Incidentally' for the group. It's an odd situation but it doesn't seem to cause trouble anymore: Rod and the Faces are mutually dependent, and the departure of Ronnie Laine in June 1973 is unlikely to make any difference to that feeling. The group play on Rod's albums as session men, while Rod sees himself as just one of the group when it comes to recording or stage appearances. They decide things among themselves when decisions have to be made. "I don't know if I could ever lead a band as such," says Rod.

The Faces live a full life as a group, unlike groups like the Who who only see

BACK TRACK

Born January 10th, 1945, the youngest of five. Signed with Brentford FC when he left school. He then went to art school in Shoreham, Sussex. Next came a 'tour' of the South of France with Wizz Jones which ended in deportation for vagrancy.

1963: Rod joined Jimmy Powell and the Five Dimensions, who had a residency at the Ken Colyer Club in London, along with the Rolling Stones. Rod and Jagger became friends at this time.

1964: January, Rod joins Long John Baldry's Hoochie Coochie Men. October, first single 'Good Morning Little School-girl.'

1965: Rod joins Steam Packet, with Long John Baldry, Elton John, Julie Driscoll and Brian Auger.

1966: Jagger produces Rod's single; 'Come Home Baby' on Decca.

1967: Rod joins Shotgun Express. 'Little Miss Understood' and 'In A Broken Dream' (re-released under the name of 'Python Lee Jackson') were recorded as solo singles. Then Rod joined Jeff Beck's new band.

1968: Rod storms America with Beck, and the amazing album 'Truth' released.

1969: 'Beck Ola' album released, and Steve Marriott leaves the Small Faces. Rod leaves Beck along with Ron Wood and they form the Faces.

1970: The Faces tour America three times. February, 'First Step' for the Faces, and 'An Old Raincoat Won't Ever Let You Down' for Rod. September, 'Gasoline Alley' for Rod, and in November 'Long Player' for the Faces.

1971: July, 'Every Picture Tells A Story' for Rod, and November, 'A Nod's As Good As A Wink' for the Faces.

1972: August, 'Never A Dull Moment' for Rod.

1973: March, 'Ooh La La' for the Faces. July, 'Sing It Again Rod'.

1974: January, 'Overture & Beginners' for the Faces.

each other when they're working. They have a reputation, not only as hotel-wreckers extraordinary, but as a real group guaranteed to liven up any situation. At a Warner Brothers' Christmas party they once took over a whole room, and devoted themselves to throwing posters out of the window and kicking a football around while Rod was seen dismantling a telephone, apparently 'repairing' it for a distraught secretary.

Rod and the Faces are one of the few groups that turn *Top Of The Pops* into a party. Their most memorable appearance was when John Peel came on with them and mimed mandolin, while Ron Wood polished his guitar and Rod sang his lyrics from a scrap of paper. They turned a routine mime into an entertainment as they so often do. And it's all done on 'Boozo The Wonder Drug'.

Rod has modestly described himself as 'just a crooner', but he's more than that — or, for that matter, more than just a show-man. The large number of albums he's now recorded show him as a distinctive and flexible singer, a fine songwriter, and an excellent judge of what are the right songs for him to sing. Also, despite his avowed distaste for recording, he isn't a bad record producer either.

One of the Lads

Rod Stewart has now been singing professionally for some nine years, so he's certainly no overnight success. He's now won himself all the traditional trappings of the fully fledged pop-star — a £100,000 Berkshire house, two Lamborghinis and a Rolls — but all this doesn't appear to have unhinged his head. He hasn't joined the Cannes jet-set, or gone to live on top of a Tibetan mountain; he's stayed out there on the boards — a full-time rock & roller. Rod has said he's glad that he's hit the heights at 28, because he hates to think what it might have done to him 10 years earlier.

The 'one of the lads' image he puts over isn't just a mask for the benefit of the public, it's very much an expression of the lad himself. "I try to be home to catch the six o'clock news," he says. "I don't feel cut off from the world. I'm quite ordinary in what I want out of life: peace of mind, good health, that kind of thing."

But you can't go on rocking forever — or can you? Anyway, Rod is quite clear about his future intentions. "If the time comes to pack it in then I'll know. When people aren't so enthusiastic I'll knock it on the head. I'll miss making live appearances, I really will; like a whole bit of me will have fallen off. It's a real crunch for people to have to give that up, but if you carry on it can all end up a bit pathetic."

In the meantime Rod Stewart has found the success he's long sought — and he's wearing it well.

Left: Rod Stewart early in 1974 wearing a scarf of the Stewart tartan.

MARC BOLAN:
Overnight success in ten years

As Marc Bolan declared in 'Children Of The Revolution', T. Rex's eighth consecutive Top 10 monster in just under two years, he's got corkscrew hair and he ain't no square — as neat a nutshell description of the man as you'll find. An immensely shrewd and sharp-eyed operator, over the years he's unerringly homed-in to the main chance.

He'll tell you exactly how and why he's successful, he'll give you the most accurate assessment of what the scene's all about. Like Paul McCartney, he understands pop. Armed with this essential talent, a sure sense of style, apparently boundless confidence, and the sort of startlingly ambiguous looks that go infinitely further than the wicked choirboy concept, he has made it as he always thought he would.

Marc was born Marc Feld on September 30th 1947 in Hackney, North London, the traditional home of the working-class cockney sparrow. At an early age he was admiring the flash and the cool of the older boys on the scene, and quickly turned on to the music they were digging. Particularly, he found a hero in Cliff Richard — a rocker, at least in the early days, and most importantly a British rocker, he showed that you didn't need to have a mean biker image to make it in rock music. Richard's appeal was sensual, but a very clean sort of sensual.

By the time the Mod craze reached its height Marc was right there in the middle of the scene, and he received his first taste of the spotlight when *Town* magazine featured him as the 'King of the Mods', the sharpest figure, supposedly, in what was at the time a very cool, sharp scene indeed.

Marc's parents weren't quite sure what to make of their son's activities at the time. He wasn't working, he listened to music, he hung out. Why didn't he get a job like a good boy? Marc tells that he came home after one day's modelling with more money than his father made in a month, and handed over the cheque — just to show that if he wanted, he could make money easily enough. No sweat or drudgery for him. It was during the same year according to Marc's official biography, that he entered show business. He did it by starting to hang around the cradle of pre-Beatles British rock, a coffee bar in Soho called the Two I's. Tommy Steele,

Marty Wilde, the Drifters (later the Shadows), and just about every other rocker you could think of has cut his teeth down in that basement.

The Two I's role was taken over by the Marquee — and indeed, by the time Marc started going there it wasn't quite the place it had once been — but if there was one particular place you went if you wanted to be discovered by a record producer or manager, that was it. However, it wasn't until three years later that Marc finally scored the hoped-for crock of gold with a recording contract. He hasn't said much about the intervening years except — and it's a key part of the Bolan myth — that he spent five months living with a wizard in Paris. Learning all the time.

Marc made his first record under the guiding hand of Jim Econimedes, a London-based American record producer who got Decca to put out 'The Wizard', a Bolan composition. Decca, for their part, suggested that Marc should re-christen himself Bolan. 'The Wizard' wasn't a hit. Neither were 'Hippy Gumbo' or 'The Third Degree', though they did attract a certain amount of attention and his name got around. Then came a pause in the proceedings, which ended when Marc started recording again as the front-man with John's Children.

Love 'n' Peace

John's Children caused quite a commotion during the three months that Marc stayed with them. They had some publicity shots taken without any clothes on in the middle of bushes, and managed to get their first single, 'Desdemona', banned by the BBC because of a line saying 'lift up your skirts and fly'. It was a minor hit.

Marc was chief songwriter, lead singer, and guitarist in the band. It was 1967, the year of the flower children — beads, incense, love-ins and a new sense of wonder and romanticism filling the air — and John's Children were, sure enough, right there with their fingers on the button, thanks to Marc. Some measure of his importance in the band can be gauged from the fact that after he'd departed they went on recording his songs. Despite this they never had a real hit, and quickly disappeared.

Marc surfaced again in 1968 as the main ingredient in Tyrannosaurus Rex, which started as a five-piece, but almost as soon as it was born contracted to an

acoustic duo. Marc sang and played his £14 Spanish guitar, and Steve Peregrine Took kept up a pattering beat on his hand drums. Took derived his colourful name from a character in Tolkien's *Lord Of The Rings* trilogy, an enormously popular and influential work that was required reading for anyone with a vaguely hippie cast of mind.

The setting for the Tolkien books was a fictitious land called Middle Earth, which also happened to be the name of the most popular social centre for the beautiful people in London, and the springboard for a high proportion of the new rock music. Two DJs, regulars at the club, gave their seal of approval to Tyrannosaurus Rex and were their first patrons.

John Peel and Jeff Dexter were probably the most influential arbiters of the new music. Peel's *Perfumed Garden* show on Radio London and, later, his *Top Gear* and *Night Ride* on the BBC, were the first and best of the 'underground' shows, and Marc and Steve, the two archetypal flower people, were given massive promotion and exposure.

The Great Leap Forward

Peel went out of his way to get bookings for the band in clubs all around the country. Jeff Dexter, known as 'The Blond Bombshell', was Bolan's double in all but hair — his long and wispy — but the two of them lived around Ladbroke Grove in London, hung around the same scenes in wildly colourful clothes, wore girls' buckle shoes, and were both short.

Peel and Dexter ensured that Tyrannosaurus Rex became a household name on the underground scene — but the hippies were hardly good consumers, and didn't have much money to spend on records. Tyrannosaurus Rex's fey, magical image was fine for the times, but their music didn't compare with the heavy stuff from the West Coast, or bands like Pink Floyd and the Crazy World of Arthur Brown in Britain. They lost out on that level, and the pop market at the time was too conservative to take Tyrannosaurus Rex's whimsical acoustic rock with its Eastern overtones. At this time the band's most successful record was 'Deborah', their first single, which managed the lower half of the charts in '68.

Despite the 'gentle vibes' tone of the band, Marc still preserved a liking for the more traditional brand of flash he'd gone for as a Mod, and this was reflected in the choice of material for their first album, 'My People Were Fair And Had Sky In Their Hair'. This album included songs like 'Mustang Ford' and 'Hot Rod Mama' — pure '50s Chuck Berry in inspiration — alongside the more fanciful 'Child Star', 'Chateau In Virginia Waters' and 'Frowning Atahuallpa' ('My Inca Love'). Marc's tumbling cascades of word and melody managed to combine, as if it were the most natural thing in the world, the tastes of the speedy city ace kid, and the strange enchanted nature boy.

It was in the direction of old-time rock that Tyrannosaurus Rex was edging over the next two years. They were one of the most prolific of recording bands, and the more they did the more it became apparent that Marc *was* Tyrannosaurus Rex. Steve Took had little to do but sing harmonies and provide a simple beat, while Marc was getting into the techniques of recording, pouring out a never-ending stream of songs, becoming a more than fair guitar player — and was *the* figure that came over.

Steve finally decided to call it a day, and split from Marc after a relatively successful first American tour. He retreated from the world of pop back into the freak scene around Ladbroke Grove, playing with such people as the Pink Fairies. Marc began looking for a replacement, and he finally met him in a macrobiotic restaurant. Micky Finn impressed Marc by owning a large and powerful motorbike, and altogether cut a considerably heavier dash than Steve.

Everybody in the music business, unwilling to bend their tongues around the impractically long Tyrannosaurus Rex, had long since referred to the band as T. Rex — it was chunkier, harder, and you didn't have to be educated to say it right. In short, it had more commerciality; shortly after Micky joined, it became the official name. The new line-up's first album was, in April 1970, the first electric one — 'A Beard Of Stars'. On record, with the aid of multi-tracking, T. Rex had finally changed into a rock band. The next step was to be able to play the music on stage. And, with a little pruning down to the basics, to make it as pure pop.

It was around this time that Marc had started working with David Bowie, another ex-Mod and scene king who was interested in making it as a pop star. There were many similarities — Bowie was something of a poet, supremely into the nuances of style, and also intent on dissolving the traditional barriers between masculine and feminine. Bowie and his wife Angela, and Bolan and his wife June seemed to be heading the same way. Bolan played a fair electric guitar on David's 'Prettiest Star', the follow-up to 'Space Oddity'; but though he was for several weeks the best-selling poet in the country with his *Warlock Of Love* book, as an artist he was working on a lighter, less obsessive level than Bowie.

Bolan: in the early days; as a sharp Mod; the '70s star.

Camera Press

John Kingaby

Marc and Micky took the final step in 1970, when Steve Currie was recruited to play bass, filling the role occupied by producer Tony Visconti on record. At first Marc took care to let people know that T. Rex was still a duo, so as not to give the image too sudden a jolt. As 'Ride A White Swan', a soft-edged pop/rock number soared up the charts to become Marc's first big hit, the rightness of his tactics was proved.

It was the start of what the papers called 'T. Rextasy'. Wild scenes started to take place in the ballrooms as the 'Bopping Imp' stood revealed as the 'Electric Warrior' and put a spell on the young girls. Marc used the voices of Mark Volman and Howard Kaylan — ex-members of an American pop band called the Turtles — to add the authentic feel to his records. Bill Legend had joined the band on drums, there was a new contract with Fly Records, and the old image was supplanted by the new raunchy, rocky Marc with the band somewhere in the background.

Easy Action

As hit followed hit, it seemed that Marc was everywhere. He was the face, he was quoted everywhere, and he was claiming to be as big as the Beatles had been five years before. The records came in quick succession. 'Get It On' and 'Jeepster' kept the name up front through 1971, the year in which the 'Electric Warrior' album was released. This album marked the high point of T. Rex as a rock band — you could see how far Marc had travelled from Tyrannosaurus Rex by the song titles — 'Lean Woman Blues' (recorded by Elvis and Jerry Lee Lewis in the '50s), 'The Motivator' (Chuck Berry was 'motorvating over the hill' with 'Maybellene' in 1955), and updated variations on the theme with 'Life's A Gas' and 'Rip Off'.

Having conquered the charts, Marc's next step was to set up his own record company, the T. Rex Wax Co., which had its first hit with 'Telegram Sam' early in 1972. There were those who thought that Marc was more concerned with his image than with producing his best music. Marc, meanwhile, was doing well enough for 'Metal Guru' and 'Children Of The Revolution' to follow their predecessors into the charts as if by automatic feed.

Towards the end of 1973 it seemed as if Marc was losing some of his enthusiasm for rock and his career in it. He'd starred in *Born To Boogie*, a film by Ringo Starr, and seemed less inclined to take his position as a teen hero seriously. 'The Groover' failed to sell as well as earlier singles, and 'Tanx', his summer album, wasn't as well received as it might have been a year earlier. The hysteria was dying down; the only big target left for Marc was to make it in America.

Like his early hero, Cliff Richard, he hadn't cracked it there when many less spectacular British bands had. Maybe, like Cliff, he was a little too clean, a little too level-headed, to make it as a rocker in the place where it all began.

BACK TRACK

SKR

MARC BOLAN
Born 30th September 1947, the second son of Simeon Feld. Of Jewish/English stock, Marc was a non-starter academically.
1962: Spotlighted in *Town* magazine as a Mod-cult leader. Frequented the 2'I's coffee bar. Spent 5 months living in Paris with a wizard. Developed an interest in mysticism and white magic. Returned to London and tried to break into the music business.
1965: Met Jim Economides, an American record producer. Signed with Decca. Recorded 'Wizard' and roused minor interest.
1966: 'Hippy Gumbo' on Columbia. Still not a big hit.
1967: The year of flower power. Marc formed John's Children and recorded 'Desdemona' (Track) which was banned by the BBC. Met Steve Took and formed the five-man Tyrannosaurus Rex.
1968: Recorded 'Deborah' (Regal Zonophone), which was a minor hit in April. In July, 'My People Were Fair' reached no. 5 in the album charts. Released 'Prophets, Seers & Sages' (R.Z.) in November.
1969: A reasonably successful tour of America. 'Unicorn' (R.Z.) released in July. Steve Took left.
1970: 'A Beard Of Stars' in April under the new name of T. Rex with Micky Finn. Also (with R.Z.) he cut 'One Inch Rock', 'Pewtor Suitor', 'King Of The Rumbling Spires' and 'By The Light Of The Magical Moon'. In December he changed labels to Fly, recorded the monster hit, 'Ride A White Swan', which jumped into the no. 2 position.
1971: This was a year of hits for Bolan. In February, 'Hot Love' (Fly) got to no. 1, and in July, 'Get It On' followed it there. In November the album 'Electric Warrior' was released and besides reaching no. 1, was also one of EMI's biggest sellers. This was followed in December by 'Jeepster' (Fly), which got as far as no. 2.
1972: Marc began to record under his own label of T. Rex Wax Co. In January, 'Telegram Sam' was released. In April, they re-released the double album 'Prophets, Seers & Sages' and 'My People Were Fair'. The 'Bolan Boogie' album came out in May along with the single, 'Metal Geru'. In July, 'The Slider' came out, which stopped at no. 5. 'Children Of The Revolution' was released in October and it went to no. 2, as did 'Solid Gold Easy Action', which came out in December. In this hit-dotted year, Marc also made the film *Born To Boogie*, which was filmed 'live' at Wembley.
1973: 'Twentieth Century Boy' was released in March and got to no. 3. In April, 'Tanx' was released, and in June, 'The Groover' – they both stopped at no. 4. In July, he went on a major American tour. The US rock papers were yet again disappointed by T. Rex, who failed even to win an encore at Santa Monica, California, in August. Marc has his share of American glitter fans, but more substantial Stateside success appears to be beyond him.

Led Zeppelin

Masters of Heavy Rock

Led Zeppelin are a 'supergroup' in every sense of the word. Since 1968, when they first came together, they have broken box-office records everywhere and have sold more than 10,000,000 LPs.

They now command more than £25,000 for a concert in the States, are the epitome of heavy rock, and the acknowledged masters of the cacophonous crescendo.

They consist of the near legendary skill of Jimmy Page on guitar, the giant voice of Robert 'Percy' Plant, the manic thrashing of John 'Bonzo' Bonham on drums, and the swirling punch of John Paul Jones (alias John Baldwin) on bass guitar. The climax of Zeppelin's 1973 US tour was a series of three concerts at New York's Madison Square Garden, pulling an audience of 25,000 people at each concert.

The Garden Explodes

At each of the performances, the Garden was absolutely jam-packed inside and out, and the group had to be wheeled into the bowels of the stadium through a heavily guarded and barricaded entrance. The group sat around relaxing until the enormous frame of manager Peter Grant pushed through the dressing-room door to bawl that the show must start. So, greeted by a huge roar from the audience, the band appeared on stage. The lights went up and a solid, unremitting wave of sound soared out from the massive PA set-up, wrenching at the audience's viscera. Plant's voice, sounding as if amplification was unnecessary, carefully manipulated the listeners, lifting them gently through a verse to bring them hurtling down with a crash of drums and guitars which escalated to an almost unbearable pitch. They were left stunned and silent in the brief respite before the next chorus. Page effortlessly churned out an intricate but weighty solo, his hands moving in a blur of speed, throwing out pattern after pattern of electrifying noise.

Alternating the mood between savage gut-rock and tender love song, Led Zeppelin pummeled their way through nearly three hours of non-stop music, and though the mood may have changed, the tension certainly didn't. But it wasn't just a case of volume and dynamics. Unlike many other contenders to the rock throne, the solidity of their music is created by a carefully woven, complete, and resilient net of musical variation in which loudness is only used as a means of contrast. The stadium thundered with applause for a full 15 minutes before the band came back for the first of their two encores. Though they put on a dazzling visual show, their musical expertise was the most potent weapon in their arsenal, and the show a breathtaking climax to a magnificent tour.

Jimmy Page is often regarded as the musical 'nemesis' of Zeppelin, a quiet and withdrawn character famed for his silent strength and emotion, emotion that only shows in his immaculate guitar style. His musical pedigree is perhaps the longest and most diverse of all the members of the band. During the early '60s, Page left school and joined Neil Christian's Crusaders, touring Britain on a continuous cycle of one-nighters until the strain made him ill. He then split to art college, playing at London's Marquee Club in an 'interval band'. There he was *spotted*, and then followed several years of session work, playing on sessions for the Who, the Kinks, and a multitude of records by nearly every major British artist and act. In 1965, Jimmy worked as a producer for the Immediate label, producing John Mayall's Bluesbreakers with Eric Clapton on lead guitar. A double-album of unfinished material recorded at Jimmy's house, featuring Jimmy and Eric Clapton, the Rolling Stones, and the Cyril Davies' All Stars, was released by Immediate in 1969, after Zeppelin had become famous.

Though he had turned down the job of replacing Eric Clapton as lead guitarist in the Yardbirds when Clapton left to join the Bluesbreakers, in July '66 Jimmy joined as bass player when Paul Samwell-Smith left. Though he had never played bass on stage before, he knew most of the group's material as he had been a friend of theirs for some time. Then, during a tour of the States, lead guitarist Jeff Beck was taken ill and Jimmy had the nerve-wracking job of standing in for him. It went so well that he and Jeff became possibly the first twin-lead players, setting audiences aflame during the Stones/Yardbirds US tour in September '66. Unfortunately, the partnership didn't last long as Beck left at the end of the year, and recordings of the group with two lead guitarists are now very rare. Jimmy stayed on until the Yardbirds, disillusioned, split in July '68.

Determined that the Yardbirds shouldn't disappear without trace, Jimmy and Chris Dreja (the Yardbirds' bass player) set out to find musicians to form the New Yardbirds. The new group was originally intended to consist of Jimmy on guitar, Dreja on bass, Terry Reid (then lead singer with Peter Jay and the Jay Walkers) as lead vocalist, and drummer Paul Francis. Reid, now a well-known solo artist, had at the time just been signed as a solo singer to Mickie Most and couldn't join. Instead, he suggested a singer called Robert Plant who had been in the highly-rated Band Of Joy. Jimmy went to hear 'Percy' Plant singing with a band called Obbstweedle, and knew he was the one. An old friend from Robert's Band of Joy days, 'Bonzo' Bonham, was thinking of leaving Tim Rose's backing band, and Jimmy also went to see him play. "When I saw what a thrasher Bonzo was, I knew he'd be incredible . . . He was into exactly the same sort of stuff as I was." The line-up for the New Yardbirds was by now almost complete.

Always rather torn in career terms, Chris Dreja decided to emigrate to the States to become a photographer (he took the back-cover shot on Led Zeppelin's first album), and ex-Jet Harris player and famous session-man John Paul Jones was brought in to play bass and keyboards. It was after their first tour, of Scandinavia, that the group decided to drop the 'New Yardbirds' name, as only one of the band had actually played in the original group. So, in October 1968 they adopted a name that Who drummer Keith Moon had thought up, and Led Zeppelin came into being. Their very first concert in London won them two encores, two standing ovations, and massive plaudits from the pop press. They had arrived.

Sexual Lyrics

The first album, 'Led Zeppelin' was released in early 1969 and confirmed that the group were more than able to transcend the gap between stage and disc. It had been recorded in only 30 hours, less than five weeks after the group had been formed. That is difficult to imagine when one listens to the superb tightness of the sound and the masterful production. Ace engineer Glyn Johns (also engineer of the Faces' albums) must take much of the credit as must Jimmy Page, the album's producer. The album was centred around aggressive rock with predominately sexual lyrics, with Page's clinically eclectic, but nevertheless brilliant, guitar playing standing out. One oddity aspect was the inclusion of 'Black Mountain Side', an acoustic steel-strung guitar number reminiscent of Bert Jansch (a fabled acoustic player who became even better known as part of the Pentangle folk group).

Though the band's album sales have always been extremely healthy, they decided very early on not to release any singles in Britain, and to keep an equal emphasis on playing live gigs. Under the expert wing of their manager, the band managed to combine one of the most energetic and successful tour careers with the regular output of one album a year. They played to sell-out venues all over the world and appeared every year at the top of the various pop polls. But the public and press were not always on their side. Their second album, 'Led Zeppelin II', released in August 1970, continued to develop the directness and power of the first, and numbers like 'Whole Lotta Love' and 'The Lemon Song' have since become classics of heavy rock. Their third album, 'Led Zeppelin III', was released only a few months later and contained, in contrast, a number of laid-back songs and several traditional folk songs written at the group's Welsh hide-out. This album, though, was well and truly hammered by the press, and for a time the group became very despondent about the whole thing.

A year later, with a couple of highly successful tours under their belts, the group braced themselves to make another LP. This time they wanted to prove that they could still be successful on record as as well as on live gigs. They decided to completely play-down the group, and the LP appeared without even the printers' name on the cover. Instead of a title, the group set a precedent by using four runic symbols, each representing the personality of a member of the band. The album was released in November 1971 and, contrary to the beliefs of many who thought they were committing professional suicide, the LP was a hit and even the pop press had to admit that numbers like 'Stairway To Heaven' were indeed musically unsurpassable, and that the band had succeeded in living up to its reputation.

It was this uneasy relationship with the press — based on the apparently arrogant refusal of the band to co-operate — and some justified comments concerning the band's originality and cynicism, that led to much of their great success as a live band being ignored. During their mammoth tour of the States in 1972, the Rolling Stones had also arrived there and, as Page says: "Who wanted to know that Zeppelin had broken the all-time attendance record at such-and-such a place when they could get shots of Mick Jagger talking to Truman Capote?" As a result, Zeppelin lost out in the publicity stakes, and their tour work was largely overlooked.

In May, 1973, their album, 'Houses Of the Holy', was released . . . and the controversy started all over again. The critics were sharply divided between those who liked Zeppelin and liked the album, those who didn't like Zeppelin and didn't like the album, those who liked Zeppelin but didn't like the album, and the vast majority who weren't sure about the album but appreciated that Zeppelin were a great group that they'd followed for years. True, the album was certainly different from much of their previous work (it even featured string arrangements in places), and the melody side took precedence over the rhythm patterns on several tracks, but

202

Centre: Jeffrey Mayer

Roger Morton

their hard rock ability still showed through.

Of much greater importance to the band and the hundreds of thousands that have seen them perform, is that the apparent loss in momentum as far as recording is concerned is contradicted by the increase in their vitality at live concerts. Quite apart from box-office successes (they broke the world attendance figure for a single group when 58,000 people paid to watch them play at La Tampa in Florida), they seem to have reached an even greater degree of 'togetherness' on stage. The switching of John Paul Jones to playing more keyboards has added another dimension to their music and, as always, they still burn off fantastic amounts of energy at each performance.

Though their recording future may still be in some doubt their next album should resolve the issue, and either way there's little doubt that they will remain one of the most exciting live bands in the world.

Chris Walter

BACK TRACK

Jimmy Page joined Neil Christian's Crusaders on leaving school, but later went to art college. 'Spotted' playing at London's Marquee club and became a top session guitarist in the early '60s. By 1965 he was producing for the Immediate Label. In 1966 he joined the Yardbirds as bass player but switched to twin lead guitar with Jeff Beck for the Rolling Stones/Yardbirds tour of the States that year.
1968: The Yardbirds split up and Chris Dreja and Jimmy Page decide to form the New Yardbirds. Singer Terry Reid suggests Robert Plant as vocalist and Plant brings in John Bonham on drums, whom he'd met in the Band Of Joy. Dreja then decided to become a photographer and session musician John Paul Jones joined on bass.

After a tour of Scandinavia, the group dropped the name New Yardbirds and at Keith Moon's suggestion they became Led Zeppelin. First concert in London brought a standing ovation and immensely favourable press coverage.
1969, March: Led Zeppelin I album.
1970, August: Led Zeppelin II album.
1970, October: Led Zeppelin III album.
1971, November: UNTITLED (Led Zeppelin IV album).
Led Zeppelin's massive tour of the States in 1972 was overshadowed in the press by the return to the road of the Rolling Stones.
1973, May: Houses Of The Holy album.

SLADE

Imagine an audience knocked out by a really great performance that's been going on for two hours; they're not as yet sated, but they've been lifted to a deafening peak. They're drooling for more, clapping, stamping, stomping, screaming, chanting, whistling, shrieking — hoarse, hot, damp, hungry for it; ready to have their minds blown for keeps. When it's a Slade gig you can forget about that being the

encore — it's like that before the band come on for their first number!

'Cum On Feel The Noize' is really one for the knockers; it was Slade's sixth hit in a row, and the first record in years to make Number One in a week. Noddy Holder and Jimmy Lea, who write the hits, have never bothered to stretch their imagination for ideas, but the simplicity of 'Cum On Feel The Noize' is audacious, and the audacity springs from complete self-confidence: Holder and Lea aren't *trying* to write hits, they *know* they're writing them. *Noize* is about the band itself. Each verse

picks out a criticism, which is then dismissed with a throwaway response and the implication that they themselves don't really understand or care what their success is all about: 'And I don't know why . . . any more.' The chorus offers the solution: that the only way to discover the real nature of Slade's music is on their terms, to 'feel the noize'.

That title phrase provides the key. Even its misspelling is characteristic. Since their first Number One, 'Cos I Luv You', Slade's song titles have, in cheerful revenge against school, displayed a string of Second Form howlers: 'Look Wot You

Dun', 'Take Me Bak 'Ome', 'Mama Weer All Crazee Now', 'Gudbuy T' Jane'. More important however is what the phrase really means. Exhortations to sing along, listen to the music, dance to the music, tap toes, and clap hands are cliches of popular song-writing, but that's not what Slade are asking. All those responses they regard as controlled, restrained — listening to the music is even passive. *Feeling the noize* is something else altogether. It's about gut sensations, physical commitment to the sound, and the sort of exhilaration and wild abandon that brings the audience to the edge of exhaustion, and has everyone on their feet, screaming out the names of their favourites. The band have built their reputation on live performances. Even their studio recordings have an on-stage presence that is heightened by the use of such devices as distortion and echoed hand-clapping. Nevertheless, despite the band's consistent success on record, their singles still work as trailers for the live performance.

Musically, none of the band — with the possible exception of Jimmy Lea, whose versatility enables him to switch from bass guitar, his main instrument, to violin and piano — are much more than competent instrumentalists, but their style doesn't make heavy demands on individual musicianship, instead deriving its strength from an overall sound. Besides the attractively simple melodies, the most obvious characteristic of Slade's music is its rhythm, which deliberately forsakes subtlety and leaves the audience in no doubt when to clap or stomp. Drums, bass, and rhythm guitar work together to this end, and the role of the lead guitar is largely restricted to straightforward riffs and chord patterns, ignoring the virtuoso possibilities of a solo. When the audience stomps, it's not just because Holder's pounding Doc Glitters are marking time; it's a natural response to the come-on offered by the noize. The same goes for the choruses, which have the audience stomping and singing along until the hall itself seems to vibrate, and the stalls are lost amid hundreds of writhing bodies. Holder and Lea write some of the strongest hooks since 1963, when the Beatles made 'She Loves You' and millions sang along. The one that lifts the chorus of 'Cum On Feel The Noize' to its highest pitch is the most natural of all:

*'So you think my singing's out of time,
Well it makes me money . . .'*

Out in front of the rhythm, the riffs, the hooks, is Noddy Holder's voice, powerful and cutting as a lumberjack's saw. He's no mere shouter, however, and although that's the range he makes most use of on-stage and at the top of the Hit Parade, he can hold back in a surprising soft falsetto when he wants to. As one of the best, and certainly one of the most distinctive rock singers in the country, he also manages to give the impression that anyone could sing like him. That's important: it makes the audience feel closer to the band, and emphasises that Slade aren't coasting along on a superterrestrial plane way above the level of their audience. Their role is almost as Super Kop leaders, with the auditorium as the terrace and them up on someone's shoulders — mainly because they're pushier — leading the chants, the songs, the clapping rituals, and the mass gesticulations. When the band is on top at a gig, they even start the chorus of 'You'll Never Walk Alone' just to be sure that the audience gets into the spirit of it all.

*'So you think I got an evil mind,
Well I'll tell you honey . . .'*

Holder is a natural-born King Of The Kop.

He's noisy and vulgar and a joker. He's the one who takes the mickey, makes saucy remarks, cracks smutty jokes, tells the girls to grab the boys, and generally instigates a bit of fun. The girls like him because he makes them blush when he catches them kissing their boyfriends, or broadcasts the colour of their knickers. (Couldn't trust him though, and Mum wouldn't like him because *she* knows the sort that get girls into trouble.) The boys reckon him because he's one of the lads: likes to have a few drinks, a laugh, get a bit rowdy — 'We get wild, wild, wild', — and pull a chick:

*'So you say I got a funny face,
I ain't got no worries . . .'*

The other reason the blokes like him is that he's no better looking than they are, and so doesn't constitute any kind of threat where girls are concerned. No girl is likely to tell her boyfriend, 'I wish you looked like him,' when *him* is Holder. And Holder plays up to the image, grimacing on-stage, pulling faces for the cameras. His appearance in general is outrageous:

*'Say I'm a scruff bag, and it's no
disgrace, I ain't in no hurry . . .'*

These days neither Holder nor the rest of the band are exactly scruffy, but they don't conform to the sartorial conventions of pop stardom. They may sparkle and glitter, and Dave Hill may have put on the bi-sexual costume of camp rock (that's why the boys don't mind him — no one who looks *that* much like a pouf could be a threat), but the style is still based on the skinhead image which first brought the band public attention in the late '60s.

The adoption of the skinhead image was an inspired publicity manoeuvre. At a time when all rock bands wore their hair long and a sizeable youth cult had boots, braces, and hair razored almost to the scalp, the stunt was doubly effective. At first it got them noticed because they looked like no other band in the country, and secondly it identified them with a large proportion of teenagers whose tastes were almost completely ignored by the mass music business. Skinheads were mostly Reggae fans, just as their Mod predecessors had picked up on blue-beat half a dozen years before. But, like blue-beat, Reggae had not infiltrated 'the business' in any significant way. Nevertheless, just as the Small Faces had been popular among Mods because they *were* Mods, Slade immediately attracted a following of skinheads, delighted to find their presence acknowledged in this way, even by a band that didn't play their music.

Anti-Social Cult

The band's association with a cult labelled as violent and anti-social by the media had certain disadvantages. Besides arousing the suspicion of all those who were alarmed by the skinheads' public image, Slade found promoters reluctant to book the band because they were afraid that either they or the audience they would

attract might cause trouble. So Slade let their hair grow, and today Holder remains the strongest link with the original audience as he struts around in braces, with his trousers short up around his shins, emitting a sort of style that has nothing to do with clothes.

*'So you think we have a lazy time,
Well you should know better . . .'*

Pop music is crowded with examples of bands, normally the ones with the better publicists, that have made it to the top with little talent and less work. But very few bands have ever hit the Big Time, as Slade did, with a reputation built up through a long background of live performances. It was this 'live' quality that stood out on 'Get Down And Get With It', which became their first hit in 1971, even though the record was made in the studio. It became an obvious number for getting the audience going, and undoubtedly a large proportion of the record's sales went to fans of the band who wanted to recapture the excitement of the live gigs.

Not that astute management hasn't been a factor in Slade's success. In Chas Chandler they have a manager who is a great believer in 'live' performances; even now he personally supervises sound-tests and rehearsals. His timing with Slade has been impeccable, and it's more than mere coincidence that their recording contract came up for re-negotiation the same week as their first hit single. Perhaps Chandler's loving care of the group stems from what happened to Jimi Hendrix after Jimi split from him.

A good manager can lift a group through the most difficult times. In July 1973, Slade were dealt a blow that would have kept many a lesser band off the road for months, when drummer Don Powell was nearly killed in a fatal car crash. Yet Slade were on the boards again in less than seven days with Jimmy Lea's younger brother, Frank, as stand-in drummer. They *still* produced that wild audience reaction which has made them famous.

Showmanship

Slade already have two American tours under their belt; the first playing second on the bill to Humble Pie, the second as top of the bill. American rock critics are making the same mistakes about Slade that the pop press did in Britain; one of them even saying that Slade won't make it in the States until they settle down and play some serious rock & roll! Slade's records however are beginning to creep up the charts and perhaps they will become 'the people's band' in the US as they have in Britain.

Slade's amazing band/audience relationship began as a reaction to the detached and egocentric manner of those late '60s rock bands; many saw them as playing basically for themselves, more interested in technical perfection than showmanship, and consequently preferring to play in the controlled conditions of a recording studio than on-stage in front of an audience. As Slade's act developed with Chas Chandler (ex-Animals' bassist) as their manager, it acquired features from the skinhead cult, from football terraces, and embellishments from other performers.

However much critics put down the live spectacle as a substitute for musical talent, no band has ever strung hits together the way Slade do just because they come over strong on stage. Besides, Slade have long passed the point of relying on critics for their reputation. They demand to be accepted on their own terms or not at all. And those terms are clearly stated in their music, most of all in that one song: so, *Cum On Feel The Noize.*

BACK TRACK

All the group, excepting Dave Hill from Devon, were born in Wolverhampton.

Jimmy Lea born 14/6/52.

Don Powell born 10/9/50.

Dave Hill born 4/4/52.

Noddy (Neville) Holder born 15/6/50.

Slade began in the late '60s as the 'N Betweens, releasing records like 'You Better Run' (Columbia), and as Ambrose Slade, 'Genesis' (Fontana). Then, as Slade, they also released 'Wild Winds Are Blowing' (Fontana).
1970: 'The Shape Of Things To Come' and 'Know Who You Are' (Fontana).
1971: 'Get Down And Get With It' (no. 15) (Polydor). October, 'Cos I Luv You' (no. 1).
1972: January, 'Look Wot You Dun' (no. 4). March, 'Slade Alive' album (no. 1). May, 'Take Me Bak 'Ome' (no. 1). August, 'Mama Weer All Crazee Now' (no. 1). November, 'Gudbuy T' Jane' (no. 2). December, 'Slayed' album (no. 1).
1973: February, 'Cum On Feel The Noize' (no. 1). June, 'Skweez Me Pleeze Me' (no. 1). September, 'My Friend Stan' (no. 2); 'Sladest' album (no. 1). December, 'Merry Xmas Everybody' (no. 1).
1974: February, 'Old New Borrowed and Blue' album (no. 1). March, 'Everyday' (no. 2).

Polydor

S.K.R

Top: '70s Slade. Right: The original skinhead Slade, as they originally began in the late '60s, in bovver boots, braces and razored scalps. From left to right, Noddy Holder, Jimmy Lea, Dave Hill and Don Powell.

Roger Morton

DAVID CASSIDY from Partridge to Peacock

David Cassidy, that spearhead of the weenybopper scene, is the perfect example of the machine-made rock star. That is not to belittle him or his work, but merely to underline a department where America has always totally dominated Britain — the creation of television vehicles to launch hitherto unknown artists upon the nation and thus make them into million dollar earning stars. You have only to recall the Monkees and the Archies to realise how successful this method has been.

And so it was that David Cassidy was picked from an audition he did for a new Screen Gems series called *The Partridge Family.* When the series eventually got on the screens in America it was the fan magazines that started the whole Cassidy machine moving. They were looking for a fresh young face to replace Bobby Sherman, who had had a pretty good run, and

so they seized upon the feline Cassidy. *The Partridge Family* was being recorded by Wes Farrell — who has the knack of making hits — and he discovered that Cassidy could sing. Although the machine then played its part, Cassidy was also artistically prepared for what was about to happen because he came from a theatrical family. His parents are Jack Cassidy and Evelyn Ward, who appeared in Broadway musicals and shows. When Cassidy senior divorced his first wife he married another actress,' Shirley Jones, who is now the screen mother of the Part- ridge Family.

Cassidy's youth, therefore, was spent in touch with the theatre, although at no time was he pushed, or really encouraged, to become an actor. The family originally lived in New York but when his parents broke up he went with his mother to Los Angeles, where he gradually became more interested in the stage. One school holiday his mother was cast in the L.A. production of *And So To Be.* The producer was looking for a young boy who could sing and act. David got the part.

When he left school he decided to return to New York because that was where all the big shows were and he wanted to become an actor. He took a job so that in the lunch hour he could tour around the agents' offices and get his first part. He got the part all right, but it was in a show that came off within days of opening, and that was the end of his New York career.

A Teenager For Ever

He went back to California and con- centrated on television bit parts, which is how he came to audition for *The Partridge Family.* It was a series which was both to imprison and create him. Twenty-six episodes a year are filmed on the Columbia film ranch in Los Angeles at weekly intervals, so it all becomes like working at a factory — especially as Cassidy has to be at the studios from 7am, when he enters make-up, until 5.30, when he usually goes off to the recording studios. It is not a life many young artists would put up with for the three years that Cassidy was with the show, but he came through it stoically his Partridge career finally ending in November 1973.

The Partridge Family story-line is simple enough. The all-white children appear to run the all-white family, and Cassidy played Keith Partridge, elder son and a perennial 17-year-old. Cassidy in fact was 23 years old by the time he was due for his release and saw no sense in being a teenager for ever.

The show started in September 1970, and even by then the first Partridge Family single — 'I Think I Love You' — was well on its way to selling five million copies. Cassidy was featured as lead singer and throughout the singing career of the Family, it is his voice and that of his screen mother and real stepmother Shirley Jones that are heard.

Darling David

Soon after his screen and record launch the marketing machine took over. As Brian Epstein had discovered with the Beatles almost 10 years before, you could earn nearly as much again on merchandising your star product, as you could in the recording studio and in performance. Soon American girls were able to buy everything from David Cassidy posters, bubblegum, colouring books, colour slides, and even have personalised official David Cassidy stationery. This latter item came in pink and had David's face permanently captured within a heart. Until recently this side of his business was run by a companion, who to fans, has become part of the Cassidy mythology. Someone whose past could be repeated by any Cassidy fan as faithfully as that of darling David himself — Sam Hyman. Sam and David had been at school together and had remained buddies ever since — at first sharing rumpled bachelor quarters in Los Angeles when neither had any money — until today when the faithful Sam resides in the guest house in David's garden. Cassidy has always explained Hyman's constant presence with the factual statement of stardom that 'you never know who your real friends are'. Hyman is one of the few people he can truly trust.

The same goes for his ever-present manager Ruth Aarons — a former ping-pong champion and a theatrical agent who had always handled his father. Although not used to the world of pop Aarons has remained an astute manager, who, re-negotiated Cassidy a lucrative contract for his last year with *The Partridge Family*.

What happened after the first airing of the TV series was truly remarkable. As the fan magazines like *Tiger Beat*, *Fave* and *16* whipped up the fan fervour his private life vanished completely — he was unable to go out on the street for fear of being mobbed, and twice had to move his address because fans invaded his home. It was a life-style still unbelievable in a Britain whose sole

Roger Morton

source of reference was Beatlemania. It was something that just hadn't happened since the Beatles, and according to the experts was not likely to happen again in their lifetime. The American music business knew differently. With teenagers maturing earlier and earlier the market was ripe for exploitation, and that, as far as Cassidy was concerned, was what happened. He recalls now, ''I was given the feeling at the beginning that they could just go out on the street and find someone else. But in fact they couldn't.' As time went on it became clear that Cassidy as a property was unique. He could not be replaced by just going on the street and finding someone else. This can be seen now that his reign as a weenybop idol is coming to an end — witness the frenetic efforts to push gleaming, clean-limbed toothsome Williams Twins — the nephews of the gleaming, clean-limbed toothsome Andy Williams. And the repeated efforts in Britain to win through with the easily forgettable Simon Turner, Darren Burn — the son no less of an EMI record executive — and Ricky Wilde — the son, no less, of that one-time British rocker Marty Wilde. What Cassidy had on his side all this time was a youthful feline quality, epitomised in his stage act where he would wear what was akin to a white or black figure hugging cat suit — with usually a giant silver buckle emphasising the lithesomeness of his waistline. Fortunately for him Cassidy has never had any of the weight trouble that has often in the past affected successful rock stars. In fact after a serious illness a few years back he has had a constant need to put on weight.

Weenyboppers

To watch him at work on a live audience is to glimpse much of the reason for his success. On his first European tour in 1973 a typical weenybopper audience, often accompanied by understanding mothers and met outside by equally uncomprehending fathers, would already be shrieking his name an hour before he was propelled on stage. The merchandising men had done their job and little girls were already armed with David Cassidy flags with his face on, as well as waving posters and expertly produced programmes. Cassidy too had done his preparation thoroughly in the picking of the musicians who backed him. He works very closely with a talented Los Angeles singer/songwriter Dave Ellinson and his beautiful long-blonde-haired wife Kim Carnes — who have a monthly column in the Cassidy fan club magazine.

Ellinson, who works on many leading L.A. sessions, picks the musicians and in the second half of the show he and his wife add the backing vocals. The musicians, therefore, are of an unusually high calibre for this sort of work — including on keyboard Alan Broadbent, a young New Zealander who helps arrange for the Woody Herman band. In Cassidy's latest sessions under a new producer, Rik Jarrold, who worked on the early Jefferson Airplane and Nillson albums, he has used even more and funkier musicians like the

legendary session guitarist James Burton.

Bum Rock

On tour the band plays the first half of the show, prior to the interval and the appearance of Cassidy. Despite their quality their efforts are largely wasted as the audience repeatedly screams for 'David, David, David'. When the moment comes, his name is roared by the compere and he is literally thrown at running pace onto the stage. It is a touch of supreme showmanship because, from the front, as his entrance is picked up by the lights he seems to arrive suddenly from nowhere.

He starts to work his audience in a cat-like way, stalking hither and thither, prowling along the front of the stage to the ecstasy of his fans. He represents purity — a safe way of living dangerously — life with a safety net always comfortingly beneath it — sexually almost asexual in the manner purveyed once before by Cliff Richard. One paper in Britain coined the phrase 'Bum Rock' to describe his act because of his habit of turning his behind slowly to the audience and wiggling it. Yet this was merely another extension of an act calculated to thrill, to offer but never to harm. Up there on the stage he looks commercially vulnerable — a little-boy-lost among the pressures of success. When he gives radio or television interviews he is prone to reflect this attitude by adopting an almost hushed little-boy voice. He has gone on record in the past, admitting that in the studio they used to try and make his voice sound higher than it was — to get an ever more youthful flavour about his work. It must be said in his defence that he has attacked these methods and finally come to a position in life where he is himself. A 23-year-old who realises what has happened — grateful for what has happened —

Below: David Cassidy with his dog. Opposite page, above: David Cassidy on stage; below: David Cassidy smiles for his fans.

SKR

Bell Records

In the spring of 1972 Cassidy surprisingly co-operated with *Rolling Stone* magazine in an interview that inevitably ended up being less than complimentary. *Rolling Stone* readers could hardly number among darling David's millions of knicker-wetting teenies. In it he talked about dope and other image shattering experiences. Yet although later in London he decried the interview and said he was mis-quoted, in the long run it was to do his career a lot of good – he was seen to be a real human being for the first time. It almost might have been cleverly engineered that way. The same with a piece in the London *Sun* newspaper during his European tour, which wrote about his liking for wine and a young lady in Madrid. His manager Ruth Aarons so liked this piece that she presented the reporter with a bottle of champagne.

And So On

Even after all this publicity the question most asked is – what is David Cassidy really like? Why should people be bothered? They don't ask it about Mick Jagger or Gary Glitter. Elton John thinks Cassidy was made paranoid by success and that he is at last coming to terms with it. Cassidy must know he will be replaced – although he has never been willing to talk about this. In Britain the Osmonds and to a lesser extent the Jackson Five are challenging his position. Like the groups in the old days, whose lifespan was rated as three years at the most, weenybop stars must wilt and lose appeal with age. They have to be young enough for a very young audience. The Osmonds hold the nap hand because their age group spreads down from the oldest Wayne Osmond, through the in-the-middle Donny to the youngest Jimmy and his sister Marie.

Cassidy has made and more importantly held his riches. He has a large single-storeyed house outside Los Angeles, with a well-lived-in feel about it (though its gravel drive is guarded by an electronically operated gate). He has land in Hawaii and is taking an increasing interest in horse-racing, with his own red and white check colours and runners at Hollywood Park. This could cause the final break with fan magazine land. After all, horseracing is harder to write about than the death of David's favourite dog Sheesh, his current Irish setter Bullseye, or his favourite long-haired black cat Boots – or even his music.

but on the other hand more determined to be treated seriously in the future.

He has an endearing sense of humour. At a press conference in the living room of his suite at the staid Hotel Amigo in Brussels during his 1973 tour he was asked by a Dutch Radio Luxembourg radio reporter how David Cassidy would approach kissing a girl. To which he replied: "First take a rope . . ."

The Cassidy Spectacular

Musically his contribution has been far less than his commercial worth. He is that precious managerial property, a personality rather than any one type of musical performer. This should guarantee his future, and already the offers reflect this. Film and stage roles are offered in almost greater numbers than musical ones. Yet Cassidy has always seemed to miss being part of the real rock scene. His close friends say that he often asks them to tell him what it is like 'on the road' in rock rather than the Cassidy spectacular with which he tours. In Britain a close friendship has built up with Elton John who, when he thought Cassidy was being laughed at by serious rock musicians in Britain during his last tour, offered to go up on stage and play piano. It was Elton John who held a dinner party during this same tour and introduced Cassidy to Rod Stewart, who proceeded to drink him under the table. This can be seen as Cassidy's attempt to shatter his weenybop image.

BACKTRACKS
1972: 'Could It Be Forever', single (no. 2). 'How Can I Be Sure', single (no. 1). 'Cherish', album (no. 2). 'Rock Me Baby', single (no. 11).
1973: 'Rock Me Baby', album (no. 2). March, triple single 'I Am A Clown'/'Some Kind Of Summer'/ 'Song For A Rainy Day'. October, 'Daydreamer'. November, 'Dreams Are Nothing More Than Wishes'.
1974: May, 'If I Didn't Care', single.

The Osmonds

There's never been a pop phenomenon quite like the Osmonds. Already they can outsell the Beatles and Elvis and produce fan mania that is wilder and more fervent than anything seen before. Without a doubt, they are *the* super teenybop heroes of the '70s.

To many older rock & roll fans, the fact of the Osmonds success is extremely depressing. The original response by the established media to rock & roll in the '50s was the creation of young, plastic crooners, whose careers were entirely moulded by managers, agents and advertising men. Today, the Osmonds and the Cassidys of this world, appear to be the direct descendants of the Pat Boones, Paul Ankas, Tab Hunters and Fabians who watered down rock & roll into pop in the '50s and '60s. To an ageing rock fan, the Osmond mania is both disappointing and mysterious.

And yet, as any teenybopper will tell you, the reason for this quite extraordinary success, or rather the key to it, is a young man by the name of Donald Clark Osmond. Born in Ogden, Utah, on December 9th, 1957 — to millions he's just simply 'Donny', the boy heart-throb whose picture can be seen any day staring from the covers of countless glossy magazines on newsstands the world over.

If the Osmonds relied on Donny alone to win their fans it would be more than enough, but this is a family act that covers all angles. While Donny takes care of the teenies, Little Jimmy, aged 10, is the darling of the weenies a spokesman for the music hungry sub-teens who enjoy their pop as much, if not more than, the next fan. What's more, he's the kind of showbiz trouper who wins the hearts of the older generations too, so that by the end of Christmas 1972 he had won over the pop audience everywhere with his 'Long Haired Lover From Liverpool' single.

These two then take care of the younger fans almost single-handed, and rely on the four older brothers of the family — Alan, Wayne, Merrill and Jay — to provide the rocking. Donny is now a regular part of the singing/playing/dancing Osmonds act, though Little Jimmy, and the only sister Marie, are still restricted to guest appearances on the shows.

The group's success is not, surprisingly, one of those meteoric-rise-to-fame tales that makes pop seem like a fairy story — more the opposite really. The four older brothers first started singing together in 1960, when their parents — Olive and George Osmond — began organising a family evening each week for a musical get-together. Mr Osmond joined in the singing, while his wife played saxophone. Before long the boys were singing regularly at family occasions, and soon the church in their home town of Ogden, Utah, heard of the act and asked them to perform at a church luncheon. The act was a success and prompted an invitation to California to appear at various churches.

213

It was while they were in California, during a trip to Disneyland, that the boys were spotted doing an impromptu session with one of the park's regular groups and invited to appear there professionally. They returned some weeks later to make their very first public appearance, and before long they had made it on to the *Walt Disney TV Show*. They were now well and truly into showbiz, and when the *Andy Williams Show* started on TV in 1962, they were signed up, and appeared regularly for the next four years.

During this period the boys also made their acting debut in a TV series called *The Travels Of Jammie McPheeters*, and Donny, at the tender age of five, joined them for the first time in a TV special called *The Seven Little Foys*. Donny had also appeared at odd times on the *Andy Williams Show*, but it wasn't until 1966 when the show closed and the boys joined the *Jerry Lewis Show*, that he became an official member of the group at the age of nine.

After the *Jerry Lewis Show*, the act began to pop up on many other TV shows and the group started to make stage appearances — at first concerts with big name artists like Andy Williams and Nancy Sinatra, then tours of Japan and Sweden. In all this time the boys had ignored the record industry. They were true children of the TV age, and went on appearing for another year on the *Andy Williams TV-Special*.

'Sweet And Innocent'

It was 1970 that saw the big change. A cynic would tell you that the Osmonds had noticed the success of a rival group of singing brothers, the Jackson Five, and decided to liven up their image and compete. In fact, it may well have been mere coincidence that turned this middle-of-the-road band into competitors for the Jackson Five's share of adulation among the young hip kids. Whatever the motives and inducements, the Osmonds did at last sign a record contract with MGM in 1970. They at once repaired to the (by now) famous Muscle Shoals studio near Memphis and made their first and biggest group hit, 'One Bad Apple'. The single, which featured Donny's falsetto lead, leapt straight to the top of the US charts and earned the boys their first Gold Disc.

More Gold Discs followed — one for the group's first album, and one for Donny's first solo single, 'Sweet And Innocent' — then followed a golden year. First the boys were given their own TV-Special in which Jimmy made an appearance; their tours abroad took them to a *Royal Command Performance* in London; and between September 1971 and September 1972 they were awarded 10 Gold Discs. This put them ahead of the Beatles who had previously gained eight Golds in 12 months, and Elvis who had gained nine.

It was right in the middle of this period that Donny launched the group to worldwide fame with his multi-million selling recording of a 1958 classic, 'Puppy Love'.

214

From then on everything he and his brothers did struck gold. Donny stayed with the well-tried ballad hits of the past, and saw one after the other go into the hit parades of the world. Meanwhile, Alan, Merrill, and Wayne concentrated on their own compositions.

By the time the group returned to Britain in October 1972, the scene was set for the biggest display of fan mania ever witnessed — including the crazy days of Beatlemania. When the boys touched down at Heathrow airport in London on the morning of October 29th, there were 8,000 screaming, adoring teeny fans cramming the airport building. The police had to fight back charging hordes determined to battle their way through a wire fence to get to the group. Again it was Donny they craved to reach. Girls of 11 and 12 sobbed as he stood on the tarmac waving to them. Afterwards he said: "It's kinda crazy that I don't yet shave properly, yet all the girls out there think I'm the most desirable guy in the world right now. It's just great. It makes me feel as if I'm flying. I just hope I don't let them down and they are not disappointed with me." Donny reckoned that the fans identified with him because he was their age, but at the same time he stayed very cool about it all. "I don't do it for the adulation," he said. "I really love our music. I'd play for free. It's my great ambition to take a degree in music."

Despite his popularity, Donny took something of a back seat when the group appeared on BBC's *Top Of The Pops* to perform their new single, 'Crazy Horses'. The record was an immediate hit, and their first in Britain.

Pretty Faced Boys

But back at the hotel a siege was taking place as thousands of fans tried to get into Donny's room. It didn't seem to connect with his eager fans that the boy had come with his brothers to perform a protest song. In fact, the song was the first to point to the musical development and moral commitment of the Osmonds. It was an anti-pollution song that, although sneered at as riding on the latest liberal band-wagon, showed there was maybe a little more to the five pretty-faced all-American boys than just showbiz schmaltz.

Since that crazy tour in 1972, the group's interests have become polarised and their future set as a sort of pop-gospelling rock band spreading the word of brotherly love that has been so much part of their Mormon upbringing. In August, 1973, they delivered 'The Plan', a concept album setting out their philosophies and beliefs. At once the group began to receive the sort of critical acclaim reserved for artists of lasting stature. It seemed they were now to be taken seriously and no longer thought of as merely a transient product of ephemeral teenybop pop.

Alan Osmond explained:

"We spent a lot of time asking people

BACK TRACK

1960: First public appearance (without Donny) at the Mormon church in Ogden, Utah — then later, professionally, at Disneyland in California.

1962: First TV appearance on the very first *Andy Williams Show*. Donny's first appearance with the group in a TV show called *The Seven Little Foys* at the age of five.
1970: The group signed a record contract with MGM. Their first hit, 'One Bad Apple'.
1971: May: Their first visit to Britain for a *Royal Command Performance*. 'Sweet And Innocent' released by the Osmonds.
    October: 'Go Away Little Girl' released by Donny Osmond.
1972: The Osmonds toured Britain.
    January: 'Hey Girl' released by Donny Osmond.
    February: 'Down By The Lazy River' released by the Osmonds.
    April: 'The Donny Osmond' album released.
    May: 'Phase III' album released by the Osmonds.
    June: 'Puppy Love' released by Donny Osmond and made no. 1 in the charts.
    September: 'Too Young' released by Donny and made no. 5. 'Portrait Of Donny' album released by Donny.
    October: 'The Osmonds "Live"' album released.
    November: 'Why' released by Donny, and made no. 3 He also brought out an album, 'Too Young'. 'Long Haired Lover From Liverpool' released by Jimmy and made no. 1. 'Crazy Horses' by the Osmonds made no. 2. 'Crazy Horses' album also released.
1973: January, 'Killer Joe' album released by Little Jimmy.
    February: 'The Twelfth Of Never' by Donny made no. 1.
    March: 'Tweedlee Dee' by Jimmy made no. 4.
    May: 'Alone Together' album released by Donny.
    July: 'Goin' Home' by the Osmonds made no. 4.
    August: 'Young Love' by Donny made no. 1. 'The Plan' album released by the Osmonds.
    October: 'Let Me In' by the Osmonds made no. 3.
    November: 'When I Fall In Love' by Donny made no. 6.
    December: 'A Time For Us' album released by Donny.
1974: March: 'I'm Gonna Knock On Your Door' by Jimmy made no. 11.
    April: 'I Can't Stop' single released on MCA, not Polydor (a 1971 recording).
    May: 'In My Little Corner Of The World Marie' single released.
    June: 'In My Little Corner Of The World Marie' album released.

---

what they wanted to know most of all and the answer was always the same. Who am I? Where am I going? What am I doing here? We felt we had a duty to provide an answer as we are kinda leaders.''

Their answer, 'The Plan', is an album entirely conceived, written, recorded and produced by the group. They even played most of the instruments themselves in what seems to have been a gigantic effort to prove to the world that the Osmonds *can* do it.

Most of their non-touring time is now spent either recording in their own 16-track studio at their ranch home in Utah, or perfecting the skills of karate — which they now employ in their stage act. Otherwise they simply pursue the sports of the idle rich like horse riding and flying.

With their recent single, 'Goin' Home', having made the Top 5 in Britain, Donny's latest single, 'Young Love', having reached no. 1, and their album earning them legions of new fans, it seems certain the Osmonds will be around for a long time.

In the midst of all the glamour and adulation, the Osmonds seem almost totally unaffected. They have been known to pose for hours in freezing streets just to please the press, they have gladly welcomed fans in to their hotel rooms and patiently signed autographs for hours when pistol-packing security guards have done their utmost to protect them. They are perhaps an incredible peculiarity in a pop world that seeks rebels rather than saints.

Because of their too-good-to-be-true image, the Osmonds face an uphill struggle if they *are* to be taken seriously. Indeed, they are apprehensive about their lack of acceptance by the hip and heavy brigades: who in turn see the Osmonds as representatives of Middle America, and their fans as falling neatly into the area forever labelled by President Nixon as 'the silent majority'. The Osmonds even chose to *support* Nixon during his last presidential campaign because they believed it was 'good to have an opinion'!

Despite these affiliations they do not enjoy the wholesale merchandising which

sees Osmond products in toy and book shops the world over, and their concern for the under-privileged has seen the formation of a foundation to aid the deaf and the blind. The boys have two older brothers, Virl and Tommy, who are both hard of hearing, and together they run the group's fan club and help administer the foundation.

Maybe they've chosen to remain in pop because it's undoubtedly the best means of global communication there is, and certainly the Osmonds will be the last to abuse the position of power and trust they now occupy among the young everywhere. But as long as pop music is taken as something more serious than just entertainment by some people, it seems that the Osmonds will continue to be the consistently controversial and loved/hated band that they have been to date.

After all, 'Puppy Love' and the rest of Donny's re-recorded hits were seen as schmaltzy betrayals of real rock & roll when they were first released . . . let alone this many years later.

Syndication International

The Jackson Five

The Jackson Five, now resident in the show-business paradise of Beverley Hills, California, originated from a dull, staid Mid-Western industrial city called Gary, which, till their advent, was best known as the setting for *The Music Man*. In that saga a wiley salesman promotes the idea of a boys' band to keep the kids off the streets and out of trouble. Joe Jackson did much the same thing, and without him there would be no Jackson Five story.

Married at 16 and a crane operator in Gary, Joe Jackson fathered nine children, six boys and three girls, and had himself harboured longtime ambitions of becoming a professional musician. He played guitar in a local group called the Falcons and several times came home from work and prepared to set off for a gig only to find his guitar had been tampered with by one of his sons.

Initially, the culprit — usually Tito or Jermaine — would get a good whacking, but Jackson eventually came to realise that his boys shared his own burning desire to create music. He then made the decision

between either furthering his own career or devoting his efforts to the encouragement of his brood. Choosing the latter course he insisted that each son learn to play an instrument. The boys would come home from school around 3pm and find the equipment already set up in the living room. Joe would rehearse them relentlessly, far on into the evening, grooming them for the eventual public debut which they began to doubt would ever materialise.

School Holidays

But Joe Jackson knew his game. He wanted them to be really ready, polished, assured, professional, and after a year they were. Winning a series of local talent contests — usually with the old Temptations' number 'My Girl' — they would spend every school holiday and weekend travelling to shows spread over as wide-ranging an area as practicable. They were their own roadies, managers and press officers. When they decided they needed a drummer and an organist to fill out the sound they took on their cousins Johnnie Jackson and Ronnie Rancifer — not especially for their undoubted ability but because they already owned their own equipment.

It was tough but the group was tight,

polished, and now quite ready for the big break. Tito on lead guitar, Marlon, Michael and Jackie doing the smart dance movements, Jermaine on bass with Johnny Jackson and Ronnie Rancifer right behind them driving the rhythm along, they performed the music they liked — and spent a fortune on singles which they would listen to and analyse assiduously — and specialised in performing Sly Stone, Temptations and obscure Smokey Robinson songs like 'Who's Loving You', originally the 'B' side of the Miracles' first hit and now a J5 standard.

Jackie studied the movements of the big name soul acts on TV and at shows, working out the Jacksons' own original dance steps. More often than not he has seen similar routines show up on the group's white shadows — the Osmond Brothers. They cut a few obscure records with a minor local record company and were appearing as second-on-the-bill with stars like Gladys Knight and the Pips and their idols, the Temptations.

Playing basketball in the city league in their spare time they met Gary's Mayor Richard Hatcher and were invited to play at one of his re-election campaign shows. Unknown to them, Mayor Hatcher convinced Diana Ross, in the city on a short

visit, to give up her afternoon off to see them. Miss Ross was overwhelmed with the latent talent she saw. Hatcher introduced her to them and, before the night was over, she was on the phone to Berry Gordy Jnr., boss of Tamla Motown Records.

The Jacksons ranged from 10–16 years of age when Bobby Taylor produced their first album, featuring 'I Want You Back'. Motown put all their renowned promotional and distributional force behind both the album and the single, and a phenomenon happened among a million or so young black kids, who, on learning that lead singer Michael Jackson was only 10 years old suddenly had someone of their own age to identify with.

Soul magazine, a popular weekly music paper run by one of the leading black radio stations, carried a weekly page devoted entirely to the Jacksons. Where 10 years earlier black kids had bopped and finger-popped in imitation of the Temptations, now elementary school boys had a group they could not only admire but with which they could identify directly. Mind you, the all-American clean-cut version was just around the corner. The Osmonds, who had been on TV – courtesy of the Andy Williams Show – for almost five years, singing pale cover versions of the Top 10, suddenly found a hit formula of their own with what was, initially, a similar style to the J5.

Not Just Bubblegum

When 'One Bad Apple' stormed up the chart for the white group it nearly provoked a fresh wave of racial riots. "Leave it to the whites to always have to follow," commented black comedian Richard Pryor, who later based an amusing routine around the fortunes of the two groups. But the furore died down as each group found its niche. Donny became the wide-smiling hero of the sweet little girls, along with David Cassidy, while older record buyers, who were into music rather than images, plus the whole of black youth, stuck firmly with the original. The Jackson Five are more than mere black bubblegum, they're a lot more than that, they've got soul.

Of course, songs like 'I Want You Back', 'Mamma's Pearl' and 'ABC' had a pretty direct appeal, but on ballad material the Jacksons showed real feel. Isaac Hayes tried his vocal chords on 'Never Can Say Goodbye' but, amazingly, it's little Michael Jackson who cuts through with lines like: 'It's that same old crazy feeling, can't do with you or without'. The melodic and emotive 'I'll Be There' sold more than four million copies in America alone. Bill Withers' classic original of 'Ain't No Sunshine' never made the chart in Britain, but Michael Jackson made it big with his cover, while, after scoring a US million-seller with his original of 'Dr. My Eyes', Jackson Browne had to look on enviously as the Jackson Five made it a British hit.

Perhaps the most important seal of approval though came in 1971 when *Rolling Stone* magazine – the rock counter-culture's bible – sent writer Ben Fong-Torres to team up with the Jacksons on

Redferns

SKR

the road. The cover story in this mass-circulation bi-monthly featured a picture of a serious looking Michael peering up at the headline: 'Why Does this eleven-year old stay up past his bedtime' while the article itself was headed: 'The Jackson Five – The Men Don't Know But The Little Girls Understand'. No one could have said it better.

America was conquered but Europe was yet to be convinced. The group had met with quite a lot of success on record but the critics found it hard to believe the reports of widespread fan mania emanating from the other side of the Atlantic. By a classic touch of irony, the Osmonds were due to arrive in England for their second tour on the same day as the Jacksons winged in for their first visit – they'd booked into the same hotel as well.

Even so, Heathrow's security officers felt there was no need for any special arrangements – not with a six a.m. arrival scheduled. And so the J5 flew in to a riot of a kind not seen since the hey-day of the Beatles. Hundreds upon hundreds of screaming, cheering, near hysterical kids fought and trampled each other in a bid to reach their heroes. Scarves, caps, pieces of clothing, clumps of hair disappeared as fans grabbed for mementos and the harassed group fought their way into their limousines.

A Family Trip

The Jackson Five really is a family trip. Great capital has been made out of their home life, pictures are splashed over the fans mags of Michael making the beds, Jermaine helping in the garden, Tito fixing his car – but that's no hype, that's really the way they are, a close-knit typical black American family which on-stage is transformed into a close-knit professional package. Jackie, Tito and Marlon are the quietest of the brothers. They love what they do but prefer to let the more extrovert Michael do most of the clowning around. Tito is the second eldest of them and the most serious both in personal life and as a musician. He has got married and is now a father. He and Jackie have decided to take courses in business management, figuring that if the frontlines of the music business don't continue to work out for them when they get older then they can use their talents behind-the-scenes.

Cringing Sex-symbol

Jackie is the eldest and he well understands exactly the way the group's fans feel since he acted the same way over the Temptations when he was a teenager. Marlon is a year older than Michael and a freak for cards, the rest nicknaming him 'Las Vegas'. Young, good looking Jermaine stands by himself as hearthrob to legions of teenage girls who are much too old for Michael's antics. He didn't plan it that way as, like most of the family, he is basically a little shy and reserved. He cringes at the title 'sex symbol' but it has helped his solo albums ring up

million dollar sales and brought film and TV offers pouring in.

As a solo singer, Jermaine is at his best on slow ballads and his version of the Shep and the Limelights' classic 'Daddy's Home' is, for many of the group's fans, the highspot of their show. Jermaine sees the solo roles of the individual brothers as a swiftly developing factor. He stated in a recent interview: "Now people know our names and they call for one of us. I'm the romantic, Tito goes funky, Jackie blows the harmonica and gives us sweet melodies . . ."

Main Man

The group show a preference for live stage work, though recording, naturally, plays a vital part in keeping them at the top. Few groups spend as much time on the road as this one. In 1973 alone, the Jackson Five have played all over the USA, toured Japan and Australia and will complete British and European tours before the year is out. The Jacksons though really enjoy what they are doing. When asked what he would like to do if he was not a singer, Michael was completely stumped: "I just don't know," he said, perplexed.

Michael is without question the 'main man' of the group. Soft-spoken, intelligent, perceptive and with an impish sense of humour he is possessed of an electric personality on-stage which makes him the immediate centre of attraction. In many ways it was Michael's particular appeal which first started the fan mania which now surrounds the group and turns each and every concert appearance into a nerve-racking experience for the security men and sometimes the group themselves. In Madison Square Garden, the 20,000 seat venue in the middle of New York City, the show had to be stopped a half-dozen times, yet on each occasion the J5 were able to get straight back into their groove where other groups might have lost their musical togetherness.

They Really Care

In December, one British pop paper that runs a weekly column on the group shipped Jermaine an enormous package of birthday presents and cards. A random sampling of the gifts included dozens of identity bracelets bearing Jermaine's name and often that of the sender, personal poems, art work and passionate love letters, one written on a pair of cotton knickers. A month later the paper received a surprise call from Joe Jackson: "We just got your package," he reported, "What do you want Jermaine to do with the mail? Answer it? Send back photos?" The journalist was stunned that they actually cared: "Let him do what he likes with it."

Jermaine replied to it all. But then, the Jackson Five do care about their fans and that's part of the reason for their continued popularity. Tamla Motown, the J5's recording company, has a slogan: 'The sound of Young America'. Perhaps the truth is that the Jackson Five are young America.

Elton John: Glamour on the Grand

Syndication International

On a hot summer night in L.A., 25,000 people had crowded into the famous Hollywood Bowl. After the supporting acts had come and gone, and with the stage bare, the spotlight fell on the female MC who, with a succession of superlatives, was announcing the star of the show. Finally the words, 'Elton John', preface a deafening roar, and as the back of the stage miraculously turns into a stairway reminiscent of Hollywood's heyday, the man appears.

He is dressed from head to foot in ostrich feathers, a jump-suit and a hat about twice his own size. Arms aloft, accepting the cheers, like royalty out for the day, he slowly minces down the steps — maintaining a precarious balance on six-inch heels. The hat is swept aside with another grand gesture as he seats himself at the piano. Is it a joke?

Yes and no is the answer, as Elton and his band swing into a two-hour repertoire of songs — co-written with Bernie Taupin — that many a serious 'artist' might envy. The feathers are removed to reveal a podgy, gold lamé-d body cavorting on stage like a mad teddy bear. And still the music goes on, a mixture of '50s rock and singer/songwriter sensitivity; a mixture of art, slush, volume and daring; the work of a serious charlatan, a musical clown — the boy from Middlesex taking L.A. by storm.

Reggie Dwight was born and raised in a suburb of London, and pursued a normal family/school life. He went to Music Academy as a teenager, as he said, "five years every Saturday morning playing my Chopin études and passing my grade examinations." But the blues were his first love, and he got involved in a Harrow-based group called Bluesology, which played semi-professionally around the London clubs, mostly using material

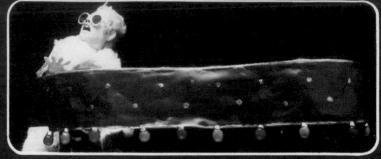

BACK TRACK

1947: Born 25th March in Middlesex, near London. Piano lessons and study at the Royal Academy of Music.

1964–'67: Playing with Bluesology, as semi-pro local group ('64–'66), backing group for visiting American soul stars ('66–'67), working around Europe ('67), backing Long John Baldry ('67).

1967–'69: Songwriting for Dick James Music, playing and singing on budget cover labels, starting collaboration with Bernie Taupin. Made couple of singles which were not at all successful.

1969: 'Lady Samantha' single and 'Empty Sky' album, both of which were fairly successful.

1970: 'Elton John' released in April to critical acclaim but low sales until Elton takes America by storm in late summer tour. 'Tumbleweed Connection' released in autumn, both albums make US Top 10.

1971: Three albums released – 'Friends' soundtrack, live '17.11.70', in April,

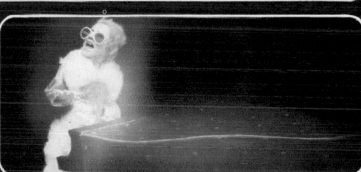

and 'Madman Across The Water' in October. All score Gold in the States, but Britain is not impressed. The amazing rise of Elton John seems to have turned into an equally amazing fall in Britain.

1972: Elton decides to drop the heavy string arrangements and get back to basics with a band. Davey Johnstone on guitar is added to Dee Murray on bass and Nigel Olsson on drums. The group go to the Strawberry Studio in France

to record, 'Honky Chateau'. It gives Elton his first no. 1 album in the States. Elton makes guest appearance in Marc Bolan's *Born to Boogie* film.

1973: 'Don't Shoot Me, I'm Only The Piano Player' released early in the year and shoots to no. 1 on both sides of the Atlantic. Elton's career obviously on the upswing again. Two singles taken from the album are both huge hits — 'Crocodile Rock' and 'Daniel'. Elton does the Royal Variety Show and

doesn't enjoy it. Rocket Records formed to promote unknown artists, to give them better royalties in particular and a better deal in general. 'Goodbye Yellow Brick Road', single, released in September, album in October. 'Step Into Christmas' released in November.

1974: 'Candle In The Wind', single, released February. 'Don't Let The Sun Go Down on Me', single, released in May. 'Caribou', album, released in June.

by then little-known artists like Jimmy Witherspoon. The group got jobs backing US soul singers like Major Lance, Patti LaBelle, and the Ink Spots, did some time in Hamburg and St. Tropez, and continued to play the London club scene. All this time Reg was working as a tea boy at Mills Music, a publishing company. Then the group got together with Long John Baldry and started earning a reasonable wage — about £30 a week each. But then Baldry had a hit record with a ballad, and the group was dragged along in its wake, playing cabaret and the like — a long way from their accustomed stomping grounds.

Reg was thinking at this time of leaving the business, but he happened to see an advert in a pop paper for 'songwriters and talent'. He turned up at an audition and was hopeless — 'you must be joking' they said — but before leaving, he had a sheaf of lyrics pushed into his hands. They came from a Lincolnshire lad named Bernie Taupin, and so the great songwriting collaboration began, conducted for the first six months almost exclusively by post.

Their Singles Sank

The next two years or so were a long grind. Reg started writing tunes to Bernie's lyrics and a few demos were made at Dick James' studio, courtesy of a young engineer named Caleb Quaye. Reg had by now finally left Bluesology and Bernie had come to London. In vain the two of them tried to write the commercial songs that Dick James demanded — a few singles were produced that sank without trace. Then a new plugger arrived at Dick James Music — Steve Brown — who convinced the two that they'd got stuck between doing what they wanted and what Dick wanted. He advised them to do just what *they* wanted and not to worry about commerciality.

So off they went for a few months, and wrote most of the songs subsequently to appear on the 'Empty Sky' album. One of them, 'Lady Samantha', was released as a single, and sold reasonably well. In the meantime, Elton John, as Reg now styled himself, was singing on budget label cover versions, mostly on those songs that had too high a range for Uriah Heep's David Byron. Then Dick James gave the go-ahead for the 'Empty Sky' album, which did well enough to justify another, this time with no financial strings, 'as long as it was good'. Elton and Bernie worked out the music in detail before recording, brought in Gus Dudgeon as producer and the arranging prodigy Paul Buckmaster to fill out the sound.

The album sold quite well in Britain, around 4,000 copies in the first week, and actually reached no. 45 in the album charts. Some of the songs were recorded by famous names ('Border Song' by Aretha Franklin), but the album didn't actually set Britain on fire. It was to be in the States that they made the breakthrough.

It was decided that the album had to be promoted on the road by a band, and so Dee Murray (bass) and Nigel Olsson (drums), both ex-Spencer Davis Group, were drafted in. They did the college circuit in Britain, but among the other gigs they arranged was one at the Troubador folk club in L.A. ''That,'' says Elton, ''was the start of all our success.'' They arrived in a double-decker bus emblazoned with 'Elton John has arrived' . . . and took the club apart. Elton's Jerry Lee Lewis finale on 'Burn Down The Mission', complete with the stool kicked away and the dance on the piano, was a particular hit. They moved rapidly on to the East Coast and caused the same sensation in Philadelphia. By the time they were headed for home, 'Elton John' was rising fast up the US album charts, and Britain was eager to know more. The ball was definitely rolling.

The 'Elton John' album was stylistically central to the music of the first four studio-produced albums, from 'Empty Sky' through to 'Madman Across The Water'. The mood is generally serious, either low-key sentimentality or a semi-gospel howl. The music is dominated by Elton's piano and Buckmaster's string arrangements, the latter becoming increasingly ominous from album to album as Taupin's lyrical concerns darken toward the depths of 'Madman Across The Water'.

The fact that Elton writes music to Bernie's words, rather than vice versa, obviously gives the words — and Bernie Taupin — a great importance. On the early albums the words tend toward the obscurely romantic, but with a breadth of subject-matter that is rare. But it was one of their most 'obvious' songs, 'Your Song', which established them as writers of ingenuous love songs:

'If I was a sculptor but then again no
Or a man who makes potions in a travelling
*   show*
I know it's not much but it's the best I
*   can do*
My gift is my song and this one's for you'

The words here are perfectly complemented by the tender voice and the swaying melody. The next album, 'Tumbleweed Connection', gave full play to Bernie's obsession with Americana, which can be seen in a wider context as an obsession with loss — sometimes known as nostalgia. This receives its apotheosis with 'Indian Sunset', which starts with Elton singing unaccompanied, and then introduces a menacingly insistent piano which gradually fades into a nostalgic resignation as the strings take up the theme of barely controlled rage:

'Now there seems no reason why I should
*   carry on*
In this land that once was my land,
*   I can't find a home*
It's lonely and it's quiet and the horse
*   soldiers are coming*
And I think it's time I strung my bow and
*   ceased my senseless running . . .'*

Strings also dominated the title cut, with its brilliantly evocative opening lines — 'I can see very well, there's a boat on the reef with a broken back' — and Elton's singing at its most seriously expressive. This album, which was the furthest logical extension of the music started on 'Empty Sky' and 'Elton John', was also the furthest away from 'pop' that Elton John was to venture. It also marked the nadir of his commercial fortunes. And that point was not to be missed.

The change which came over Elton's music on 'Honky Cat' and the following albums, was really no more than a change of emphasis. He has always been something of a rock & roller at heart, as a couple of cuts from each of the earlier albums bear witness to. Talking once about playing on the Hollies' 'He Ain't Heavy', he said that ''they thought they were making art. I was just having a good time.'' The 'live' album, '17.11.70', which was released before 'Madman', conveyed Elton the raver far more than did any of the studio albums. But his audience weaned on the singer/songwriter values of the early '70s, didn't want to know. Taupin's lyrics may never have exactly bared his soul, but they did sound serious, and rock & roll was not considered a serious medium. But then again, seriousness was one thing, morbidity was another. Couldn't Elton write 'Your Song' over and over again with nice piano and strings? The answer was no — Elton may think his work has built-in obsolescence, but he's serious about the fun he produces. The way out of the impasse had to be a return to more of a 'pop' style but without losing any of the old trademarks.

First Time Guitar

In early '72, Elton went to France to record in the 'Strawberry Studio' Château. And this time he had a band with him, not a collection of session men. Folk-guitarist Davey Johnstone, late of Magna Carta, had been added to Dee and Olsson. This, as Elton put it, ''took the pressure off the rest of us.'' Guitar, which until this time had been pretty inconspicuous on Elton's records, now became an important part of the group's sound. The massive string arrangements of the earlier records were cut back accordingly. The result was a clearer sound, in which Elton's voice and piano could be counterpointed by guitar rather than drowned in strings. It was a rock & roll band on record.

This album, produced in France, was suitably called 'Honky Chateau'. One of the singles taken from it, 'Rocket Man', obligingly rocketed up the charts. One of Bernie's most perceptive lyrics — the exploration of the cosmos reduced to a lonely job, 'burning out my fuse up here alone' — was backed by a flowing melody, interspersed with the electronic wails of a synthesiser. It marked the beginning of Elton's second wave of popularity in Britain, and carried him over the hump in the States, after the over-production in quantity/quality of 1971.

As 'Honky Chateau' was becoming Elton's first no. 1 album in the States, the band were already back there cutting

Ed Caraeff

The two extremes in a successful music team, Elton John and lyrics-man Bernie Taupin.

another one, to be titled 'Don't Shoot Me, I'm Only The Piano Player'. The first side turned out to be 'my discotheque album'. Three singles were released from the album, two of them in particular – 'Daniel' and 'Crocodile Rock' – really hitting the jackpot. It is a happy album, a long way from the doom of 'Madman'. The piano rocks along over Olsson and Dee's thumping beat and Davey plugs in the gaps with some amazing guitar-playing for someone who'd only just turned electric. Elton sings like he's really enjoying himself.

The lyrical content has also shifted since 'Madman'. Bernie's obsession with old America is not so all-pervasive, the '50s music scene and the '40s film scene are rapidly becoming the prime targets for his nostalgia; 'long nights crying by the record machine, dreamin' of my Chevy and my old blue jeans'. And still on each album there are a couple of gems in the sensitive love song department and songs on many a matter, from crime to rednecks, from schooldays to teenage-idols. In the meantime Elton swept across the States and Britain playing to packed houses, and becoming more outrageous each time.

The 'Goodbye Yellow Brick Road' album released in autumn '73, seems in many ways to sum up all that's gone before.

Being a double album it has space to include just about everything. All the things that Bernie and his audience have lost – the American West, Marilyn Monroe, a simple male chauvinist view of women and vice versa, '50s rock & roll, sanity – are paraded in an apocalyptic procession. The band really knew each other by this time, and the combination of their musical skills, Elton's singing, and the duo's writing, produced a few really remarkable songs. The one about Marilyn, for example, is only flawed by a couple of Taupin's lines (he does have a tendency towards uneven writing within songs). The chorus is perfectly constructed, sung beautifully over a fine, distinctive melody, illumined by flashes of Davey Johnstone's guitar.

*'And it seems to me you lived your life
  like a candle in the wind
Never knowing who to cling to when the
  rain set in
And I would have liked to have known you
  but I was just a kid
Your candle burned out long before your
  legend ever did'*

The fine moments on this record suggest that Elton had finally begun to put the pieces of himself together. He seemed to have bridged the gap between pop and

rock, between fun and dedication, between being a clown and being an artist. He has always been all of these, but before, the various parts used to get up and bite each other. Part of his audience would tug him one way and part the other. Perhaps now he had got to the point where he could tug them together.

'Saturday Night's Alright For Fighting' is a good example. Perhaps one of '73s best singles, Davey's crazy, rocking guitar riff and Elton's rockabilly piano put it in a class of its own. *That* and it's easy to imagine Elton up there on stage prancing round in his gold lamé, strutting his stuff . . . straight-talk is always surprising. In one music paper it was argued that 'diversion not revolution, sentiment not existential angst, fun not solemnity, and professional competence not good intentions are what a large section of today's audience seeks in its performers, and these Elton has in abundance'. But is that fair? David Bowie's claim to super-stardom rests on his proven ability to get past these dualities, and it is arguable that Elton and Bernie have achieved something similar, if at a different level of seriousness. When the 'madman across the water' starts dancing the 'crocodile rock', then something is up in the State of the Nation, even if no-one knows what it is.

225

Alice Cooper Super-Ghoul

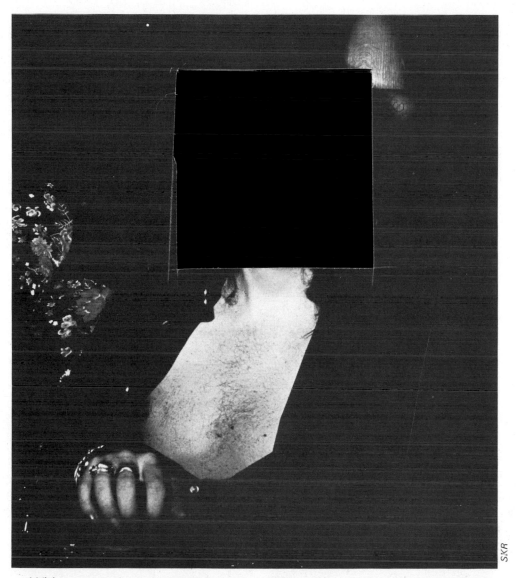

SKR

Black-shirted, bare-chested Alice Cooper without his evil and satanic make-up.

Without warning, an empty beer bottle comes hurtling out of the darkness, slashes through the glaring beam of the spotlight, and begins its rapid descent. With a resounding crash, the bottle misses its target, smashes into the battery of flickering footlights, and shatters into a million lethal splinters to indicate that all is not well.

'I hate ya', hollers the human missile-launcher, as with menacing glazed acid eyes, he lurches towards the stage where the rancid blood-splattered Monster is being viciously beaten-up by a gang of cheesy thugs to the sound of a savage and strangely sinister rock & roll raunch.

'I hate yer, I hate yer, I hate ya all', he continues to yell, as with the strength of a team of fresh pack-horses, he bulldozes his way through the tightly packed crowd of gawking thrill-seekers.

Only 20 feet now divides this would-be assailant from the battered object of his frenzied disgust.

Venomous abuse spills from his lips, and with one violent motion he casts aside a sobbing young girl as if she were a discarded rag doll. She falls to the ground and stays there. Her one desperate attempt to restrain this madman from attacking her plastic, fantastic, make-believe lover proving to no avail. All she can do is whimper, 'I love you Alice . . . I love you Alice . . . for God's sake, somebody stop him, don't let him kill my Alice.'

Freed of his sobbing shackle, her escort reduces the crash barrier to matchwood and begins to scale the stage which is the last remaining obstacle.

The killer is now staring up into the eyes of his intended victim. But instead of fleeing for his life, this prime cut of mortuary steak falls to his knees and goads him on.

Gore and Decadence

Are we about to become eye-witness to a mindless slaying? Is the forever-damned spirit of Lee Harvey Oswald a rock & roll fan? Thankfully, we are never to find out, for the police pounce, secure the maniac in a strangle-hold, and drag him away pleading 'let me go, let me go . . . I wanna kill him . . . can't you see I gotta kill him.'

Granted a stay of execution, the victim staggers to his feet, laughs aloud, and addresses the 25,000 spectators: 'you're crazier than me, and that's what I like.'

Believe it or not, this is no cheap publicity hype, but the kind of response that inevitably takes place once an Alice Cooper concert has climaxed in a finale of gore and decadence.

Any guy who intentionally cavorts around under the good old apple pie 'n' ice cream pseudonym of Alice Cooper, sets himself up as Public Animal Number One by inferring that he's a stubble-chinned transvestite, beer-gutted necrophiliac, satanic baby-killer and prize rock & roll freak, has just gotta be a shrewd pro. Then, when he's seen swanning around swish night-spots with the likes of Zsa Zsa Gabor, Jack Benny, Salvador Dali and a Richard Nixon look-a-like, you just know that's where he's at.

The facts are these. Alice Cooper has emerged from out of the mass media cess-pit to become the only true Superstar of America's instantly disposable consumer culture. Sure, the silent majority of God-fearing Americans may find everything about Cooper to be totally repugnant and un-American, but then, this is the whole object of the carefully calculated exercise.

Make no mistake about it, behind that hideously smeared make-up, Alice Cooper — leader of the first post-Charles Manson nihilistic rock band — is as All-American as

227

George Washington, the Ku Klux Klan, massage parlours, instant TV dinners, the Boston Strangler, topless bars, greasy cheeseburgers and Napalm.

A grotesque graven image, who in six years flat succeeded in trampling any remaining remnants of Flower Power firmly under a tatty stacked heel, burying the spirit of Woodstock in the bottom of a stinking trash can, while callously mirroring what he considers to be the true face of America — the once beautiful — a society preoccupied with sex and violence. For love and peace substitute hate and depravity.

He's Dorian Grey branded with the mark of death and the sign of the almighty dollar on his forehead. A self-made Franken-stein's Monster, a depraved schizophrenic free of all censorship, and the most astute image-manipulating entertainer of his generation.

Though Cooper's contrived performance may lack the psychological plausibility to seriously erode the morals of the youth culture, it is nonetheless far more effective in terms of stirring up public outrage and condemnation than the real-life catastrophe and carnage that invariably dominates every TV newscast.

Living is Fun

But then Cooper is the first to confirm that it's all just a charade. ''On stage, I'm Bela Lugosi, but away from it, I'm just good ol' Fred McMurray. Personally, I really hate the idea of death'', he reveals, ''because I have so much fun living. Death is the only thing that I really fear, because like everyone else, I know nothing at all about it. That's why I play with death and make fun of it on stage. As far as I am concerned, it's not that our act plays on the idea that people like to see blood. We're just as human as everybody else. It's just that we like the idea of blood-lust just so long as it's us who are portraying it. We do it strictly for the audience. We're their outlet. We aren't condoning violence, we're relieving it. Just because I hack the head off a baby doll doesn't mean some kid has to run out and re-enact that situation with a real child.''

A responsibility towards one's audience is the least thing Cooper is concerned with. ''I never get repulsed by an audience's behaviour'', he insists. ''In fact, I often think that it's real healthy. When I'm down on my knees hacking that baby doll's head off I imagine that the girls out there, screamin' for the bits, would secretly like to change places with me. To be quite honest'', continues the mock bi-sexual bogey man, ''I think I'm doing an artistic thing on stage . . . something that's never been done in rock until I came along. Not only am I giving them music, but also an image for them to think about.''

With the second coming of rock Americana in the mid-'60s, there was a bumper sticker that circulated for a relatively short period, which announced: 'We Are The People Your Parents Warned You About'. Had it been conceived a couple of years

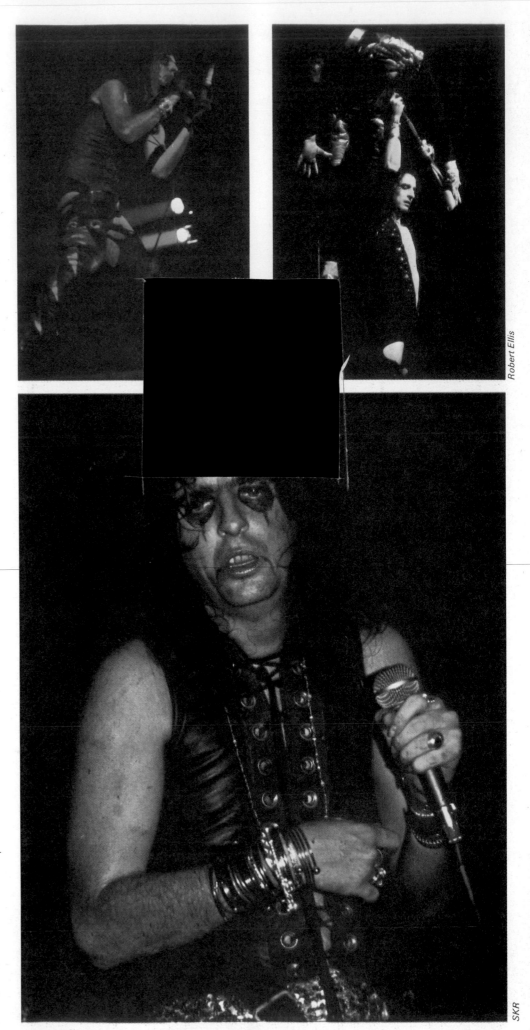

Robert Ellis

SKR

228

Robert Ellis

Alice Cooper resplendent in silver-studded catsuit (not to mention the gaping hole at thigh level) nearly manages to look attractive.

later, it could have been utilised as the holly in Alice Cooper's Christmas crackers. For despite his admissions of innocence, in the eyes of middle-class America Alice Cooper will always be hounded as a pervert, renegade, and blatant purveyor of bad taste. He accepts this with pride and satisfaction:

"Bad taste", says Cooper, "believe me, there's not such a thing nowadays as bad taste." Like a Vampire drawn to the warm life-giving blood of his victim, he establishes, "I ask you, how the hell can there be such a thing as bad taste when the top box-office draws are movies like *Straw Dogs*, *A Clockwork Orange* and *Deep Throat*."

Not since the Kama Sutric pelvic thrusts of Presley and the posturing bum wiggling of rubber-lipped Jagger has any one individual managed to totally alienate his elders, win over the youth market, and blatantly rake in a few million dollars in the process.

Whether the public wish to admit it, or for that fact are aware of it, Alice Cooper is the Patron Saint of materialistic America. He is showing them their worst side, rubbing their nose in it and then charging admission for the pleasure of such experience.

Lullabies of Homicide

You can sell the public anything, and Alice Cooper is a shrewd enough cookie to realise that as long as he continues — with snake, axe, make-up, guillotines, gallows, lullabies of homicide, and the rape of both the living and the dead — to aggravate the acute paranoia rampant amongst the over-protective Mothers of America, his success is guaranteed.

The image may well be an explicit sick one, but one that has paid off most handsomely. Perhaps the whole Alice Cooper phenomenon can be summed up by the photo on the inside sleeve of his 'Billion Dollar Babies' album, which depicts Alice and his band decked out in expensive white satin suits and wallowing in heaps of Uncle Sam's freshly-minted Greenbacks. The story that this picture tells is that it's his money in our pockets, and he wants it back. Every red cent of it.

Like virtually all of America's second generation rocksters, young Vince Furnier — the son of a Preacherman — was immediately inspired beyond belief by the Fab Four.

The year was 1964, and it didn't take but a few minutes for this bratty, skinny sophomore attending high school in Tucson, Arizona, to round up a bunch of his punko pals to terrorise the Top 40. It was his idea to form the band, so natch' he was

229

the one who became the front man.

Resplendent in their bright yellow corduroy Carnaby Street-styled jackets, the Earwigs — as they called themselves — were the hit of the local Catholic Youth Club hop.

Along with acquiring Beatle caps they changed their name to the Spiders, and then after hearing a Yardbirds' record, the Nazz. They cut a couple of records, but nothing happened.

They moved to California where they starved in one room. The only gigs they could get were accompanying the fist-fights that broke out between the Blacks and the Mexicans in tatty gin-mills around L.A. Then one night out of sheer frustration Vince changed his name to Alice, applied lipstick, powder and paint to his face, and staggered on stage.

"We wanted to draw attention to ourselves", Cooper states with almost total recall, "because we just weren't getting anywhere fast."

Breaking into a laugh, he continues, 'we had bruises all over our bodies from the foot-poles . . . that's how much

promoters refused to touch us. So we decided to go on stage and do anything that we wanted. Some nights we used to stagger on stage so drunk, I'd pass out at least three times during a set. Surprise . . . surprise, people dug it and quite often they used to come along just to see what would happen to us. I'd just stand in the middle of the stage and pass right out and the crowd would cheer. The band would pick me up, I'd get back together again — take a swig of this gawdamnawful cheap Ripple wine — and crash out once again."

However, not all audiences responded so positively. At one gig, two thousand people walked out and the only person who stayed was Frank Zappa. It was Zappa's opinion that anyone who could induce such a strong audience response, be it positive or negative, must have something going for them. They signed to his Straight label, cut two albums and split. It wasn't until they cut their 'Love It To Death' album which contains their own little masterpiece 'I'm Eighteen' that people suddenly realised that they were more than some kind of boozed-up pseudo-

faggy freak band with badly twisted minds.

But though the simulated sexuality in their act was never ever more than tongue-in-cheek, they continued to upset the community.

"People are both male and female biologically", Cooper pronounces, "yet the typical male American thinks that he's all-male . . . 100%. What he's gotta realise is that he has got a female side." Because as Alice Cooper, Vince Furnier chooses to display both sides of the coin, it only adds to the confusion.

So when the last words of abuse have been screamed, the dolls hacked beyond recognition, the snakes put back in the baskets, and Cooper has paid the supreme penalty of being publicly executed, how do you expect people to react when, with a gleam in his mascaraed eye, he casually infers: "actually, there's no point whatsoever to our act."

And that's when the dollars come pouring in. It's Cooper's money in our pockets and he'll do anything you ask just to grab it back. Now that's what you could call real smart.

SKR

BACK TRACK

Born Vince Furnier in 1948, son of a Pennsylvanian minister.

1964–68: Played in a group calling themselves first the Earwigs, then the Spiders, then the Nazz — based in Tucson and Phoenix, Arizona.
1968: Moved to Los Angeles and later in the year met Frank Zappa. Was given a recording contract and had become Alice Cooper by early '69.
1969: Moved to Detroit.
1970: Albums 'Pretties For You' (Straight) and 'Easy Action' (Straight) released.
1971: Moved to New York and then to Connecticut. Recorded 'Love It To Death' (Warners) which was produced by Bob Ezrin and reached no. 32 in the album charts. In November 'Killer' (Warners) was released and reached no. 28. Also two singles, 'Desperado' and 'Under My Wheels'.
1972: 'School's Out' (Warners) reached no. 4 in the album charts. 'Be My Lover' released in March. 'School's Out' (single) released in June and soared to no. 1 in the Top Twenty. 'Elected' was released in November and made no. 4.
1973: 'Billion Dollar Babies' (Warners) got to no. 1 in the album charts. 'Hello Hurray' made no. 5 in the singles charts and 'No More Mr Nice Guy' reached no. 9. 'Special' single issued through *NME*, 'Slick Black Limousine'. 'Pretties For You' and 'Easy Action' were re-issued by Warners as a double-album, 'Schooldays: Alice Cooper The Early Recordings'. In December 'Muscle Of Love' album released.
1974: January, 'Teenage Lament' was released and reached no. 12.

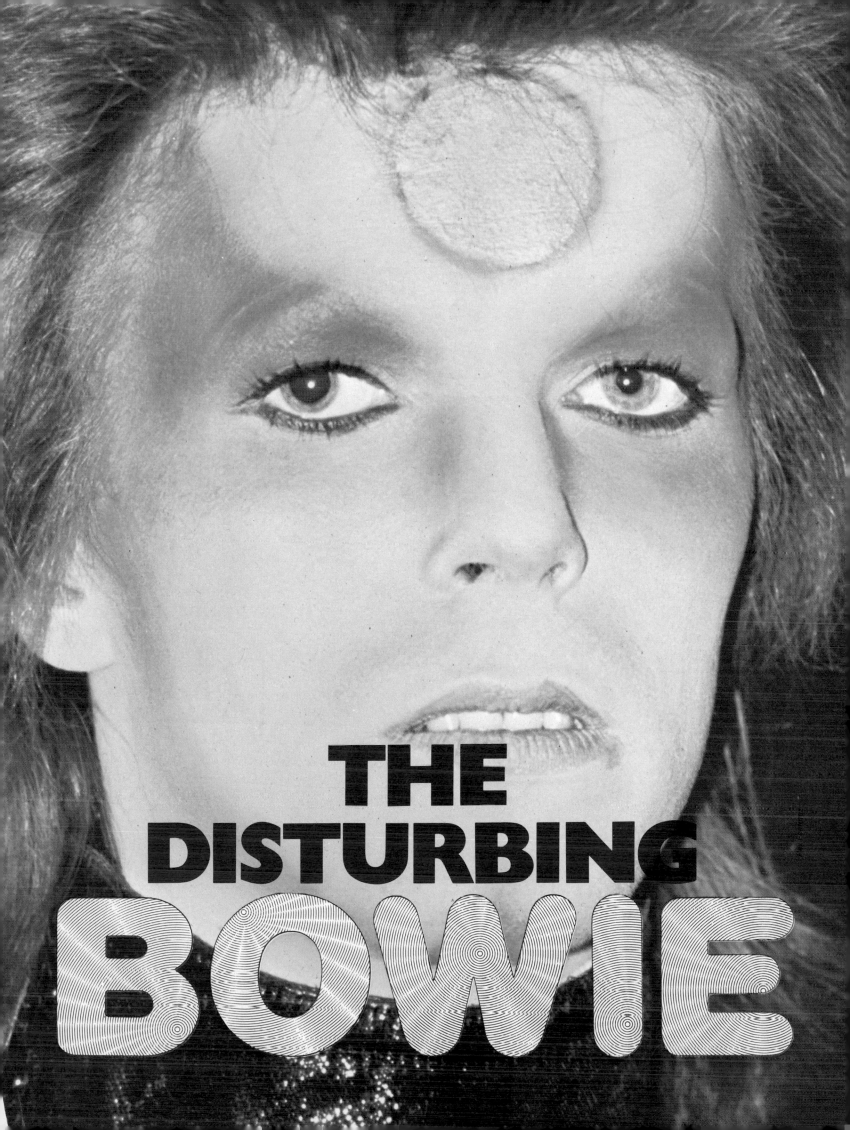

THE DISTURBING BOWIE

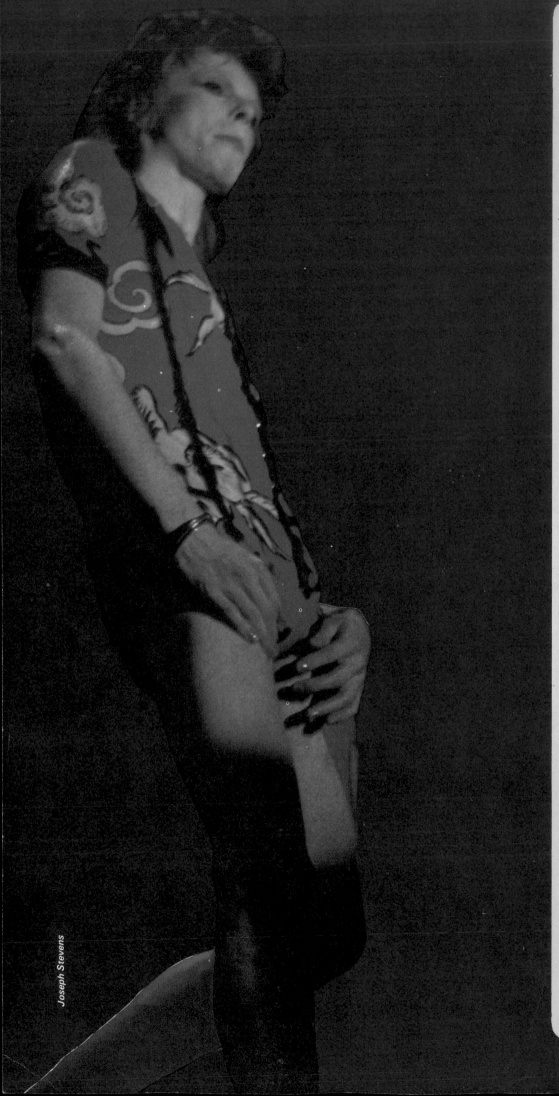

Joseph Stevens

By the time that David Bowie took his final bow from the whole touring scene at London's Hammersmith Odeon in July 1973, he had probably become the best-loved and most-hated performer in the rock world. His admirers called him a prophet, a demi-god, a superman; while, in common with many another artist who seemed to be breaking new ground, he had been the subject of frenzied attacks from all directions. His detractors branded him a fraud, a hoaxer, a pretentious charlatan and worse, but Bowie himself shrugged it all off with the elan of a true star. "There have been some fairly petty things said," he murmured.

So what was all the fuss about? Why would one of America's most important daily papers call David Bowie 'the most intellectually brilliant man currently using the medium of the long-playing record', while a British music paper would sneer about 'another nail in the coffin in which the whole Bowie mystique will soon be laid to rest'? It wasn't Bowie's theatrical stage act was it? Maybe it had something to do with his much-publicised bisexuality. Or, if not that, could it be that the intense crystal-gazing of some of his lyrics proved rather too much for them to stomach?

The cause of all this comment was born in Brixton in 1947, the son of the public relations man of a children's home. He dropped out of art school to work in an advertising agency, while playing in various groups like the Conrads, David Jones and the Lower Third and others. When the Monkees began to terrorise the planet in 1967, David Hayward-Jones became David Bowie and the Buzz. Photographs taken around then show him looking curiously similar to the Bowie of the '70s.

Lauren Bacall

Bowie had made an album for Deram and a couple of singles for Pye, but it wasn't until late 1969 that he emerged with his first big hit. This was 'Space Oddity', which appeared on the Mercury label in the wake of *2001* and the first moonshot. This tragi-comic tale of the spaceman who was unable to get back connected instantly in the public mind, and was followed by an album called 'David Bowie' (later to be re-issued as 'Space Oddity'), and a single called 'The Prettiest Star', the latter featuring Marc Bolan playing lead guitar.

Neither album nor single was successful, and Bowie seemed to have joined the long list of one-hit wonders. He retired from the music business for a year and a half, and ran an Arts Laboratory in Beckenham in partnership with a lady called Mary Finnegan.

Eventually, the apathy of the local community caused Bowie to abandon the project. "People were simply coming to be entertained," he recalled, "and the essence of an Arts Lab is participation."

Meanwhile, his record company were less than overjoyed by his semi-retirement, and demanded another album. What they got was the classic 'The Man Who Sold The World', a strange and foreboding album which took a few years to achieve the appreciation it deserved. On the cover, Bowie reclined languidly on a chaise-longue, enticingly clad in a long flowing dress and looking exactly like Lauren Bacall — this at a time when stubble and denims were the order of the day. Clearly, something more was afoot than simply another has-been folkie trying to make a comeback.

If the cover was startling, the album was infinitely more so. The music was the heaviest of heavy rock — taut, claustrophobic and menacing. The songs were harrowing exercises in paranoia; complex essays on themes of alienation and madness. Bowie's imagery was literate, economical, witty and immensely sophisticated, and doubly outstanding at a time when the stoned burblings of the Acid Age had only just slipped into memory. The album was produced by Tony Visconti, who also played bass on it. The other musicians were both formerly members of a Hull blues band called the Rats; guitarist Mick Ronson and drummer Mick 'Woody' Woodmansey.

Hunky Dory

'The Man Who Sold The World' shook up a lot of American critics, and the album sold a healthy 50,000 copies in the States; but Britain didn't seem ready for it, and it just rolled over and died. A year was to pass before Bowie recorded his next album, and in that year a number of important changes took place. He parted company with Tony Visconti, and formed a partnership with Ken Scott, who had engineered his last two albums. Even more important, he teamed-up with Tony DeFries, a young lawyer to whom he'd taken his tangled financial affairs, and who became his new manager. DeFries immediately negotiated a new recording contract with RCA, and thus equipped with a new producer, a new manager and a new company, Bowie went back into the studios to record 'Hunky Dory'.

'Hunky Dory' was lighter in texture than 'The Man Who Sold The World', but, if anything, heavier in terms of content. In fact, Bowie wasn't softening up at all. Even 'Oh You Pretty Things', which had been taken into the charts by no less a personage than Peter Noone himself, was about the need for the present human race to realise its own infinite possibilities and 'make way for the Homo Superior'.

Among the more straightforward songs on the album was 'Kooks'; a sweet little tune dedicated to Bowie's son Zowie and his wife Angie. 'Song To Bob Dylan' expertly pastiched its subject; while 'Queen Bitch' was Bowie's tribute to Lou Reed and the Velvet Underground. Finally, there was 'The Bewlay Brothers', undoubtedly Bowie's strangest song, and one that Bowieologists are still trying to unravel — Bowie himself is politely unhelpful when

Redferns

asked to elucidate any further about it.

After the release of 'Hunky Dory', Bowie took one tremendously important step. He cut his long blond hair into a feathery Mod cut reminiscent of the mid-'60s, dyed it a fluorescent orange, and, in the company of Ronson, Woodmansey and bassist Trevor Bolder (who had played on 'Hunky Dory') began to play concerts. Also, he gave an interview to one of Britain's leading rock weeklies, admitting that he was bisexual. And that really put the pigeon among the cats. Britain's first openly gay rock star! Who could resist such a divine spectacle? It was a stroke of pure genius. Bowie was made.

Bowie and his band wore tight quilted jumpsuits that looked as if they'd been left over from a gay version of *Star Trek*. Ronson peroxided his hair blond, Trevor Bolder dyed his six-inch-long sideboards silver, and Woodmansey adopted a blond version of Bowie's own hairstyle. They looked like gay vandals from some horrific future (not for nothing had Bowie seen *A Clockwork Orange* several times), and the instant they first stepped on stage, every other group in Britain looked completely out of date. This was clearly a totally different kettle of piranha from the inept flounderings of mere sensation seekers — these guys meant business.

Straight

Of course, the whole thing was something of a hoax. The band were as straight as could be, and despite the publicity Bowie's preferred company was that of his wife and child — hence 'Kooks'. Paradoxically, but perhaps predictably, his alleged gayness and his marriage only served to increase his following of both girls and boys, who faithfully reproduced his hairstyles, clothes and make-up as part of a familiar pattern of teen adulation that has been part of the rock & roll experience all along.

But the qualities which made Bowie artistically viable for somewhat older listeners who weren't really into dressing up, were the same ones that had won him a faithful cult audience long before Ziggymania. Basically, Bowie's greatest strength lay in his songs. No-one seemed to be writing songs for the '70s which cut so deep into the feelings that many had recognised in themselves, but had failed to analyse. His band too was amazing — as tough a power trio as anyone had heard, but tight, controlled, and willing to channel all their formidable energies and skills into the power blasts of those songs. The album that put it all together was released in the summer of 1972, and it was entitled 'The Rise And Fall Of Ziggy Stardust And The Spiders From Mars'.

It was probably Bowie's finest and most complete performance on record. While its two predecessors had included individual songs that surpassed the 'Ziggy' material, this album really made it as a whole. Its setting was five years before the end of the world, and its theme was the life of the rock & roll star. Remember, Bowie was not yet a big star at the time that the 'Ziggy' songs were written, and so he was able to look at the situation with a certain amount of detachment. The album's opening number 'Five Years' lets down the backdrop, and the remaining songs on the first side (with the exception of Ron Davies' composition 'It Ain't Easy', a leftover from the 'Hunky Dory' sessions) examine various aspects of the situation. But it's the second side of 'Ziggy' that shows Bowie really getting his hands into the meat.

Ziggy Stardust and the Spiders From Mars are the archetype rock & roll band, and the songs chart their career from the first time Ziggy gets up to sing in a small club, right through to his superstardom when leeches and hangers-on bug him non-stop, inter-group jealousies develop, and the final apocalyptic moment arrives when 'the kids had killed the man I had to break up the band'. As a kind of alternative ending, there's 'Rock And Roll Suicide', when the forgotten idol roams the streets forlorn and nobody wants to know anymore. That 18-minute song cycle stands as a veritable tour-de-force, a total brain-bruise, and it made David Bowie almost as big a star as Ziggy himself. Tony DeFries leapt in fast and made sure everybody realised it: no interviews and no pictures except by Bowie's authorised photographer. The press, as

Below left: The Bowie family; his wife Angela and their son, Zowie. Below right: The changing face of Bowie; an early 'image'.

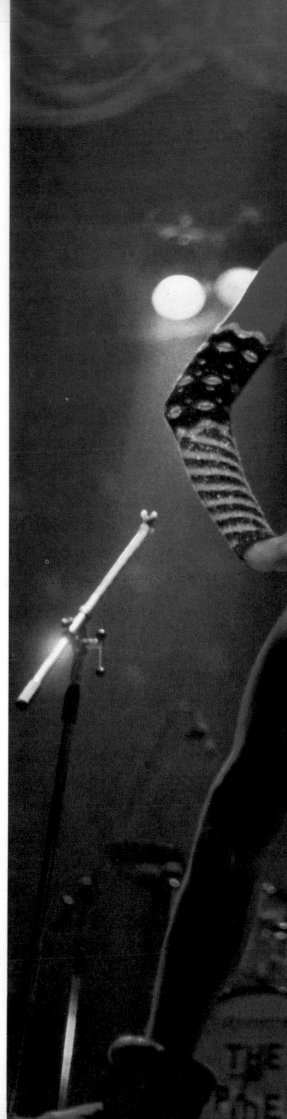

Joseph Stevens

well they might, struck back the only way they could — by mounting an all-out campaign against Bowie's records and performances.

Regular Superstar

But the live shows just got more and more extravagant. Costume changes, elaborate lighting, the complete works. At one concert at the Rainbow in London, Bowie was even joined by a team of dancers led by the great mime Lindsay Kemp, one of his early mentors. At this same concert a lot of industry people got very uptight because the support group, Roxy Music, were not allowed to rehearse in the hall, and their record company were not permitted to set up advertising stands in the foyer, or to give away posters and badges to the audience. Again, with only a few exceptions, the critics jumped on Bowie with both feet.

Following a moderately successful American tour, Bowie went into the studios to record his next album 'Aladdin Sane', comprising songs written on tour and reflecting his impressions of 'God's Own Country'. The main innovation on this album was the piano work of veteran New York jazzman Mike Garson, but the band had never played better, and the album contained some stunning moments. To the critics though, and to many of Bowie's followers, this album appeared something of an anticlimax compared to past glories. It was viciously put down, but nevertheless became Bowie's biggest seller so far, and the focus of a stage act with which he made a stormy and controversial tour of Britain. It began in chaos at the packed 18,000-seater Earls Court Stadium in London, where poor acoustics and minimal visibility ruined the proceedings for vast numbers of the audience. At subsequent performances, however, Bowie delivered shows of such total virtuosity that few, if any, of his fans were disappointed and the rock press at last found some sympathy, and even praise, for the man whose big gig in London had been a flop.

But the stresses and strains of that last tour were enough to convince Bowie that further 'live' performances were out of the question. So, in July 1973, after a gig in London featuring Jeff Beck, Bowie at last renounced the stage for the recording studio and movie lot.

So much for history, then. In the final analysis, why is David Bowie so deeply disturbing? Why did so many people feel threatened by his very existence? Reasons are manifold. Firstly, some folks found him 'cold' and 'contrived'. On the face of it, there's some substance for this charge; but Bowie never claimed to be a spontaneous boogier. The creative processes that go into producing work like Bowie's are far more complex and precise than those of most of his contemporaries, and this very complexity renders any impression of spontaneity laughable. Also, every aspect of Bowie's operation has equal importance. The clothes, the performances, the records, the composing — they are all part of the total experiment in living that Bowie carries on every moment of his life.

Bowie's particular vision of the world and the life-styles that go with it, mean that his influence goes far beyond a bunch of songs and a stage act. From now on, it seems as though Bowie will be 'leading from the back', as his career opens up and he is beginning to concentrate on work in the studio and various film projects. But to backtrack. On the eve of his big teenage breakthrough, Bowie sang in 'Star' from the 'Ziggy' album:

'I could do with the money,
I'm so whacked out with things as they are,
I'd send my photograph to my honey,
And I'd come on like a regular superstar'

and ended with this line:

'I could make it all worthwhile as a rock
and roll star.'

As in all good fairy stories, the charm worked. He did it just like he said he would. It leaves you wondering if 'Rock And Roll Suicide' — the song he finished his last 'live' gig with — had perhaps been written for that very occasion.

235

Cat Stevens

JKA

On October 1st, 1966, a single was released by an unknown 17-year-old from Soho, London. The song was 'I Love My Dog', and the singer was Cat Stevens. Even in a good year like 1967 the song shone out; it was catchy, imaginative, well arranged. Above all else, it managed to combine a rhythmic complexity with a simple melody.

It was a minor hit, but the follow-up, 'Matthew and Son', was a smash. Throughout 1967, Cat continued to turn out singles of a high quality, characterised by arranging flair and interesting tempo changes. They were certainly more adventurous than the standard two-verse-and-chorus structure which was always predominant in pop music. And not one of them was a love song . . . extraordinary for the singles market.

Perhaps for this reason, the later singles didn't sell quite as well as the earlier ones. Still, he was voted the 'Brightest Hope For 1968' in a music paper poll, and the future seemed fairly rosy. Then he was taken ill and disappeared from the scene for two years while recovering from TB. The market to which he returned in 1970 was different from the one he had left. In 1967 there had been a demand for superior singles; but by 1970, people capable of producing them had mostly gone over into the album market. Cat came back with an album, 'Mona Bone Jakon', in which he displayed the essential singer/songwriter talent, an ability to express himself, to reveal *his* innermost feelings in a way that made sense to other people and deepened *their* own experiences.

'Mona Bone Jakon' was a fine album, and perhaps it's still — for all its lack of the later gloss — his finest. All the pop talents are in evidence, and the newer singer/songwriter ones as well. The result is interesting, melodic music — a rare commodity. In 1967, Cat had said that he intended to 'start complex and end up simple'. He was on the way.

The style Cat Stevens evolved on 'Mona Bone Jakon' was further elaborated and refined in the three albums that followed — 'Tea For The Tillerman', 'Teaser And The Firecat', and 'Catchbull At Four'. Perhaps 'Teaser' is the most representative, with the vibrant acoustic guitars of Cat and Alun Davies strummed in the imaginative rhythms that Cat seemed capable of producing *ad infinitum*. Behind them, bass and drums add depth to the sound; above them Cat's voice changes expressively with the moods of the songs.

The subject matter on 'Teaser' is fairly typical of his work as a whole. There are a few songs of love's sadness, a few of his self/world awareness, one song half in Greek, one song of wonder, and one of the mysterious. The love songs are simple and perceptively honest, and all musically just right.

Timing Conjures Tension

'Peace Train' is as good an example as any. The lyric itself would be nothing on its own, but, given the driving force of the rhythms and tempo changes behind it, it becomes a statement that is emotionally convincing. Between singing 'I've been thinking lately about the world as it is' and singing 'why must we go on hating', there is a pause of just the right length. That might seem a small point, but it is such timing that is Cat Stevens' main strength. Timing conjures tension, and tension marks the great songs. The disappointing feature of Cat's 1973 release, 'Foreigner', was the disappearance of such tension with the abandonment of the acoustic blend he had perfected. Perhaps he thought he had taken it as far as he could. In any case, the new piano-fronted sound was far less likeable, his singing sounded forced, and his lyrics generally empty of any significance.

Some artists try to get across what they think other people should realise, they try to provide a *lamp* for everyone. Others seek to portray things as they see them, to provide a *mirror* so clear that anyone looking in it will see things much more clearly.

Cat Stevens has been drawn, inextricably, towards being a lamp. He's found a way for himself, and his music is mostly concerned with letting others in on the secret. But doing this is not without its dangers, as Dylan found out. By putting yourself forward as an answer, you get trapped in the role of a saviour. Dylan created a context where anything he said related back to all the rest. Cat Stevens' problems arise, paradoxically, because he has never created such a convincing context. His tendency to play the preacher has been reinforced by his closeness to the world of 'pop', leaving him unable to lay himself open.

His best music has been when he has opted for the other approach, that of recounting situations with a minimum of preaching, that of being just a mirror. When he sings:

'I'm always thinking of you
But my words just blow away,
*   just blow away*
It always comes back to one thing honey
And I can't think of right words to say'

. . . and counterparts it musically with just the right fragility, just the right guitar lines descending again and again into hopelessness, then the effect is stunning. If he would go back to that sort of approach, then who knows what he could do.

Gary Glitter

In 1960, the little-known Paul Raven, a London club singer, recorded 'Tower Of Strength'. After that, it took 12 years and a change of name and image before Paul actually became that hit-making tower of strength to millions of young kids all over the world . . . in the person of that hairy-chested, lovable glitter-man . . . Gary Glitter!

Gary Glitter has none of the long, hard leanness of Jagger or Chuck Berry, the beautiful nakedness of Bowie, or the delicate, slender frailty of Bolan. Gary's is a thicker, manlier presence made up of hairy chest, strong thighs, garage mechanic's eyes and a boxer's movements. Whatever the adjectives, however, Gary's is an image that most definitely appeals to the '70s generation of nubile little females.

To have chanced on a name like Gary Glitter, right at a time when 'glitter rock' was just becoming an established phrase, was either a brilliant stroke of luck or an amazingly perceptive P.R. job. Gary and glitter both seemed to break into the music scene at one and the same moment . . . and from the beginning Gary always seemed to have an edge over the other advocates of glitter rock; for with names like Bolan, Bowie, Sweet and Wizzard, it was never so clear from the start that they too were very much part of the glitter scene. By the end of 1973, though, it had become quite clear that *that* had been a 'glitter year'. From Britain's glitter stars, through to Sylvester of San Francisco and Iggy Pop of Detroit, camp and sequins had quite obviously been the order of the day.

Entertainers have never made a point of reflecting the dress of the man-in-the-street and sadly enough, the costumes and sparkle of glitter rock have remained firmly the property of the stage. Streets and homes are as far as ever from being awash with a brilliant flood of sequins and other artefacts of the shine world, and the only really noticeable fall out has been via the few bold blades who adorned their jean-suits with rows of metal studs, or even indulged in a touch of sequined embroidery.

Dressed Up Rock

The definitive glitter-star, Gary Glitter has taken rock once again into the realms of the costumier. Even though his music was hard put to keep pace with the inventiveness and boldness of his dress, his audiences nonetheless adored it. And his fans have never been the poodle-hugging, happy mums who cheered Liberace; they are perhaps the youngest weenyboppers the music business has ever had to contemplate. Often too young to be actual record-buyers, many of Gary's young followers must have surely relied on the good humour of big sisters and brothers or indulgent parents to buy their records for them.

To many of the kids, Gary is no doubt a replacement for that fairy-on-top-of-the-xmas-tree, or that large bride doll that has so recently been outgrown or maybe dropped. Whatever the reasons, the fact remains that Gary Glitter's fans are *really* young . . . and as ardently as they love Gary, they also probably love David Cassidy, Donny Osmond or the Jackson 5. However impossible the combination might seem from the outside — from the clean-cut, sweet-smiling, young teenybopper stars to this hard-rocking, pelvis grinding Gary — the tinies seem to take it all in their stride.

Back in the '50s, the little 'uns tended to grow up in a Saturday morning cinema world of Batman, Superman, Tarzan and Roy Rogers. They had their allotted two hours of fantasy amid yells and hollers and face-sized lollipops that were good for hiding behind when the baddies seemed to be winning.

Tarzan In Tinsel

In the '70s, though, kids by the hundred get dressed up in their glitter gear, their bright eyes concealing all yawns as their mums and dads escort them to a Gary Glitter concert. There, they sing and chant and shout to the easy words of the glitter-rock songs. As the excitement increases, they mount the seats until soon their little legs are standing high on the backs of their seats, and their arms are pounding forth in Hitler-like unison. They really get off on Gary, he is their biggest and sparkliest superman of all, and they seem well-pleased with their hero. The kid's feelings for their hero defy all reason, and Gary himself has no explanation to offer for it. *He* doesn't know why his primitive heartbeat rhythm has won him such a loyal, contented and young audience. The kids can certainly dress themselves up to look like Gary, and they do, but the disparities are just so many. But then again, Superman, Batman and Tarzan never did look like their young fans either.

And when the concert's over, the little ones trot out in tired happiness, to their waiting parents, who invariably have a collective look of bewilderment and anxiety about them. The parents, moreover, certainly have a lot more in common with Gary in regard to age, habits and waist-lines than their offspring do.

Gary was born Paul Gadd in the small country town of Banbury, in Oxfordshire, England (of 'Ride A Cock-Horse To Banbury Cross' fame.) Life there was quiet, peaceful and uneventful, and Gary recalls that he had a reasonably happy childhood — although he didn't know a father, his uncle, John Gadd, was a very loving father-substitute. At the age of six, Paul would be singing, while his uncle played guitar. As Gary himself recalls, "I used to idolise him, I used to think he was where it was at. Even now, I really dig him. If circumstances had been different for him, I think he would have made it big on the music scene too. He taught me my first rudiments of E, A and B7, that kind of thing. My

grandfather was a pro as well, busking on the Brighton pier, things like that."

Then, at the age of 11, Gary moved to London, as his mother had re-married. Gary's memories of school from then on aren't particularly happy ones: "I used to talk to teachers like they were on an equal footing, I'd say, 'let's discuss this', and they'd say, 'we don't discuss it, you do it'. They wanted me to become an army cadet and things like that. I knew exactly what I wanted to do when I left school at the age of 14 — I was going to be a rock & roll star. . . . It took a lot of time, but I've done it."

Playing The Blues

At the time, Gary had a friend called Brian Ramsay, who always used to be tapping, tapping on everything. So eventually, Gary's stepfather agreed to be the guarantor on a drum-kit. This was in 1959. Gary and Brian then teamed up with Pete Rainer, who was a brilliant guitar player, and although there was no bass player, just Gary, the three of them were off — singing and jigging around.

"I like blues, I *love* blues. I could sit there for hours just playing Sonny Boy Williamson and things like that. I'm very much into black music, not so much the soul thing, though I dig Stevie Wonder. I used to see Alexis Korner a lot in the old days when there were just four places to go to — the Top 10, the Two I's, the Freight Train and later on, the Marquee.

The atmosphere used to be electric — Adam Faith, Cliff Richard, Vince Eager and Marty Wilde . . ."

Shortly after this, Gary became the resident singer at Le Conda club in London, where people like Connie Francis used to sing. He wasn't allowed to do too much rock & roll there, but used to sing numbers like, 'Dream Lover' and 'She Was Only Sixteen'. "I got all the rock & roll out of my system at the Two I's, doing stuff like 'Hound Dog'," Gary now recalls, "Everyone who was around at the time all sang the same things. No one had any arrangements or anything. It was all American stuff — Eddie Cochran, Gene Vincent, things like that — and America was a million miles away then."

In 1960, Gary (by now known as Paul Raven) recorded his first single, 'Tower Of Strength', which he since reckons must have been the worst record *ever* made. After that it wasn't until 1962 that he cut his second single, 'Walk On Boy'. This one sold about 30,000 copies, but from then on he found it very difficult to get suitable material as he had decided he didn't want to do any more cover versions, which was what most people were recording at the time.

"It wasn't until I started writing with Mike (his manager, Mike Leander) that I got into any decent material. Before, I never got any of the top-drawer stuff from the publishers: I used to get all the dregs at the bottom. Now they'd probably bring out the whisky and the cigars. Then, I couldn't even get a cup of tea."

For the next couple of years after that,

Gary did whole theatre tours with easy-listening people like Tony Newley, Ronnie Corbett and Bernard Bresslaw . . . and found it invaluable experience: "Everybody needs to do some kind of apprenticeship, and that was mine. I learnt so much from the lighting-men upwards." This pattern continued until 1964, when the Northern invasion took over Britain, when the Liverpool lads were the kings of the road. Then, from the Beatles down, you *had* to have a Liverpool accent. According to Gary, it was the end: "It was terrible, I'd go along to auditions, talking like this (does an excellent imitation of some '60s Liverpool lads singing 'Money, Money, Money') . . . but it was hopeless. I'd get a bit excited and revert back to my cockney. If you didn't speak with a Liverpool accent in London, in 1964, you just never made it."

Assistant Producer

So, Gary ended up working on the pop music TV show, *Ready, Steady, Go!* for a year, as a kind of assistant producer. It was there that he first met Mike Leander, who had just produced 'As Tears Go By' for Marianne Faithfull. Mike asked Gary to join a band he was forming to go on tour with the Bachelors. It was a really big band, on the same lines as Blood, Sweat and Tears, and they were doing great Spector-type arrangements.

It was then that Gary met John Russell, who has since become his trombone and sax player in the Glittermen. The two of them soon decided to get a band together and take off for Germany: "We played in clubs, it's a great thing. You learn so much about yourself. You get so bored with what you're doing that you find new areas to express yourself in the whole time. Nobody can get that in 1974 in London. There's nowhere for anyone to play. You play for an hour if you're lucky. I used to play at the Star Club for a total of eight hours, and there might be five other bands on as well. When we weren't playing, we'd all be in the beer parlour next door, or else we'd be watching the other acts, and they included people like Ray Charles and Fats Domino. It was great; I learnt so much about myself and how to entertain people. And the things I do now, I used to do then, except I'd do them seven times a night. I was very fit. Altogether, it was a very cushy number, but I shouldn't have stayed so long, I guess."

During these years, Gary (who was still Paul Raven at this time) had still been in contact with Mike Leander. Mike was very much at the top of his league – as well as Marianne Faithfull, he had produced Billy Fury and Lulu. He had also become a successful songwriter after his first hit with 'Lady Godiva'. In 1967 he also produced four singles and two albums for Cliff Richard, not to mention the Beatles', 'She's Leaving Home'. So, Gary eventually persuaded Mike to travel to Germany and watch him work. That was all it took for Mike to realize that Gary had something going with his 'crowd participation thing', and so his next move was to persuade Gary to write his own material.

However, it wasn't until Gary went to Berlin and saw a Little Richard show that he realized the potential that rock & roll had: "He was brilliant. He's still good now, it's just that he needs to rap a lot to get his breath, he's getting old."

The show was, in fact, enough to convince Gary to sell up everything to enable him to return to Britain for a year and work on his songwriting. The results of this industry were 'Rock & Roll Parts 1/2' and 'I Didn't Know I Loved You Till I Saw You Rock & Roll' . . . and so Gary Glitter was born.

Gary's first record owed its success to the discotheques that played it, rather than the radio. Beyond that, his subsequent successes have, he feels, been due to the efforts he's put into his live shows: "I'm not afraid of gigs. I like it. At the beginning, we did so many gigs throughout Britain, we just didn't stop. It must be terrible for those guys who write and suddenly find themselves with a smash hit on their hands, and they're told to get out there and gig. I get a real buzz out of going on stage."

In the following two years, Gary's hits came thick and fast: 'Do You Wanna Touch Me?', 'Hello, Hello, I'm Back Again', 'I'm The Leader' and in December, 1973, 'I Love You Love Me Love'. This single went straight into the charts at no. 1, something that hadn't happened in the pop scene, since the Beatles days. His two albums, 'Glitter' and 'Touch Me' were equally successful although his critics were many and it took a long time for the music press to concede that he had anything going for him at all. They derided his simple lyrics and all-enveloping drum beat, but Gary remained sure of what he was doing:

"I like the naïve lyrics and it can be hard to write such simple words. 'Long Tall Sally saw Mary having it in the alley' – you can't get any simpler than that. I've never said, 'play our album and you'll discover new depths'. I say, 'bung it on at a party and you'll have fun'. My place is making music to bop to."

Hollywood Glamour

Gary's stage act is reminiscent of an unrehearsed Busby Berkeley stage show with floating staircases and long lines of luscious ladies, swaying and smiling. Although the show lacks precision and style the kids do not seem to notice. This Hollywood glamour scene is shattered by a thundering mass of black motor bikes revving around amidst a cloud of heavy smoke, deafening the audience with their roars, followed on by Gary, driven in astride the pillion seat of a silver chopper – he and his bike are as one, a gleaming, gliding star-studded package, guaranteed to cause explosive excitement.

Gary's act is nothing if not physical and energetic. He knows how to get an audience going and keep them going. His seven-strong band too, is comprised of very competent musicians who are excellent in their clockwork timing. Gary can

I. Dickson

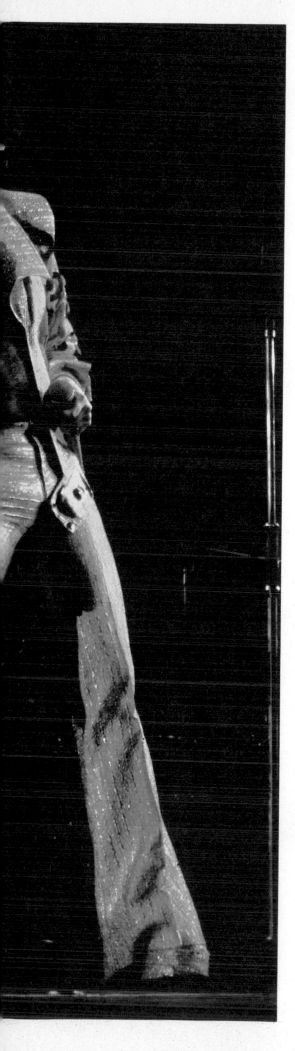

fool around with his stacked-boot walking and clenched-fist shaking, mounting up audience responses until, when he finishes, the band comes right in without any heavy signalling. They bop along at the back just perfectly, with typical '50s sax breaks, choreographed leg-stepping and body-rocking; plus supporting him brilliantly with zippy guitar streaks. The overall effect is screamaramas to end all screamaramas . . . but it's the thudding, pulsating drums that really win the show for the band, as they fill the air with their simulated heartbeat and get Britain's tens of thousands of weenies, wobbling along on their well-stacked wedgies.

Gary's music seems to attract much intellectual derision and his audiences tend to be mainly working-class; the middle classes tending more towards the rarefied world of ELP, Pink Floyd, Frank Zappa, Led Zeppelin and perhaps Bette Midler. But Gary's kids can hear the words and understand them, even if they might put their own interpretation on them as they run around the playground shouting, 'I'm the leader of the gang'.

According to Gary, "the record-buying kid is maturing so much earlier now, they're nine and 10 and maybe even younger. When I started writing songs, I treated it as a lot of fun, and I think they're slowly progressing, slowly getting better. Mike and I, as a team, are only two years old now. We're capable of writing better, but I don't want to go too quickly. We've got an audience and I want to take them with me, and I don't want to blow it."

In the years since Gary has made it, he has successfully toured Britain several times — from small unknown halls to his breakthrough at the Wembley Rock & Roll Revival in the summer of 1972, and then on to the Palladium and his triumphant successes at the Rainbow, where such artists as Stevie Wonder and David Bowie have taken the London audiences by storm. Gary has also had two smash tours of Australia, and it remains to be seen how long he will wait before tackling the US.

Starving

Gary has already moved into the film world, with a film made at the end of 1973. Based on his performances, plus all the people involved in the production of his show and with Gary himself, it features four live numbers, 'Leader Of The Gang', 'Sidewalk Sinner', 'I Love You Love Me Love' and 'Touch Me'.

In the meantime, the question that many rock critics have been asking is, 'what will it be like to be stuck with the Glitter image and especially the name after '73?' As Gary explained further, "I enjoy working, because I've starved at times. Films are really interesting to me. I want to get into the film thing, because I think there's something in me that could come over really well. I'm stuck with the glitter image thank goodness, and I'm stuck with it for the rest of my life. And there will always be somebody, somewhere who'll say '1973, wasn't that a funny time, when

we all put glitter in our hair and wore those incredible clothes and boots . . . weren't we silly'. And then, they'll all say, 'Oh, yea, he's on down the road at the Variety Club or something' . . . and they'll all come trooping along. And they'll be there, with their pints of beer or whatever, remembering the good old days at the Rainbow or wherever they saw me."

Satin And Sequins

Gary is definitely a star of the '70s. His image is a different one from that presented in the '50s by the leather, grease and duck-tail rockers, but he does have the exaggerated pelvic movements. His bare chest, dimpled navel and satin-concealed crutch are afloat in sequins and lurex and silver lamé — and it's all very much part of the show. The frenzied, hypnotic beat of the drums emphasizes that it is a physical feeling he aims for, not a psychedelic one. With Gary on stage, in fact, there is little space left for the mind to ruminate on higher planes — it's a here-and-now show, a masterpiece of come-on.

Yet he is also reminiscent of the '30s, that extravagant era when actors and actresses were filmstars-cum-goddesses. Supreme creatures who had swopped Mount Olympus for the high-flying luxury of Hollywood. Immortals, occasionally glimpsed by swooning earthlings, who admired and fantasized over their style, but never dared to approach it.

Gary Glitter could, in fact, have been a working-class hero of the '60s, if he'd been lucky enough to have been born in Liverpool. Instead, he has taken the rocker music of the '50s, combined it with the style of the '30s, and given the world a real rock star for the '70s.

Nonetheless, one daily newspaper began an article on G.G. by saying: 'Mr Gary Glitter is 19-49-29. And those are just his ages'. Gary retorted by saying, "I know I look a bit clapped out some of the time, but 49 is a bit heavy." And heavy is one thing that Gary is not. He's warm and friendly and has that quick, fall-about cockney wit that encircles him like a magic cloak. His very name invites an avalanche of mockery, but remember what the over-35-year-olds were saying when the Beatles hit the scene: 'Beatles, what kind of name is that' . . . and so on and so on. After the Beatles, the names hardly seemed to matter and certainly they weren't used to establish an image of musical integrity, yet they were accepted without a second thought. All the more surprising, that everyone blanched at the sound of Gary Glitter, a name derived from a 10-minute think-tank with some old friends.

Maybe it's time that the critics got off Gary Glitter's back. After all, Bob Hite of Canned Heat is known as Bob the Bear, not Bob the Slob; and there's been no mention of George Melly the Belly. As for age, the final cross that Gary has been lumbered with, surely it's OK to say he's somewhere between David Bowie and John Lennon, as are Cliff Richard and Bob Dylan.

A sort of singing Rocky Marciano in black leather and sequins, Gary uses motorbikes, dancing girls and the whole bag of tricks to put on a show that has the tinies leaping gleefully out of their seats.

Ian Dickson

BACK TRACK

Born: May 8th, 1944, in Banbury, Oxfordshire, England.
1959: Formed his first group, and played the London clubs.
1960: First record, 'Tower Of Strength'.
1962: 'Walk On Boy' was released.

1963: Did theatre tours.
1964: Worked as an assistant producer on the TV show, *Ready Steady Go!*
1965: Left Britain to work in clubs in Germany for the next 5 years.
1970: Returned to Britain. Worked on the 'Jesus Christ-Superstar' album.
1971: Songwriting, session work.

1972: 'Rock & Roll Parts 1/2', success.
1973: January, 'Do You Wanna Touch Me' (no. 2). March, 'Hello Hello I'm Back Again (no. 2). July, 'I'm The Leader Of The Gang I Am'. September, 'I Love You Love Me Love' (no. 1).
1974: March, 'Remember Me This Way' (no. 3).

Chris Walter

Gilbert O'Sullivan

Gilbert O'Sullivan — the kooky Irish kid turned champion of easy-listening pop — is the enigma that proves the rule. He's stylish but introverted, reclusive but eccentric . . . and loved by many different factions of the record-buying public from teenies to grannies.

Raymond O'Sullivan was born in Waterford on December 1st, 1946. Somehow he's *so* perfect, he could almost be a plastic mock-up of the real thing. In these days of flash and raunch, lipstick and

campery, 'G' stands out as a successful anachronism. He's a genuine, good old dyed-in-the-wool, poet/musicman. He's never pretended to be a rock & roller, and his only concession to that frenetic culture is the introduction of electric piano.

The point is, it just isn't fair to consider Gilbert in rock & roll terms. The smooth, innocuous arrangements — done with the help of one Johnny Spence — leave those rambling rhymes in the clear, and Gilbert's personality positively gleams through. Soon after 'Nothing Rhymed', his first hit in 1970, an astonished music press, still labouring under clouds of misdirected

intellectual fantasy, was forced to admit 'real talent'. Praise indeed for the times, but the fact that Gilbert had turned his back on the rock business and opted for Gordon Mills nonetheless created a lot of suspicion. Why should a singer/songwriter with such obvious appeal get drawn into the glamour of Tom Jones and Engelbert Humperdinck — the other Mills protégés?

So, right from the start, the new star had to contend with praise tempered with rather meaningless criticism, like why did he wear those ridiculous clothes? Ridiculous? Why of course not! It was either very clever management, or very clever Gilbert.

243

And if we are to believe it, the latter was true.

Gilbert's ready answer to all that criticism about hype and how his music made it unnecessary, was that he loved wearing suits that were two sizes too small. He liked his 'pudding basin' hair and cloth cap. He preferred wearing army boots. As someone said at the time: 'An interesting example of the introvert with an enormous instinct for the extrovert; hence the carefully cultivated image'.

But wasn't it all much simpler than that? Didn't the lad who started writing songs at art college in 1967 have the drop on us all? While the world was revelling in the psychedelic excesses of the late '60s, here was a young man with short hair, unusual clothes, and straight, tuneful songs sung in a George Formby style. It was bound to shock!

It's not surprising that such an individual comes from a large family including two sisters and three brothers. He always considered himself to be the black sheep, and, coming to England in 1960 after his father died, he gradually veered towards the loner's life. When his mother bought an upright piano so that one of his sisters could learn to play, the lessons naturally fell to him when she refused them. ''I hated them,'' he has since said. ''After a while I packed them in. Mother moved the piano into the garden shed and that's where I started writing. I was always the odd one out — the scruffy art student with painted jeans and long hair. My mother hated it.''

But hairy Raymond kept at it until he was finally prompted to send some tapes to record and publishing companies. That was in 1967, while he was in his last year at college. With monotonous regularity, the tapes would be returned, mostly unopened.

His next step was perhaps obvious by today's standards, though in 1967 it may have seemed the antithesis of what youth culture was all about: he moved to the big city to get closer to the action, and found a job at a large store. It just so happened that one of his workmates had a recording contract with CBS. So, Raymond handed over his tapes . . . and the company became interested. At first they could only offer him a publishing contract, but he stuck out and they finally agreed to give him a chance. It was the start he wanted;

BACK TRACK

Real name Ray O'Sullivan. Born December 1st, 1946, in Waterford, Ireland.

244

it was not the break he really needed.

The contract required one single a year, and — by his own admission — the first was terrible, mainly because of an incompatibility with the production team. Both Mike Smith (producer) and Keith Mansfield (arranger) had just had chart hits with the likes of the Tremeloes and Love Affair. Raymond's songs, 'You' and 'What Can I Do', however, were of a totally different nature.

Another song, 'Disappear', was recorded, but Raymond reckoned the finished product sounded worse than his original demo made in the shed at home. As a result, he got the company to add a string quartet to the original tape . . . and that became the first single.

Musical Chairs

Although people really liked the record, basically it failed. Mike Smith then said he must release 'You', and when that crashed as well Raymond wanted out. Major Minor was the next company to take an interest. He would be a big star they assured him, and duly released 'I Wish I Could Cry' and 'Mr Moody's Garden'. The only significance of this disc being the adopted name of its singer. Then it was just Gilbert — the O'Sullivan only being added at Gordon Mills' instigation.

Gilbert believed in that particular single, but watched dismally as the record company went about destroying the feel by adding flutes and suchlike. Again he wanted out, and this time he'd only lasted six months compared with the 18 months with CBS.

Next came a period of quiet re-thinking, a time for deciding how to do things properly. Obviously a manager was needed, and already one or two music biz people were sniffing around. Gilbert, however, was taking care. He informed inquirers that a list of possible management candidates was being drawn up. Robert Stigwood was one of the names he put on his list, Paul McCartney he also considered.

The thing was that it had got to be someone big enough to promote the talent he knew he had. Already the '30s image was formulating in his head, and he was acquiring a few items for his wardrobe. Abruptly he decided to approach Gordon Mills, a man he admired. This was the second start, but still his career fizzed like a damp squib. Mills told him to go away and write more songs, come back in a year, and in the meantime continue as a clerk.

Then, once he had signed, Mills justified the wait by producing his first hit almost immediately. The single was 'Nothing Rhymed', the prototype of the sound that was to make Gilbert very famous very quickly. It got to no. 7 in the charts.

As Gilbert himself observed: "It was lyrics people could talk about. I got great publicity. I was irresistible really what with the clothes, the hair and the lyrics." At the time he also had this to say about his image: "Don't think I like cutting my hair. It looks out of place. I'm sure it embarrasses some people. Some people feel

1969: Signed with Gordon Mills.
1970: 1st single for MAM, 'Nothing Rhymed' (no. 7).
1971: 'Under The Blanket We Go'. 'We Will' (no. 28). 'Himself' album. 'No Matter How I Try' (no. 5).
1972: 'Alone Again' (no. 3). 'Ooh Wakka Doo Wakka Day' (no. 9). 'Claire' (no. 1). 'Back To Front' album.
1973: 'Get Down' (no. 1). 'Ooh Baby' (no. 14). 'I'm A Writer Not A Fighter' album. 'Why Oh Why Oh Why' (no. 5).
1974: 'Happiness Is Me And You' (no. 20).
Chart positions courtesy of NME.

'Long live Gilbert, the cloth cap is dead', seems to be the message of this shot. Gilbert's metamorphosis from the spotty, overgrown schoolboy to the fine-featured, handsome creature (right), has been one to amaze and delight the general music public.

sorry for me but I like it. Some artists say 'don't categorize me', I'm saying 'you can't categorize me'. Anyway, people like me are good for the business.''

In that first rush of success he was quite outspoken, perhaps because — like a clown — he could hide behind the mask of his new-found image. It wasn't until later, after hits like 'No Matter How I Try' and 'Alone Again' (the one that broke him in the States), that the great O'Sullivan charisma began to build. Maybe it was a by-product of the star machine that had made Engelbert and Tom. Anyhow, Gilbert was by now installed in a bungalow on the Gordon Mills estate, and was to be seen by the odd journalist who could get to him as a pipe-smoking collector of artifacts. His bits and pieces included anything to do with his heroes Charlie Chaplin and Buster Keaton, the Beatles and Bob Dylan, and the pile was forever mounting.

Into Long Pants

Meanwhile, his records, including a first album 'Himself' were doing great business. By Spring 1972, Gilbert had decided to make subtle changes to his image. The trouser length was dropped below the knees, and the big 'G' T-shirts were introduced.

That was the start of a continuing process which saw him gradually transform himself from the boyish figure of 1970 to the hairy-chested he-man image that harmonized well with his two stable mates.

At the same time, his records moved gradually away from the fairly slushy efforts on his first album, through the up-tempo treatments of 'Back To Front' (1972), to the comparative sophistication of 'I'm A Writer Not A Fighter'.

Throughout, Gilbert O'Sullivan maintained his rhyming jumbles of words that sometimes sounded like a story, and often like an incomprehensible hodge-podge of ideas. The important point must be, however, his ability to trigger knowing smiles from listeners who have found themselves in the situations he sings about. He's a storyteller without any heavy messages. 'They are real slices of life', is a comment often aimed at his lyrics.

Having conquered both the States and Britain — they called him 'the scream machine' — and also the world record market, Mr. O'Sullivan wasn't going to go far wrong. His appeal was broad enough to take him onwards if the boppers finally tired of his romantic tunes and clean-living image . . . ''I'm too shy to mix with people'' . . . The matriarchal matrons could always be relied on to sweep him to their ample bosoms. Most of all, Gilbert O'Sullivan has style, and showbiz looks after its own.

The Sweet:
Teenage Hell Raisers

'Funny, Funny' hit the charts in January 1971, and was both the first hit for Brian Connolly, Mick Tucker, Andy Scott and Steve Priest – the Sweet – and for Nicky Chinn and Mike Chapman, the songwriting team whose commercial ear for the Top 10 has sold the group over 8,000,000 singles since then.

In fact, although it is often assumed that the Sweet were formed as an outlet for Chinn and Chapman's potential hits, Brian Connolly, the group's lead singer, and Mick Tucker, the drummer, were playing together as long ago as 1968 in Wainwright's Gentlemen, a soul band which included such notables as Ian Gillan and Roger Glover, who were later to find huge success with Deep Purple. Also in the band were the founding members of the bubble-rock group, White Plains, remembered for 'My Baby Needs Loving'.

In 1968, Connolly (then known as Brian McManus) and Tucker, formed the Sweet with Steve Priest (a former solicitor's clerk) on bass guitar and vocals and Frank Torpky on lead guitar and the group recorded their first single, 'Slow Motion', on the Fontana label. Its only interest now is purely historical, as it sank without trace, and a move to EMI gave no greater cause for optimism when the

Sweet's three releases for the company, 'Lollipop', 'All You'll Ever Get From Me' and 'Get On The Line' similarly flopped.

Meanwhile, the group gigged around the UK and Europe, pausing to replace Frank Torpky, first with Mick Stewart in March, 1969, and then with Andy Scott in October of 1970, the same year that they came under the management of Nicky Chinn and Mike Chapman.

Songwriters/Producers

Chinn and Chapman are songwriters who specialise in turning out specific songs for specific artists, with the sole intention of producing chart successes. In the States, writers seem to be more concerned that the end product of their labours should have a semblance of artistic merit as well as a chart hit, and so there has been the growth of the songwriter/producer – a role that is virtually interchangeable – and which Phil Spector exemplifies. In the UK, however, the overriding preoccupation has almost always been that of total commercial success. Nicky Chinn and Mike Chapman seem to have fitted perfectly into this latter line of thought. Until they found the Sweet, success had evaded them. With the Sweet, they have succeeded in producing worldwide single smashes.

In retrospect, there was really no reason why the Sweet should not have become a

very successful group. They had reasonably good looks; by 1970, two years on the road had made them fairly accomplished on their instruments (Andy Scott's late arrival to the group did not preclude him from this, as he had spent six months backing the Scaffold) and they were sufficiently aware of audience reaction to know how to manipulate a crowd from the stage. However, it is doubtful that the group could have consistently scored up hit after hit unless they had joined forces with their songwriter/managers and their producer, Phil Wainman.

A new recording contract with RCA Records resulted in the team's first record appearance in the shops in January 1971. Its title was 'Funny, Funny' and soon it was high in the singles' charts and although it was a distinctly bubblegum record, it can now be seen to have shown that right from their very first hit record, Chinn and Chapman were almost obsessed with providing songs which relied virtually totally on the 'hook' – the part of the record, usually the chorus, which is repeated several times and which, after only two or three hearings, has the listener humming along to it whether he likes the song or not.

The Sweet's only ambition appeared to be to have hit singles as a bubblegum group. Just before 'Funny, Funny' was released, Brian Connolly stated that their objective was: "To concentrate on tight, four-part vocal harmonies and be a popular group, as opposed to heavy. We want to give people a good, melodic, danceable sound, and that seems pretty scarce these days.'' 'Funny, Funny' was almost a justification of this wish, as the vocals – and especially the 'hook' – virtually obscured the instrumental backing.

Their first hit, though, was securely under their belts and after that there was no stopping the newly-found success formula of the group. 'Co-Co', their next single, followed its predecessor into the Top 10 with a chorus that seemed to have been written in Swahili, and although there was a brief halt to the Sweet's growing success in the late summer of 1971 when 'Alexander Graham Bell' only reached the no. 30 spot, the momentum was regained with the release in January, 1972 of 'Poppa Joe', which was to be their third Top 10 single in Britain.

'Alexander Graham Bell' had had far less stress placed upon its vocals and 'hook' lines than 'Funny, Funny' and 'Co-Co', and instead had relied more on a sound which integrated the vocal harmonies with a more forceful instrumental backing. After its relative failure and before the release and success of 'Poppa Joe', Nicky Chinn said: ''We tried something different with 'Alexander Graham Bell' but obviously the public preferred the out-and-out bubblegum sound of 'Co-Co' and 'Funny, Funny'.''

This was something of an understatement as the public had preferred the out-and-out bubblegum sound of 'Co-Co' to the extent of having bought more than two million copies of the single throughout the world. So when 'Poppa Joe' was followed by 'Little Willy' – which was once again in the proven hit mould – it seemed that the Sweet's chart entries would forever be aimed at the weenybopper audience and would consist of a strong 'hook', vocal harmonies, and an adequate but minimal instrumental backing.

'Blockbuster'

In September of 1972, however, 'Wig-Wam Bam' was released. Although this remained largely true to the formula of the Sweet's previous successes – and did in fact turn out to be a massive hit – the vocals and instruments were stronger and sounded more forceful and more purposeful than on the previous singles. It was in many ways a transition single, paving the way as it did for the change of musical emphasis that came with 'Blockbuster', the group's first record of 1973 which quickly reached no. 1.

'Blockbuster', once again written by Nicky Chinn and Mike Chapman and produced by Phil Wainman, heralded 1973 in with the sound of wailing police sirens and a driving heavy beat – a far cry from 'Funny, Funny'. But the essential 'hook' lines were still there, although the rest of the lyrics were virtually indistinguishable when heard on an average, pocket-sized transistor radio, buried as they were beneath the galloping, incessant beat, and

Foreground: drummer Mick Tucker.

Redferns

it seemed as if their only raison d'être was to fill in the gaps between the screaming forth of the title.

The Sweet have always been unacceptable to music critics, who have generally savaged their records without mercy. But with or without critical acclaim, the Sweet have steadily gathered a mighty legion of fans throughout the world since their meeting with Chinn and Chapman. Sweet records, by the beginning of 1973, were selling in vast quantities almost everywhere in the world and the group had toured extensively throughout Europe and especially in Germany, where they were one of the most consistent chart-topping groups. Once again, critical acclaim for their live appearances in Britain was virtually non-existent, but it was down to the fans to pack out the halls, and pack them out they most certainly did. By Christmas of 1972, it was a rare gig for the Sweet when the audience were not in ecstasy by their third number.

A stage act, as such, did not exist and apart from bashing out their hits, Who numbers and a medley of early rock & roll songs were usually included. The group, however, seemed to take little notice of the critics and 1972 was a formative year for the Sweet. Taking advantage of the glam-rock mood created by T. Rex, David Bowie and Slade, the four group members indulged themselves similarly and took to wearing make-up and dressing in hot-pants, massive stack-heeled boots and other equally camp costumes. Brian Connolly emerged as the front-man, both on stage and off, mincing and pouting across the stage and emphasising his sexuality with fairly lewd innuendoes and explicit gestures. In keeping with this new visual image, his voice took on an

effeminate lilt, a lilt that was first fully heard on record on 'Blockbuster'.

After the initial shock and great success of that record, which in the true traditions of good pop singles was totally electric and seemed to be an Identikit record of every other glam/glitter number, Chinn and Chapman turned out another record very much in the same vein, 'Hell Raiser', which wasted no time in hanging around and went straight in at no. 1.

This success was somewhat marred by the fact that a month before its release, at the end of April, 1973, the Sweet had topped the bill at London's Rainbow Theatre, the High Temple of contemporary music, and had once again been critically lambasted, although yet again their fans, who by now seemed to have an average age of around 13, had poured adulation on the group, despite their equipment having broken down shortly after the set started.

Hit Formula

'Ballroom Blitz', the third high energy single from the group, came out nearly five months later in September and was yet another variation on the hit formula which had produced the last two 'new-look' singles. This was not surprising as, shortly after 'Hellraiser's' success, Mike Chapman had been quoted as saying: 'I now write everything around one chord'. With this single, the Sweet did begin to gain some critical respect, however. One British music paper critic wrote: 'how come their clever records aren't intellectually acceptable in Britain when such as Status Quo can get by with the tiredest of clichés?' Ironically, perhaps, 'Ballroom Blitz' was held off the no. 1 spot by a freak hit, 'The Van der Valk Theme' by the Simon Park Orchestra.

1973 was completed for the Sweet by a sensational stage performance at the Rainbow, once again, just before Christmas. For this Rainbow show everything worked perfectly, including a variety of fairly suggestive films and the taped special effects for their 1973 hits. Criticism, however, could be levied at the group for their lack of communication with the audience, and the almost deliberately arrogant manner with which the Sweet seemed to attempt to remain remote and thereby attain a god-like status.

By the end of 1973, the group had become one of the premier singles' bands in Britain, and they had also developed a highly sophisticated stage act. 'Little Willy' had proved something of a surprise by getting to no. 3 in the US over a year after it had been a hit in Britain. However, they had had only two albums released in Britain – 'Funny How Sweet Co-Co Can Be' and 'The Sweet's Biggest Hits' – neither of which had met with any great success. Gary Glitter on the other hand was selling large quantities of his albums throughout Europe. So, overcoming this lack of success was obviously to be the next goal. By now they had also a further problem. To what extent was their future in the hands of Chinn and Chapman?

Index

Acknowledgments:
Jacket: Portraits by Philip Castle.
Photographs by Syndication International.
(US edition: Photographs by (front flap) Syndication International; (front, left) Syndication International; (front, centre) Joe Stevens; (front, right) Roger Morton; (back) Redferns; (back flap) Syndication International).
Pages 4–5: Redferns.